D1410431

The COMPLETE ILLUSTRATED ENCYCLOPEDIA *of* Cats & Kittens

Publisher and Creative Director: Nick Wells
Project Editor: Cat Emslie
Assitant Project Editor: Victoria Lyle
Picture Research: Victoria Lyle and Gemma Walters
Art Director: Mike Spender
Layout Design: Dave Jones and Imagefile Ltd
Illustrator: Ann Biggs
Digital Design and Production: Chris Herbert
Copy Editor: Colette Campbell
Proofreader: Victoria Garrard
Indexer: William Jack

Special thanks to: Claire Walker, Carmen Herbert, Julia Rolf and Fiana Muhlberger

13 15 17 16 14

1 3 5 7 9 10 8 6 4 2

This edition first published 2013 by
FLAME TREE PUBLISHING
Crabtree Hall, Crabtree Lane
Fulham, London SW6 6TY

www.flametreepublishing.com

ISBN 978-0-85775-880-4

A copy of the CIP data for this book is available from the British Library.

Printed in China

The COMPLETE ILLUSTRATED ENCYCLOPEDIA *of* Cats & Kittens

Lee Harper & Joyce L. White

FLAME TREE
PUBLISHING

Contents

History, Culture & Anatomy 10

Care & Management 64

The Breeds 146

How to Use This Book

This book is divided into three main chapters, each designed to enhance an understanding of cats, their practical care and enjoyment, and the various breeds that exist.

History, Culture & Anatomy

This is an introduction to cats—their status and development throughout history and their involvement in human culture, such as art and literature, along with their physical characteristics and behavior.

Care & Management

This chapter offers a practical guide to cats, taking you all the way from becoming a cat owner through to taking care of it and even breeding cats. If you are interested in showing off your beloved pet, learn about cat shows and how to enter.

The Breeds

This chapter begins with a closer look at the evolution and domestication of cats. It explains the genetics that influence the appearance of cats, what a "breed" is and how they develop, as well as the way breeds are classified. Feral cats and new breeds are also discussed. This is followed by a comprehensive section detailing almost all known breeds of cats that exist today, divided into shorthairs and longhairs and organized within those sections by similar origin or appearance. A look at the wildcat breeds of the world ends the celebration of our feline friends.

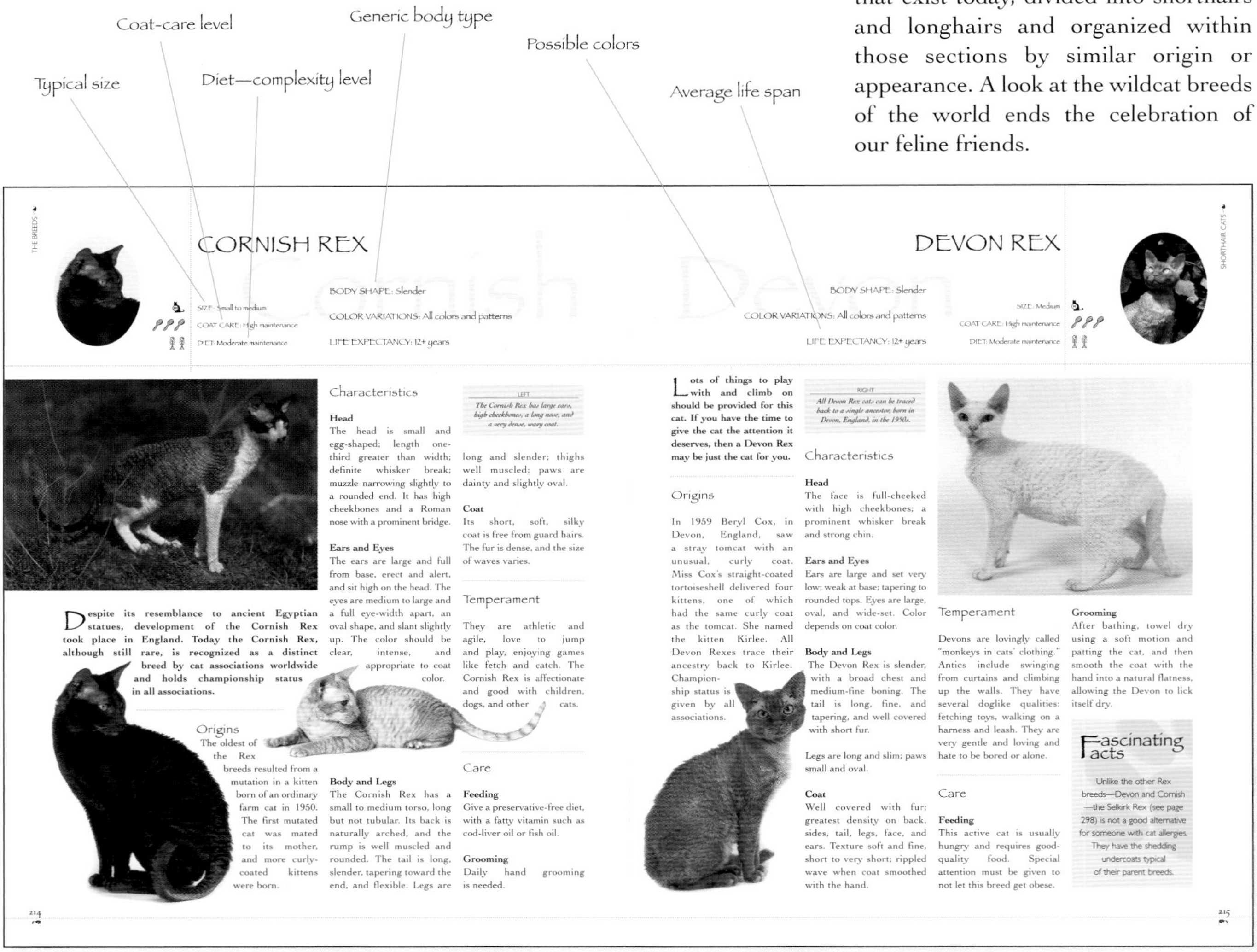

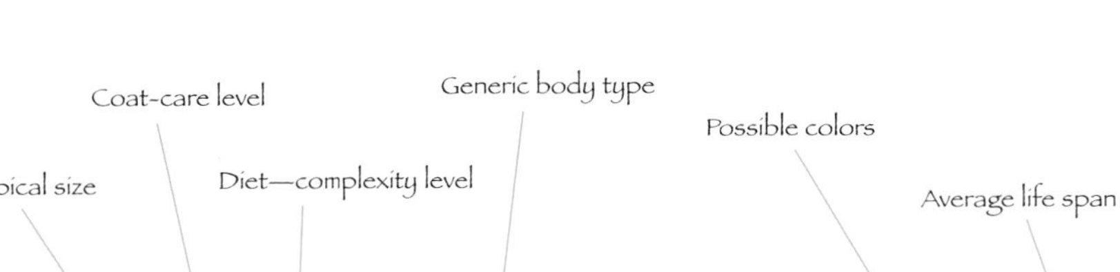

THE BREEDS

CORNISH REX

SIZE: Small to medium
COAT CARE: High maintenance
DIET: Moderate maintenance

BODY SHAPE: Slender
COLOR VARIATIONS: All colors and patterns
LIFE EXPECTANCY: 12+ years

Despite its resemblance to ancient Egyptian statues, development of the Cornish Rex took place in England. Today the Cornish Rex, although still rare, is recognized as a distinct breed by cat associations worldwide and holds championship status in all associations.

Origins

The oldest of the Rex breeds resulted from a mutation in a kitten born of an ordinary farm cat in 1950. The first mutated cat was mated to its mother, and more curly-coated kittens were born.

Characteristics

Head
The head is small and egg-shaped; length one-third greater than width; definite whisker break; muzzle narrowing slightly to a rounded end. It has high cheekbones and a Roman nose with a prominent bridge.

Ears and Eyes
The ears are large and full from base, erect and alert, and sit high on the head. The eyes are medium to large and a full eye-width apart, an oval shape, and slant slightly up. The color should be clear, intense, and appropriate to coat color.

Body and Legs
The Cornish Rex has a small to medium torso, long but not tubular. Its back is naturally arched, and the rump is well muscled and rounded. The tail is long, slender, tapering toward the end, and flexible. Legs are long and slender; thighs well muscled; paws are dainty and slightly oval.

LEFT
The Cornish Rex has large ears, high cheekbones, a long nose, and a very dense, wavy coat.

Coat
Its short, soft, silky coat is free from guard hairs. The fur is dense, and the size of waves varies.

Temperament

They are athletic and agile, love to jump and play, enjoying games like fetch and catch. The Cornish Rex is affectionate and good with children, dogs, and other cats.

Care

Feeding
Give a preservative-free diet, with a fatty vitamin such as cod-liver oil or fish oil.

Grooming
Daily hand grooming is needed.

214

DEVON REX

BODY SHAPE: Slender
COLOR VARIATIONS: All colors and patterns
LIFE EXPECTANCY: 12+ years

SIZE: Medium
COAT CARE: High maintenance
DIET: Moderate maintenance

SHORTHAIR CATS

Lots of things to play with and climb on should be provided for this cat. If you have the time to give the cat the attention it deserves, then a Devon Rex may be just the cat for you.

Origins

In 1959 Beryl Cox, in Devon, England, saw a stray tomcat with an unusual, curly coat. Miss Cox's straight-coated tortoiseshell delivered four kittens, one of which had the same curly coat as the tomcat. She named the kitten Kirlee. All Devon Rexes trace their ancestry back to Kirlee. Championship status is given by all associations.

RIGHT
All Devon Rex cats can be traced back to a single ancestor, born in Devon, England, in the 1950s.

Characteristics

Head
The face is full-cheeked with high cheekbones; a prominent whisker break and strong chin.

Ears and Eyes
Ears are large and set very low; weak at base; tapering to rounded tops. Eyes are large, oval, and wide-set. Color depends on coat color.

Body and Legs
The Devon Rex is slender, with a broad chest and medium-fine boning. The tail is long, fine, and tapering, and well covered with short fur.

Legs are long and slim; paws small and oval.

Coat
Well covered with fur; greatest density on back, sides, tail, legs, face, and ears. Texture soft and fine, short to very short; rippled wave when coat smoothed with the hand.

Temperament

Devons are lovingly called "monkeys in cats' clothing." Antics include swinging from curtains and climbing up the walls. They have several doglike qualities: fetching toys, walking on a harness and leash. They are very gentle and loving and hate to be bored or alone.

Care

Feeding
This active cat is usually hungry and requires good-quality food. Special attention must be given to not let this breed get obese.

Grooming
After bathing, towel dry using a soft motion and patting the cat, and then smooth the coat with the hand into a natural flatness, allowing the Devon to lick itself dry.

Fascinating Facts

Unlike the other Rex breeds—Devon and Cornish—the Selkirk Rex (see page 298) is not a good alternative for someone with cat allergies. They have the shedding undercoats typical of their parent breeds.

215

Size

This icon indicates the average relative size of the breed in terms of bone structure and weight (not height), according to generally agreed standards. Normal domestic cats generally range in size from 5 lbs (3.3 kg) to 18 lbs (8.2 kg).

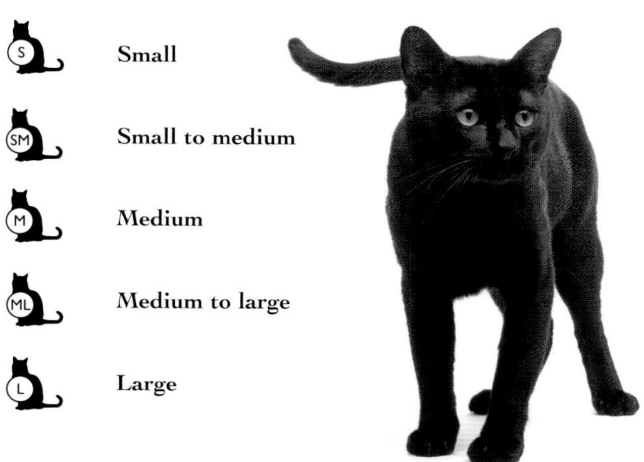

Coat Care

These icons give the approximate level of grooming and coat care necessary for the breed.

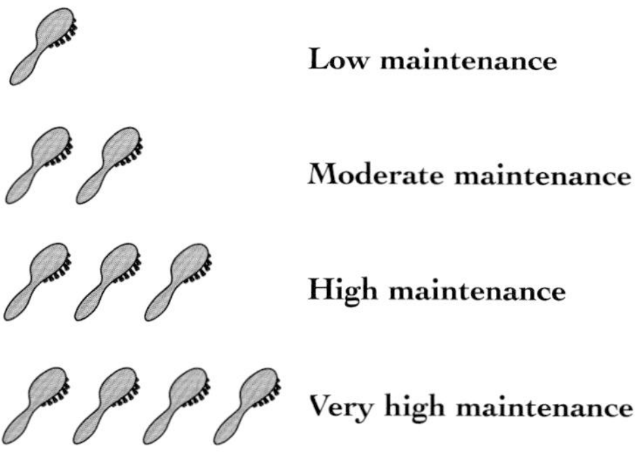

Diet

This is not as much an indication of how much a breed eats but instead gives a general idea of how high maintenance or complicated the cat's feeding requirements are.

Low maintenance

Moderate maintenance

High maintenance

Very high maintenance

Body Shape

This gives the body-shape type of the breed, for example "cobby" or "oriental" (*see* pages 155–56).

Color Variations

This gives the various possible color and pattern combinations in which the cat can occur (more precisely, those "allowed" by the official bodies). They are only a guide, and additional reading is recommended if you'd like to know more specific standards.

Life Expectancy

This gives an average range for the age to which you can expect the individual breed to live.

This at-a-glance information is followed by a more in-depth discussion of the breed, including a look at its origins, history, development, and status today; its physical characteristics, temperament, and behavior; and the care it needs (such as feeding and grooming).

Throughout the book, many "Fascinating Facts" are listed in order to provide bite-size chunks of information and amusing facts on the subject in question or on cats in general.

Reference Section

At the end of the encyclopedia, there is a list of useful addresses and contacts—from cat registries to humane societies; there is also a list of titles suggested for additional reading to expand on the subjects and breeds covered here. A glossary explains any terms that might be unfamiliar or sums up what you have already learned, and a thorough index will allow you to instantly locate an individual topic.

Introduction

"The smallest feline is a masterpiece." **Leonardo da Vinci**

I have a secret. It's personal. I'm having a love affair . . . well, actually several . . . I am referring to my cats, for I have more than one. I allude also to the incredible difference my cats make in my life. Companionship, entertainment, and emotional support—they give me all this and more. How can words really express the comfort and sweetness of a kitten purring in your lap? Or the joy of watching a mother cat cuddling her newborns for the first time? Or the amusement of watching a cat's reaction to its reflection in a mirror? There is no yardstick that is long enough or high enough or wide enough to measure just how much my cats add to the richness of my life. And millions of people around the word share my feelings.

Why Cats?

Cats give us someone to talk to. They reduce stress and help us live longer and more fulfilled lives. They even keep mice away. A purring cat and a glowing fireplace make winter manageable. Cats turn everyday household objects into toys and make us more aware of the birds outside. They serve as unpredictable alarm clocks. Cats inspire us to be better mothers. Cats perform acrobatic feats right in our own living rooms. Cats make a windowsill more beautiful. Even a worn-out couch seems elegant if a cat rests on its cushions. Cats make us smile. Cats inspire poets and playwrights and give us cool cartoon characters. Cats teach us how to land on our feet. Cats let us indulge our desires to spoil someone. Cats remind us that life is a mystery and help us feel connected to the wild. They teach us the luxurious art of stretching out and show us how to lick our wounds and carry on. Cats create a kindred feeling with other "cat people." Cats open up our hearts.

The Complete Illustrated Encyclopedia of Cats has been written specifically to provide cat owners (or potential owners) with the wealth of information that will allow them to better understand, appreciate, and enjoy the feline member of the family. This book should prove to be an invaluable reference and an inspired addition to any cat-lover's library.

Every Aspect Covered

Understand how your cat sees its world. Discover more about feline psychology, anatomy, and the instincts cats inherit from their wild ancestors. A home without a

cat is only a house, so for the potential kitten buyer, this book includes detailed descriptions, photographs, histories, and characteristics of more than 60 breeds of pedigreed cats.

Whether choosing a pedigreed cat or a mixed breed, this volume provides tips on how to pick the purr-fect kitten—one that is ideal for your lifestyle, interests, and circumstances. Included is information on how to feed, groom, and train even the most demanding or unruly cat. Learn how to choose a great veterinarian. Detailed information about common feline diseases and ailments will help you better protect your cat's health. Instructions in feline first aid may even provide knowledge that might save your cat's life in an emergency.

Going Further

If you are interested in entering the world of breeding felines, this book also includes specific information regarding the cat's life cycle, mating behavior, pregnancy, and birthing that should prove to be invaluable. Enjoy reading about the history of cat exhibitions, or learn the basics you need to know before entering your cat in its first show. You can even learn a little about the wild counterparts of our domestic friends, the wildcats of the world—including everyone's favorites, the Big Cats, such as lions and tigers. Plus there are many fascinating facts about cats; for example, did you know that Sir Issac Newton invented the cat flap? Or that a Siamese mother cat gave birth to a single litter of 19 kittens?

Owning a cat brings with it many responsibilities . . . but to cat lovers around the world, owning a cat is a privilege.

Lee Harper
Editor,
ShowCatsOnline.com
Mockingbird Persians
& Exotics

History, Culture & Anatomy

CATS IN HUMAN HISTORY

"God made the cat in order to give man the pleasure of caressing the tiger," (author unknown). From ancient times, humans and cats have shared a unique relationship. Of all the domesticated animals, it is the cat that seems closest to its wild roots—and therein lies its mystique. Despite the dog's reputation as man's best friend, it is the cat that is the most popular pet in homes throughout most of the world.

For the Love of Cats

There is an estimated 600 million house cats worldwide. With a human population of roughly 6.6 billion, that means there is one cat for almost every ten people on the planet. Moreover, the popularity of the feline continues to grow.

BELOW

Owning a cat can be therapeutic and an antidote to the stresses of fast-paced, modern life.

A 2007 survey by the American Pet Products Association found the country with the most cats is the U.S., with 88.3 million felines; almost 15 million more cats than dogs. China rates second, with around 55 million felines. In the United Kingdom approximately one out of every four households has a family cat. In the U.S. more than one third of households have a feline. Ninety-two percent of pet cats are mixed breeds.

What makes the cat so popular?

More than 50 percent of people surveyed say they keep a pet for love and companionship. The fast pace of life, increased stress levels, and demanding work of the modern world often means individuals lack the time or energy to develop close relationships. A pet can help fill that gap and be both rewarding and therapeutic.

Cats make ideal pets. They are less demanding than a dog, are clean, fastidious, and relatively quiet. A cat is happy to live an indoor existence, making it adaptable to anyone living in an apartment building. The cat also has a definite mystique—loving yet independent, elegant yet playful, cautious yet bold, mysterious yet familiar.

RIGHT

Many farms keep working cats as a way of controlling the rats and mice.

Working Cats

Most house cats enjoy a privileged lifestyle; the feline equivalent of royalty with servants providing all their comforts. Yet some cats work for their living, for the cat is the world's most accomplished rat catcher—a job respected since the earliest recorded history. In ancient times the cat was recognized and valued for its ability to keep the granaries of the world free from rats and mice. Some historians theorize that the Egyptians held the domestic cat in such high esteem due to this special feline talent.

Not all mouse-catching felines have worked in an agricultural setting. Accounts from Exeter Cathedral in England from 1305–1467 include a salary for a succession of cats. The wage was to supplement the diet of the official cat, who was expected to control the pest population of the cathedral.

In 1883 a cat named Peter also received a salary to rid the British Home Office of rodents. The tradition of employing a black cat to control vermin in the British Home Office continued for almost one hundred years.

Feral Cats

Not all cats maintain a close relationship with humankind. Wild or "feral" cats are the descendants of domesticated felines that have gone stray or been abandoned. Once homeless, feral cats live and breed according to their own resources. Although the mother cat may once have been a family pet, when she gives birth in the wild her offspring are never socialized with humans. The kittens are feral. While some ferals live a solitary existence, they are more commonly found in large groups called feral colonies. The largest feral cat population in the world is in Rome, Italy, where between 250,000–350,000 feral cats live, organized into around 2,000 colonies and residing in such famous landmarks as the Coliseum and Vatican City.

Fascinating Facts

A group of cats is called a clowder. A group of kittens is a kendle.

Throughout Time and Around the World

More than any other domesticated animal, the cat has endured wild swings of fortune in its relationship with man. At one time revered as a god, the cat has also been reviled as a devil. Yet no matter its status, the cat has always fascinated humankind. Whether living in the boiling hot desert or in a frozen fjord, from a mud hut to an exotic palace, from ancient tombs to the modern urban jungle, the domestic cat has endured and thrived throughout the ages.

Descended from the Wildcats

Fifty million years ago, during the Eocene Period, a weasellike creature called miacids hunted in the forests. From this fierce creature the meat-eating carnivores evolved. The biological order, carnivora, is divided into several families including Felidae, the family of large and small cats. The family Felidae is divided into six genus, including Felis, which includes the smaller felines such as the bobcat, ocelot, serval, and the domestic cat.

There has been plenty of debate over the evolutionary relationship of the small wildcats and the modern domestic cat (*Felis silvestris catus*). DNA evidence published in 2007 concluded that domestic cats have descended from at least five founding females of the African (also known as the "North African" or "Sardinian") wildcat (*Felis silvestris lybica*). As the first cats accompanied man in his travels, there was probably subsequent interbreeding between the domestic cat and other subspecies of wildcats, including the European wildcat (*F.s. silvestris*), the Central Asian wildcat (*F.s. ornata*), the sub-Saharan African wildcat (*F.s. cafra*), and the Chinese desert cat (*F.s. bieti*).

ABOVE

Our domestic cats belong to the same genus as the smaller wildcats, such as this tree-dwelling Margay.

LEFT

Recent scientific research has shown that the African wildcat is a direct ancestor of the domestic cat.

Fascinating Facts

Cats have been domesticated for only half as long as dogs. The word "cat" first came into popular use during the 300s, when Palladius recommended the cattus be used to protect the artichoke gardens from vermin.

LEFT
A statue of Bast, the Egyptian goddess of love and the moon, who had the head of a cat.

In from the Wild

It is difficult to pinpoint exactly when cats were first domesticated. Ancestors resembling modern cats first appeared around ten million years ago, but they were completely wild and did not associate with humans. The record of the cohabitation of cats and humans is buried in the mists of time. Ancient man was a nomadic hunter. As civilization progressed, humans lived a more settled lifestyle and learned to farm, growing grain crops such as wheat and barley. Stockpiling a portion of the harvest each winter, the grain attracted rats, mice, and birds, and these attracted wildcats. Gradually the wildcats and humans formed a mutually beneficial relationship. It is easy to imagine the cats becoming tamer and eventually fully domesticated.

The oldest archaeological evidence of a domesticated cat was found in the ancient Neolithic village of Shillourokambos on the Greek island of Cyprus. There are no wild cats native to Cyprus, yet the remains of a small cat were discovered buried just 15 in. (40 cm) from a 9,500-year-old human grave, suggesting that the cat may have been brought to the island as a treasured pet and buried with its master.

The next evidence of domestication was found in Haçilar, Turkey, where images of female figurines dating back to the 500s B.C. were discovered carrying catlike figures in their arms.

The Golden Age of the Cat

The first wall painting of a cat wearing a collar, a definite sign of domestication, appears on a fifth dynasty Egyptian tomb in Saqqara (Old Kingdom, circa 2500–2350 B.C.). By the twelfth dynasty (Middle Kingdom, circa 1976–1793 B.C.), small cats with flecked coats were frequent subjects in Egyptian art. By the twenty-second dynasty, the golden age of the Pharaohs, King Osorkon endowed a white cat with supreme power in a temple ceremony. Cats became divine.

So valued were the cats that even King Ptolemy Aultete, father of Cleopatra, was unable to save a Roman who had accidentally killed a cat. The man was hanged. The Persian king, Cambyse II, won the battle of Peluse by demanding that his soldiers strap cats to their shields. The Egyptians surrendered rather than injure the felines.

LEFT
A typical Egyptian bronze sculpture of a cat wearing a decorative collar, dating from around 600 B.C.

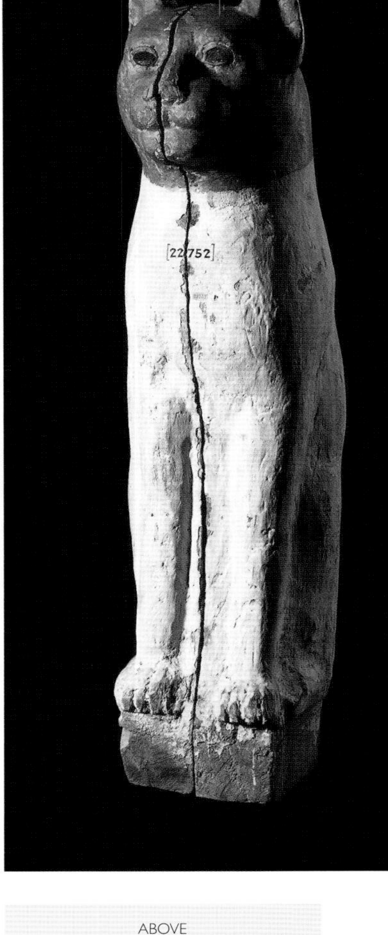

ABOVE

The Egyptians valued cats for their hunting abilities, as suggested by this painting from around 1400–1425 B.C.

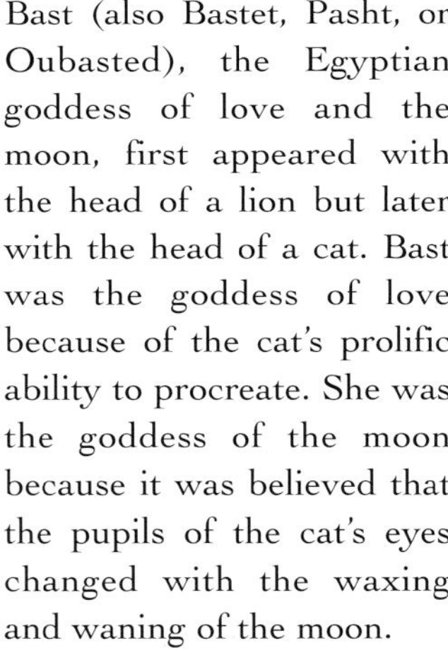

Bast (also Bastet, Pasht, or Oubasted), the Egyptian goddess of love and the moon, first appeared with the head of a lion but later with the head of a cat. Bast was the goddess of love because of the cat's prolific ability to procreate. She was the goddess of the moon because it was believed that the pupils of the cat's eyes changed with the waxing and waning of the moon.

Ship Ahoy

Although the Egyptians created laws that forbade the removal of their sacred cats, the ancient sailors of 1000 B.C. were quick to see the advantage of having cats aboard ship during long voyages to protect their food supplies from damage by rodents, so Phoenician and Greek sailors smuggled cats out of Egypt.

The cats brought aboard the trading vessels may have "jumped ship" at various ports, and in this manner cats spread throughout Asia and Europe. Archaeological evidence indicates that the Romans were the first to bring cats to the British Isles. As the powerful seafaring nations crossed the Atlantic Ocean in the 1600s, they in turn introduced the domestic cat to the new world.

ABOVE

The ancient Egyptians mummified cats and buried them in coffins made out of bronze or wood, like this one.

BELOW

A Roman mosaic from Pompeii; it is believed that the Romans introduced cats to the British Isles.

The Far East and the Orient

Cats reached China in around A.D. 400. The silk growers of China appreciated the cat's hunting abilities and used them to prevent rats and mice from destroying silkworm cocoons at a time when silk trading was vital to the economy. By the A.D. 1100s the yellow and white "lion-cats" were especially valued as pets.

Cats were introduced in Japan in around the 500s. According to custom, every temple owned two cats in order to keep mice away from the manuscripts. In the Middle Ages, the Japanese distinguished good-luck cats by their tortoiseshell fur and malevolent cats by their forked tail and their ability to change themselves into witches. Disciples of yoga felt the sleeping position of the cat was the ideal position to regulate vital body fluids.

BELOW

In Japan, these ceramic cats with one paw raised are placed in front of a home to ensure good fortune.

A symbol of purity, cats became the bridge between Buddha and his faithful followers. In Japan the Kyoto palace opened its doors to a white cat that had given birth to five kittens. A temple was dedicated to the cat named Maneki Neko, called the beckoning cat, seated with one paw raised in greeting.

In the 1100s Sultan El - Daher - Beybars bequeathed a park for stray cats called Gheytel-Qouttah, or The Cat Orchards; its feral cats were fed for many years.

RIGHT

Cats are revered in many different religions; Buddhist monks in the Far East raised sacred cats.

The Arabs of the 600s believed cats had a pure spirit, unlike the unclean spirit of dogs. According to legend, when Mohammed's cat, Muezza, was sleeping in the prophet's sleeve, the prophet chose to cut the garment rather than disturb his companion. The grateful cat was affectionately stroked by his master's hand three times, thereby granting the cat seven lives and the ability to always fall on his feet.

In the Far East, Buddhist monks raised sacred cats , and Sanskrit from 1000 B.C. mentions a pet cat. Indian epics Ramayana and Mahabharata, 500 B.C., also refer to pet cats. Indians worshipped a feline goddess of maternity, Sasti, the protector of children. There was a time when Hindus were obligated to feed at least one cat. The Siamese cat of Siam (Thailand) could only be owned by royalty and was bestowed as a gift to visiting dignitaries.

BELOW

Cats were used in China to control the rats and mice that threatened the silk trade.

ABOVE

The spread of the Plague via rats helped restore the reputation of the cat as a valuable companion.

BELOW

In the 1800s cats became a popular subject for paintings, such as this one by Julius Adam.

Reviled in Europe of the Middle Ages

And so the domesticated cat spread throughout the world, admired for its hunting ability, fertility, and beauty . . . until the Middle Ages. Because cats were associated with femininity, sensuality, and sexuality, the Church of the Middle Ages attributed evil powers to felines and set out to destroy the myths and pagan worship associated with the cat. Cats became symbols of evil and Satan. Hundreds of thousands of cats were crucified, tortured, skinned alive, or thrown into the fire as companions of witches. Once a demigod, the cat's fall from grace lasted almost 200 years.

The Plague

As the feline population dwindled, the rodent population thrived. By 1799 bubonic plague, the Black Death, spread rampant through Europe, transmitted by the fleas on gray sewer rats. The cat's skill as a hunter of vermin was desperately needed. Its reputation was salvaged. Owning a cat was back in style. The British Royal Navy decreed that every ship must carry two cats on board in order to ward off rodents.

The return to popularity

While the cat was once more acceptable, it was not viewed as a pet in the same way as a dog. Then in the late 1800s, Louis Pasteur's theories regarding microscopic microbes led to people developing a phobia about animals carrying germs. With their reputation for cleanliness, cats were exempt from the fears of contamination. Thus began another period of feline popularity. Writers, philosophers, and artists became inspired by the feline form and personality.

LEFT

In the Middle Ages, cats belonging to women considered witches were often burned alive with their owners.

Fascinating Facts

In the Middle Ages cats were believed to have venomous fangs and were considered the cause of all kinds of problems, ranging from stale beer to the spread of diseases.

BELOW

George Sheridan Knowles' Kittens *(c. 1890–1930) shows how cats had once again become acceptable as pets.*

RIGHT

One of the most familiar cat breeds is the Siamese, with its colorpoint coat and deep blue eyes.

ABOVE

Longhair pedigree cats include the Norwegian Forest Cat; this image shows a Silver Tabby variety.

BELOW

The Egyptian goddess Bast can be depicted either as a cat or as a cat's head on a woman's body.

The Modern Age

As the popularity of cats grew and their beauty became recognized, it was inevitable that people would want to compare their cats with those of others. The first contemporary cat show was held in 1871 in England and was organized by Harrison Weir, considered the father of the cat society. Enthusiasts began selective breeding of the domesticated cat, establishing pedigree records, developing new breeds, and breeding to type. The number of cat breeds grew from a mere 20 in 1960 to over 70 breeds recognized by various cat registries around the world by the end of the 1900s. New hybrid breeds continue to be developed right up to the current day.

Mythology and Folklore

Cats have figured in the mythologies of cultures throughout the world and across the centuries. Bast is the well-known Egyptian goddess of the moon and sexuality, who is either depicted as a cat or having the head of a cat on a woman's body. The Egyptian Sun God, Ra, changed himself into a cat to do battle with the serpentlike darkness. In Roman times Libera, the mythological personification of Liberty, was portrayed as a cat because cats hate to be constrained. In Celtic mythology, Grimalkin is a gray cat that possesses magical powers. Freyja, Norse Goddess of Love and Beauty, had a chariot drawn by two horse-sized, winged, gray cats. In Japanese folklore, Raiju, the demon of lightning, assumes the shape of a cat. If a tree is struck by lightning, it is said that Raiju's claws have scratched it. Maneki Neko, the familiar, lucky, waving cat of Japan, is believed to have originated from Chinese folklore from the 800s. Siamese god-kings believed their souls passed into a cat upon their death, where the soul rested for the cat's natural life span before entering Paradise. Tjilpa are the ancestral totemic cat-men of aboriginal Australia.

Fascinating Facts

Because the Burmese people treasure their cats, a British officer during the Second World War painted images of cats on the army vehicles to gain Burmese support for Allied forces.

BELOW

The Egyptian Sun God Ra (right) changed himself into a cat in order to fight against darkness.

BOTTOM

The Norse goddess Freyja rides in her chariot drawn by two gray cats.

The Cat as Good Luck

There are many legends associated with cats and luck.

- In Yorkshire, England, it is lucky to own a black cat but extremely unlucky to come across one accidentally.
- In the early 1500s a visitor to an English home would kiss the family cat to bring good luck.
- The Celts thought black cats were reincarnated beings able to divine the future.
- The Scots believed a strange black cat on the porch brings prosperity.
- Charles I, King of England, owned a black cat that he felt brought him luck and had it guarded day and night. The day after the cat died, he was arrested. In England it was believed that if a black cat lived in the house, the daughters would have plenty of suitors. In Britain it is bad luck if a white cat crosses your path but good luck if a black cat crosses your path. In the U.S. it is the opposite.
- Early Americans believed that if a cat washed her face, the first person she looked at would be the first to be wed.
- The Dutch of Pennsylvania place a cat in the cradle of a newlywed couple in the belief that she will grant their wish for a child. For the Dutch to see a white cat on the road is lucky, but it is unlucky to see a white cat at night.

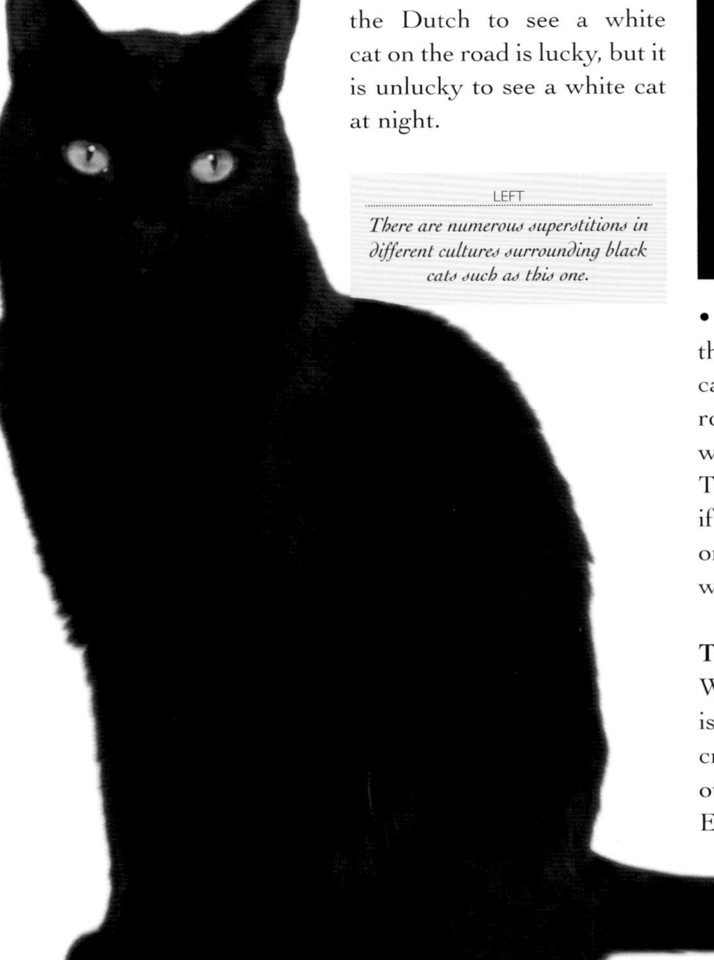

LEFT

There are numerous superstitions in different cultures surrounding black cats such as this one.

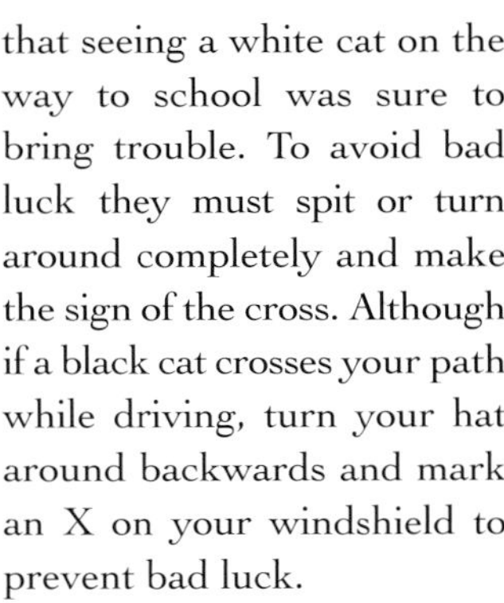

- French peasants thought that if you released a black cat at a junction where five roads connected, the cat would lead you to treasure. The French also believed that if you found one white hair on a black cat, Lady Luck would smile upon you.

The Cat as Bad Luck

While many people believe it is bad luck if a black cat crosses your path, there are other superstitions too. Some English children believed that seeing a white cat on the way to school was sure to bring trouble. To avoid bad luck they must spit or turn around completely and make the sign of the cross. Although if a black cat crosses your path while driving, turn your hat around backwards and mark an X on your windshield to prevent bad luck.

- The French believe it is bad luck to cross a stream while carrying a cat. It is considered bad luck to pass a black cat after nine at night and bad luck to see a white cat at night.
- It is believed that cats can steal both a baby's breath or steal a dead person's soul.

Cats and the Weather
In mythology the cat was believed to have great influence on the weather.

- Witches who rode on storms took the form of cats. The dog, an attendant of the storm-king Odin, was a symbol of wind. Cats came to symbolize heavy rain, and dogs symbolized strong gusts of wind. This may be from where the phrase "it's raining cats and dogs" originated.
- A Welsh superstition states when the pupil of a cat's eye broadens, there will be rain.
- If a cat cleans behind its ears it will rain, and a cat sneezing once means there will be rain.

In China the presence of a black cat foretold of poverty. If a cat sneezes three times, the family will catch a cold. There is actually truth to the belief that some cats can predict earthquakes. It appears they are sensitive to vibrations undetectable by humans.

The Cat at Sea
Sailors believed that if a cat licked its fur against the grain, it meant a hailstorm was coming; if it sneezed, rain was on the way; and if it were frisky, the wind would soon blow. If a cat ran ahead of a sailor to the pier, it was believed that would bring good luck; if the cat crossed his path, his luck would be bad.

- Fishermen's wives kept black cats, believing that the cat would prevent danger from befalling their husbands at sea.
- Loudly mewing cats meant that it would be a difficult voyage.
- A playful cat meant that it would be a voyage with good and gusty winds.

ABOVE
Some people believed that a visitor was on its way if a cat cleaned its face and paws in the parlor.

BELOW
Sailors traditionally thought that a loudly mewing cat carried a warning of a difficult voyage.

BELOW
Black cats were kept by fishermen's wives in order to prevent harm from reaching their husbands at sea.

Seeing into the Future
In Egypt priests predicted the future by interpreting the behavior of the sacred cats kept in the sanctuary. Some people believed that if a cat cleans its face and paws in the parlor, a visitor is approaching.

The Cat and Death

The mysterious cat is often associated with death.

• Malaysians venerated the cat as a godlike creature that eased their journey from hell to paradise in the afterlife.

• In India it is believed that a reincarnated soul may be "liberated" by throwing a black cat into a fire.

• Early Christians believed that two cats fighting near a dying person, or on the grave shortly after a funeral, are the devil and an angel fighting for possession of the person's soul. In Italy in the 1500s, it was believed that if a black cat lay on the bed of a sick man, he would die. Similarly German folklore states that if a black cat jumped on the bed of a sick person, it meant death was near. In Ireland having your moonlit path crossed by a black cat was thought to foretell death in an epidemic. In French Normandy seeing a tortoiseshell cat foretells death by accident. In the mountains of Transylvania it was believed that if a cat jumped over a dead body, the unfortunate corpse was doomed to eternity as a vampire. A person who drowned a cat would someday suffer the same fate. A farmer who kills a cat will see his cattle die mysteriously. An Irish superstition says that killing a cat brings seventeen years of bad luck. In Finland it was thought that black cats carried the souls of the dead to the other world.

Fascinating Facts

An ancient Chinese legend maintains that the cat is the product of a lioness and a monkey—the lioness endowing her offspring with dignity and the monkey with curiosity and playfulness.

BELOW

Early Christians thought that two cats fighting near a dying person both wanted possession of the soul.

Literature

Cats have been portrayed in literature since ancient times.

• Although the Old Testament makes no mention of cats, the Babylonian Talmud mentions their admirable qualities and encourages the breeding of cats "to help keep the houses clean."

• Cats feature in the writings of Homer, Virgil, and Ovid; Ovid tells of the transformation of Apollo's sister, Diana, into a cat.

• Aesop tells the fable of a cat turned into a woman by Venus to be with the man she loves. In human form, the cat remains a cat after all, chasing a mouse across the room.

• During the Middle Ages the cat often represented witchcraft, deceit, evil, or cruelty in literature.

• By the Renaissance in the 1500s, while cats still suffered from a tarnished image, opinions were changing. Du Bellay composed a two-hundred-verse epitaph to Belaud, his beloved cat.

• Into the 1600s fable writers still portrayed cats as selfish or mischievous creatures. Charles Perrault's *Stories or Tales From Olden Times* (1697) featured a clever, loyal cat, Puss in Boots, who helps his young master triumph in life.

• In the 1700s one of the first works truly celebrating the cat, *Les Chats* by De Moncrif, was published in 1727.

• The British writer Rudyard Kipling penned *The Cat That Walked by Himself* (1902). T. S. Elliot, Nobel Prize-winning British poet and playwright, was a cat lover who wrote an entire book of poems about cats, *Old Possum's Book of Practical Cats* (1939). This was later set to music and became the long-running musical, *Cats*.

In children's literature, felines remain popular figures. The Cheshire cat described in Lewis Carroll's children's classic, *Alice's Adventures in Wonderland*, (1865) could slowly disappear, leaving behind only its grin. Nursery rhymes abound with feline characters—from the three little kittens that lost their mittens to the cat and the fiddle. Dr Seuss' *Cat In The Hat* is now an iconic feline.

LEFT

In Aesop's tale a cat is turned into a human, but she is unable to resist chasing a mouse.

Cats also figure in mysteries, science fiction, and melodramas. Mrs. Murphy is a cat that helps her human solve mysteries in a series of novels by Rita Mae Brown. Her cat, Sneaky Pie Brown, is credited as coauthor. *The Cats of Ulthar* take revenge upon the murder of a kitten in H. P. Lovecraft's story of that name. Binky is the real-life cat that inspired Susan Becker's book *All I Need to Know I Learned from My Cat*.

LEFT

Charles Perrault's Puss In Boots *features a smart cat who ensures the success of his young master.*

BELOW

Alice encounters the Cheshire Cat in an illustration from a 1921 edition of Lewis Carroll's classic tale.

Art

The profile of a cat carved into a piece of bone dating back to prehistoric times illustrates that the feline form and face has often served as inspiration for artists.

ABOVE
Cats have inspired artists for thousands of years; this is featured in a hunting and fishing scene.

• A bronze statue of a mother cat and her kitten was recovered from the Saite period (730–332 B.C.).

• Egyptians carved cats on walls.
• A Roman vase from 450–400 B.C. shows a cat and a pigeon at the feet of two women.
• A mosaic from Greco-Roman times depicts a cat seizing a duck.
• A cat confronts a dog in another bas-relief from the 400s B.C.
• A bronze Islamic incense burner from the 1100s shaped like a cat features an inscription that says: "Valor, power, and glory."
• A Venetian painting circa 1480, *Birth of the Virgin*, includes the household cat.
• A 1493 woodcut shows a Venetian doctor visiting a plague patient while a cat sits on guard.

LEFT
Jan Cornelisz Vermeyen's The Holy Family By The Fire *(c. 1532–33) showing a cat by the Virgin's feet.*

• Cats were often depicted in Asian art as protectors of crops and silkworms.
• Chinese painter Shên Chou, one of the first great masters of the Ming Dynasty, featured cats in 1494.
• Albrecht Dürer's 1504 engraving of Adam and Eve includes a cat in the Garden of Eden.
• *The Holy Family By The Fire* (c. 1532–1533) by Dutch artist Jan Cornelisz Vermeyen shows a cat by Mary's feet.
• The Mogul miniature from the 1500s, *Noah and the Flood*, features a cat on the ark.
• In 1654 Rembrandt etched *The Virgin and Child with Cat*. Judith Leyster painted *Laughing Children With a Cat* in 1629. Dutch artist Jan Steen painted *The Cat's Dancing Lesson*, oil on panel.
• A blue and white earthenware jug from Southwark, England, circa 1670 is in the shape of a cat.

BELOW
A slightly perturbed cat in Laughing Children With a Cat *by artist Judith Leyster, who painted in the 1600s.*

Fascinating Facts

There is a legend that many little kittens were thrown into a river to drown. The mother cat wept and was so distraught that the willow trees on the bank felt compassion and held out their branches to the struggling kittens that clung to them and were saved. Ever since that time, every spring the willow trees wear gray buds that feel as soft and silky as kitten tails. That is why they are called "pussy willows."

• Alexandre-François Desportes' *A Cat Attacking Dead Game* features a cat with dead game birds.
• William Hogarth included a scene depicting the abuse of cats in his 1750 series of engravings entitled *The Four Stages of Cruelty*.
• In *Don Manuel Osorio de Zuñiga* (1787), Goya painted a child teasing a cat with a bird at the end of a string.
• Japanese artist Hiroshige Utagawa features a Japanese bobtail in an 1868 woodcut, *Cat In A Window*.
• Manet's shocking, realistic nude etching *Olympia* includes her black cat.
• French Impressionist Auguste Renoir's 1887 oil on canvas, *Julie Manet With Cat*, depicts the young woman hugging a small brown tabby cat.
• An 1894 poster advertising sterilized milk features images of cats by Théophile-Alexandre Steinlen.
• In 1903 French artist Pierre Bonnard included cats in a series of brush and ink illustrations for Jules Renard's *Histoires Naturelles*.
• Russian painter Marc Chagall's *Paris Through The Window* features his cat gazing out on a dreamlike Eiffel Tower.
• *Cat and Yellow Butterfly* was painted in the first half of the 1900s by Chinese artist Hsii Pei-hung.
• German expressionist Gerhard Marcks created a woodcut titled *Cats* in 1921.
• Picasso's 1939 oil painting *Cat and Bird* symbolizes the cruelty of nature.
• The 1962 woodcut *Woman and Cats* is by American printmaker Will Barnet.
• The poster for the New York Art Expo of 1983 features a cat by artist Marty Neumeier. By the 1900s feline art entered a period that ran the gamut from superrealism to fantasy, the latter exemplified by the art of Susan Herbert, a leading and prolific cat artist with nine books in print.

ABOVE
Cats often featured in domestic genre paintings such as Marguerite Gerard's The Cat's Lunch.

BELOW
Julie Manet With Cat *(1887) by Auguste Renoir, depicting the daughter of Berthe Morisot and Eugène Manet.*

BELOW
Alexandre-François Desportes painted a very fortunate feline in A Cat Attacking Dead Game.

Movies and Theater

Cats in Live-action Movies

Felines have often been cast as main characters, especially in Disney movies.

- In 1963 a Siamese cat, Tao, costarred in the movie *The Incredible Journey*, adapted from a novel with the same title by Sheila Burnford.
- Sassie, a Himalayan, costarred in the 1993 remake of the same movied and the 1996 sequel *Homeward Bound II: Lost in San Francisco*.
- 1964 Disney movie *Three Lives of Thomasina*, originally a book by Paul Gallico, tells the story of an orange tabby cat that uses up three of her lives before returning to her first owner, a little girl.
- *That Darn Cat* is a Disney movie adaptation of the book *Undercover Cat*, first produced in 1965 and remade in 1997. It tells the story of a cat, DC, that helps solve a kidnapping.
- *The Adventures of Milo and Otis* is an award-winning, live-action movie about an orange tabby, Milo, and a fawn pug, Otis. Originally a 1986 Japanese movie, the English language version was released in 1989 in the U.S.
- Snowbell is the white Persian featured in the *Stuart Little* movies.

Even as minor characters, cats on the big screen are memorable. Blofeld's unnamed white Persian cat from three James Bond movies has inspired many imitations and spoofs.

- Duchess, from the 1995 film *Babe*, and Mr. Jinx, a Himalayan cat from *Meet the Parents* and its sequel *Meet the Fockers*, are all memorable characters.

Fascinating Facts

Garfield's creator Jim Davis does not own a cat. His wife is allergic to them.

RIGHT

The animated film Cats & Dogs *by Lawrence Guterman told of an ongoing battle between the two species.*

ABOVE

Snowbell the white Persian, the sworn enemy of mouse Stuart Little in the movies with the same name.

ABOVE

Macavity the Cat, from a production of Andrew Lloyd Webber's popular stage musical Cats.

Cats in Animated Movies

Cats are natural choices for animation.

- The casts of *The Aristocats* and *Gay Purr-ee* are mostly feline.
- *Cats & Dogs* postulates an ongoing war between cats and dogs dating back to ancient times.
- In 2004 the Puss in Boots character was introduced in the blockbuster sequel, *Shrek 2*.
- *Fritz the Cat*, a 1972 animated movie based on the comics by Robert Crumb, was the first animated movie to receive an X-rating in the U.S. It was ranked 51st in the greatest animated movie of all time list by the Online Film Critics Society and number 56 on Channel 4's list of the 100 Greatest Cartoons.

Cats On Stage

Any discussion of feline characters in the theater is sure to include British composer Andrew Lloyd Webber's successful 1981 musical *Cats*, based on poet T. S. Eliot's 1939 children's book, *Old Possum's Book of Practical Cats*. This musical was a huge success, both in London's West End and New York City's Broadway. It won seven Tony Awards and was the longest-running show on Broadway until its final performance on September 10, 2000.

BELOW

Tom's schemes to catch Jerry the mouse were never successful and usually backfired on the hapless cat.

ABOVE

The first feline star—Pat Sullivan's silent-movie era Felix the Cat—seen here sitting on some cheese.

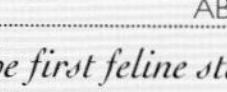

Comics and Cartoons

The first great feline star was Pat Sullivan's cartoon hero "Felix the Cat," a black and white cat that debuted in the silent-movie era in 1928. In the 1930s the gray cartoon feline, Tom, chased Jerry, the mouse, with little success.

- In 1945 Sylvester the cat spluttered "Sufferin' succotash!" when thwarted by Tweety Pie, the canary.
- Heathcliff, a cartoon tabby always in trouble, debuted in 1973, moving to television in 1980.
- Garfield is the comic strip cat known for his laziness, sarcasm, and appetite.
- An animated Garfield starred in the 2004 movie, *Garfield, The Movie*, and in the 2006 sequel, *Garfield: A Tail of Two Kitties*.

The Cat in Advertising

Naturally commercials advertising cat food feature feline actors. A few cats have attained star status pitching their particular brands.

- In 1963 Arthur the cat appeared on British television in the first of 309 advertisements for a cat food. His trademark was using one paw to scoop and eat food straight out of the can.
- Glitter, the silver tabby British Shorthair, worked as the spokescat for Whiskas.
- Finicky Felix was the feline that could not resist Friskies cat food.
- SH III, a Chinchilla Persian, appeared in Fancy Feast advertisements and the movies *The Jerk* and *Scrooged*.
- Morris, the egotistical orange tabby that appeared in a series of U.S. commercials for 9 Lives, was played by a series of similar-looking cats.

Fascinating Facts

The original Morris was rescued from a Chicago-area animal shelter. Besides serving as a spokescat, this philanthropic cat makes public appearances on behalf of homeless pets nationwide.

LEFT

Garfield began his career as a comic strip character before hitting the big screen in 2004.

RIGHT

Arthur the cat made hundreds of advertisements in which he would scoop cat food directly out of the can.

Famous cats

Many real-life cats have earned fame: Grampa was the oldest recorded domestic cat – he was born in Texas in 1964 and lived 34 years; *The Guinness Book of World Records* names Himmy to be the heaviest cat, at 46 lbs; CopyCat is the first cloned cat; Morris II, the successor to the original advertisement cat, ran for president in 1988; Oscar, a hospice cat, was written up in the New England *Journal of Medicine* for his uncanny ability to predict which patients were going to die; and a cat called Willard was credited as coauthor of two research papers in physics written by his owner at Michigan State University.

The British Navy has a history of loyal serving felines. Simon, of H.M.S. *Amethyst*, is the only cat to have won the PDSA's (People's Dispensary for Sick Animals) Dickin Medal for his morale-boosting activities during the Yangtze Incident in 1949. The most famous seafaring cat, however, is Unsinkable Sam, the mascot of the British Royal Navy, who served as ship's cat of the *Bismarck*, H.M.S. *Cossack*, and H.M.S. *Ark Royal*, surviving the torpedoing of all three ships.

Macavity is a British cat who regularly rides the bus to visit a fish and chip restaurant near his home. Hamlet is the world's most traveled cat, flying over 370,000 mi. (600,000 km) when he got stuck in a Canadian airplane for seven weeks. Fatty, a London cat, lived in St. Faith & St. Augustine's Church by St. Paul's cathedral in wartime Britain and received a PDSA Silver Medal for bravery in caring for her kitten when the church was bombed. In 1996 a small cat saved her kittens from a fire in Brooklyn, suffering horrible burns in the process. Named Scarlett by the fireman who rescued her, she embodies the power of a mother's love.

ABOVE

The first cloned cat, born in December 2001 in Texas and shown here at the age of seven weeks.

LEFT

The Dickin Medal, modeled here by Luna the cat, was awarded to Simon of H.M.S. Amethyst in 1949.

BELOW

Cats are popular on military ships as good luck symbols; this feline was the mascot of U.S.S. Macdonough III.

Famous owners

Sir Isaac Newton, one of the leading scientific intellects of all time, invented the cat-flap for his favorite cat, Spithead. when his cat fell asleep on his right. Sir Walter Scott, author of Rob Roy and Ivanhoe, was painted at his desk with his tabby, Hinx, lying nearby.

Albert Schweitzer, 1952 Nobel Peace Prizewinner, became ambidextrous by writing with his left hand

ABOVE

Author Mark Twain gave his cats interesting names — Beelzebub, Appollinaris, and Zoroaster.

BELOW

English Prime Minister Sir Winston Churchill remembered his tomcat Jock in his will.

Charles Dickens' cat kept him company in his study as he wrote, demanding his attention by snuffing out his reading candle.

Author Mark Twain, creator of Tom Sawyer and Huck Finn, chose unusual names for his cats (Blatherskite, Beelzebub, Appollinaris, and Zoroaster) "to practice the children in large and difficult styles of pronunciation." Sir Winston Churchill, Prime Minister of England, owned an orange cat named Jock that slept in the statesman's bed, joined his master during mealtimes, and attended all the wartime cabinet meetings. Churchill included Jock in his will. President Abraham Lincoln entered presidential office accompanied by a cat, and Theodore Roosevelt had a polydactyl gray cat named Slippers. The first Siamese cat brought to the United States was a gift to President Rutherford B. Hayes.

Fascinating Facts

According to Chinese astrology, people born in the Year of the Cat are considered decent, smart, and with a high regard for others. They are also aloof and oversensitive. Years of the Cat include: 1963, 1975, 1987, 1999, and 2011.

ABOVE

Sir Isaac Newton, scientific intellect and cat-lover, who invented the cat-flap for one of his pets.

ANATOMY, PHYSIOLOGY, AND APPEARANCE

While effortlessly fitting into our modern environment, the domestic cat's unique physical appearance and mental abilities are the hereditary gifts of its historical role as a nocturnal hunter. Like its wild cousins, the family cat possesses retractable claws, remarkable night vision, a sharp sense of hearing, and a highly flexible, muscular body. The cat's physical attributes are complemented by its active intelligence, excellent memory, sharp analytical skills, and an aptitude to learn from experience . . . and of course its inexhaustible curiosity.

Skeleton and Physique

The Skeleton

The feline physique is designed for powerful and fluid movements needed to stalk and capture wild prey. The cat skeleton is composed of 230 bones compared to the human's 206. Allowing for a variation in tail length dependent upon the breed of cat, almost 10 percent of a cat's bones are in the tail. The cat has 30 vertebrae in its backbone, five more than a human. The extra bones allow for the backbone's flexibility, contributing to the cat's athletic prowess. The cat's clavicle bones are free-floating, which is why its body can fit through any opening its head can pass through.

The overall skeleton provides a framework for the body. The ribs and sternum (breastbone) protect the heart and lungs from injury, while the skull protects the brain and eyes. There are specialized bones in the ear that allow the cat to hear.

ABOVE

The long bones of a cat's legs are usually fully formed after around one year of growth.

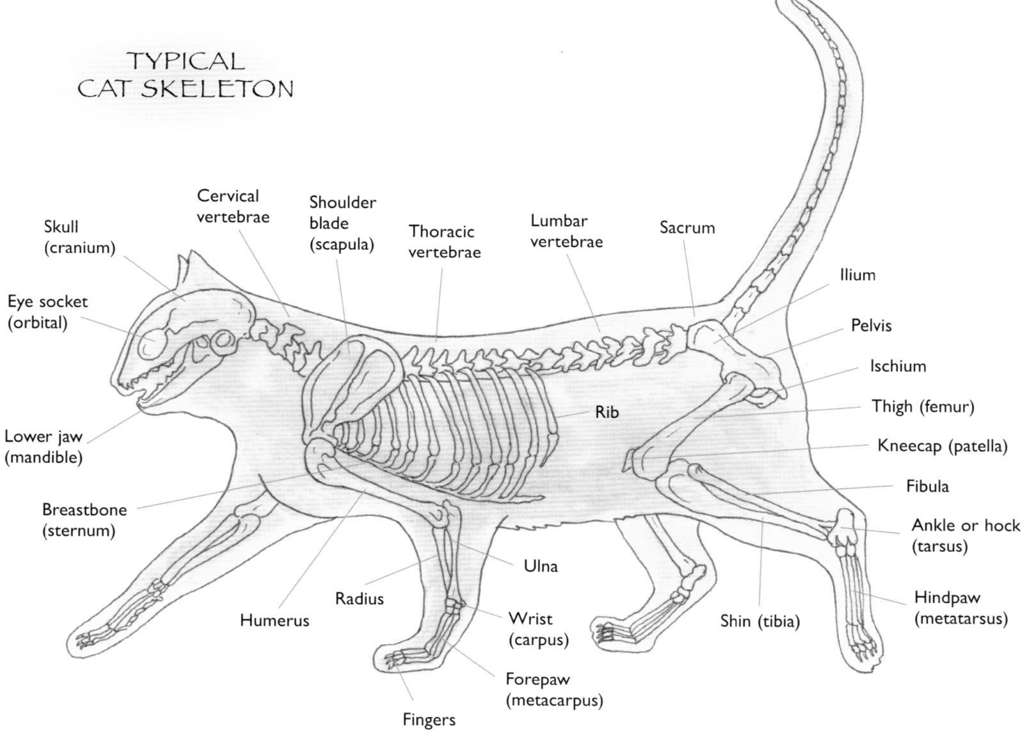

The cat skeleton is composed of four types of bones: long, short, irregular, and flat. The long bones of the legs are elongated cylinders with hollow shafts that contain the marrow that manufactures red blood corpuscles. Short bones, including the toes and kneecaps, have a spongy core surrounded by compact bone. The vertebrae of the spine are irregular bones, similar in composition to short bones except for the unusual shape. Flat bones consist of a thin central layer of spongy bone sandwiched between two layers of compact bone and form the skull, the shoulder blades, and the pelvis.

Fascinating Facts

At 2¾ in. (7 cm) tall and 7½ in. (19 cm) long, Tinker Toy, a male blue point Himalayan, held the record as the smallest domestic cat.

RIGHT

The striated muscles enable the cat to make voluntary movements, like walking and stretching.

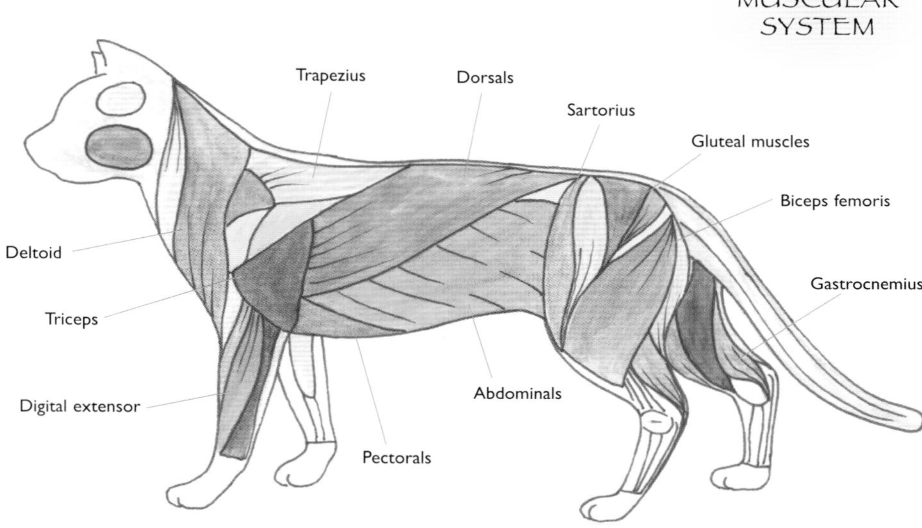

Bones are living organs composed of calcium and phosphorus, with their own blood supply and nerves. The long bones of the legs grow from immature bone located near the ends, called the epiphyseal or growth plates. Once growth is complete, usually around one year of age, the growth plates "close," becoming hardened with calcium and minerals, a process called mineralization. Until the growth plates harden, they are especially vulnerable to injury. Epiphyseal fractures are common in kittens near the wrist (carpus) and the knee (stifle).

The Muscular System

The cat has 500 skeletal muscles. There are two basic types of muscles: smooth and striated. The smooth muscles are involuntary—the individual has no control over their function. They are the muscles associated with the internal organs such as the intestines, stomach, and bladder. Striated muscles are predominately attached to bones of the skeleton and are under the conscious control of the individual. The striated muscles are what allow the cat to walk, eat, and to move its eyes, ears, and tail.

Development of the muscles reflects the physical needs and abilities of the cat. The hindquarters of the cat are thickly muscled so that the hind legs can provide the explosive power needed to leap and pounce on prey when hunting. The strong muscles of the cat's lower bottom jaw enable it to grasp and hold its prey securely.

Claws

Like its skeleton and musculature, the cat's specialized claws and dentition evolved from its hunting past. The cat has five toes and claws on each front foot and four on each back foot. The fifth claw on the front foot is located higher on the inside of the leg and is called the dewclaw. The dewclaw acts like a thumb, aiding the cat to grip when attacking prey or climbing. Cats become stuck in trees because their claws are constructed perfectly to climb up, but they curve the wrong way to climb down.

Claw Retracted

Ligament relaxed

Claw Extended

Ligament contracted

CLAW RETRACTION AND EXTENSION

The claws are made out of keratin, the same protein that forms the outer layer of the skin and human nails. A blood vessel called the "quick" runs through the center of the nail. The quick does not reach the end of the actual point of the claw, allowing you to trim the nail. If you cut into them, the nail will bleed.

What makes the cat unique in the carnivore family is that its claws retract, allowing the cat to silently stalk its prey. As the cat attacks, specialized ligaments contract, and the claws flash out to grip the prey. Because the claws retract when not needed, they stay very sharp.

The Polydactyl

While most cats have a total of 18 toes and claws, some cats are more generously endowed. Polydactyl is the name used to describe cats with extra toes and claws—sometimes up to seven on each foot.

Also known as hyperdactyl or supernumerary digits, extra toes are not a rare trait in felines. The innermost extra toes on the front paws are often opposable, allowing some cats to use their front paws like hands in an almost humanlike manner. While polydactylism can be hereditary or a spontaneous mutation, it is a condition and not a breed of cat. The most famous colony of polydactyl cats was owned by American writer Ernest Hemingway. The multi-toed descendents of Hemingway's original cats still live in his former home in Key West, Florida, where they are protected by law.

Fascinating Facts

The cheetah is the one breed of cat that does not have retractable claws. Renowned as the fastest land mammal, the cheetah can attain a running speed approaching 70 mph (112 km/h). It does not hunt by stealth but by chasing down its prey. Its non-retracting claws provide the traction that help it run and corner at high speeds, similar to the way the cleats on an athlete's shoes help running in sports events.

LEFT

Extra toes are not uncommon in cats; this polydactyl kitten has six toes on each of her front paws.

The Teeth

Feline dentition is designed for tearing and biting, not chewing. In the wild the cat tears a piece from the carcass and swallows it whole. Teeth come in four types. Incisors are small front teeth, closely spaced, ideal for ripping and scraping flesh off bone. The canines are the pointed fangs or eyeteeth made for holding prey down, killing, and ripping. Because cats do not chew in the classic sense, the premolars and molars slice food into chunks small enough to swallow. The premolar and first molar function to cut meat like a pair of scissors. The cat's teeth are symmetrical on each side of the jaw, but they differ in number from the top jaw to the lower jaw. The upper jaw contains six incisors, two canines, six premolars, and two molars. The lower jaw contains six incisors, two canines, only four premolars, and two molars.

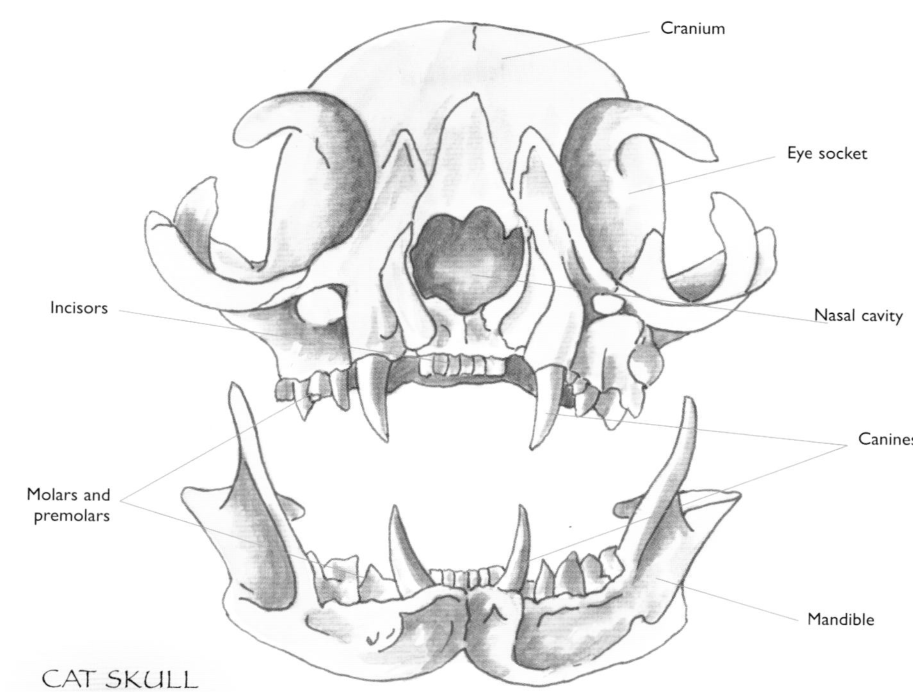

CAT SKULL

Like a human baby, a kitten is born without teeth. The deciduous or "milk teeth" begin to appear at around four weeks of age. By six weeks of age, 26 deciduous teeth are present: 12 incisors, four canines, and ten premolars (no molars). Between 13 to 30 weeks of age kittens lose their baby teeth, and the permanent adult teeth come in. By six months old the kitten has 30 permanent teeth. By comparison a dog has 42 permanent teeth.

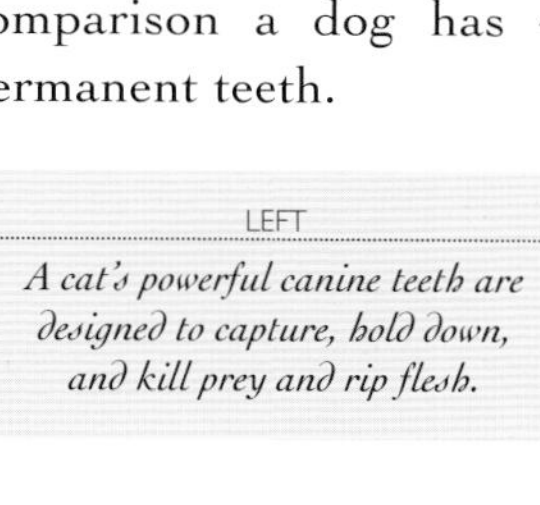

LEFT

A cat's powerful canine teeth are designed to capture, hold down, and kill prey and rip flesh.

Skin and Coat

The Skin

Cats have especially loose-fitting skin that allows them to defend themselves by wiggling around in the grip of a predator. The veterinarian also finds this convenient when giving an injection or fluids under the skin. The scruff is the loose skin at the back of the neck. The mother cat grips her kittens by the scruff to carry them. Even as an adult, most cats usually become quiet and passive when gripped by the skin on the back of the neck; from there the expression "scruffing" the cat. This behavior can be useful to subdue an injured or uncooperative cat. Never attempt to carry an adult cat by the scruff, as it is too heavy and should be supported under the rump and chest. The tough outer layer of the skin is called the epidermis. As the outer cells erode, cells underneath mature and move up to replace them. The thickness of the epidermis varies. The more exposed areas, such as the head and back, are thicker than less exposed areas, such as the armpits and belly.

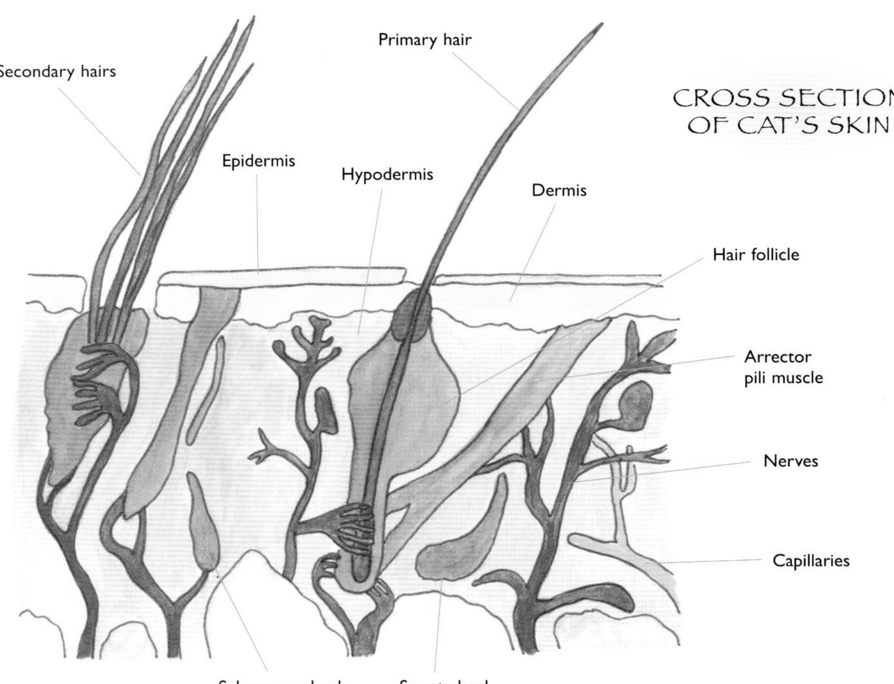

ABOVE

A cat's loose-fitting skin allows it to be carried safely when young, as well as to escape predators.

BELOW

The outer layer of a cat's skin is thicker on the more exposed areas of its body, such as the paw pads.

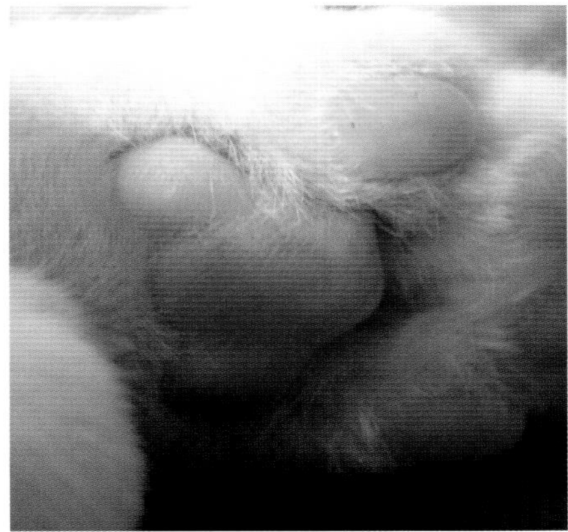

The deeper layer of the skin, called the dermis, contains hair follicles, blood vessels, nerves, and sebaceous oil glands. Cats do not sweat through their skin but through their paw pads and nose. They lose water by panting rather than sweating. Hair follicles and sebaceous glands are more numerous on the back than on the belly.

The Coat

Like claws, hair is composed of keratin. Each hair follicle can grow a single hair. A kitten is born with all the hair follicles it will ever possess. Most cats have four basic types of hairs: guard, awn, down hair, and vibrissae. The average adult cat has around 1,000 down hairs for every 300 awn hairs and 20 guard hairs, although the ratio can differ by age and breed. Newborn kittens lack primary guard hairs, which is why their coats are short and soft.

ABOVE

A cat does not sweat through its skin like a human but through its paw pads and nose.

RIGHT

A kitten's coat is shorter and softer than that of an adult, as the guard hairs have not yet developed.

Types of Hairs The guard hairs make up most of the outer topcoat of the cat. They are slender, taper toward the tip, and are longer and thicker than the down or awn hairs. Guard hairs protect the undercoat and act as a waterproof outer "jacket." The cuticles on guard hairs have microscopic barbs that are very rough. The awn hairs make up the "middle" coat of the cat. These are "intermediate-size" hairs with rough, broken, or cracked cuticles. They provide insulation and protect the down hairs underneath. The down hairs are the hairs closest to the skin and form the cat's undercoat. They are the shortest, finest, and softest hairs. Like a feather comforter, the down hairs keep the cat warm because they have microscopic crimps or waves that trap air, making them such good insulators. Cat hair clings to clothes because it is electrostatic, the guard hairs have small barbs, and because the awn hairs have cracked cuticles.

RIGHT

The sensitive vibrissae hairs are shown here plainly on the cat's face.

Vibrissae are thick, specialized hairs that are very sensitive to touch. The most apparent vibrissae hairs on the cat are its 24 whiskers, arranged in four rows on each side of the muzzle. Whiskers are more than twice as thick as ordinary hairs, and their roots are set three times deeper in a cat's tissue. Vibrissae are also found on the upper lips, the cheeks, above the eyes, and on the wrists of the forelegs.

Whiskers provide sensory information about the slightest air movement—a valuable tool for a nocturnal hunter. Cats use their whiskers in the dark to identify things they can't see or to navigate through underbrush.

BELOW

Longhaired cats have exaggerated guard hairs, forming a thick, soft, and luxuriant coat.

BELOW RIGHT

The coat of the Devon Rex contains no guard hairs, resulting in a different feel and texture.

Fascinating Facts

If you touch a cat's whiskers, the cat will automatically squint the eye on that side. It is nature's way of protecting the eye from injury from twigs or brush. If a cat becomes so overweight that its sides stick out farther than its whiskers, it will lose its sense of perception and stability.

Fascinating Facts

Cats have thinning hair between the top of their eyes and their ears. In the wild this gives the impression that the cat's eyes are open when it is asleep, discouraging possible predators.

RIGHT

Sphynx cats give the impression of being hairless but in fact have down hairs on some parts of their bodies.

Breed Differences There is a wide variation in different breeds regarding the size, shape, and distribution of the types of hairs. For example, Persians have guard hairs that are exaggerated in length. American Wirehairs have all three hair types, but all are short and curly. Cornish Rex have no guard hairs at all. While the Sphynx appears hairless, it has a light sprinkling of down hairs on some areas of its body.

Hair Growth and Shedding Cats continually shed old hair, replacing it with new living and growing hair. Anagen is the first phase, during which the new hair grows beside the old hair, which is subsequently lost. Catagen is an intermediate stage, and telogen is the resting phase when the follicle becomes dormant. Different follicles are always in different phases, so the cat is never hairless.There is no such thing as a non-shedding breed. Shedding is governed by age, amount of sunlight, temperature, breed, sex, hormones, allergies, and nutrition. Indoor cats who live mainly under artificial light usually shed continuously. Strictly outdoor cats shed for several weeks during major seasonal changes, mostly in the spring and fall. While the hair coat changes in appearance and texture, the number of hair follicles remains the same.

BELOW

The thinning hair between a cat's eyes and its ears makes it appear to be awake when it is sleeping.

Red

Colors and Markings

There are two basic colors in cats—black and red (often referred to as orange). All other colors and patterns are the result of modifying genes that trigger changes to the basic colors.

Colors and Patterns

Solid or self-colored A cat of one coat color. The basic solid colors are white, black, and red. White is a dominant masking gene. Although the cat has genes for other colors, white is the only color expressed visibly. A modifying gene dilutes the color black to blue, more commonly but incorrectly called gray. Red is diluted to cream. The chocolate modifying gene changes black into chocolate and blue into lilac but has no effect on the red gene. Other modifying genes produce brown or cinnamon.

Parti-colored A two-toned cat. Cats with a mix of red and black are tortoiseshells. The dilute is called blue-cream. The genes for black and red are carried on the X chromosome, often called the sex chromosome. Female cats have two X chromosomes (XX), while a normal male only has one (XY)—that is why parti-colors are females. The occasional male tortoiseshell, blue-cream, or calico is the result of the male having an extra X chromosome (XXY).

> **Fascinating Facts**
>
> One out of every 1,000 tortoiseshells will be male.

White

LEFT

A calico cat; this coloring is very rare in males and only occurs if the cat has an extra X chromosome.

Tortoiseshell-and-white (Calico)

Brown

Cinnamon

Black

Cream

Lilac

ABOVE

The shade of this lilac cat's coat is a result of the chocolate modifying gene altering the blue color.

Blue

LEFT

This Korat cat is an example of the blue solid-color, which is a dilution of the basic black.

Blue-cream

Tabby A coat pattern, not a color. It can be combined with any variety of other coat colors and patterns. Tabbies come in four main patterns. The mackerel tabby is the most common pattern. These tabbies have an "M" pattern on the forehead, striped rings around their tail and legs, a "necklace" of stripes on the front of their chests, and bands of solid or broken stripes running down the sides of their bodies. The classic tabby also has the distinctive "M" on the head but has whirls of colors ending in a "bull's-eye" on the side of the cat and a butterfly pattern across the shoulder. The Ocicat and the American bobtail are good examples of a spotted tabby pattern, which typically has distinct spots arranged in lines reminiscent of a mackerel tabby pattern. Finally a flecked tabby, such as seen on an Abyssinian, has hairs with distinct bands of color on them, breaking up the tabby patterning into a salt-and-pepper appearance. Ghost striping or "barring" may be seen on the legs, face, and belly.

Fascinating Facts

It is believed that the term "tabby" comes from Attibiah, an ancient district in Baghdad, where artists wove beautiful, watered, silk fabric called tabby cloth, later called taffeta.

With white (bicolor) The piebald or spotting gene adds patches of white to any other combination of color and pattern. White spots on the chest are called lockets, and white feet are known as mittens or gloves. A single spotting gene produces a cat with less than half white—often in the classical tuxedo pattern with white on the paws, chest, belly, and nose. If the cat has two spotting genes, it will be more than half white, sometimes appearing all white except for the head and tail, a pattern called van. In the Japanese bobtail, the pattern is called Mi-Ke.

BELOW

A mackerel patterned tabby, with the characteristic "M" on the forehead and striped necklace.

Classic Tabby

Mackeral Tabby

Flecked Tabby

Spotted Tabby

LEFT

The single spotting gene results in a cat having white patches that make up less than half of its coloring.

Single Spotting Genes

Two Spotting Genes

Single Spotting Genes

Pointed Most people are familiar with the Siamese and Himalayan cats, with their striking coat pointed pattern. The pointed cat has a pale body color with the head, tail, and legs having a darker color.

Fascinating Facts

The Oriental breed of cat has over 300 recognized colors.

Shaded or Smoke This coat pattern occurs when an inhibitor gene causes color to be confined to the tip of the hair. If the amount of color is mostly on the tip of the hair, the color is called "shaded." If the color is more than halfway down the shaft, the cat is a smoke. If the cat is a tabby, the inhibitor changes the base color of the tabby, producing a silver tabby.

Seal Point

Red Point

DEGREES OF HAIR TIPPING

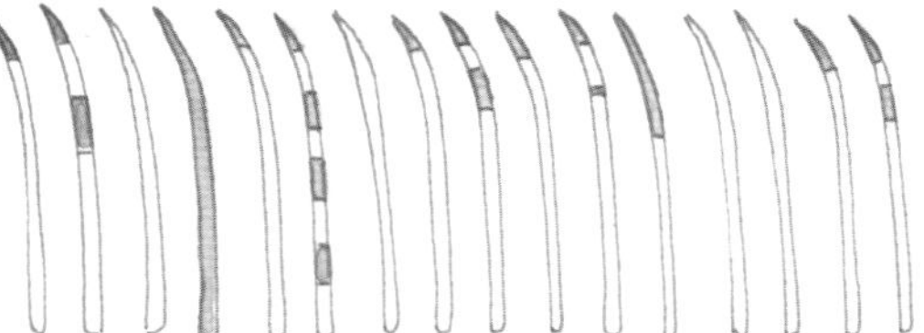

Uneven "confused" banding—shaded type

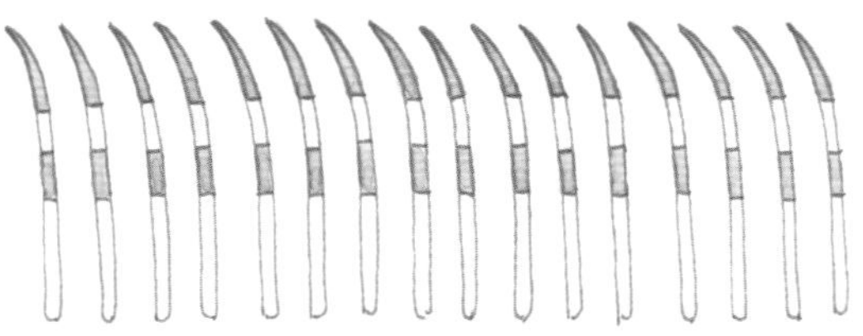

Even banding—Abssinian type ("flecked")

Is Color a Breed?
Color and pattern do not determine a cat's breed. A breed is determined by the physical characteristics described in each breed's standard, while the same colors and patterns can be seen in many different breeds. Mixed breed cats have all the same colors and patterns that are seen in purebred cats.

BELOW
Pointed cats, such as this Ragdoll, have a pale body with a darker color on the head, tail, and legs.

Blue Point

Different Names —Same Color
In discussing colors of cats, it can be confusing—there are different names for the same color. The correct term "red" is commonly referred to as "orange," "rust," "yellow," "ginger," and "marmalade." Cream is often called "buff," "tan," or "blonde." Different cat registries call the same color by different names. A calico in one organization is a "black tortie and white" in another registry and a "tricolor" in a third.

Smoke

Shaded

Fascinating Facts

While most kittens are born the color they will be as an adult, pointed kittens are born white and the color develops on the extremities over time.

BELOW
Some colors, such as calico, are confusingly given different names by various organizations.

Sight

Because the cat is a nocturnal hunter, sharp night vision was an evolutionary development that helped it become a successful predator. Contrary to popular myth, a cat cannot actually see in the dark. It can, however, see extremely well in very dim lighting conditions.

The cat's eye has several adaptations that help it see in low light. Compared to the human eye, the cat's eye is larger and rounder. Cats' eyes have more receptor cells and more neurons in the visual centers of the brain.

Light passes through the cornea and pupil of the eye and strikes the retina. The cat's retina has fewer cones but more rods than the human eye. The cones perceive color, while the rods are sensitive to light. While a cat sees fewer variations in color than a human, it sees better in low light conditions. While cats see fewer colors, they are able to distinguish more shades of gray. Since their prey species are usually shades of gray, (mice, rats, and birds) this visual feature works well out in the wild. The cat's pupil contracts to a slit instead of a circle, giving the cat more accurate control of the light entering the eye, especially in bright sunlight. The slit blocks more light than a round pupil can. Because the cats' eyelids close at right angles to the vertical pupil, the cat can further reduce the amount of light by bringing its eyelids closer together. This combination allows the cat to make very delicate adjustments and gives its vision a sharp depth of field.

ABOVE

In darkness, a cat's pupil widens to let in as much light as possible.

LEFT

In bright light, a cat's pupils narrow from a circle to a slit, preventing excess light from entering the eyes.

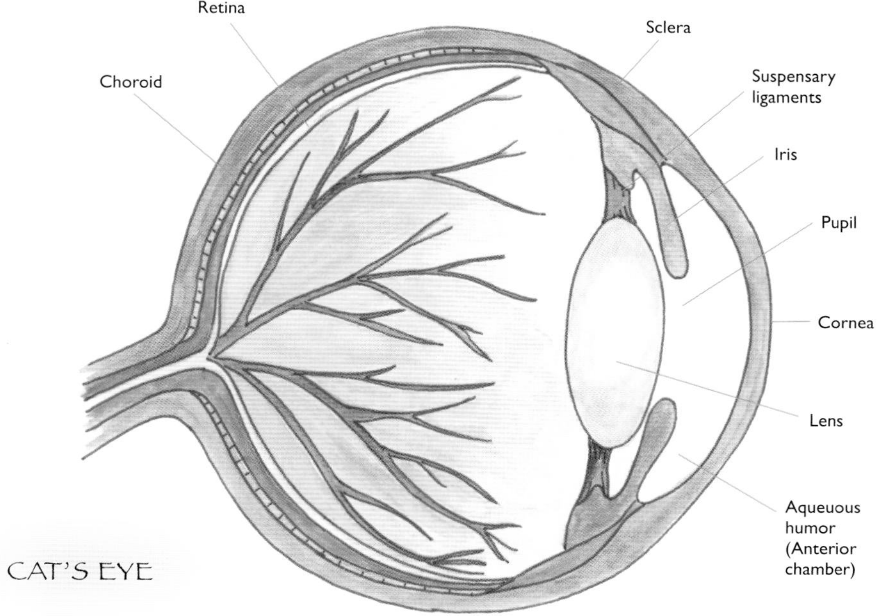

CAT'S EYE

Fascinating Facts

The lion hunts by day, not by night. Because the lion does not need the same sensitivity to light as the cat, its eyes contract to tiny circles, not vertical slits.

The feline's eye has an extra inner layer of cells called the *tapetum lucidium*, that has a multiplying effect by reflecting extra light to the retina. The glow of cat's eyes in flash photography is largely due to light reflecting off the tapetum.

The eyes of the cat face forward so that the field of vision of each eye overlaps. This stereoscopic vision allows the cat to assess distance and location accurately when hunting prey. Because the eyes are deeply set in the face, the cat's field of vision is only around 185 degrees. With limited peripheral vision, the cat must turn its head to see better from side to side. Instead of the fovea that gives humans sharp central vision, cats have a central band known as the visual streak.

In addition to upper and lower eyelids, the cat has a third eyelid called the nictitating membrane or haw. The clear membrane moves across the eye as the eye moves within the socket, removing dust or debris. Lachrymal glands produce tears that wash and lubricate the eye. When a cat is sick, the third eyelid will partially close, although it is often visible in a sleepy, contented cat. Because the eye is lubricated by the nictitating membrane, the cat blinks less often, an advantage when hunting in the wild.

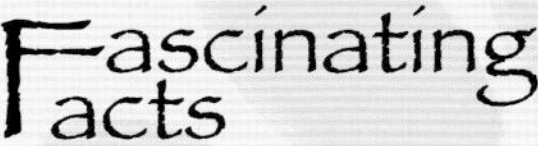

Fascinating Facts

Kittens usually open their eyes at seven to ten days, but some breeds can open them in as little as two days, and occasionally a kitten is born with its eyes open.

BELOW

A cat's eyes are lubricated by the nictitating membrane, which means it needs to blink less often.

Hearing

The hearing of the cat is outstanding—even sharper than that of a dog. In fact, of their six senses a cats' hearing is the most acute. This excellent hearing is an evolutionary advantage that helped cats hunt for their prey. The cat's ear consists of three sections. The external outer ear is called the pinna, or earflap. In most breeds of cats, the external ear is erect and points forward.

Thirty-two individual muscles in each ear allow it to swivel and pivot up to 180 degrees to scoop in sound waves and better pinpoint the exact source of a sound. Each ear moves independently of the other. The sound waves funnel down the ear to the eardrum, that stretches across the ear canal. The middle ear has three small bones that convert the weak sound vibrations of the eardrum into small, strong vibrations of the cochlea of the inner ear. The inner ear converts the vibrations into nerve impulses, which pass along the acoustic nerve to the brain. The cat's brain decodes the signals and recognizes them by comparing them with sounds stored in its memory bank. In this way a cat learns to identify specific sounds. At lower-pitched frequencies, there is little difference between the hearing of cats, dogs, or humans. People hear sound frequencies up to 20,000 cycles/second. Dogs hear up to 35,000 –45,000 cycles/second. However, cats can hear sounds of an amazingly high pitch—up to 100,000 cycles/second. That is two octaves above what humans can hear and includes ultrasonic sound waves. It is also the high-pitched range of sounds made by mice and other small rodents—the food source for a cat out in the wild.

ABOVE

A cat's ears can move independently from one other and can swivel up to 180 degrees to aid sound location.

RIGHT

The cat's ability to hear extremely high pitches can help it locate prey when it is hunting.

Cats are experts at telling the exact direction from which a sound originates. The cat determines the direction of the source of the sound by differences in the time of arrival and intensity of sound received by each ear. A cat can differentiate between two sound sources separated by as little an angle as 5 degrees. At a distance of 60 feet, a cat can distinguish between two sounds that are only 18 inches apart. A cat can tell the difference between two sounds from the same direction but at different distances. Their sharp hearing makes it possible for the cat to distinguish between very similar sounds. In a crowded room filled with people and other felines, a cat can distinguish the sound of its owner's footsteps.

The cat's ability to hear even the faintest noise can sometimes be a concern in a noisy situation. A cat may be upset by the noise of a vacuum cleaner or loud music or outdoor noises such as a lawn mower or traffic.

RIGHT

Cats have an amazing ability to distinguish between sounds, although loud noises can frighten them.

BELOW

A cat born with one blue eye is often deaf in the ear on the side of the blue eye.

Smell, Taste, and Touch

Its sense of smell is perhaps the most important of the cat's senses because it is critical to its hunting, feeding, and sexual behavior. A cat's sense of smell is around 14 times that of a human's. The cat has approximately 60 to 80 million olfactory cells that gather and identify the most subtle scents. By comparison a human has only 5 to 20 million olfactory cells, which means cats smell things of which we are not aware. Even the olfactory region of the cat's brain is larger than expected.

The Flehmen Reaction

Cats have a specialized scent organ located in the roof of the mouth just behind the front teeth. Called the vomeronasal sac or Jacobson's organ, it is a small pouch lined with receptor cells and connects to the nasal cavity. When a cat smells certain scents, especially musky or sexual ones, it stretches its neck, opens its mouth, and curls its upper lip. This is termed the Flehmen Reaction. The tongue gathers minute particles of scent and then is pressed to the roof of the mouth, transferring the scent molecules to the Jacobson's organ. Opening the mouth slightly enables the ducts to open up, connecting to the nasal cavity. The appearance of the cat as it brings air into the Jacobson's Organ looks like a smile or a grimace.

Taste

It is not unusual for a cat owner to be surprised by the sandpaper kiss of a cat. What makes the cat's tongue so rough is the numerous hard projections called papillae on the surface. The papillae form backward-facing hooks containing large amounts of keratin, the same material found in human fingernails. The hardness and strength of these hooks helps the cat hold prey. The hooks also provide the abrasiveness that is so effective when a cat grooms itself.

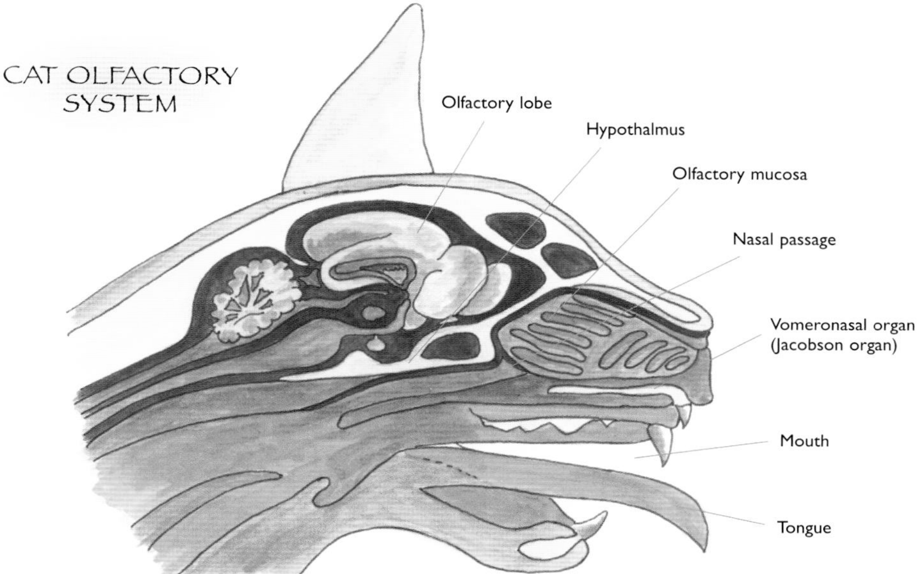

ABOVE
A cat's sense of smell is vital to many facets of its life.

BELOW
The rough surface of a cat's tongue is covered in hard, backward-facing hooks called papillae.

The cat has two sets of taste buds. The ones on the tip and the sides of the tongue are mushroom-shaped papillae that contain some of the largest taste buds. At the very front of the tongue are smaller, circular, "fungiform" papillae. These two sets of taste buds make a cat's sense of taste extremely sensitive. In 2005 it was discovered that the cat family lacks the T1R2 protein, one of two proteins necessary to taste sweetness. Most scientists believe this mutation

Fascinating Facts

No matter how tasty it might be, if a cat cannot smell the food, it will probably not eat it.

may have led to the cat's role as a strict carnivore. Their modified sense of taste would cause them to ignore plants, a large part of whose taste appeal derives from their high sugar content. Instead cats favor a high-protein carnivorous diet, which stimulates their taste receptors.

In addition to flavor, a cat's tongue is sensitive to the texture or "mouth feel" of a particular food. The cat's tongue also reacts to temperature, preferring foods at room temperature.

Water is an essential ingredient and is involved in virtually every function of a cat's body. A cat drinks by making its tongue into a spoon shape. It flicks its tongue quickly in and out of the water, swallowing after every third or fourth lap. A cat's water intake will vary depending on the air temperature and humidity, the cat's activity level, and its diet. Cats fed canned cat food with its high moisture content will not drink as much water as those eating dry food.

Sense of Touch

Like humans, cats have touch receptors all over their body that transfer sensations of pressure, temperature, and pain from nerve cells to the brain. The most sensitive places on the cat's body are the face and front paws. These are the body parts the cat uses most while hunting. The skin of the pads on the underside of a cat's paw is sensitive to pressure but not to a delicate touch. It is the hairs on the tip of the paw that are very sensitive—not the pads.

LEFT

Cats drink by making their tongues into a spoonlike shape and flicking liquid into their mouths.

The nose leather (the fleshy part of the nose) is also very sensitive to touch. It is also receptive to temperature and humidity—like a barometer.

The cat's whiskers also play a critical role in sensation. A cat has around 24 movable vibrissae or whiskers in four rows on each upper lip on each side of its muzzle, in addition to a few on each cheek, tufts over the eyes, bristles on the chin, the inner forelegs, and at the back of the legs.

Richly supplied with nerve endings at their base, whiskers give cats extraordinarily detailed information about air movements, air pressure, and anything they touch. The upper two rows of whiskers can move independently from the lower two rows for precise measuring. As air swirls around objects, whiskers vibrate, detecting very small shifts in air currents. This enables a cat to sense the presence, size, and shape of obstacles without seeing or touching them—a great advantage when hunting in the dark. The structure of the area of the brain region, which receives information from the vibrissae, is similar to that found in the visual cortex, implying a cat's perception through its whiskers is similar to seeing. When a cat's prey is too near for accurate vision, its whiskers move to form a basket shape around its muzzle to detect the prey's location. A cat may rely on the whiskers in dim light, where fully dilating the pupils would reduce its ability to focus on close objects. The whiskers also spread out roughly as wide as the cat's body, making it able to judge if it can fit through an opening.

Fascinating Facts

When cats walk or run they step with both left legs, then both right legs, and so on.

BELOW

Cats can use their whiskers to help them locate other animals when they are too close to see them accurately.

BELOW RIGHT

A cat's nose leather is very sensitive and responds to changes in temperature and humidity.

CAT BEHAVIOR

"Thousands of years ago, cats were worshipped as gods. Cats have never forgotten this," (author unknown). Feline behavior has intrigued humans for hundreds of years, probably because much of the domesticated cat's behavior reflects the patterns inherited from its wild ancestors. This is part of the charm and mystique of the cat. Gaining an insight into how and why a cat reacts to its environment enhances the owner's enjoyment and appreciation of their pet. Many things that a cat does in its home are simply extensions of instinctive habits from the wild.

Cat Psychology

The Catnap and Nocturnal Activity

The average cat sleeps for 13–18 hours a day. Newborn kittens sleep almost non-stop. This is an instinctive behavior that protects them in the wild, as while they are asleep they cannot wander away from the nest. Sleeping, the kittens also make no noise that might attract a predator. As the kittens grow, their proportion of sleeping to time awake gradually changes, until they attain typical adult sleep patterns. Like people, cats will sleep more as they enter old age.

Around one third of a cat's sleeping time is spent in a deep sleep, during which it may dream. Twitching muscles, meows, and growls and purrs often accompany dreams. Unlike humans, cats spend many hours sleeping relatively lightly. During light sleep, the body

Fascinating Facts

Two out of three owners allow their cats to sleep on their beds at night. This can keep your toes warm and allows you to fall asleep with a soothing purring in your ear.

Fascinating Facts

The primary active compound of catnip is Nepetalactone. This is chemically similar to human hallucinogens.

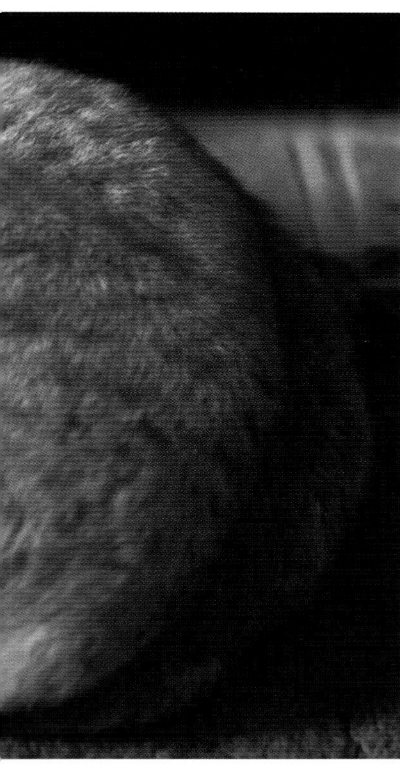

temperature lowers slightly, the muscles are slightly tensed, and the blood pressure remains normal. A cat can go from a light sleep to being fully awake instantly. Because a cat in the wild is a nocturnal hunter, some cats will tend to sleep all day and then wander around the house at night.

A cat can sleep anywhere but prefers a sleeping place that feels safe. Some cats like to be up high and choose a shelf in a cupboard. Some prefer enclosed spaces, like under the couch. During hot summer days a cat may prefer the cool porcelain of a bathroom sink. In the winter most cats cuddle up to a warm spot near a heater. Temperature also affects the cat's sleeping position. When cold, cats tend to curl up in a ball and put their face between their paws to reduce body heat loss. When hot, they will sleep stretched out with the belly turned upward to release the body heat.

The Catnip Response

Catnip (*Nepetia cataria*) is a plant native to North America. Fresh leaves of the catnip plant have a mintlike scent, while dried leaves smell like alfalfa. Watching a cat respond to catnip amuses most people. Pawing, clasping, rolling onto the side, and rhythmic kicking with the back feet is behavior similar to that displayed when they detect and capture prey. Some cats enjoy catnip and revel in its effects, while other cats appear to avoid it, despite prior displays of catnip sensitivity. Generally, male and female cats of reproductive age are more sensitive to catnip than very young or old cats. Catnip is not toxic to pets.

ABOVE RIGHT

Cats can sleep anywhere but often seek out a warmer spot when the weather gets cold.

RIGHT

Some cats respond to catnip, while others remain unaffected.

Inappropriate Biting
Just like human babies, kittens have the urge to chew and bite when they are teething. Or a cat may scratch or bite without warning when you are petting it, as a result of overstimulation. To correct either situation, distract the cat with a toy that is a more acceptable object for aggression.

Bad Litter Tray Habits
If a previously clean cat begins scratching outside the litter tray, this is a signal that the cat is not happy about something. It may be that the tray needs to be cleaned or it is uncomfortable with the feel of the litter, the smell of the litter, the type of tray, or even the location of the tray.

Clawing Furniture
Contrary to popular belief, when a cat claws the furniture it is not sharpening its claws. Scratching helps the cat remove the old claw sheath to expose the new, sharp ones. Cats also scratch on objects to mark their territory by stimulating the release of a scent from glands located between the paw pads.

Kneading
Young kittens instinctively knead their mother's nipples with their tiny forepaws while nursing. The kneading stimulates the flow of milk. When a kitten kneads the lap of his owner, it is mirroring the same happiness that it felt nursing at its mother's belly. While most people recognize and appreciate the privilege a cat bestows when kneading on their person, if the kneading is uncomfortable, too enthusiastic, or continues too long, the cat can be gently discouraged by simply distracting it. Keeping the cat's nails clipped short helps too.

Burying Food
If a cat does not like the taste of wet food on a plate, it may try to "bury" it by scratching repeatedly on the floor or covering it up with whatever might be in the area—a mat, bed, or toy. Even if the cat likes the food, if there is more than it can eat at one meal, it will scrape its paw along the floor as if covering the food. This is an instinctive behavior left over from when a wild cat would bury the remains of a kill to eat later.

Fascinating Facts

Cats can suffer a mid-life crisis, especially if they are bored. They need to be mentally and physically stimulated throughout their life.

ABOVE
Toys can be used to distract cats that bite during petting as a result of overstimulation.

BELOW
Cats scratch to remove their old claw sheaths and also to scent-mark their territory.

Running Water

The sound and motion of water pouring from a tap is mesmerizing to many cats. It is probably a feast for the senses as it stimulates hearing, sight, smell, and touch. Many cats prefer to drink from a running tap, as the water is fresh. Water that has been standing even a few hours loses some of its oxygen content, which changes its taste.

The Foot Attack

Even the most domesticated cat may feel the urge to practice its predatory skills. Some cats make up elaborate prey games, hiding underneath furniture or behind a door waiting for their owner to stroll by and then leaping out and attacking their feet. The cat is not trying to hurt you but is simply reacting to an instinctive urge to hunt. The cat can be discouraged by providing it with more playtime or providing it with a feline playmate.

Retrieving

In the wild, when a cat takes down prey it will often carry it to a safe spot to consume it. The indoor cat's equivalent of this behavior is to retrieve objects in the same way a dog plays fetch.

Sucking, Nursing, or Chewing on Materials

Thought to be a behavior more common if a kitten has been weaned too early, some cats will suck or nurse on material or objects. While some kittens outgrow this behavior, putting something on the item that is distasteful to the cat, such as paprika, cologne, or a citrus scent, can discourage the behavior. Some cats seem addicted to chewing on photographs or paper. Some people believe that some cats detect a slight odor or that the coolness and texture of the plastic feels and tastes good on the cat's tongue.

A related activity is called "pica," an abnormal compulsion to eat things that are not usually eaten. While rare, some cats, especially the Oriental breeds, are noted for snacking on everything from sweaters to phone cords.

LEFT

Cats can be distracted from the desire to ambush their owners by providing them with a playmate.

Instinct and Learning

The size of the average cat brain is 2 in. (5 cm) in length and 1 oz. (30 g) in weight. Since the average cat weighs around 7 lbs (3.3 kg), the brain is less than 0.9 percent of its total body weight, compared with the average human's brain, which accounts for two percent of its body weight.

Cats learn by trial and error, observation, and imitation. The cat's learning abilities are aided by an excellent memory. Cats can remember and recall information much longer than dogs—up to 16 hours, as opposed to a dog's five minutes. In one study it was discovered that cats possess visual memory ability comparable to that of monkeys. The feline short-term working memory is less impressive, however. One study showed that dogs were better than cats in short-term memory tests.

While a cat is born with strong instincts, its aptitude for gathering and analyzing information and learning through experience serves it well. A kitten first learns by imitating its mother. As it grows more independent, it does something and then observes the results. If an action is pleasant, it is likely to repeat it. If not it will be less likely to do it again.

RIGHT

Cats learn about cleanliness from their mother and will use a litter tray from the age of five to six weeks.

A kitten can be seen imitating hunting behavior very early on, at around one month old. If it is an outdoor cat, the mother will bring prey, dead or alive, by the time the kitten is six weeks old. By two months of age the kitten will have learned how to hunt, and by six months it will be a confident hunter capable of satisfying its needs, all by imitating its mother.

RIGHT

A tomcat marks his territory by spraying concentrated urine on some bushes.

The kitten is also taught hygiene and cleanliness from its mother. The mother keeps the birth nest clean by licking and eating the urine and feces of her nursing kittens. As a kitten starts walking and starts eating solid foods, the mother cat will no longer clean the kitten's rump. A kitten will not soil its own bed and will use a litter tray by the time it is five to six weeks old, if one is accessible.

The mother cat is constantly grooming her newborn kittens, and the kitten imitates her licking behavior. Like a human baby, a kitten explores its environment by putting things in its mouth. This is how it learns what is food and what is not. It is trial and error combined with watching what its mother eats.

Territoriality

In the wild cats are territorial. The male stakes out a territory as his food source. He will also protect the area for his female and his kittens. A male may even attack and kill young kittens sired by another male to eliminate competition.

Cats mark their territory by spraying concentrated urine. While usually associated with tomcats, whole females and some neutered males will exhibit spraying behavior. A cat will remark its territory if the previous scent markers have been washed away by weather or cleaning. The usual reason for a previously clean cat to begin urine-marking indoors is a reaction to stress. Commonly the introduction of a new cat to the household will upset a cat. Feeling threatened or stressed by the presence of the strange cat, the resident feline will mark the home as "his."

Fascinating Facts

Cats have self images. Whether it is good or bad depends on the owner, because they will live up or down to the expectations.

LEFT

Cats have scent glands on the sides and back of their heads, which they rub on things to mark ownership.

The cat has glands that secrete scents in several areas of its body but especially concentrated around the sides and back of the head. When a cat rubs its head along your legs, it is marking you—sending a message that you belong to it. Similarly the cat will rub on furniture in the home. The outdoor cat will rub against walls, fences, bushes, and trees.

Marking trees with its claws is another message a cat leaves to be interpreted by other felines. The higher the marks, the larger and more dominant the cat that made the marks, so a cat stretches as far up as it can when scratching on a tree. When the cat digs its claws into the tree, it also leaves a scent message from glands between the paw pads.

Curiosity and the Cat

The cat is famed for its inexhaustible curiosity. Its inquisitiveness is the result of the mixture of its lively intelligence, highly tuned senses, and its evolutionary instincts as a predator.

RIGHT

Cats are well known for their curiosity, and they cannot resist peeking into nooks and crannies.

Movement and Balance

Generally, the size and shape of the average domestic cat has remained relatively constant throughout its association with man. Whether sprinting after prey or stalking in slow motion, the cat is built for speed and coordination. A cat in good shape can run 30 mph (48 km/h). The cat is a sprinter, however, and not a long-distance runner.

Cats are digitigrades: they walk directly on their toes. Cats are capable of walking very precisely because they place each hind paw almost directly in the print of the corresponding forepaw, minimizing noise and visible tracks and providing sure footing. The cat, the giraffe, and the camel are the only mammals that walk by moving the front and hind legs first on one side and then the other.

RIGHT

A cat's tail is essential for balancing while jumping.

A cat is able to jump more than five times its own height in one single leap. When preparing for a jump, the cat closely observes the place it intends to jump to, calculating the distance and exact angle before making the leap. Like Nijinsky, the cat then jumps with style and

elegance no matter the distance, the tail acting to balance the cat in the air. Rarely does a cat injure itself, even when the jumps are very large or a landing is miscalculated.

Jumping down is a little more difficult. Most cats try to shorten the distance they have to jump by putting their front paws as close as possible to their target and then pushing off with their hind legs.

Fascinating Facts

A cat has a resting heart rate of between 100 and 140 beats per minute. With increased activity or excitement, its heart rate can be as high as 240 beats per minute.

LEFT

As these prints from a South African desert show, cats walk on their toes and place their paws in line.

The Self-righting Reflex

Perhaps one of the most unique feline characteristics is a cat's innate ability to balance itself and land on its feet when falling from a height. While not infallible, a falling cat is usually able to twist itself around to land on its paws. This is called the self-righting reflex. A kitten begins to demonstrate this reflex at three to four weeks of age, and it is usually perfected by the time the kitten is seven weeks old.

BELOW

These images show the series of movements a cat uses to balance itself while falling from a height.

RIGHT

Many cats can climb trees easily enough, but coming down is not as easy, sometimes resulting in falls.

The vestibular apparatus of the inner ear of the cat contains three semicircular canals. Like a carpenter's level, these structures work with the brain to sense and maintain balance. When a cat falls with its legs higher than its body, impulses from the vestibular apparatus are analyzed at lightening speed and combine with visual information to transmit a message to the cat's neck muscles to orient correctly.

Because the cat has a highly flexible spine and floating collarbone, the head is able to twist into an upright, horizontal position, independent of the rest of the body. Next the front feet rotate until they are facing the ground. Finally the hind legs swivel around until the cat has completely balanced itself in mid-air.

The hind legs touch down first, relaxing to act as shock absorbers. The spine arches to further minimize impact, and the front legs relax to lessen the possibility of injury. Like a skydiver, a falling cat will reach a point in its fall where it is no longer accelerating. This is terminal or maximum velocity. The average cat reaches a speed of 60 mph (100 km/h) after falling five storeys. Small size, light bone structure, thick fur, and spreading the legs to increase drag all slow down the descent.

Once a cat has balanced itself, reached maximum velocity, and is no longer receiving the stimuli to balance, it goes into "free fall" and relaxes. The relaxed cat is less likely to sustain injury as it lands.

Fascinating Facts

Andy, a cat owned by Florida State Senator Ken Meyer, owns the record for a non-fatal fall, surviving a 200-ft. (60-m) fall.

RIGHT

If this precarious-looking cat were to fall, it would balance itself and then relax, minimizing impact on landing.

ABOVE

Cats will often clean a companion when they have completed their own grooming.

Self-Grooming

If there were an animal Olympics for self-grooming, the cat would win the gold medal. Cats are enthusiastic self-groomers, spending a large amount of their waking hours grooming. So addictive is the grooming behavior that after thoroughly cleaning itself, a cat will often attempt to groom a companion, whether another cat, a human, or the family dog. Mother cats are dedicated to cleaning their kittens. It is not unusual to hear a young kitten squeal in protest as "mom" holds it down and licks, licks, licks. A cat may groom meticulously after being petted, possibly in an attempt to remove the scent of the person who touched it.

Anyone having experienced the rough kiss of the family cat realizes that the feline tongue is not smooth. It is actually covered with hard, strong, backward-facing hooks called papillae that are very useful for cleaning the cat's coat. Acting like a comb, the tongue removes dirt, oils, and loose hair as it licks the coat. The cat will use its tongue to lick all the parts it can reach. A grooming session typically begins with a thorough licking from shoulder to flank followed by the underside, tail, and hind legs. Special attention is paid to cleaning around the anus and genital regions. Paws are inspected, biting any debris that may be stuck in the hair between the pads.

RIGHT

Cats clean their paws meticulously in an effort to remove anything caught between their pads.

RIGHT

During a thorough grooming session, a cat works its way around its body, cleaning each area in detail.

LEFT
Cats usually assume a seated position for cleaning the face and ears.

LEFT
Cats are sensitive to changes in the weather; some believe that a cat cleaning its face predicts rain.

Once the cat has groomed all the areas it can reach with its tongue directly, it moves on to grooming the difficult to reach areas like the face and behind the ears. Assuming a sitting position, the cat will continuously lick the inside of a front paw and leg until it is wet. It then rubs the wet paw along the side of its face and cheeks, around the eye, the forehead, and behind the ear. Once it completely cleans the side of its head, it changes paws and repeats the procedure on the other side of its face.

So efficient is the abrasive tongue at removing dead hair from the coat that the cat often ingests so much loose hair that it forms a ball in the cat's stomach. Unable to pass through the digestive tract, the cat usually vomits up the ball of hair. If the hair does enter the intestine, there is a danger it may become impacted in the gastrointestinal tract. This is one reason why it is important to comb your cat frequently, especially during shedding season. Longhaired cats need daily grooming. Shorthaired cats should be groomed once a week.

Fascinating Facts

The Japanese waving cat, Maneki Neko, is the figure of a cat with a raised paw as if to say hello. It actually represents a cat cleaning its face. In many cultures there is a belief that if a cat cleans its face, rain will follow. The sharp senses of the cat detect minute environmental changes that precede the weather pattern, making a cat uneasy. The cat cleans its face to ease its anxiety.

Hunting

Despite hundreds of years of domestication, most cats display an instinct to hunt if given the opportunity. This predatory behavior has been passed down to the domestic cat through the mists of time. While cats are born with a hunting instinct, killing and eating prey are generally learned behaviors. While a cat may catch and kill a mouse, it might not eat it, even if it is hungry, unless it has been taught to.

Kittens begin to show hunting behavior from as young as six weeks of age. Programmed from birth to chase, kittens practice hunting skills by crouching, pouncing, play fighting, and fake attacking with their littermates. A mother cat might use her tail to help teach her babies hunting skills, using it as a "tease" to teach them to stalk. If the mother is an outdoor cat, she will bring small, dead prey to her kittens. She will eat in front of them, encouraging them to join her. Next she will bring injured prey and encourage her kittens to play with it. She will kill it in front of them. Slowly the kittens learn that prey can be caught and eaten. Eventually the kittens accompany the mother as she hunts and learn to catch and kill on their own.

RIGHT

Kittens are taught to hunt by their mother and begin practicing their skills from an early age.

Cats will exhibit teaching behavior not only toward their own kittens but also other cat's litters. Some cats even include their human owners in the lesson, bringing home dead prey and dropping it on the doorstep. The hunting feline patrols a specific territory. The size of the territory varies depending on the availability of prey. Most adults are solitary hunters, although at times cats hunt in cooperation. The cat kills with a lethal bite through the spine at the base of the neck. If a cat isn't hungry, it will delay or even defer killing the prey, instead opting for the excitement of repeated stalking, capturing, and playing with the victim.

LEFT

Most domestic cats retain the hunting instinct, although not all kill and eat their prey.

Why do cats often appear to torture or play with their catch before killing it? There are several theories. One theory is that these cats lack confidence. They may still be wary of their prey, which if not killed quickly can fight

Fascinating Facts

Towser held the record for most mice killed (over 28,000) through until at least 1997. Tibbles single-handedly wiped out the Stephen's Island wren. Recent studies indicate that cats kill a minimum of 55 million birds in the U.K. alone.

and bite back. Another theory is that domestic cats that live in a relatively rodent-free environment lack the opportunity to catch real live prey. When they finally do catch a mouse, they want to prolong the "great" event as much as possible. "Birding" is a distinctive teeth chattering kind of noise that some cats seem to reserve for when they see birds or squirrels or feathers. Indoor cats may just be showing their excitement or frustration at seeing potential prey that they cannot reach.

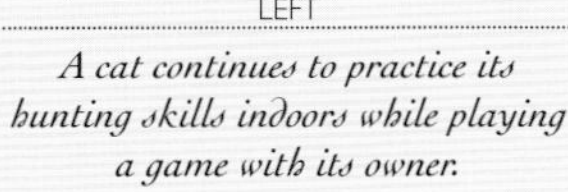

LEFT

A cat continues to practice its hunting skills indoors while playing a game with its owner.

Communication

Cats communicate by smell, vocalizing, body language, and marking.

Vocalizations
Cats have a wide range of vocalizations that include murmurs, meows, spitting, hisses, and growls. These can be divided into three broad categories: closed mouth, vowel patterns, and intense vocalization patterns.

Fascinating Facts

Cats almost never meow at another cat. They use this sound mainly to communicate with humans.

RIGHT
Spitting, hisses, and growls are all examples of intense vocalization patterns and can mean the cat is upset.

Purring, mating vocalizations, and the closed-mouth "mrrrr?" uttered when a cat seems to be asking a question are closed mouth vocalizations. Vowel patterns include the more typical "meow" and are produced when the cat opens and closes its mouth when making the sound. Cats meow for various reasons but most often because they want something like food, to be pet, attention, or to go outside. Intense vocalizations are made when the cat holds the mouth open throughout the sound when aroused, demanding, or upset. These include growling, hissing, and screaming.

BELOW
Cats can meow for a number of reasons, but it often indicates that they want food or attention.

Some cats are "talkers," meowing repeatedly or for an extended period, especially in response to the human voice. Oriental breeds, such as the Siamese, are renowned for being chatty.

Purring Part of the admiration humans feel for the feline is its unique ability to purr. Small cats, including the domestic cat, purr on both the inhaled and exhaled breath. The big cats purr only when they breathe out. Cats can purr with their mouths tightly closed. Kittens are born blind and deaf yet purr in response to their mother licking them. Kittens can purr with their mother's nipple in their mouth. Because a kitten cannot nurse and meow at the same time, it purrs while nursing to let its mother know it is happy. Their mother purrs so that they can find her, and purring acts to comfort both of them. Kittens do not purr in response to human touch until around six weeks old.

This phenomenon of suckling and purring at the same time can occur because purring is not a vocal sound. The purr does not come from the true vocal cords. No one really knows for sure where the purr sound comes from, although there are several theories on the subject.

Cats purr when they are happy but also purr when in pain. Pain stimulates the hypothalamus to release endorphins to help block the pain. But maybe it doesn't really matter how a cat purrs or why it purrs. It is enough that they do purr.

ABOVE

The forward-held ears of this cat indicate that it is alert and interested in something.

Body Language

Cats easily convey their feelings through body language. Everyone recognizes the raised back and flattened ears of a frightened feline.

Expressive Ears A cat's ears are used for more than just hearing. The angle of a cat's ears is an important clue to its mood. If the ears prick forward, the cat is showing interest. Ears pointed to the side mean the cat is thinking and considering its next move. If the ears are plastered flat against its head, beware—the cat is not happy. Ears back and down indicate fear.

Tail Talk Besides contributing to a cat's overall beauty and balance, the tail indicates the cat's emotional state. The way your cat holds its tail and each movement of the tail communicates what it is thinking and feeling. You just need to learn how to speak "tail talk."

Held erect for its full length, the tail is used as a greeting. If the tail is held erect and gently quivering, the cat is displaying affection. If the tail is erect but the tip is tilted over, this means the cat is in a friendly mood but has reservations. If the tail is held upright but curved to one side, it indicates a desire to play. The tail straight up is a request for food. If the tail is raised slightly and softly curved, the cat is beginning to be interested in something. If the tail is curved over the cat's back, it means it is expecting something to happen.

LEFT

An erect tail with the tip tilted over indicates that a cat is feeling friendly but has its reservations.

Fascinating Facts

Cats purr at around 26 cycles per second, the same frequency as an idling diesel engine. A cat's purr may be able to heal bone fractures, increase bone density, and control pain. Scientists discovered that vibrations between 20–140 Hz aid bone growth and help heal fractures, torn muscles, and ligaments, reduce swelling, and relieve pain. A cat's purr not only matches this vibration, but its dominant frequencies are 25 and 50 Hz—the optimum frequencies for bone growth and fracture healing.

ABOVE
Female cats hold their tails erect and to one side when they are in season and ready to breed.

If the tail is fully lowered and tucked between the hind legs, it indicates the cat is feeling submissive. If the tail is lowered and still but the tip is twitching slightly, the cat is feeling mildly irritated. If the tail is wrapped around the cat's body, it usually indicates that the cat is contented, although sometimes it can be the defensive posture of a nervous cat.

If the tail waves slowly and gently to and fro, it indicates pleasure. The tail flicks of a seated cat indicate irritation or indecision. A tail tip of a cat quivers when excited. A tail that wags back and forth and then pauses and repeats the sequence is annoyed. A tail slashing back and forth in wide arcs means that the cat is angry and that you should watch out.

If the tail is arched over the back and puffed up, the cat is feeling defensive. If the tail is puffed up and held straight up and the back is arched, the cat is feeling aggressive and may be ready to attack. If the tail is lowered and fluffed, the cat is fearful. Tail held to one side by a female cat indicates that the female is in season and inviting a sexual advance.

Scent
Cats recognize one another by their scent. Scent glands called temporal glands are situated above the eyes on the sides of the forehead. Cats mark objects, including people they consider "theirs," by rubbing the side of their heads along their object of affection. Cats mark their territory with urine. Other cats smell the urine and recognize the message.

Fascinating Facts

Whiskers are also an indication of the cat's mood. Whiskers point forward when the cat is inquisitive and friendly, and they lie flat on the face when the cat is being defensive or aggressive.

BELOW
Two cats sniff each other in greeting; cats recognize each other by their scents.

Care & Management

GETTING A NEW CAT

The cat is a special creature, beautiful and elegant in form, with mystery in its eyes and music in its purr. The unconditional love and companionship provided by owning a cat is enjoyed by millions of happy owners around the world. When you decide to invite a cat to be a part of your life, you will be rewarded with a lifelong friend, but the decision to adopt a kitten is not one to be entered into lightly.

Points to Consider

Like a happy marriage, sharing your life with a cat requires careful planning and preparation beforehand to be a success. With modern advances in veterinary medicine, it is not unusual to see a cat enjoying good health into its late teens and twenties. Welcoming a feline member into the family is a major commitment and responsibility and not a step to be taken impulsively. While the cute kitten in the cardboard box with a sign "free to a good home" seems like a bargain, before you let your heart rule your head, first consider the financial costs of owning a cat. The cost of maintenance of your kitten will vary depending on where you live, so investigate the cost of products and services in your area. Things to consider include:

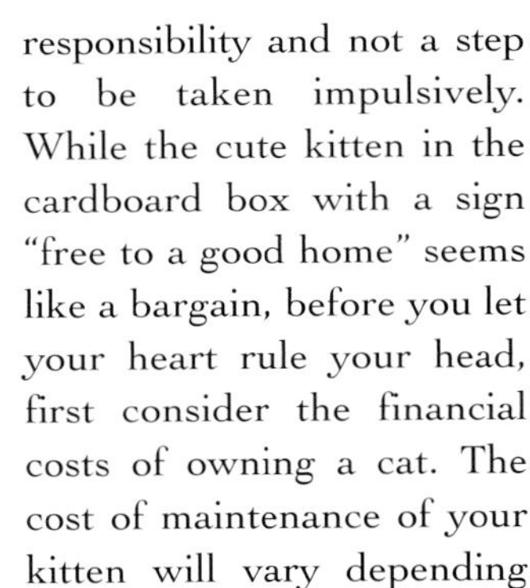

Food Choose a good quality cat food formulated for kittens.

Litter tray and Litter A simple litter tray is not expensive. Factor in the cost of litter.

Spay or Neutering There will be a one-time expense to spay or neuter the kitten.

Vaccinations The kitten will require a series of vaccinations for Feline Enteritis, Calici, Rhinotracheitis, and Rabies plus yearly boosters.

LEFT
Your cat should receive an annual checkup when it goes to the vet for its booster vaccinations.

Worming A fecal check will determine if your kitten needs to be wormed.

Fascinating Facts

On September 6, 1950, a four-month-old kitten belonging to Josephine Aufdenblatten of Geneva, Switzerland, followed a group of climbers to the top of the Matterhorn in the Alps.

Annual Checkup When your cat goes to the vet for its annual booster vaccinations, it should receive a thorough checkup, including a dental and blood profile.

Dental Care A cat may require regular yearly teeth cleaning, especially as it enters middle age.

Emergency Veterinary Care No one can predict if your cat might have a health crisis, but you should have money available to pay unexpected veterinary fees.

BELOW
As long as a cat is well loved and taken care of, the size and location of its residence is unimportant.

Pet Insurance Pet health insurance is an option to consider to ease the financial burden of veterinary care.

ABOVE
Children's abilities to take care of a cat or kitten must be considered before committing to a new pet.

Boarding If you frequently go on vacation or business trips and must board the cat, investigate the costs of an appropriate facility.

Once you have added up the approximate costs and are confident that you can afford to have a cat join your family, next consider how a kitten will fit into your home life.

If you have children, are they old enough to understand how to treat a cat? Who in the family will have the responsibility of taking care of the cat? Even if you hope to teach children responsibility by assigning to them some of the "kitty chores," an adult should supervise. How do other members of the family feel about getting a cat? Do you have other pets, and how will they adjust to a new cat?

Do you have the time to spend with a cat? Contrary to popular opinion, most cats need and enjoy attention. A neglected cat is more likely to get into trouble just to relieve the boredom. You may wonder if you have room for a cat. If there is enough room for you, there is enough for a cat. The cat in a huge mansion is no happier than the cat in a small apartment on the twentieth floor—as long as both are given plenty of love.

Choosing Your Cat

Once you are sure a cat is the right pet for you, there are more decisions to be made before you actually go looking for that special feline. Do not be seduced into purchasing an appealing kitten on the spur of the moment. Consider your lifestyle and preferences before choosing a healthy, well-socialized kitten with the needs, temperament, and personality that best work with you and your family.

Male or Female

If you do not intend to become a cat breeder, the sex of your kitten is immaterial to its role as a family pet. While some people swear male cats are more affectionate, others passionately prefer a female. The truth is that since most kittens are neutered or spayed by six months of age, there really is not a lot of difference between the sexes. It is much more important to look for the right personality, instead of limiting your choice based on the sex of the kitten.

BELOW

While mixed-breed kittens cost less and are easier to find, more information may be available for pedigrees.

Mixed Breed or Pedigreed

"Moggies" is a British slang term for a domestic cat of unidentified parentage. Mixed-breed kittens are readily available and less expensive than pedigreed cats. When choosing a moggie, the only drawback is that you have little information about its medical or genetic history, so have a vet examination before losing your heart to a kitten that may have a major health issue. On the other hand, you may have fallen in love with a breed's look and personality. Perhaps you are considering showing your cat or eventually breeding it. The advantage of a purebred, more correctly called a pedigreed cat, is that it is more of a known equation. It offers predictability. While cats are individuals and will vary, cats of the same breed are likely to share the look and personality traits characteristic of its breed. Seek out a reputable breeder who has carefully chosen quality breeding stock and is skilled at raising and socializing kittens. Many breeders provide expert advice to their kitten buyers long after the original purchase.

Kitten or Adult

The appeal of a kitten is difficult to resist. While a kitten requires an enormous amount of time and care, it is compensated by the delight of watching it grow and develop. However, an older cat may be a better choice if you lead a hectic lifestyle or have children under three years of age, who may be too young to be trusted to treat a kitten gently.

For various reasons, a new home might be needed for an adult cat due to divorce, allergies, a change in family circumstances, or a pedigreed cat may be retiring from a breeding career. Grown cats have the advantage of maturity and are already vaccinated and neutered. There is also the satisfaction of providing a home to a cat, that if not for you, may never find a home, since people naturally gravitate to kittens. One thing to consider: adult cats in shelters may have been turned in due to behavioral problems, typically bad litter tray habits. If selecting an adult cat from a shelter, try to determine the reason its last home gave it up.

Special-Needs Feline

You might want to consider adopting a special-needs cat, one that is blind, an amputee, or has a health problem that is managable with medication, such as diabetes. Often considered unadoptable, opening your heart and home to a special-needs feline is rewarded with love and companionship that more than compensates for the extra care that may be required.

BELOW

Giving a home to a special-needs feline, such as this one-eyed cat, can be a rewarding experience.

Fascinating Facts

A kitten purchased from a reputable breeder usually comes with a contract and serves as a guarantee against genetic problems.

ABOVE

There are always many adult cats in need of good homes for a wide variety of reasons.

A Reputable Breeder

If purchasing a pedigreed cat, it is best to buy directly from a reputable breeder. Cat breeders can be located through cat clubs, visiting a local cat show, advertisements, or on the internet. When you purchase a pet kitten from a breeder who shows their cats, the pet kitten has received all the extra care, nutrition, and attention to genetics as the show kitten in the same litter. Most breeders offer a contract with a written guarantee, although the conditions of the contract may vary. If you have purchased a pedigreed kitten as a pet from a breeder, there are generally two possibilities regarding registration papers. The breeder will either give you the pink and/or blue slips signed "Not for Breeding" and "Spay/Neuter," or they will withhold the papers until they have received your veterinarian's confirmation that the kitten has been spayed or neutered. With the papers in hand, you can then register your kitten.

Not all private breeders are reputable, and the informed buyer should interview breeders to separate the good ones from the bad. The term "Backyard Breeder" or BYB is used to describe a breeder whose primary motivation is making a profit, often resulting in producing substandard, unhealthy kittens.

ABOVE

Longhaired cats require more grooming, but hairs from shorthaired cats get everywhere.

Longhair or Shorthair

The grooming requirements of a longhaired cat such as a Persian are significant. Even a mixed breed with semi-longhair will require regular combing to avoid matting. A shorthair requires less grooming, but the shed hair may be more difficult to remove from clothes and furniture.

One Cat or Two

Two cats are more than twice the fun and less than twice the work. Once you have adjusted your lifestyle to accommodate one cat, adopting another requires little extra. It is not unusual for someone to go to a shelter or a breeder to adopt one kitty and come home with two. The kittens may be so adorable you cannot choose between them, so you decide to take both. Two cats are very entertaining, as they play and interact with one another, adding an extra portion of fun to the home.

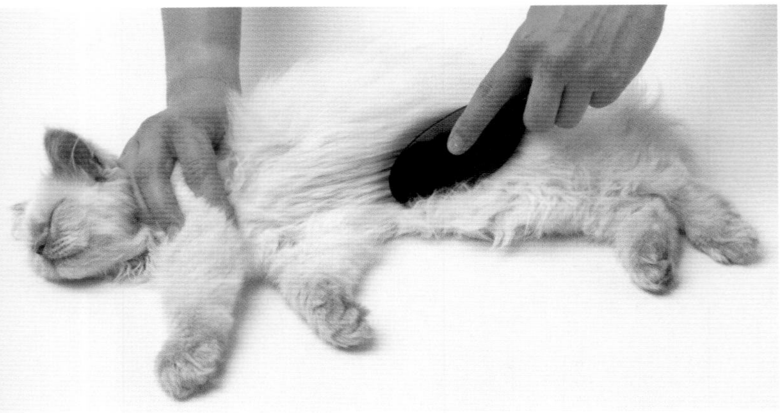

Feline and Breed Rescues

Feline or breed rescue groups are typically staffed by volunteers and funded by donations. Most depend on volunteer foster homes to care for the cats until a permanent home can be located. Foster homes assess the cat's health and behavior, providing medical care and remedial training if necessary before offering the cat up for adoption. You can often find a pedigreed cat from a breed rescue for a significantly lower price than from a breeder. You must pass a rigorous screening test before you will be approved as a prospective home.

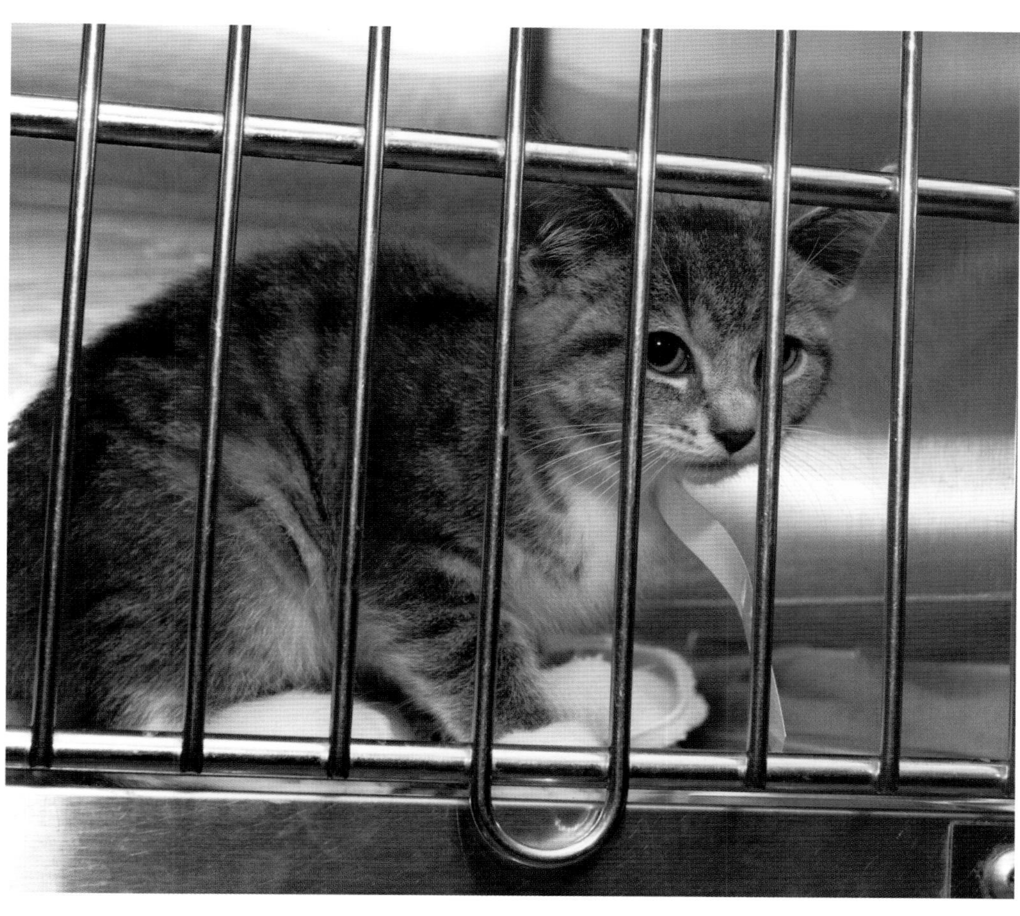

"Free to a Good Home"

If you are looking for a mixed-breed kitten, word of mouth or a classified advertisement may lead you to someone with kittens to give away, unfortunately usually the result of failure to spay an outdoor cat. Question the owner about the kitten's history, whether it has had vaccinations, and any illness in the litter. Ask to see the mother cat in her home environment to evaluate her temperament. You'll also get a better idea of the conditions the kitten has been living in, whether there is any indication of illness in the rest of the litter, and the condition of the mother cat.

Humane or Animal Shelters

With the exception of a no-kill shelter, kittens and cats at a humane society are almost always destined for euthanasia if not adopted. Adopt a cat or kitten and you may be saving a life. The drawback is that you will have little information about the kitten's medical or genetic background. Shelters charge an adoption fee, which often includes vaccinations and neutering.

Fascinating Facts

Talking to your cat establishes a stronger bond.

ABOVE

Adopting a cat or kitten from a shelter may incur a small fee to cover neutering and vaccinations.

Pet Stores

Pet stores are the place to buy food and accessories for your cat, but not an ideal place for the purchase of a kitten. Most pet stores get their animals from "kitten mills"—commercial operations breeding for profit and not to preserve or promote specific traits of the breed. There is some risk as to whether such kittens will be of good temperament or health, as the parents cannot be seen, and often little or no information is available regarding their background or breeding. Some large stores, such as PetSmart, have arrangements with local rescue groups to allow them to show their rescued cats, usually on the weekends.

ABOVE

Cats and kittens should always travel in the safety of a securely closed cat carrier.

Care of the New Kitten

You've chosen your kitten. Everyone is excited! The day has arrived to bring the new family member home. The best time to welcome your kitten to its new home is on a weekend, when you will have a couple days to settle it into its new surroundings.

Bringing Kitty Home

A cat carrier is essential to the safe travels of your kitten. As much as you may prefer to snuggle the cat in your lap on the trip home in the car, a cat should always travel in the safety of a carrier. If you hold the kitten in your arms in the car and it is startled by a honking horn or noisy traffic, it may struggle loose, scratching or biting. Once loose it could cause an accident by scrambling under the brake pedal or distracting the driver. Be safe, not sorry.

Place a small blanket or towel in the bottom of the carrier for the kitten to snuggle on. The stress of traveling can lead to an "accident," so bring paper towels and replacement bedding, just in case.

The First 24 Hours

The first 24 hours with your new kitten are the most important time. The kitten may feel lonely, missing its littermates or frightened and insecure in its unfamiliar new environment. Begin by confining it to one room, usually a bedroom, preferably of an adult family member. The kitten's most immediate needs are to learn where its food, water, and litter tray is in its new home. Make sure they are all visible.

Bring the kitten into the room in its carrier and open the door. An extroverted kitten may come bouncing out, ready to explore its new environment. The shy kitten may feel intimidated and not come out immediately. The cavelike carrier is comforting. Don't force the kitten. Let it take its time, while encouraging it to come out. Sit on the floor—it is less intimidating. Speak in soft, soothing tones. Use a small teaser to see if you can encourage the kitten to play, but also allow the kitten time to investigate its surroundings. Once the kitten seems comfortable in its new room, offer it food or a treat. Introduce it to the litter tray.

BELOW

When a kitten is first brought home, it is best to confine it to one room, preferably a bedroom.

Everyone in the family will want to pet and hold it, especially children. It is easy for the kitten to feel overwhelmed. Do not introduce it to too many family members at one time. Warn small children to sit quietly, and let the kitten come to them rather than allowing them to chase it. They need to understand that the kitten is not a toy and must be given its own space.

At bedtime place the kitten in its bed. Sometimes a kitten will feel safer in the carrier, so leave it on the floor with the door open. Do not allow the kitten to sleep on your bed unless that is something you are going to permit it all the time.

Once the kitten feels secure in "its room," open the door and let it explore the rest of the home at its own pace. If you have another cat or dog, confine it so the kitten has a chance to investigate the home without having to encounter another animal. As the cat gains more confidence, the time will come to introduce the kitten to other family pets.

Veterinary Exam

Within 24–72 hours of bringing your new kitten home, take it to your veterinarian for a complete and thorough checkup. Your veterinarian will be able to confirm the kitten is in good health, free of parasites or hidden health problems. If bought from a breeder, a vet check is often part of their contract and validates the purchase.

This is the time to have the kitten microchipped. A small electronic chip is inserted just under the skin between the shoulder blades. A hand-held scanner can read the number that is registered in your name. It allows your kitten to be identified if it is lost or stolen. If your kitten has not seen a veterinarian previously, this is also the time it should receive its initial vaccinations.

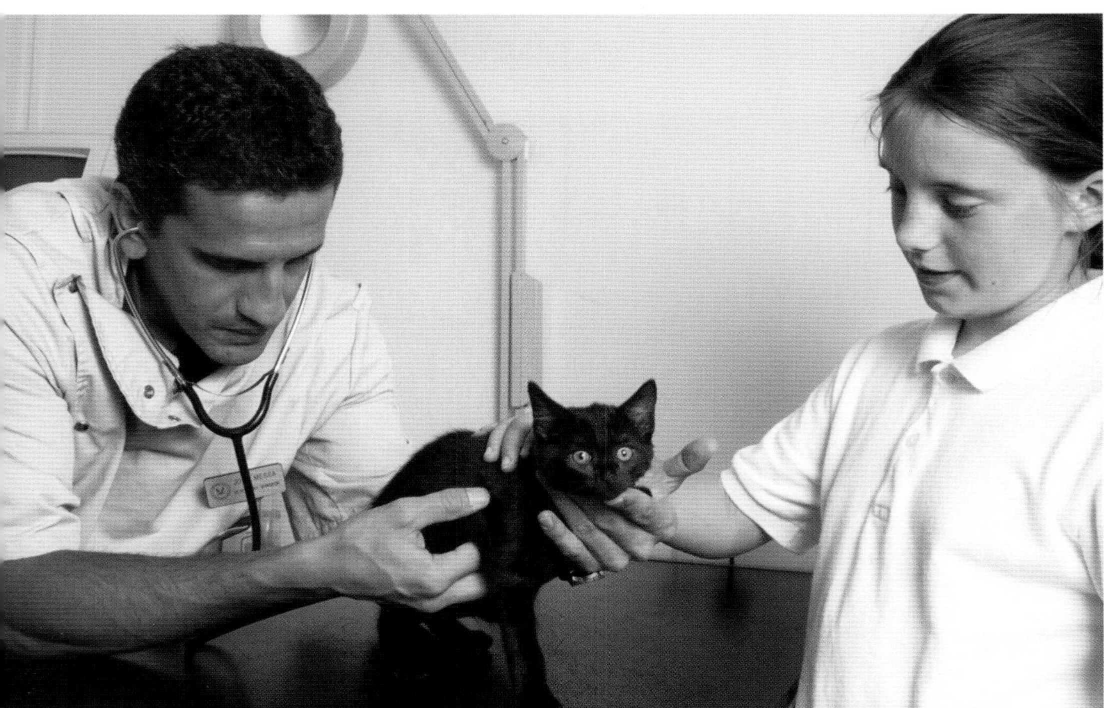

LEFT
Kittens should be taken to the vet for a general checkup within three days of arriving at your home.

Carrying the Kitten

Handle the kitten gently. Rough or sudden movements may startle it. To carry it, slip the palm of one hand under its stomach and support its bottom with your other hand.

Fascinating Facts

Cashew, a 14-year-old Labrador Retriever owned by Terry Burns in Middleburg, Pennsylvania, is blind and deaf. Her best friend is a red tabby cat named Libby, who is Cashew's seeing-eye cat. She guides Cashew around obstacles, leads her to the food dish, and even sleeps next to her every night.

Introduction to Another Cat or Dog

Always supervise the introduction of the kitten with other family pets. Begin by allowing the kitten and resident pet to sniff one another underneath the door. They may even play a game of footsie. This allows them to become accustomed to one another's scent. An adult cat may feel territorial and resent the kitten initially. Don't be surprised if there is some initial growling or hissing. This is not unusual. You can use a pet gate to separate a dog from the kitten. Or put the kitten in a cage, allowing the dog to approach and investigate but preventing a physical confrontation. Act as a chaperone until you are confident the animals will get along together. Often they will end up the best of friends within a few days.

BELOW

Introductions between a new kitten and a resident cat or dog should be conducted with care.

Playtime

The new kitten will needs plenty of play activities. This is an excellent time for bonding. You are taking the place of its siblings. The kitten will want to chase and play with your fingers and hand, even your feet and ankles. If the kitten becomes too rough or aggressive, say no and blow softly in its face.

Personality Test

There are a few simple tests you can perform to gain insight into your kitten's personality:

Testing for Socialization Observe your kitten. A well-socialized kitten will watch you, follow you, play with your feet, and make eye contact. A badly socialized kitten may hide from you or run away when you approach. If your kitten acts afraid of you, you will need to begin the socialization process over again. Spend plenty of time playing with the kitten, hand feeding it, gaining its trust.

The Toy Test Roll a small ball in front of the kitten and see whether it chases it or ignores it to test how well it reacts to things in its environment.

Testing For Dominance Roll the kitten on its back and gently stroke its stomach. If the kitten allows and enjoys the massage, it has learned to accept parental authority. If it struggles and resists, it is trying to be dominant.

The Noise Test Stand a small distance behind your kitten. When it is not looking, clap your hands loudly three times. If the kitten turns to you and comes to investigate, it is confident. If it runs away, it has not been brought up to accept new noises and sensations.

ABOVE

Kittens are very playful and may chase and attack your fingers, hands, and feet.

YOUR CAT'S ENVIRONMENT

Part of the excitement of adopting a new kitten is the preparation that goes into getting the house ready for the new arrival. Before you bring your new kitten home, there are preparations to complete, things to buy, decisions to be made. First of all, what are you going to bring the kitten home in? Then, where will it sleep? How often will it need grooming? And what will happen when you go on vacation? These are just a few of the questions we will help you answer.

The New Home

Carriers

For the safety of your cat, always travel with it in a carrier. Carriers come in several styles. The most economical is a simple cardboard carrier, often available from your vet or pet shop. Hard plastic or fiberglass carriers last longer, are more secure, easily cleaned and disinfected, and fold away for convenient storage. They are warm and cozy and provide a feeling of security for the kitten. Wire carriers are easy to clean and their openness allows for air circulation in the summer, but they can be cold and drafty in the winter and provide little refuge for a frightened feline. Soft-sided carriers are lighter to carry but offer little protection if thrown around in a car accident. Wicker carriers are aesthetically pleasing but difficult to clean.

ABOVE
Plastic carriers are long lasting, easy to clean, and provide a secure environment for a frightened cat.

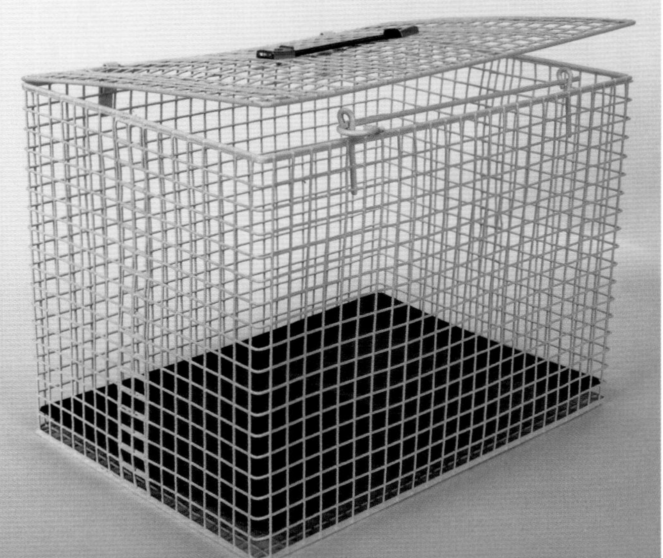

While most carriers have a door in the side, some carriers open from the top. If a cat is difficult to get in or out of the carrier, the top-opening design makes it easier. Carriers come in different sizes, so choose a size large enough to be comfortable for your cat when it reaches its adult size. Some carriers come with wheels and over-the-shoulder straps to make travel easier. You can buy a cage cover to prevent drafts in cold weather.

Fascinating Facts

Some kittens, especially shorthairs, prefer a tentlike bed. It keeps them warmer and provides privacy while napping.

LEFT & CENTER

Sleeping is a subject in which cats excel, and there is a wide range of cat and kitten beds available.

Beds

Most kittens enjoy having their own bed, even something as simple as a cardboard box with an old towel on the bottom. Cut one side low enough that the kitten can enter and exit easily. If adding a foam cushion, choose one with a washable, removable cover.

Fascinating Facts

A cat has extremely sensitive whiskers and may refuse to eat or drink if its whiskers brush the sides of the bowl, so use shallow bowls and plates, especially for flat-faced breeds such as Persians.

Bowls

The kitten will need separate food plates and water bowls. Avoid plastic, as it can cause a skin condition called rodent ulcers on the mouth of some cats. Plastic also scratches, providing an ideal place for bacteria to grow. Ceramic or stainless steel is a better choice. Avoid double bowls with water on one side and food on the other. The food tends to slop into the water and vice versa. Wash and refill both food and water bowls at least once daily.

Food and Water

Abruptly changing a cat's food can lead to digestive disturbances, so initially continue feeding the kitten the food it is accustomed to eating. Use bottled water to avoid stomachaches, gradually switching to your home tap water.

Litter Tray and Litter

The new kitten will need a shallow tray filled with the brand of cat litter to which it is used to. As the kitten grows, buy a bigger tray so the kitten always has plenty of room. A covered litter tray helps contain the litter and odors, and a removable plastic liner makes changing litter easier. Self-cleaning litter trays feature an automated, electro-nic cleaning arm. If you have multiple cats, allow for one more litter tray than the number of cats. Litter options include clay, scoopable, absorbent crystals, and pine or paper pellets. Scoop and dispose of waste at least once daily. Change the litter completely and wash the tray weekly.

Scratching Posts and Cat Trees

Provide a carpeted or sisal scratching post to avoid damage to your furniture. A tall cat tree will give the kitten plenty opportunity to climb and exercise. Place the post in a place that is easily accessible to the cat—near a favorite spot for napping is a good location. Sprinkle with catnip to encourage the cat to use the post. When the cat uses the post, provide positive reinforcement with petting and praise.

for your kitten. Always purchase a breakaway collar, so that if the collar is caught on something it will not injure your kitten. Most cats can also be taught to walk on a leash.

BELOW

The tools that you use to groom your cat will depend on the length and texture of its coat.

Grooming Tools

Grooming tools vary depending on the cat's coat. At a minimum, purchase a fine-toothed comb, brush, blunt-tipped scissors, and nail clippers. Other options include a wide-toothed comb, a flea comb, hard rubber brush, grooming glove, and chamois.

Collar and Leash

A collar with a tag is the easiest form of identification

The Indoor Cat

RIGHT

Cats may be tempted to play with wires, so it is important to insure electrical cords are covered in plastic tubing.

The most important thing you can do to insure you and your cat will have a long life together is to keep your cat indoors. Studies prove that indoor cats live longer and healthier lives than outdoor cats. The indoor cat is less likely to be injured in a fight or car accident or acquire an infectious disease. Responsible breeders of pedigreed cats often make keeping a kitten indoors one of their conditions of sale.

Cat-Proofing Your Home
Like a child, a kitten can find dangers in its new home. You will need to cat-proof your home before introducing the kitten. Block off small spaces in which it could become stuck, cover exposed electrical outlets, and close windows, etc. Kittens love to chew, especially when teething around four to five months old. Putting nasty tasting products such as Bitter Apple (a bitter-tasting liquid available at most pet stores) on objects the kitten is attracted to can discourage chewing. It is especially important to wrap electrical cords in plastic tubing to prevent the kitten from biting through and being shocked.

Dangerous When Eaten
Cats have a very different physiology than humans; some things are harmless to humans but toxic to cats. These foods include onions, green tomatoes, raw egg yolk, raw potatoes, grapes, raisins, bones, and aspirin. Chocolate, if ingested in sufficient quantities, can cause cardiac arrest. Many common plants, such as philodendrons and ivy, are dangerous if eaten. The traditional poinsettia at Christmas is a beautiful plant but is also toxic to cats.

Kittens are playful and curious—and will put anything in their mouths. Examine all toys for possible danger in the same way you would for a human baby. Toys should have any parts or decorations removed from them that a kitten might swallow—plastic eyes, ears, noses on a toy mouse, for instance, can be pulled off in play and ingested.

Be sure to dispose of dental floss where the kitten cannot get into it. All cats eventually tip over a garbage can to investigate, so if it doesn't have a lid, do not put used floss in your bathroom garbage basket.

ABOVE
Your cat or kitten may find its way to a warm surface, which could be dangerous in the kitchen.

Other Dangers Kittens love to sleep where it is warm—including a clothes dryer, so always shut the door when the machine is not in use, and always check before turning it on. If a kitten falls in a toilet it can drown, so close the lid. If you have a reclining chair, be aware that a kitten may be asleep under it and be caught in the mechanism. Avoid leaving the cat alone with yarn, string, or toys attached to a string because the cat could accidentally swallow the string or become entangled, causing a serious emergency.

Enriching the Cat's Environment
Once your home is safe for the kitten, you will want to provide an environment that encourages your indoor cat to be active and entertained and both mentally and physically healthy.

Toys and Games Select different types of toys, including soft balls, hard balls, balls with bells, catnip toys, teasers, toys with feathers, laser pointer, or a racetrack. Cats are curious creatures that enjoy having places to play hide and seek. Open cardboard boxes and paper bags make safe and inexpensive toys to enrich your cat's playground. It is amusing to watch how a cat can pretend that it is hidden completely when its head is in a paper bag while the rest of the body remains outside. Cut a few holes to peek through, and your cat will enjoy it even more. A cardboard box with holes cut into it placed over a catnip toy or ball will allow your cat to reach through and bat at the toy.

ABOVE
Curious kittens can drown if they fall into a toilet, so it is recommended to leave the lid down.

RIGHT
Cats enjoy playing with a range of toys, including chew toys, balls, catnip, string, and cardboard boxes.

RIGHT
Cats like to view the world from a high vantage point and will often climb up pieces of furniture.

High Up Cats like to see the world from an elevated angle. They seek high places to nap and enjoy observing the world around them. Provide window perches or indoor climbing trees for the cat to climb. For the older cat that is having trouble jumping to high places, you can construct a series of shelves with sturdy boxes to allow the cat to climb by jumping from box to box.

Treats Treat balls are also available that dispense treats slowly as the toy is played with. The same can be done for your cat's food. They can be placed in various locations of the house, so your cat will have to search for its food. Some cats enjoy drinking from a running tap because the water is fresher. Consider adding a drinking fountain for cats to keep the water moving continuously.

Playtime Cats like to chase, pounce, and hunt. You can attach feathers or rolled-up pieces of cardboard to a wire or wave stuffed animals on a stick to create a toy that bounces around. These toys encourage your cat to jump and "hunt" like a real lion. You can make time to play with your cat, even if just for a few minutes of the day.

LEFT
Giving your cat some catnip could serve as a treat; many cats have a strong reaction to the plant's scent.

Room with a View Rare is the cat that does not appreciate a room with a view. The window should be closed or protected well enough so the cat cannot escape. Add a shelf so the cat can sit and see out comfortably. This gives the cat the opportunity to observe the world outside and sniff some fresh air. Many cats will stay by a window with a good view for hours, especially if there are squirrels or birds outside.

Children Involve children when thinking of ways to keep your cat active. Children can play with the cat using toys, such as throwing ping-pong balls or playing with a toy attached to a string. Under adult supervision, a laser pointer beam could be used for cats to chase. For very young children, the key to safe play with the kitten is adult supervision.

Outdoor Time Finally, cats can be trained to use a leash when outdoors with their owner. Although most cats do not walk down the street alongside their owners like dogs, cats can get accustomed to having a leash on and knowing their limits. A harness attached to a leash is most commonly used. Being on a leash prevents the cat from getting lost or hit by a car while allowing it to enjoy the sights, sounds, and smells of the great outdoors under your supervision. Remember that it is a good idea to have a collar with ID tags on when your cat is outdoors in the event that it escapes from the harness. Never leave a cat tied up, even for a few minutes, as the leash could get caught somewhere and strangle the cat or the cat may escape.

ABOVE

A cat enjoys an al fresco nap on its owner's balcony, overlooking the backyard.

BELOW LEFT

By using a leash with a harness attached to it, you can let your cat experience the outside world.

The Outdoor Cat

Some cats live an indoor/outdoor life, spending part of the day indoors and part outdoors. One advantage of allowing your cat outdoors is a reduction in litter tray chores. You will, however, need to respond to the cats every meow at the door to be let out. And there is always the possibility of complaints from neighbors who do not appreciate the cat doing its duty in their yards.

The outdoor cat may develop a more independent personality as its wild instincts surface, bonding more with the outdoor environment than with its human family. The greatest drawback of allowing your cat outdoors is the risk to its life and health.

Fascinating Facts

If your cat gets trapped in a tree, put an open can of her/his favorite food at the bottom of the tree and go inside. Most cats will find their way down within a few hours.

The Dangers Faced By the Outdoor Cat

While a cat may enjoy the stimulus of the great outdoors, it is also faced with a long list of dangers. The outdoor cat is subject to injury or death by vehicles, intentional or accidental poisoning, fighting with other cats, exposure to parasites or infectious diseases from other cats, injury or death by dogs or predators, and becoming lost. It may be picked up by animal control or be the cause of complaints from neighbors.

Identification

The outdoor cat should have some form of identification in case it becomes lost or injured. A breakaway collar with a tag including your name, address, and phone number is essential. A second tag with your vet's information is an added bonus. Because a cat can lose its collar, it is important that it is microchipped. In case the cat goes missing, be sure to have a good, clear photograph to help others recognize your cat.

BELOW

Outdoor cats are prone to many health risks, including the possibility of being run over.

BELOW

If your cat goes outside, it is important to give it a collar, preferably complete with an identification tag.

Cat Flap

A cat flap is a hinged flap built into a door, wall, or window to allow a cat to enter and exit a house, freeing their human from the need to open the door while offering a degree of protection against wind and rain entering into the house. Cat flaps are popular in some countries, especially in the United Kingdom, where it is believed that around 90 percent of cats have access to the outdoors. The downside of the cat flap is that it can allow other animals into the house, and cats can also bring mice and birds into the house through the flaps.

RIGHT

A cat flap offers plenty of freedom but can also allow unwanted visitors into your home.

Building an Outdoor Enclosure

If you were going to allow your cat outdoors, the ideal solution would be to have a cat-proof backyard. There are special fencing systems available that can be added to existing fences to make them more difficult for a cat to climb. Another option is to build an outdoor enclosure. It can be stand-alone or attached to the home and allows your cat the best of both worlds—a feeling of freedom of the outdoors while being protected from the danger of the outdoors.

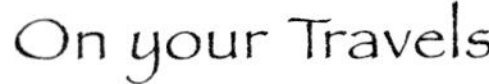

On your Travels

Home Alone

If fed a diet of dry cat food, most cats can be left home alone for two days. A full bowl of dry food or a feeding tower will be more than enough. A large bowl of water, a water bottle, or a running tap will provide water. You could ask a helpful neighbor to check in once a day. Cats are sometimes anxious and distressed when left alone for longer periods of time. Some cats are upset at the change in routine, so leave the television on. Two cats will keep one another company, though they may also get into more trouble if they are restless during your absence.

ABOVE
A cat can be left alone for a day or two if provided with water and a plentiful supply of dry food.

ABOVE
A boarding cattery can be an option for full-time pet care while you are away on vacation.

The Pet Sitter
Some cat owners in urban areas prefer to have a cat sitter visit the home daily or in some cases live in if they are going to be gone for an extended time. Start with a recommendation from a friend, neighbor, vet, or check the Yellow Pages under "Pet Sitting Services." Have the prospective pet sitter visit your home to meet your cat before actually hiring them. Watch how the sitter interacts with your pet —does your cat seem comfortable with the person? If the visit goes well, hire the sitter while you go on a weekend away before leaving for longer periods.

The Boarding Cattery
While most cats are happier remaining in their own home, as long as they have a social personality they can also be fine in a quality boarding facility set up specifically for cats. Ask to see the cattery with plenty of advance notice. All boarding facilities are not equal. The best cat facilities offer an indoor-outdoor area, allow you to bring your cat's bed, toys, and favorite food, and are far from barking dogs.

Travel by Car
Contrary to popular opinion, many cats make good car travelers. The key is to take them on enjoyable rides while they are young so they become comfortable with car travel. Take the kitten on frequent short trips; a trip to the supermarket and back. The kitten will soon take car rides for granted—just part of a cat's normal routine.

Travel by Airplane
Many airlines permit you to travel with your cat in the cabin if the carrier is small enough to fit under the seat in front of you where your feet normally go. You will be required to purchase a pet ticket. Alternately, the cat can fly in cargo in a special area reserved for live animals. It must be in an airline-approved carrier. Every airline has different requirements and restrictions regarding flying with a pet. Contact the specific airline you plan on flying to obtain their specifications. You will be required to show proof of current vaccinations and obtain a health certificate within ten days of travel. Exhibitors often fly with show cats, and most cats are good flyers. Some airlines offer frequent flyer miles for pet travel.

Use of Tranquilizers
It is not usually recommended to tranquilize a cat for travel. Reactions to tranquilizers vary, and it can actually make them more agitated.

FEEDING

Good nutrition is the foundation of raising a healthy cat. Cats are carnivores; however an all-meat diet is not balanced. In the wild, when a cat captures a mouse, it consumes everything that is edible—flesh, organs, bones, and entrails. Because the mouse is herbivorous (plant-eater), when the cat eats the stomach and intestines that contain seeds and plants, it receives the trace elements and vitamins needed for a nutritionally balanced diet.

Commercial cat foods are specially formulated to provide the cat's complete nutrition. The foods are standardized, convenient, and less expensive than preparing homemade diets. The main advantage of feeding a commercial food is the assurance that the cat is eating a balanced diet that includes all the elements necessary for proper growth and development.

An adult cat requires around 50 calories per 1 lb (450 g) of weight per day. A very active feline may need more; a less active cat requires less. Most adult cats seem to thrive on either self feeding or being fed two meals a day. A cat's general appearance is a good indicator of whether its diet is satisfactory. A well-fed cat has good weight, a shiny coat, bright eyes, and appears happy and content. Signs of poor nutrition include low body weight, dry coat, flaky skin, dull eyes, bad breath, and strong smelling stools.

Changing Foods

It is best to feed the new kitten the food it has been eating. If the kitten is purchased from a breeder, ask for their feeding recommendations and schedule. Once the kitten is settled in its new home, you may investigate other feeding options. A new food may initially upset the kitten's digestive system, so any change should be introduced in stages. Mix the new food in with the old in steadily increasing proportions over the course of a week. A slow transition avoids the risk of the kitten developing diarrhea. The best food in the world is no good if your cat will not eat it, so palatability is a critical component in choosing any food.

Fascinating Facts

The chlorine in fresh tap water irritates sensitive parts of the cat's nose. Let tap water sit for 24 hours before giving it to a cat.

Do not be misled by the phrase "meat by-products." By-products refer to heads, feet, feathers, entrails, etc. and are not a high-quality protein source.

Premium or Economy

Because a food is expensive does not mean it is necessarily better for your cat. Many mid-priced foods have good nutritional profiles. Some economy brands of cat food, however, are made from inexpensive ingredients not good enough for human consumption and not easily digested. If a food is difficult to digest, you may have to feed more of it for your cat to receive the same nutritional value as feeding less of a higher quality food.

Dry, Canned, or Semi-Moist?

With the wide selection of commercial cat foods available on the market today, it can be a challenge selecting the type and brand that best meets your cat's nutritional needs. Cat food comes in three basic types: dry kibble, canned food, or semi-moist foods in pouches. Dry foods are relatively inexpensive, convenient, and have the advantage of remaining fresh in the bowl all day, allowing the cat to feed freely. This is especially useful for kittens that eat multiple meals in small servings throughout the day. Dry food should be stored in a cool, dry place, either in the closed original bag or a container with an airtight lid to keep it fresh. There is some evidence that crunching on hard kibbles helps reduce tartar build up. Dry foods usually contain 8 to 10 percent water compared to 80 percent water in canned food, so cats fed dry food often drink more water.

ABOVE

Moist food does not last once it has been served, so you should only give your cat an amount that it can eat.

Canned food and semi-moist foods may be tastier than dry food but will spoil if not eaten immediately. Care should be taken to offer only as much food as the cat will finish in a single meal. Canned food should be refrigerated once opened, and any leftover wet food should be thrown out after each meal.

Protein Content

Cats are obligate carnivores, which mean they need to eat a food with high protein content from meat, poultry, or fish. The breeding cat's diet should be 30–40 percent protein, while neutered cats need around 25 percent. Pet food labels list their ingredients on the label. Look for the first ingredient to be a species-specific protein such as chicken, beef, or fish.

Fascinating Facts

Feeding dog food to a cat can cause blindness. Dog food lacks taurine, a nutrient essential for cat health. Taurine keeps their hearts healthy and their eyesight sharp.

RIGHT

There are many different types of dry foods on the market; they stay fresh and are good for your cat's teeth.

Life Stage Diets

Choose a food that is made to meet the specific nutritional requirements for the stage of life of your cat. Kittens have higher nutritional demands needed to develop and grow. As a cat enters its golden years, it can suffer from age-related problems including a weaker immune system, less efficient digestive system, decreasing senses of smell and taste, arthritis, and urinary problems. Senior cats may benefit from a diet lower in phosphorus and with a moderate level of fiber to help prevent constipation, and cat foods for older cats are often formulated to stimulate the senior cat's appetite.

Lifestyle Diets

Cats that go outdoors may need a food higher in protein and calories than cats living exclusively indoors. Some studies suggest as many as one out of four pet cats are overweight. Commercial foods are available with reduced fat content and high protein levels that help the obese feline lose weight without losing muscle mass.

BELOW

Some cats are prone to putting on weight, but there are many types of diet cat food available.

Special Diets

There are different cat foods specifically for felines with food allergies, sensitive stomachs, heart or urinary problems, dental disease, and coat or skin problems. Hairballs can cause vomiting and diarrhea, but specially formulated food helps improve digestion and movement in the intestines. Foods are available to meet the nutritional needs of specific breeds of cats, including Persians, Maine Coons, and Siamese. There are even cat foods that claim to reduce the amount of stool and its odor.

LEFT

To avoid your cat from becoming undernourished, ensure that the food you buy is adapted to your pet's age and condition.

Fascinating Facts

The nutritional requirements of a pregnant or nursing cat are around double those of a non-breeding cat. During lactation, cats need all the food they can get.

RIGHT

Different breeds have different nutritional requirements, and so there is a range of specifically formulated foods.

Homemade Diets

Some cat owners believe in homemade or raw meat diets. Care must be used if preparing homemade meals for your cat. While you can easily control the quality of ingredients, you can never be entirely sure of its nutritional balance. Home-prepared food is usually more expensive than commercial, perishable, and time consuming to prepare.

Supplements, Treats, and Table Scraps

If you are feeding a good-quality food, it is not necessary to add a supplement. An occasional treat from your plate shouldn't hurt, as long as it does not take the place of a cat's normal food. Several human foods are very toxic or dangerous to cats. Never feed pork, chocolate, onions, green tomatoes, raw egg yolk, raw potatoes, grapes, raisins, bones, or dog food to your cat, just to name a few.

ABOVE AND BELOW

Grapes, onions, and chocolate are among the foods that you should not feed your cat.

LEFT

Cats may be given milk occasionally as a treat, providing they do not show signs of lactose intolerance.

Water

Your cat should always have access to fresh water. Water bowls should be cleaned and refilled daily. Contrary to popular opinion, cow's milk is not good for cats. Not only is it difficult for a cat to digest, it often causes diarrhea.

TRAINING

When it comes to behavior, some cats are naturally "purrfect" (or almost), while others have a little more tiger in them. Whether your cat bites your hand, plays in the middle of the night, or climbs your leg while you prepare dinner, such antics require behavior modification. There are various techniques that can be used to encourage more acceptable behavior in your cat. You can even take it further and train them to perform simple "tricks" and agility maneuvers.

Positive Reinforcement

Cats are not dogs. The training techniques that work well with our canine friends are not especially effective with the feline psyche. Cats work best when rewarded with treats, so discover a food that your cat responds to as a reward. It may be a cat treat, a sliver of cooked meat, or a tiny taste of chicken baby food. Of course, do not ruin their properly balanced diet. Once your cat performs the task requested, reward it with both a treat and praise.

You should never hit your cat as punishment, but there are other forms of discipline that are effective. A spritz of water from a spray bottle or water pistol will often discourage unwelcome behavior. The key is to not let the cat realize the spray came from you, if possible. In closer quarters, blowing in the cat's face can be an effective deterrent. The puff of air can be varied in strength, number, and duration to best fit the cat and the behavior. Loud clapping, rattling cans, imitating a cat's hiss, or a blast from an air horn are also effective deterrents with some felines.

BELOW

When attempting to train your cat, edible rewards can be one of the most effective methods.

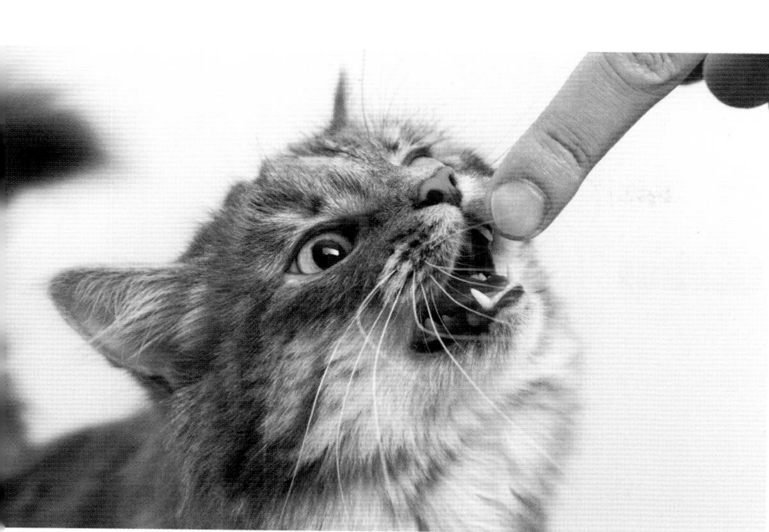

Common Unacceptable Behavior

Biting Unwarranted biting is not acceptable from your cat under any circumstances. If it happens, pinch the cat's tongue and hold on for a few seconds.

Jumping up on Counters Jumping on kitchen counters can be very dangerous—your cat could walk on a hot stove top. If your cat jumps up when you are there, keep a spray bottle handy and spritz the cat as it is in mid-leap. If it jumps up only when it thinks you are not looking, watch unobserved and just as it is thinking of jumping up, blow a whistle.

Digging in the House Plants A cat may be tempted to use the dirt in a plant pot as a litter tray. Simply fill the top of the container with small stones.

Scratching on Furniture The best thing you can do for your furniture is to train your kitten to use a scratching post. Place several scratching posts conveniently around the house. Praise the cat when it uses them. If a kitten starts to scratch on furniture, say "No" loudly and take it to the scratching post. If a cat starts to claw furniture, spritz it with water or startle it by tossing a newspaper or car keys toward it. If you cover up a favorite scratching spot with aluminum foil or double-sided tape, a cat will often be discouraged. A mild menthol, vinegar, or citrus scent also repels some cats. Once your cat realizes that these places are not fun to scratch, it will prefer the scratching post.

BELOW

Jumping up on counters can be dangerous, so it is important to train your cat not to do this.

Inappropriate Urination If your cat is urinating or defecating outside the litter tray, a veterinary checkup is necessary to eliminate a possible medical reason. If there is no health problem, confine the cat to a small room with a cat bed at one end and a litter tray at the other. Praise your cat for using the litter tray. If you catch your cat in the act of urinating or defecating outside of the tray (or even starting the digging motion), startle it by tossing a can with a few coins inside it toward the cat (but not at it) to make it stop. You could also use a whistle or water gun. Clean the area where the cat has urinated inappropriately, and then spray it with cologne or place a plastic runner upside down with the spikes pointing up to discourage the cat from returning to the spot. Double-sided tape, pet repellents, or a scat mat are other options.

Midnight Crazies Some cats come to life at night. The cat stampedes through the house, playing with toys and often jumping on beds, hoping the human occupants will "come out and play." Keep it confined to one room at night, and try to change its activity patterns by playing more with it during the day and especially before bedtime, so it is more likely to be tired.

Chewing Cats chew on inappropriate objects such as clothing, electrical cords, or papers. Make the objects taste unpleasant by spraying them with vinegar, tobasco, or Bitter Apple.

Fascinating Facts

Cats do not think that they are little people. They think that we are big cats. This influences their behavior in many ways.

ABOVE

Playing with your cat before bedtime can help tire it out if it is prone to bursts of nocturnal activity.

Teaching Your Cat Tricks Cats are not only capable of learning simple commands; they enjoy the interaction with their owner and look forward to being a "star." So as not to confuse them, work with one command at a time. Be consistent and patient, letting your cat work at its own speed. Reward the cat enthusiastically at the first sign of understanding.

Come With a food treat in hand and preferably when your cat is hungry, call "come." As it comes to investigate, praise it and give it the treat. The cat will quickly learn to associate the food with the command. Never call a cat to punish him or to do something to it that it may not enjoy—like a bath or medication—as the association will change into a negative one.

Shake a Paw With your cat sitting in front of you, touch his paw and say "shake." As soon as it lifts the paw, shake it and give him a treat and praise.

Sit Up With your cat in a sitting position, hold a treat over its head and say "sit up." Do not give it the reward if it stands or grabs at the treat but repeat the command and try again. When it sits up, give it the treat immediately.

ABOVE

You can teach your cat to sit up by dangling treats above it while giving the command.

BELOW

To ensure your cat does not get a nasty shock, cover all electrical wiring with plastic tubing.

RIGHT

A cat from the Moscow Cats Theater performs an impressive trick with trainer Yuri Kuklachev.

Playing Fetch To teach fetch, it helps if your cat has an oral fixation. It should like carrying things around in its mouth. If you notice a kitten walking around with a toy in its mouth, give it plenty of praise. The more excited your cat is about the fetch object, the more likely it will "grab" it and carry it. Throw the toy and command "fetch." Unlike teaching other tricks, a food reward is less effective in encouraging a cat to fetch. The reward is that the object is thrown again. The cat must enjoy the game of fetch or else it will simply chase the ball without returning it to you.

LEFT

In extreme cases, cat agility courses can include obstacles such as flaming hoops.

Agility Training and Competition

A new competition offered at some cat shows is called cat agility. Similar to dog agility, a cat and its handler negotiate an obstacle course designed to demonstrate the cat's athletic ability, speed, coordination, and the quality of the animal's training relationship with its owner. The event is timed, with points taken off for obstacles missed or incomplete. Typical obstacles include ramps, platforms, tunnels, jumps, hoop, weave poles, and steps. The handler uses a long teaser or wand to direct and encourage the cat to go over, through, or around the obstacles. The course is completely fenced in so that a cat cannot go astray.

GROOMING

The term "grooming," as used here, implies all the things that can or should be done by you in order to maintain your cat's appearance—including keeping the nails clipped, combing and brushing the coat, bathing, cleaning the ears, and even brushing their teeth. Although cats are very good at grooming and cleaning themselves, they need a helping hand from their owners to remain in peak condition. Grooming is important not just for aesthetic reasons but also for health ones—especially because it allows you to check for any physical changes while carrying out the grooming process.

Nail Clipping

Begin clipping the kitten's nails early on and it will get used to the procedure. Trim once every week or two. Select a scissor-style, cat nail clipper with two cutting edges or cuticle trimmers on human toenail clippers. Place the cat on a table or your lap. Hold the cat's paw, and extend the retracted claw by pressing the toe between your thumb and forefinger. If the nail is white, you will see the "quick," the blood vessel that runs through the center. Trim the nail to within 1⁄10 in. (2 mm) of the quick in one quick motion. If you accidentally cut into the quick and it bleeds, use a blood stop powder or a septic pencil to stop the bleeding.

Fascinating Facts

The state of your kitten's claws is an indicator of its health. Too hard or too soft are signs of possible deficiencies or bacterial infection.

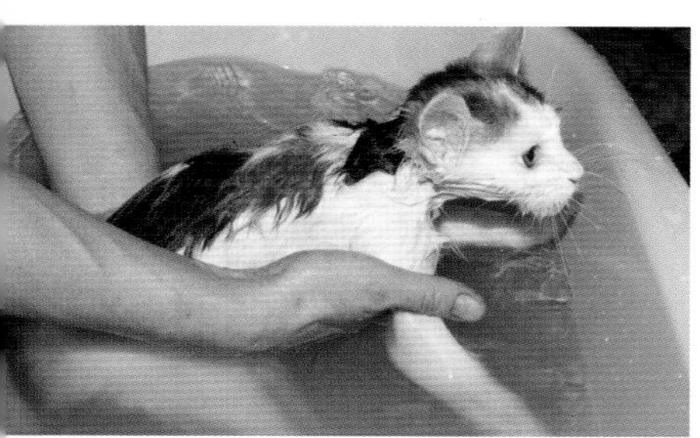

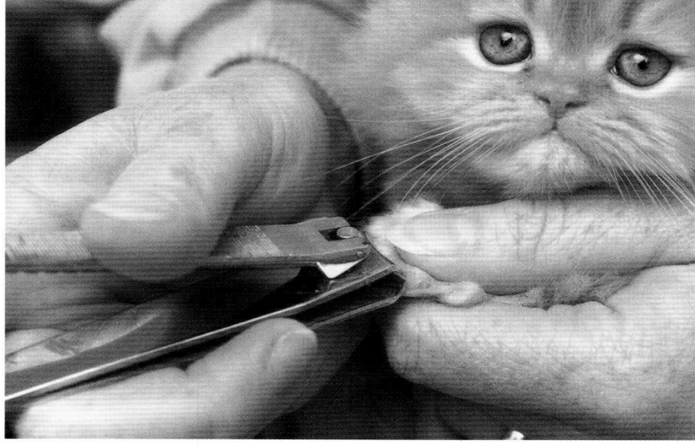

Combing

Regular combing helps remove the dead hair that can result in hairballs. A comb penetrates the coat better than a brush. Begin at the head, working toward the tail and down from the back, working to the stomach. Comb in the direction of the hair and then against it to gently remove dead hair. Lift the chin and comb the chest. Roll the cat on its back in your lap and comb the underside. Be especially careful when working around the genital area.

A weekly session with a small, close-toothed comb is usually sufficient for a shorthaired cat. After combing, repeat with a hard rubber brush and if you like, finish off by rubbing with a chamois or silk cloth.

Longhaired cats, especially Persians, require daily grooming with a wide-toothed comb. Repeat with a fine-toothed comb. Pay special attention to the rear breeches, checking for dried feces that may be stuck on the hair. Knots can be gently teased out, while mats are a job for a professional groomer. During the spring and summer when the cat is shedding, comb more frequently.

Bathing

All cats can learn to get used to being bathed. Bathing washes loose hair down the drain, reducing hair shed on the furniture and removes excess oil, keeping the cat clean. A cat can be bathed as often as you like, as long as you use mild shampoo. Show Persians are often bathed twice a week.

ABOVE

If you clip your kitten's nails from an early age, it will grow accustomed to the process.

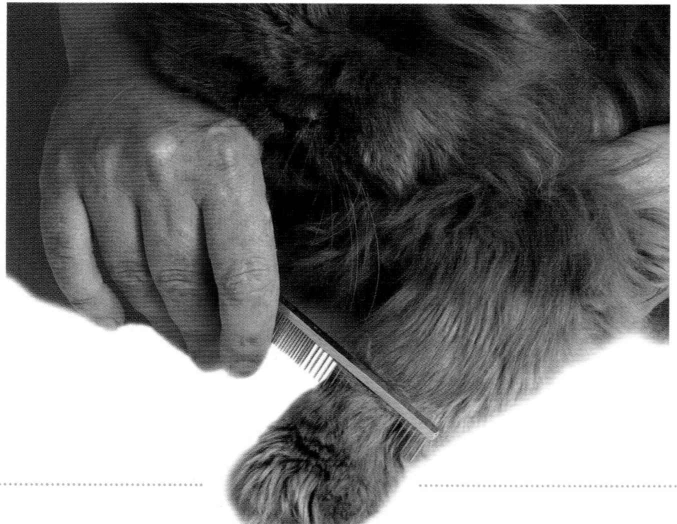

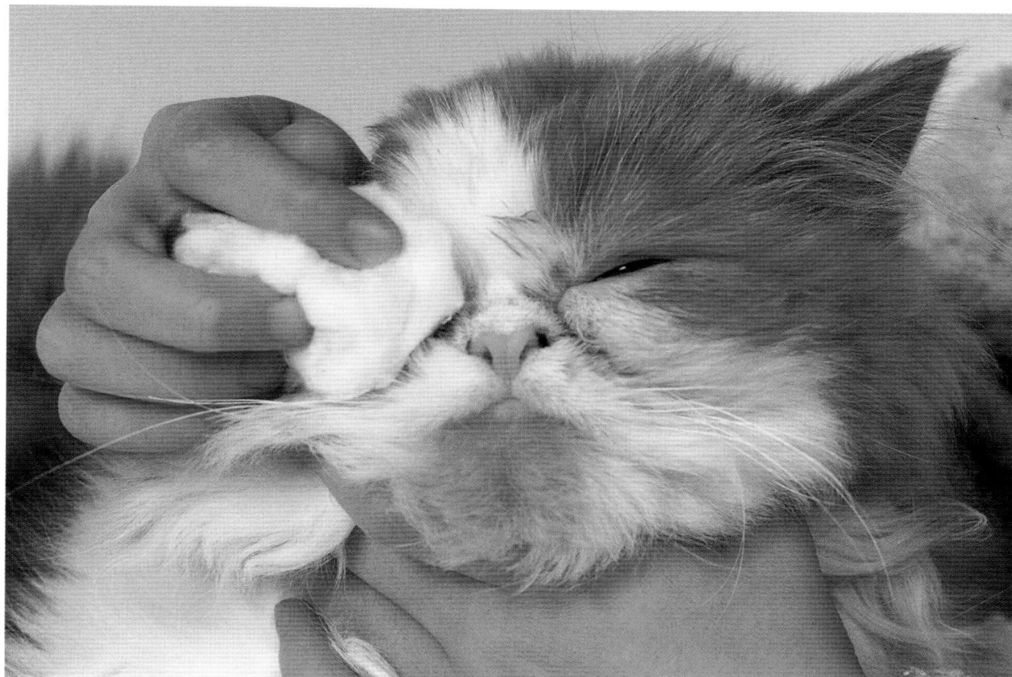

A convenient place to wash the cat is the kitchen sink, especially if it has a spray nozzle. Place a rubber mat in the bottom to stop the cat from slipping. Place the cat in an empty sink, wet the coat using the spray, and then fill the sink with water halfway. Dilute the shampoo and work through the coat from head to tail, from back to stomach. Finish with a conditioner, and rinse thoroughly.

Avoid getting water in the eyes or ears. Some cats, especially flat-faced cats such as Persians, accumulate tears under the eyes and in the creases that run on either side of the nose. A face cloth dampened with warm water is sufficient to clean the face, especially the build-up of secretions around the eyes. Dry nasal secretions in the corner of their nostrils can be removed with a cotton ball or tissue.

Squeeze as much water out of the coat as possible with your hands. Wrap the cat in a towel to absorb more moisture. Finish drying the hair with a hairdryer. Professional pet dryers are available that dry faster.

Cleaning the Ears

Use a cotton swab or make-up pad moistened with warm water or mineral oil to clean the inside of the external ear. Never use rubbing alcohol, as it is dehydrating. Do not probe down into the ear, as you may cause injury. If there is an especially obvious and unpleasant looking discharge, consult your vet.

Brushing Your Cat's Teeth

Tuna-flavored toothpaste and a finger brush can be used to brush your cat's teeth and help prevent tartar build-up.

ABOVE

A cat's ears can be cleaned by gently folding them back and wiping with a dampened pad or cotton swab.

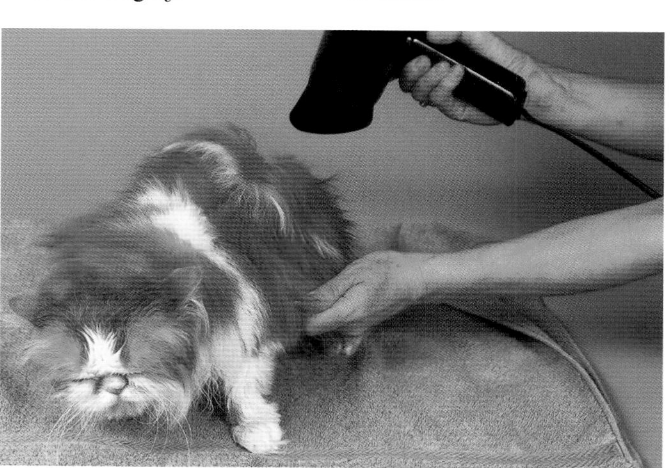

BELOW

Brushing your cat's teeth can help prevent tartar build-up; tuna-flavored toothpaste is available.

HEALTH

You've done your homework, found an adorable new kitten, "cat proofed" your home, and chosen an appropriate carrier, bed, food, and toys. Now you look forward with excitement to the joy the new feline will bring to your life. In exchange you will need to provide love and attention, good nutrition, and medical care including regular checkups at your vet's. There are also a certain amount of feline ailments that it are worth knowing a little about in order to be alert to changes in your cat's health.

Routine Health Care

Checkups
Within 24–72 hours of bringing the new kitten home, it is time for its first visit to the vet. This will give your vet the opportunity to gather basic information regarding the kitten's health and to begin its medical record. The vet will evaluate the kitten's general body condition, take its temperature, listen to the heart and lungs, check the eyes, and look in the ears and mouth. A thorough physical examination will include checking for parasites.

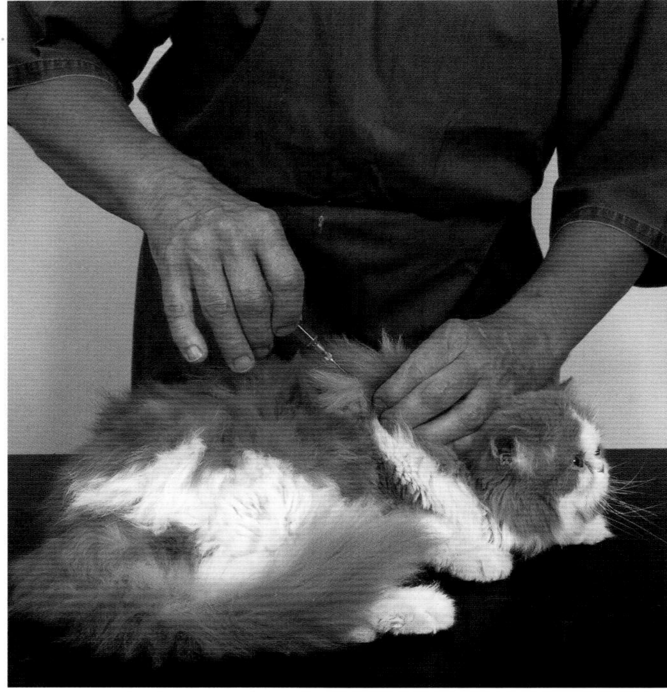

LEFT
Boosters to your cat's initial set of vaccinations are usually recommended every year.

Worming Bring a fresh bowel movement to test for internal parasites. If necessary, the kitten will be wormed.

Vaccinations Bring information you have been given regarding vaccinations the kitten has already received. Most vets recommend that kittens be vaccinated against several common infectious diseases. A single vaccine called FVRCP protects against a combination of diseases; Feline viral rhinotracheitis (FVR), Feline calicivirus (C), and Feline panleukopenia (P). The first inoculation is usually given at eight weeks, with a booster at 12 weeks. A rabies inoculation is given at 16 weeks. Boosters are recommended annually.

Depending on individual risks, vaccinations against feline leukaemia (FeLV) and chlamydia are an option.

Spaying and Neutering
A female cat should be spayed and a male neutered if they are not to be used for breeding. The traditional age for spaying and neutering was once six months, but with improvements in anesthesia, many vets now offer early procedures, sometimes as young as seven weeks of age, as long as the kitten weighs a minimum of 2 lbs (1 kg). This practice is especially common in animal shelters.

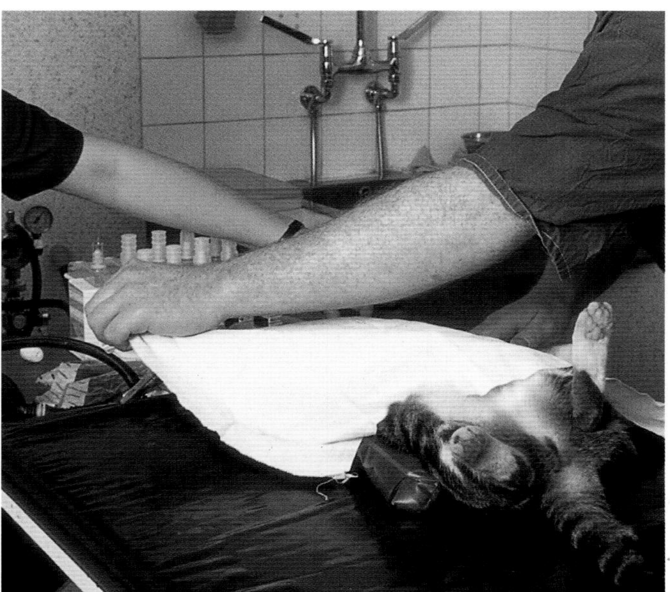

BELOW
Your cat should be spayed or neutered if you are not planning to breed from it to prevent unwanted kittens.

Fascinating Facts

Early desexing does not appear to have any long-term health risks to cats and may even be beneficial for male cats. It is a myth that spayed or neutered cats are destined to become fat.

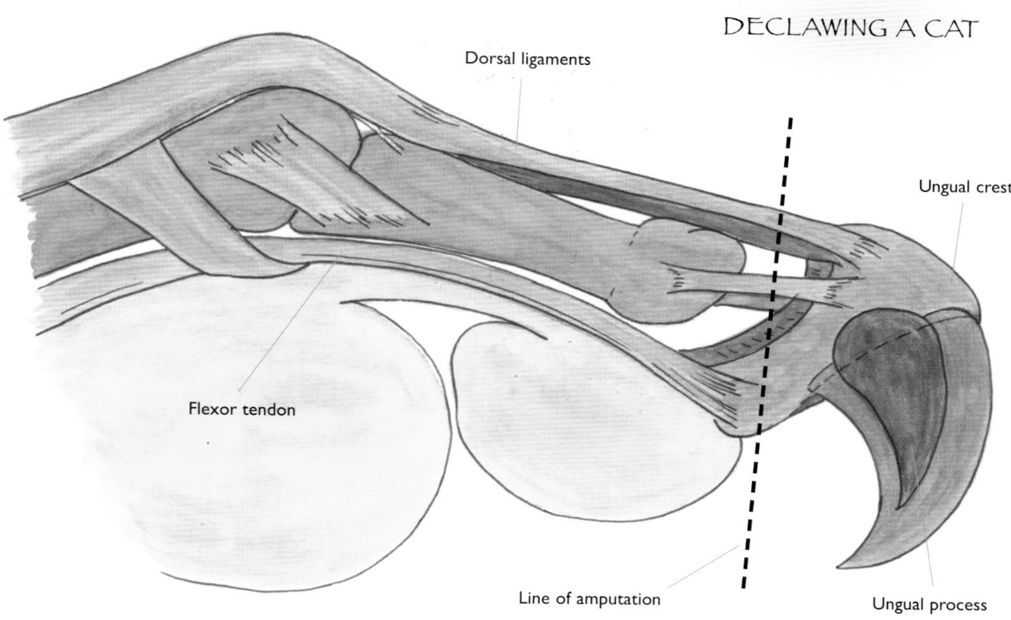

Declawing and Tendonectomy

Cats in the wild use their claws to climb, hunt, and mark their territory. This instinctive behavior can lead to destruction of furniture if the indoor cat is not trained to use a scratching post. If a cat has not been taught to use a scratching post, some owners consider having the cat declawed, a controversial elective procedure. Illegal in some countries including Great Britain (except for medical reasons), declawing is the surgical removal of the claw by amputating the last digit of the toe. Most breeders of pedigreed cats include a clause in their kitten contract stating that the cat must not be declawed. Many vets refuse to perform the surgery except as a last resort in cases of extreme behavioral problems.

A tendonectomy is the surgical removal of part of the flexor tendons. The claws are left in place, but with the flexor tendon severed the cat cannot extend the claws, preventing use of the claw to scratch. While less invasive than declawing, a tendonectomy also fundamentally alters the function of the cat's foot and nails.

"Soft Paws" is a vinyl nail cap that fits over the claw and can be effective if it remains in place. But a little effort in training the young kitten to use a scratching post is worth it for the cat's mental and physical well-being.

Dental Care

Over time tartar deposits build up on the teeth, causing inflammation of the gums, bad breath, and in extreme cases can lead to teeth falling out. Tarter is not difficult to remove, provided it has not been allowed to become too thick. Heavy deposits of tarter require special dental tools. An improper diet, especially one deficient in calcium and phosphorus, can lead to poor tooth health.

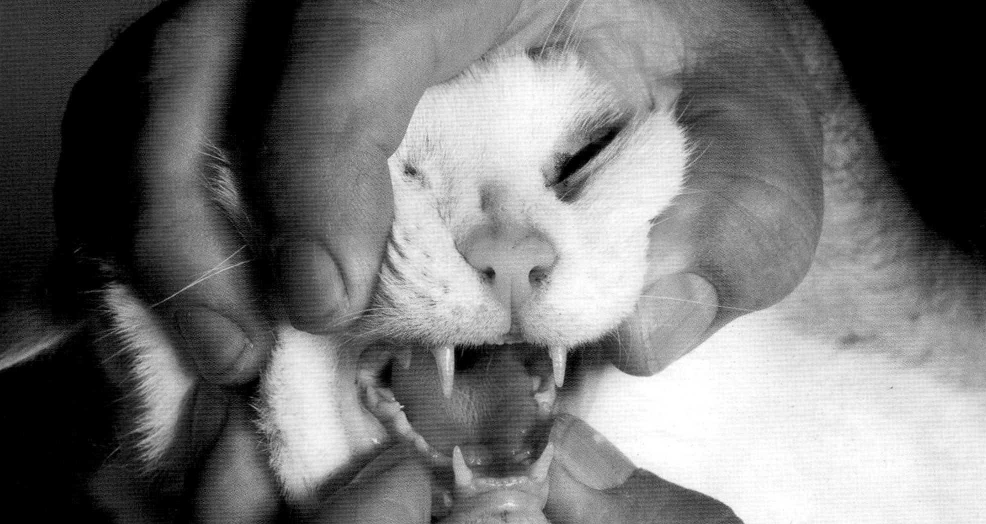

LEFT

It is important to keep your cat's teeth and gums healthy as well as tartar-free.

Signs of Illness

The Healthy Cat

A cat in good health appears sleek and well muscled but not fat. The coat is glossy and soft to the touch, with no excessive shedding except in the spring. The skin is free from sores, eczema, or fleas. Bowel movements are regular and well formed, with little odor and at least one per day as an adult. The normal rectal temperature is 101–102° F. The mouth should be free from sores, the gums pink with no sign of gingivitis, and little or no breath odor. Eyes should be bright, without redness or discharge. The nose and ears are clean and free from discharge, although a healthy cat may occasionally cough or sneeze. The cat has a healthy appetite, appears alert, curious, active, playful, and purrs contentedly when petted.

RIGHT

If your cat seems to sleep excessively, it could be an indication that it is in need of veterinary attention.

Indications of Illness

Most felines are proud, often hiding any symptoms of illness. This is a natural instinct in the wild to avoid being perceived as vulnerable by predators. Because a cat cannot tell us if it is not feeling well, the responsibility falls to the owner to be observant, sensitive to signs that something is wrong. To complicate matters, often the difference between a minor problem and something serious is only a matter of degree. Kittens and elderly cats are more vulnerable. When in doubt, call your vet. Signs of illness requiring veterinary attention include:

- Any significant behavioral changes
- Not eating or drinking for more than 24 hours
- Drinking excessively or sitting with the head hanging over the water bowl
- Vomiting repeatedly in one day, vomiting repeatedly over several days, or if vomiting is accompanied by fatigue, listlessness, diarrhea, or blood. Cats may vomit for a variety of harmless reasons, but prolonged vomiting is indicative of serious trouble
- Listlessness or sleeping more than usual
- Excessive shedding, bare spots, and sores on the skin or a dull, dry, and lifeless coat
- Constipation, diarrhea, bloody stools, or difficult bowel movements
- Frequent urination, straining while urinating, dark or blood-tinged urine, or inability to urinate. Going in and out of the litter tray repeatedly, crying while urinating, or producing little or no urine are all signs of an infection or a blocked bladder
- Loss of control of bowels or bladder
- Fever
- Excessive sneezing or coughing

- Pawing or scratching at the head or ears
- Change in pupil dilation
- Eye(s) squinted shut for more than four hours
- Heavy, thick, or discolored mucus from eyes and nose
- The third eyelid is visible (though in some cats a portion of the third eyelid is visible at all times, and it is not always a sign of illness)
- Blood from mouth, eyes, ears, anus, penis, or vulva

ABOVE

In some cats, as here, the third eyelid is always visible, whereas in others it may be a sign of illness.

ABOVE RIGHT

Checking the condition of your cat's mouth and gums can help ascertain its state of health.

- Pale gums or ears
- Swellings or abscesses on the face, legs, or tail
- Wounds, cuts, contusions
- New lumps or swellings anywhere on the body, especially ones that are growing
- Any injury that has a bad odor
- Limping or holding up a leg
- Sudden weight loss or gain
- Distended stomach
- Obvious pain or sensitivity to being touched or held
- Disorientation or loss of motor skills
- Difficulty or heavy breathing
- Limping or refusal to walk

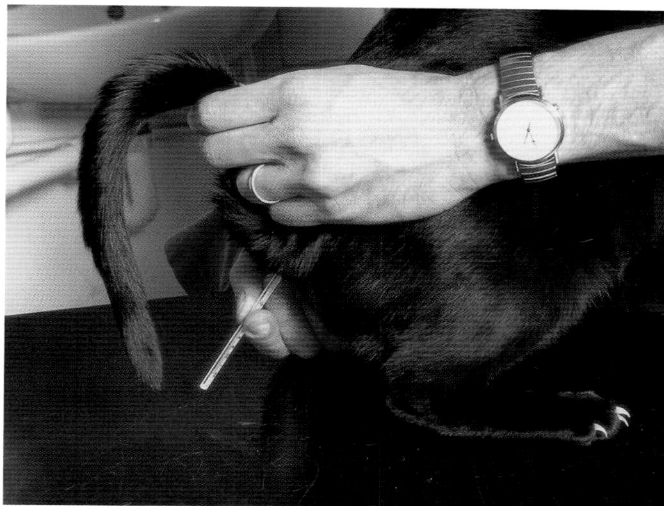

Fascinating Facts

Genghis Khan was a famous cat hater, as were Alexander the Great and Julius Caesar. The same streak of ailurophobia (cat hate) affected the personalities of Napoleon Bonaparte, Benito Mussolini, and Adolph Hitler . . . all men determined to dominate the world.

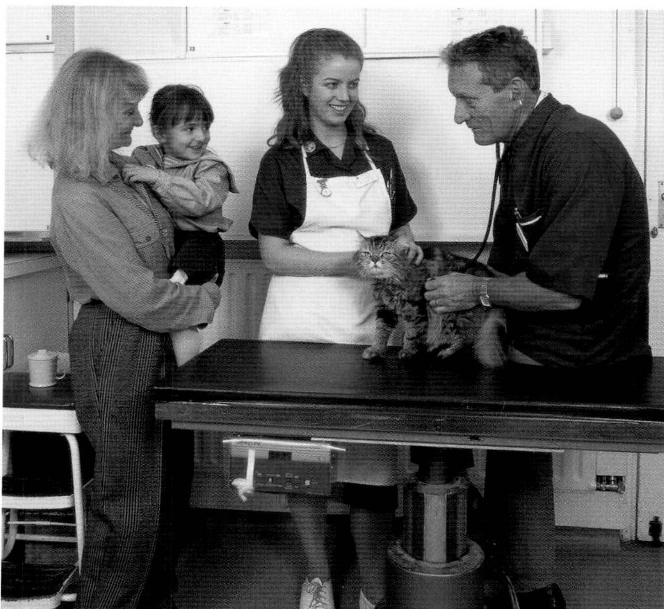

Feline Ailments

External Parasites

External parasites are found feeding on the skin and hair of the cat and are more common in cats that spend time outdoors.

Ear mites are microscopic parasites that live in the ear canal, feeding on fluid in the tissue. Symptoms include black, waxy discharge, shaking the head, holding the head or ear at a strange angle, or scratching the ear.

Fur mites, sometimes called walking dandruff, infest the skin, causing itching and flaking and can infect people.

Fleas are tiny insects that feed on blood and create mild to severe discomfort. If swallowed, they can transmit tapeworms. Symptoms include itching, dark, comma-shaped flecks in your cat's fur or skin, or sleep and play areas. Some cats develop an allergic dermatitis to fleabites.

Ticks are picked up almost exclusively outdoors, preferring to attach themselves around the neck and ears, causing an inflammatory reaction where they attach. Never pull on a tick to remove it as you risk leaving the head's tick under the skin, which can cause a painful reaction.

BELOW

The dark flecks in this cat's coat are evidence that there are fleas present.

LEFT

A deer tick feeds on a cat; ticks should never be pulled out, as the head may remain under the skin.

ABOVE

There are various remedies on the market for treating your cat or kitten if it has parasites.

Internal Parasites

Kittens are far more susceptible to internal parasites than adult cats. The major internal parasites are divided into two categories: "worms" and microscopic protozoa.

Roundworms These spaghetti-like worms lodge in the kitten's small intestine, form balls, and can cause intestinal obstructions. They can be detected by the presence of microscopic eggs in the kitten's feces. Symptoms include vomiting, diarrhea, and a distended stomach.

Tapeworms are common intestinal parasites acquired when a cat ingests an infected flea or outdoor cats eat rabbits, mice, or other rodents. Tapeworms are segmented worms that attach to the intestinal wall and cause bloating, diarrhea, and sometimes damage the coat. They can be detected by the presence of white segments like grains of rice in the stool.

ABOVE

Kittens are especially susceptible to numerous internal parasites.

ABOVE RIGHT

Ringworm is a highly contagious fungal infection and can spread from cats to their owners.

Hookworm Though these are uncommon, symptoms include weakness, anemia, and diarrhea.

Heartworm is less commonly seen in cats than dogs but can be fatal. Testing and preventive medications are recommended for cats at high risk.

Giardia are microscopic protozoa that attach to the mucous membrane of the small intestine, causing incomplete digestion, diarrhea, and gradual loss of weight.

Coccidia are parasites of the digestive system contracted from infected mice or birds or the feces of infected cats. Symptoms include diarrhea, weight loss, and listlessness, especially in kittens.

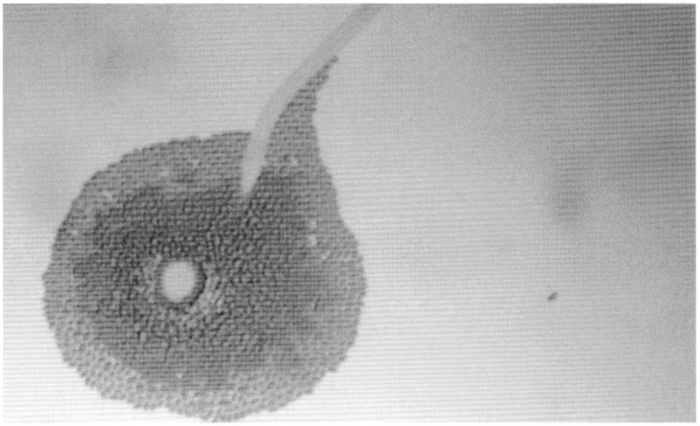

Toxoplasmosis is a serious disease transmitted by eating contaminated food or by contact with infected nasal discharge, saliva, and feces of carrier animals. Young cats are most susceptible. Symptoms include fever, loss of appetite, cough, jaundice, emaciation, heavy breathing, and nervous system disturbances. Most infected cats develop a natural immunity. If transmitted to a pregnant woman, Toxoplasmosis can cause miscarriage or birth defects. For this reason pregnant women should avoid cleaning litter trays, or at least wear protective gloves.

Skin Problems

Ringworm is a fungal infection characterized by small, round, crusty, hairless spots, especially around neck and ears. It is resistant, widely spread, and contagious to most animals and humans. Treatment is lengthy, and both animals and their environment need to be treated.

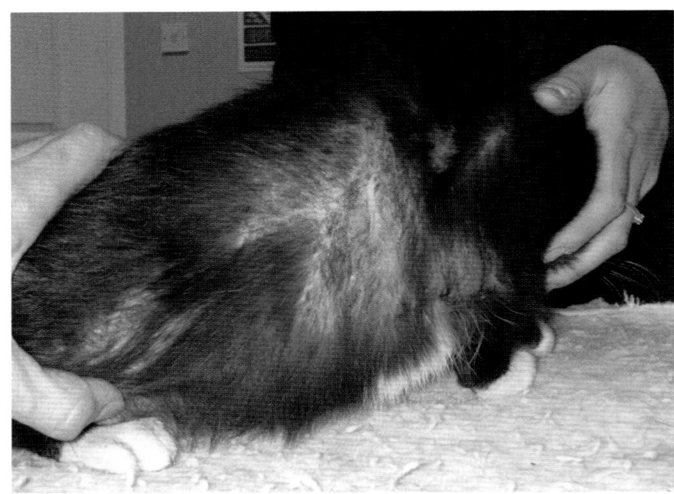

ABOVE

This cat is suffering from a form of allergic dermatitis, a skin condition that has a variety of causes.

Abscesses are small swellings on the skin caused by an accumulation of blood, lymph, or fluids resulting from an animal bite, scratch, insect sting, or a vaccination site reaction. Symptoms include swelling, pain, or sensitivity to touch, loss of appetite, irritability, and fever. Ice or cold cloths may reduce the swelling, but surgical drainage is often necessary.

Feline Acne looks like dirt on the chin and is the result of small, oily, black clogs in the chin, like blackheads, that may develop into red, itchy bumps, which may in turn become infected. Treatment varies but may include daily cleaning with an antibiotic soap, followed by a topical ointment and antibiotics.

Stud Tail is a condition that occurs when the skin's sebaceous glands near the base of the tail are overactive, producing excessive oil that blocks the hair follicles and forms blackheads. More common in breeding males, it is also seen in neutered males and female cats. Treatment includes cleaning the skin, application of topical medications, antibiotics, and shaving the hair.

Rodent Ulcer, sometimes called an eosinophilic ulcer, appears as a small sore on the margin of the cat's lower lip. While unattractive, a rodent ulcer is not painful and usually responds well to an injection of corticosteroid.

Allergic Dermatitis is a skin disease caused by an allergic reaction, which can result in itching and hair loss.

Common Ailments

Vomiting is a symptom that may be caused by disease, excitement, obstruction, parasites, poor liver and kidney function, and poisoning. If a cat has persistent vomiting and you know it has not eaten poison, withdraw food for 12–24 hours and limit water intake. If the vomiting continues, consult your vet.

Diarrhea can be an indication of parasites, poor diet, tumors, injury, or chemical irritants. True diarrhea is watery or bloody. Treatment includes a change of diet and medication to help solidify the bowel movements.

Constipation, which is infrequent or difficult bowel movements, is caused by little exercise, poor diet, hairballs, intestinal blockage, or tumors. Symptoms include lethargy, poor appetite,

BELOW

Vomiting in cats can be a symptom of many things; if it persists for long periods, consult your vet.

Fascinating Facts

Henry III, King of France (1551–1589) believed he must always appear to be bold and fearless, and he did his best to keep his image intact. But he had an Achilles heel. If a cat happened to wander into his presence, the king would faint dead away.

LEFT
Diabetes is caused by an insulin deficiency; overweight cats are especially prone to this illness.

LEFT
Constipation can be treated by introducing roughage to your cat's diet or administering a laxative.

distended abdomen, and hard feces. Treatment includes adding roughage to the diet or administering a laxative or enema to move the blockage.

Halitosis or bad breath may be caused by certain foods, intestinal disturbances, urinary ailments, or infections of teeth and mouth.

Diabetes can affect a cat of any age but is more common in older or overweight felines. It results from high blood glucose (sugar) levels caused by an insulin deficiency. Symptoms include increased thirst and appetite with accompanying weight loss. Diagnosis is confirmed by blood and urine tests. Treatment includes insulin injections and feeding a carbohydrate /sugar-restricted diet.

Arthritis is the progressive deterioration of joint cartilage. Symptoms include stiffness, limping, reluctance to climb or jump.

Asthma is an allergic respiratory condition in cats resulting in sneezing, coughing, wheezing, and difficulty breathing. Symptoms can range from mild to life threatening.

Prolapsed Rectum occurs when part of the rectum is pushed outside the anus, usually due to straining with diarrhea. It appears as a red tub hanging out of the anus. It requires surgery as soon as possible.

Cataracts are more common in older cats. They cause cloudiness in the lens, leading to poor vision or blindness.

valve. Many kittens are born with murmurs and outgrow them later in life. Many cats with murmurs live long, healthy lives. There is a small risk that murmurs can lead to congestive heart failure.

Pneumonia may be caused by a virus or bacteria, as a primary infection or secondary to another disease, such as enteritis. Symptoms include a harsh cough, thick, often bloody nasal discharge, raspy, heavy breathing, and fever. Treatment includes antibiotics and support therapy. Pleurisy is a common complication that causes the cat to breathe heavily and be short of breath.

Chlamydia is highly contagious. Symptoms include inflammation of the eyes and nasal passages, sneezing, ocular discharge, nasal drainage, tearing and salivation, and coughing. It may be transmitted to humans. Specific antibiotics are effective.

More Serious Ailments

Gastritis is a general term used to describe inflammation of the lining of the stomach. The main symptom is vomiting, although it may be mild and self-limiting or so severe as to be life threatening, necessitating hospitalization and intensive, supportive care.

Calicivirus is a contagious upper respiratory infection spread by direct contact with an infected cat or object.

ABOVE

Fatigue and exercise intolerance in your cat could be a symptom of cardiomyopathy.

Symptoms include sneezing and coughing with discharge from the eyes and nose, fever, and loss of appetite. Calicivirus and Feline Viral Rhinotracheitis infections account for 95 percent of upper respiratory infections in cats.

Cardiomyopathy is a disease of the heart muscle, which results from either a very thickened heart muscle, resulting in very small heart chambers (hypertropic cardiomyopathy) or a stretched heart muscle with very large heart chambers (dilated cardiomyopathy).

LEFT

Excessive salivation or foaming at the mouth can indicate a variety of ailments.

Both forms result in a heart that is unable to function correctly to pump blood throughout the body. Symptoms include shortness of breath, fatigue, and exercise intolerance.

Heart Murmur occurs when there is turbulence in the normal flow of blood through the chambers of the heart, usually due to a faulty heart

Cystitis is an acute or chronic inflammation of the bladder caused by stones or infection and can be painful and debilitating. Cystitis may exist as a primary ailment or as a complication of another disease. Symptoms of cystitis include frequent urination, straining, pain, bloody urine, vomiting, and bloating.

Ear Hematoma is an accumulation of blood between the skin and the ear cartilage, often following an injury from head shaking caused by an ear infection. Symptoms include pawing at the ear, shaking the head, a soft swelling inside or outside of the ear, pain or sensitivity when touched, and heat in the affected parts. Surgical drainage is required.

Hyperthyroidism is a common disease in middle age to older cats caused by excessive secretion of thyroid hormone. Symptoms include weight loss, enormous appetite, poor hair coat, hyperactivity, heavy breathing, coughing, vomiting, and diarrhea.

RIGHT

A vet checks a cat's ears for signs of infection or other abnormalities, such as ear hematoma.

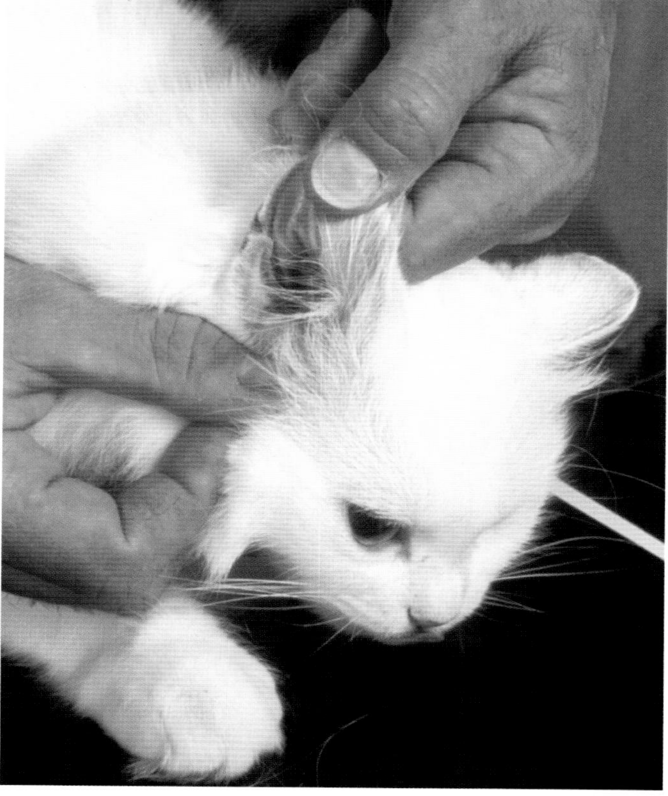

Impacted Anal Glands result when the two secretory organs located on either side of the anus become blocked. Symptoms include excessive licking or dragging of the rear end (scooting). In severe cases, the anal gland may abscess.

Inflammatory Bowel Disease (IBD) is a chronic disease of the gastrointestinal tract. It can be a frustrating disease and frequently causes vomiting and diarrhea in affected cats. Food allergies, chronic bacterial infection, or autoimmune disorders may play a role.

Keratitis is an inflammation or ulceration of the cornea of the eye usually resulting from an injury. Symptoms include sensitivity to light and occasionally a bluish-white clouding of the eye. The treatment is similar to that for conjunctivitis. It can advance if not treated.

BELOW

Weight loss can have many causes, but in an older cat it could be a symptom of hyperthyroidism.

BELOW

A kitten suffering from conjunctivitis—an inflammation of the membrane lining the eyelid and eyeball.

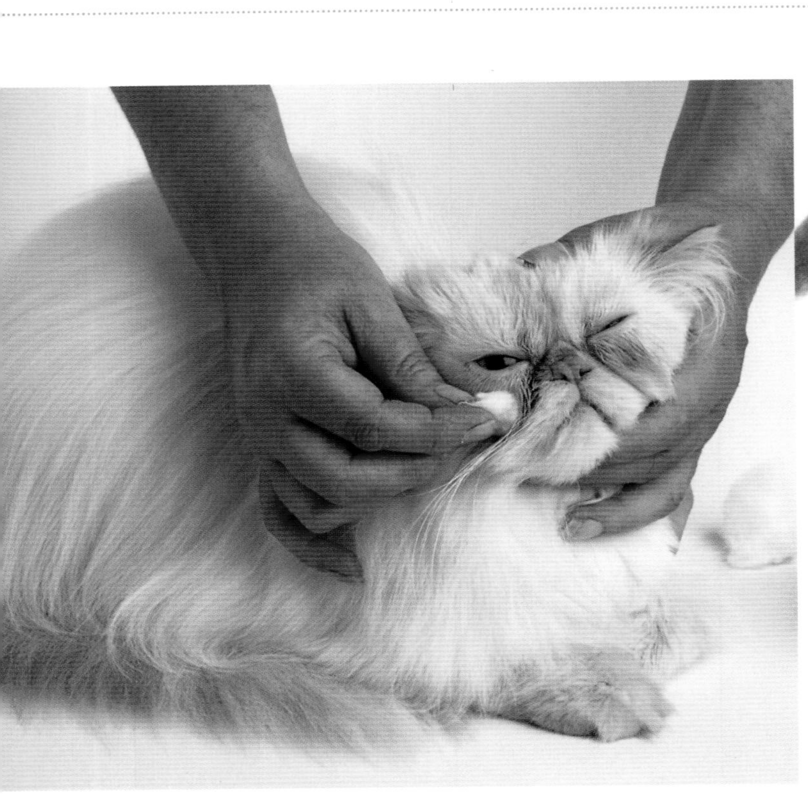

ABOVE

FIV is a contagious disease, commonly contracted as a result of fighting with an infected cat.

LEFT

Cleaning around your cat's eyes gently with cotton balls can help prevent eye infections.

Conjunctivitis is an inflammation of the membrane lining the inner surface of the eyelids and the front part of the eyeball. Symptoms include redness, squinting, and sensitivity to light. It may be caused by irritants, injury, disease, or a foreign body in the eye. Provide some relief by washing the eye with warm water. Treatment depends on the cause but may include antibiotic eyedrops.

Pneumonitis is a highly contagious virus resembling the common head cold in human beings. The incubation period ranges from six to ten days, with symptoms lasting as long as six weeks. Symptoms include running eyes, nasal discharge, sneezing fits, and salivation. Though rarely fatal, secondary infections are common. Treatment includes antihistamines, antibiotics, cleaning the eyes and nose, and applying eye ointment. The effectiveness of the pneumonitis vaccine is limited, protecting the cat for around six months at most and is only recommended if a cat is in a high-risk situation.

Potentially Fatal Illnesses

Feline Immunodeficiency Virus (FIV), also called Feline AIDS, is a contagious viral disease spread through contact with an infected cat, with wounds sustained while fighting being a common means of infection. It is a serious, often fatal disease that suppresses the immune system. This virus only affects cats and is not transmittable to humans. Symptoms include chronic infections or bouts of illness, anorexia, diarrhea, vomiting, pale mucous membranes, and chronic fever. FIV positive cats should be isolated from other cats to prevent spreading the disease.

BELOW

If your cat's eyes are running, it could be a sign that it has an eye infection.

RIGHT
The feline leukemia virus (FeLV), which is highly contagious and can be fatal.

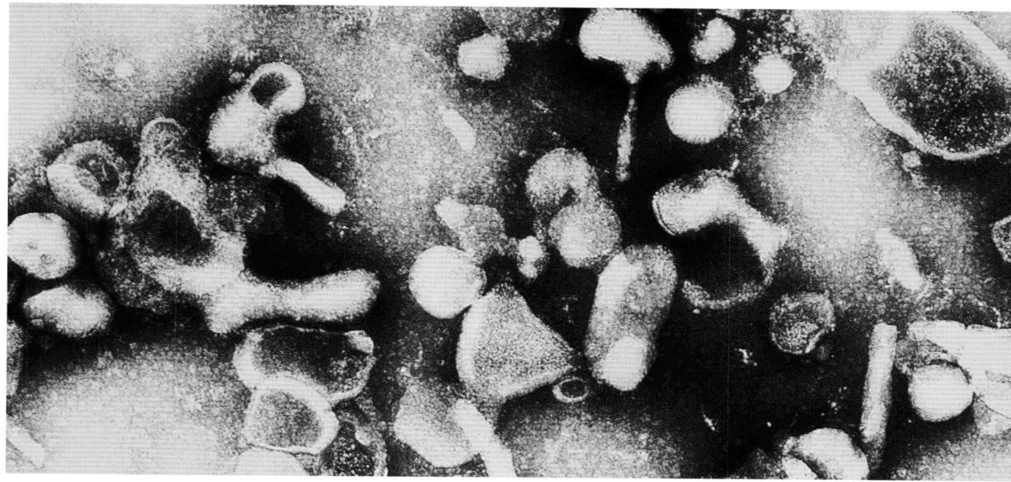

Feline Infectious Anemia (FIA) is caused by a microscopic parasite that attaches to the red blood cells and destroys them, causing low red blood cell count.

Feline Infectious Peritonitis (FIP) is a highly contagious virus spread via urine, feces, and saliva. The wet form is seen with a bloated abdomen filled with fluid. Other symptoms include anorexia, depression, weight loss, and dehydration. The dry form has similar symptoms along with lesions on the eyes. FIP can be hard to diagnose and cats who contract this virus rarely survive.

Cancer All types of cancers are found in the cat, including cancer of the skin, mammary glands, bones, blood, and blood tissues. Symptoms include lumps on the skin or bleeding from the rectum or reproductive organs. Older cats should be examined regularly by a vet for symptoms of early cancer. Many cancers can be cured if diagnosed early.

Feline Leukemia (FeLV) is a highly contagious virus spread via saliva, urine, tears, and milk, most often contracted through fighting or as a nursing kitten. There is no cure. Exposed cats may not develop symptoms but become carriers, spreading the disease to other cats. The virus suppresses the immune system, causing severe anemia and cancer. Symptoms include fever, anorexia, weight loss, and anemia. Testing is recommended as a part of a routine preventive cat health care program. Vaccination is recommended for those cats at high risk, such as outdoor cats. A positive cat should live as an indoor-only cat in order to not spread the disease to other cats.

Feline Lower Urinary Tract Disease (FLUTD), sometimes called Feline Urologic Syndrome (FUS), is a collection of diseases that affect the urinary system of the cat. Male cats suffering from FLUTD can develop a life-threatening obstruction of the urinary tract called a blocked bladder. Symptoms include poor litter tray habits, excessive licking of the genitals, and incontinence.

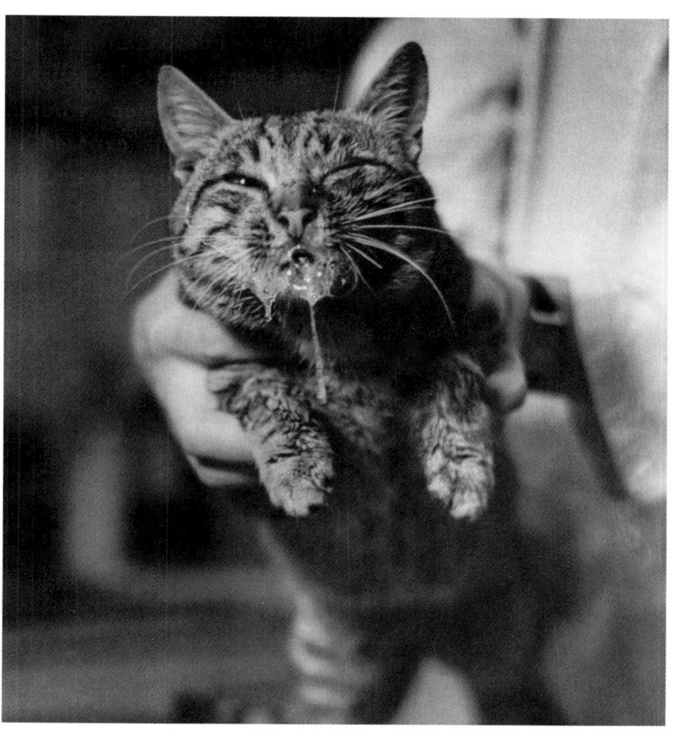

Blocked Bladder occurs when material, usually bladder stones, prevents urine from exiting the bladder. The cat's bladder becomes distended and sensitive to the touch. If not relieved, the cat will become toxic, and death may follow within 48 hours. Immediate veterinary attention is necessary.

Feline Viral Rhinotracheitis (FVR) also called "cat flu," is a highly contagious, airborne, upper respiratory virus. Symptoms include sneezing and coughing, with discharge from the eyes and nose, fever, and low appetite. Young kittens and elderly cats are more susceptible, and many require hospitalization to recover.

LEFT
Cat flu is an airborne virus and results in sneezing, coughing, fever, and loss of appetite.

Upper Respiratory Infection (URI) is common, especially in young cats. Symptoms of URI include sneezing, coughing, runny eyes, runny nose, lack of appetite, and wheezing. Vaccination against calicivirus and feline rhinotracheitis (feline herpes virus) should be part of a preventive cat health-care program, as these diseases are frequent causes of upper respiratory infections in cats.

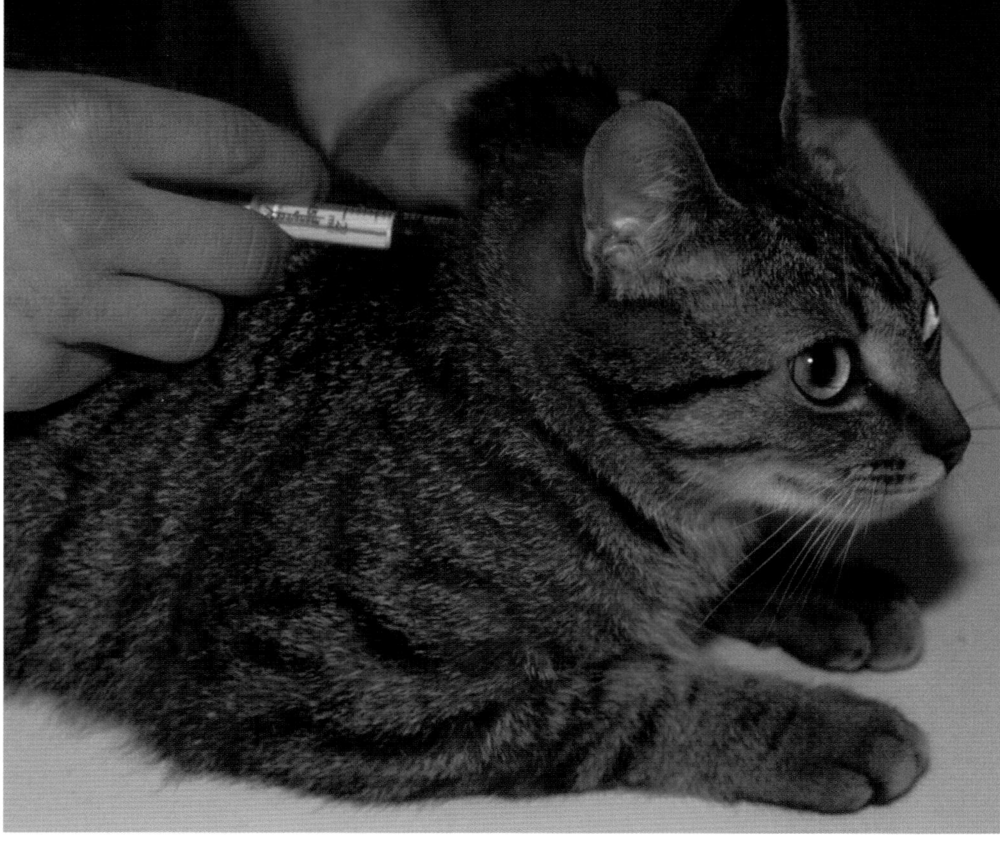

ABOVE

There is no known cure for rabies, but your cat can be vaccinated against it.

Kidney Disease is common in senior cats. Symptoms include excessive thirst and urination, lack of appetite, vomiting, and lethargy.

Panleukopenia, also known as feline distemper, is a highly contagious viral disease spread by contact with infected animals or their secretions. Symptoms include vomiting, diarrhea, weakness, dehydration, tremors, loss of coordination, and low white blood cells. Cats need to be hospitalized and receive intensive care. Mortality rate is high.

Rabies Rabies is a virus that affects the nervous system and is always fatal. There is no known cure. Symptoms include behavior change, difficulty swallowing, excessive salivation, hind limb paralysis, depression and eventual stupor. The disease is spread through the saliva of infected animals and can be transmitted through a bite or an open wound. Vaccinated pets exposed to rabies should be revaccinated and observed for 90 days. Unvaccinated pets exposed to rabies should be isolated for six months. Rabies vaccination is an essential part of a preventive cat health care program, and many communities have laws requiring the vaccination of pets against rabies.

BELOW

Cats suffering from panleukopenia need intensive treatment and therefore must be hospitalized.

Vaccine Associated Sarcoma is a tumor that develops at the site of a vaccine injection. Because it is difficult to surgically remove a tumor in the shoulder area, most vets vaccinate in the hip area rather than in the scruff of the neck.

Feline Injuries and First Aid

No matter how well you attempt to keep your cat safe, there is always the possibility that an accident may occur.

ABOVE
Bandages, in a range of sizes, are a key component of any feline first aid kit

Knowledge of basic cat first aid combined with a well-stocked feline first aid kit may save your cat's life in an emergency. Do not forget to keep the phone number of the vet and emergency clinic in the first aid kit.

The Feline First Aid Kit—Medicines and Ointments
- Wound disinfectant such as Betadine or Nolvasan
- Triple antibiotic ointment for skin
- Antibiotic ophthalmic ointment for eyes, such as Terramycin
- Eye wash solution
- Sterile saline
- Anti-diarrhea medicine
- Cat laxative in paste form
- Diphenhydramine (Benadryl) for allergic reactions
- Cortisone spray or cream to reduce itching
- Ear-cleaning solution
- Hydrogen peroxide used to make a pet vomit
- Activated charcoal to absorb ingested poisons
- Rubbing alcohol
- Hairball remedy
- Petroleum jelly

The Feline First Aid Kit—Bandages
- 3 in. sq. (7.5 cm sq.) sterile, non-stick gauze pad
- 1 in. (2.5 cm) and 2 in. (5 cm) rolls of gauze bandage
- 1 in. (2.5 cm) and 2 in. (5 cm) rolls of elastic adhesive tape
- Cloth strips
- Cotton swabs
- Cotton balls

The Feline First Aid Kit—Tools
- Digital Rectal Thermometer
- Muzzle
- Short blade, blunt tip scissors
- Tweezers
- Nail clippers
- Metal, fine-toothed comb
- Disposable syringe/ eye dropper

Feline First Aid Artificial Respiration If the cat has stopped breathing, lay it on its side on a flat surface. Open the mouth. If an object is blocking the airway, grab the tongue and pull it out. Use fingers, surgical pliers, or a hemostat to pull it out. Once the airway is clear, lift the chin to straighten out the throat. Use one hand to grasp the muzzle and hold the mouth shut. Put your mouth completely over the nose and blow gently; the chest should expand. Blow just enough to move the chest. Wait for the air to leave the lungs before breathing again. Continue giving 20 breaths per minute until the cat breathes on its own.

BELOW
A feline first aid kit should include items such as tweezers, bandages, an eye dropper, and blunt-tip scissors.

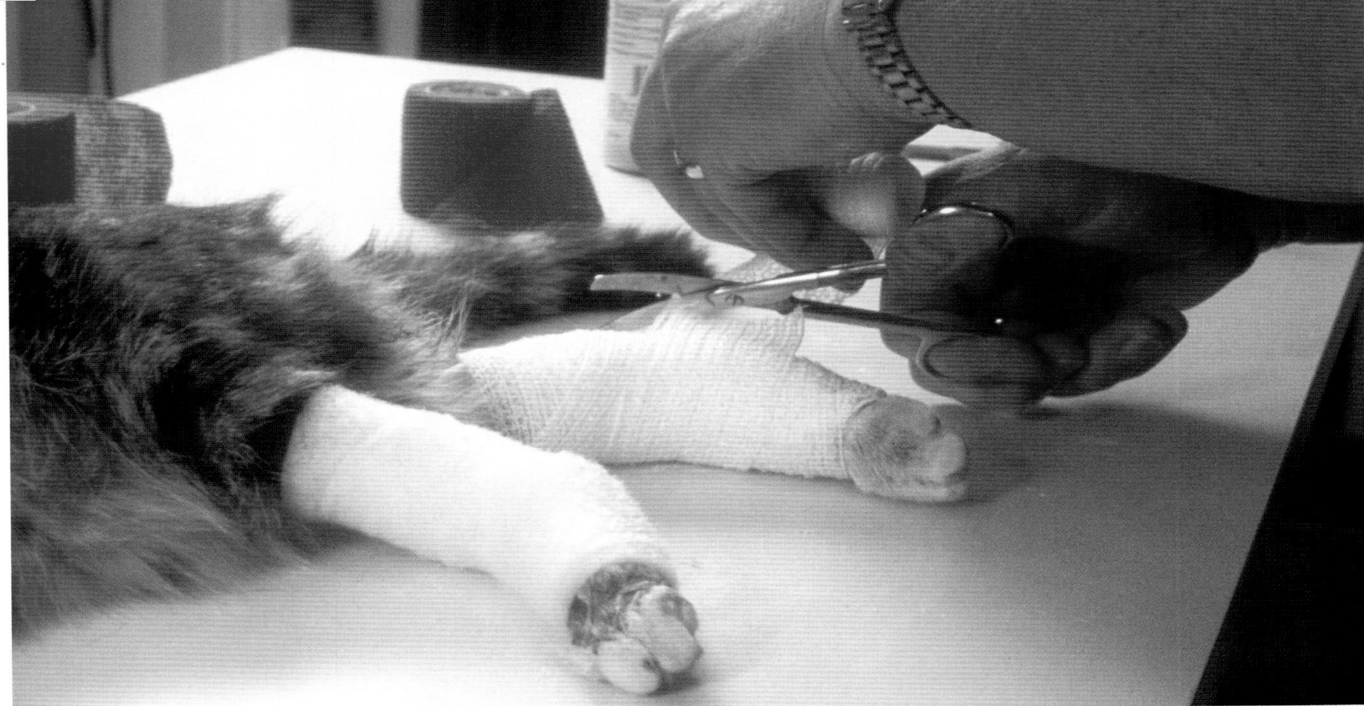

Bleeding Minor bleeding will stop on its own. However, if the bleeding is more serious, apply a cold-water compress and then a pressure bandage of gauze and secure it with tape. If bleeding from a leg or tail is profuse, apply a tourniquet by tying a strip of cloth between the wound and the body. Rush to the vet.

Broken Bones If your cat has sustained a broken leg, fold a thin towel snugly around the injured limb and secure it in place, or simply place the folded towel beneath the injured limb to provide support during transportation. Do not try to set the fracture or apply anything on an open wound. Keep the cat warm to prevent shock.

Burns A superficial burn appears red in color and blisters, while a deeper, more serious burn will appear whitish. Immediately apply ice or cold water to a minor burn for 20 minutes. Serious burns require immediate veterinary attention.

CPR If your cat's heart has stopped beating, lay your cat on its side on a flat surface. Place the palm of your hand on the rib cage over the heart. Place your other hand on top of the first. For kittens, put your thumb on one side of the chest and the rest of your fingers on the other side. Compress the chest around one inch. Squeeze and release rhythmically at a rate of 80 to 100 compressions per minute. If also performing artificial respiration, alternate one breath with five compressions.

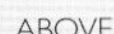

ABOVE

If your cat has a broken limb, it is best to try and hold it in place until professional help can be given.

Drowning If you find your cat or kitten in water, apparently lifeless, make sure the airway is clear and then hold the cat by the hind legs, swinging it upside down, back and forth between your legs, to force water out of the lungs by centrifugal force.

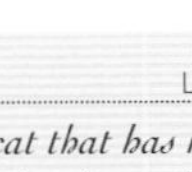

LEFT

A cat that has received an electric shock—from chewing on wires, for example—should be checked for burns and may require CPR.

ABOVE

Cats cannot resist catching insects, but this can result in bites or stings to the mouth and paws.

RIGHT

Paleness of the gums is one of the symptoms a vet will look for in a cat that may be suffering from shock.

Electric Shock Cats chewing on electrical wires may receive an electrical shock. If the cat is unconscious, check for a heartbeat by feeling the chest just behind the foreleg, perform CPR if necessary, and then rush the cat to the vet. Check the mouth and tongue for electrical burns as they need medical attention.

Insect Bites and Stings Cats are fascinated with bugs. Paws and mouths are the most common location for an insect bite or sting. Symptoms include swelling and allergic responses. Remove stinger, apply ice, administer an antihistamine, and seek veterinary care.

Poisoning If you know your cat has eaten something poisonous, but not caustic, induce vomiting by feeding 5 ml (one teaspoon) of 3 per cent hydrogen peroxide every 10 minutes until the cat begins to vomit.

Trauma/Shock Symptoms of shock include pale gums, rapid heartbeat, glassy eyes, and cold, clammy skin. Keep warm, and rush to the vet.

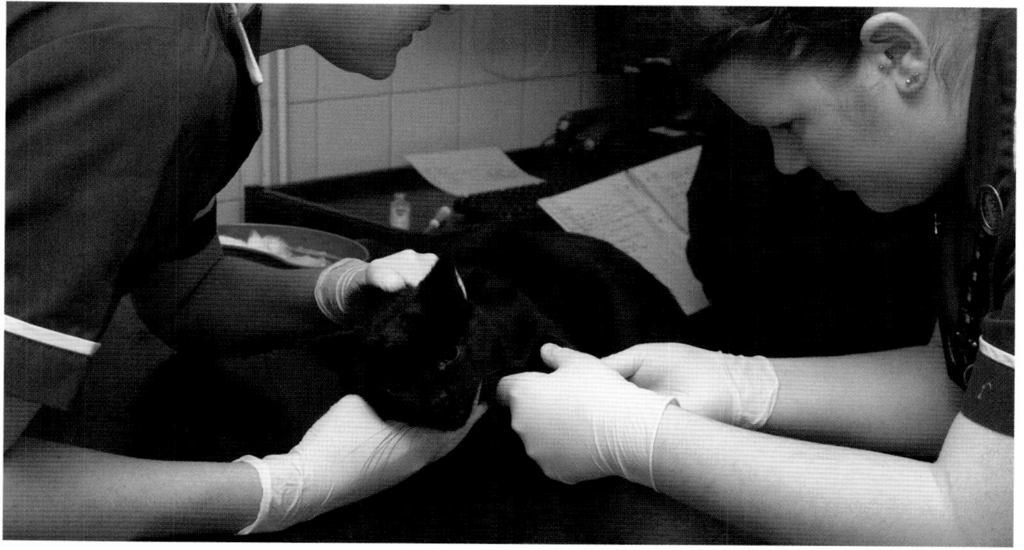

Treatment and Medication

Choosing Your Vet

A vet is your partner in the health care of your cat. A good vet can be hard to find, so make sure you find one before you need one. You should have confidence in your vet's medical knowledge, and you must be able to communicate well and feel comfortable with them. To find one that works best with you and your feline friend, consider what you want in a vet. The vet should be an experienced diagnostician competent in the latest veterinary procedures and interested in cat-specific medicine. Ideally the veterinary hospital should be a clean, well-maintained facility in a convenient location with available parking, convenient office hours, and easy payment methods. Is there a separate facility for feline patients away from the dogs? What is the range of services that the veterinary hospital provides? Is there an onsite X-ray machine, in-house laboratory facilities, ultrasound machine, laser, dental X-ray machine, or endoscope? Ask about training and experience with high-tech machines and procedures. Is there an emergency service? If the practice has multiple vets, can you specify which vet will treat your cat? Does the vet specialize in surgery, dental care, eye care, or allergies? Are the support staff friendly and helpful?

BELOW

When choosing your vet, it may be worth checking if they have the facilities to take X-rays.

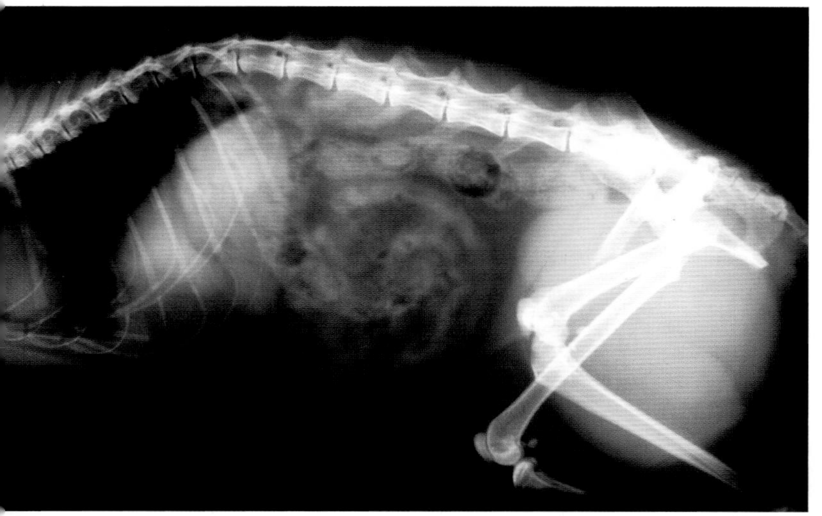

To find a good vet, ask for recommendations from cat owners in your area, groomers, or a local pet store. When moving, ask your former vet if he can recommend a vet in your new

BELOW

Once you have found a vet that meets your requirements, take your cat in for its first checkup.

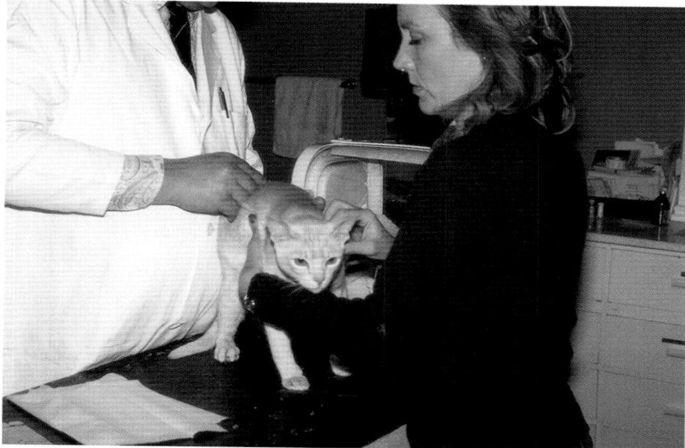

area. When receiving a recommendation, ask why they like that individual vet. The "why" is as important as the actual recommendation. Some owners prefer a "cats only" vet that concentrates all their efforts on feline-specific issues. The vet with a general small animal practice may be a better choice if the attitude of the vet and facilities better meet your needs.

Once you have narrowed your list of recommendations to conveniently located vets with office hours, payment policies, and emergency procedures that meet your needs, visit the hospitals and take a tour. No one vet or facility is likely to perfectly meet all your needs, so decide what your priorities are. Once you have made your choice, make an appointment for the vet to see your cat for an initial checkup.

Home Care

Once a sick cat has been examined by a vet, diagnosed, treated, and returns home, it is important to keep it warm, quiet, well fed, watered, and to follow up on medications or treatment the vet recommends.

Taking Your Cat's Temperature

A cat's normal rectal temperature is 100.5–102.5° F (38.1–39.2° C). Sphynx and Rex breeds may have a slightly higher normal temperature of 102–103° F (39–39.5° C). Feeling the ears, nose, or head is not considered a reliable method to determine temperature.

ABOVE RIGHT

Being able to go to a vet with easy payment procedures takes the anxiety out of a visit there.

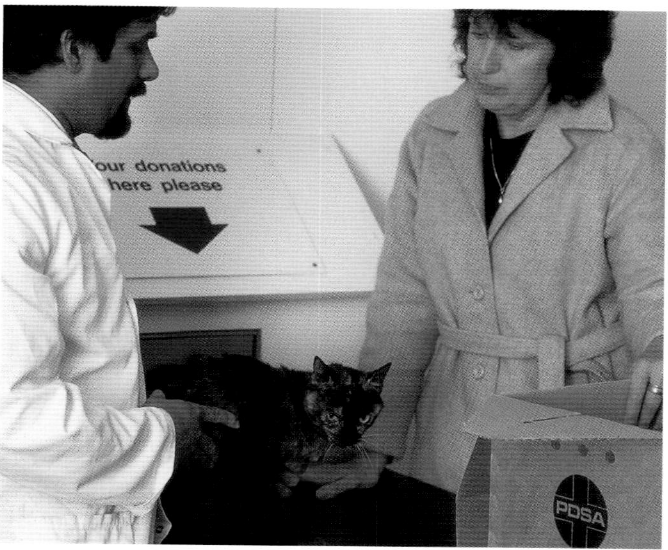

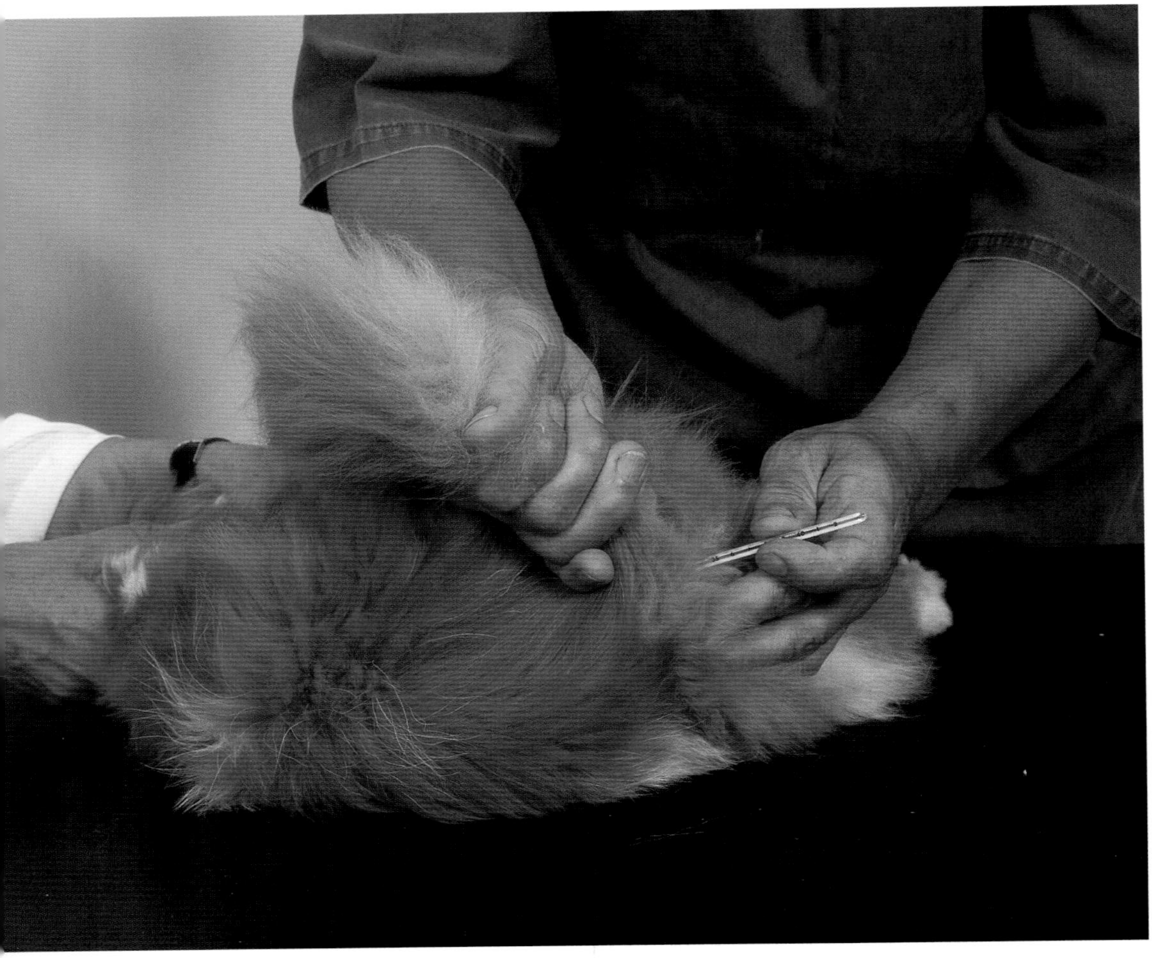

The easiest thermometer to use is a digital, rectal thermometer. Choose one with a flexible tip. Coat the tip with petroleum jelly. Place the standing cat on a counter, hugging its body to yours. Grasp the tail at the base and raise it, holding it firmly so the cat will not sit down. Gently insert the bulb portion of the thermometer into the anus using a twisting motion. Insert the thermometer around 1 inch, leaving it in place until the thermometer beeps. Remove the thermometer, and read the temperature. A high temperature could indicate an infection. A temperature below normal may indicate shock.

Ear thermometers can also be used in cats. They are generally fast and easy, but it is essential to use a proper technique to obtain an accurate reading. The normal ear temperature in cats is 100.0–103.0° F (37.8–39.4° C). The ear thermometer works by measuring infrared heat waves that come from the eardrum area, so it is important to place the thermometer deep into the horizontal ear canal. The first few times you use it, take both ear and rectal temperatures and compare. The results should be very close if you are using the proper ear technique.

Taking Your Cat's Pulse

To take a cat's pulse, use light fingertip pressure on the inside of the cat's thigh where the femoral artery can be felt. The femoral artery pulsation determines the pulse rate. A normal rate is around 110 to 135 beats per minute, varying with age, exercise, excitement, and condition of the cat. Respiration should be 25 to 40 per minute. In shock, the pulse is fast and weak.

Taking Your Cat's Heartbeat

In a difficult situation where you cannot take the pulse by touch, it may be possible to observe the heartbeat by watching or feeling the chest. One rise plus one fall equals one breath. Cats at rest take around 30–50 breaths per minute.

LEFT

A rectal thermometer is the most reliable way of checking your cat's body temperature.

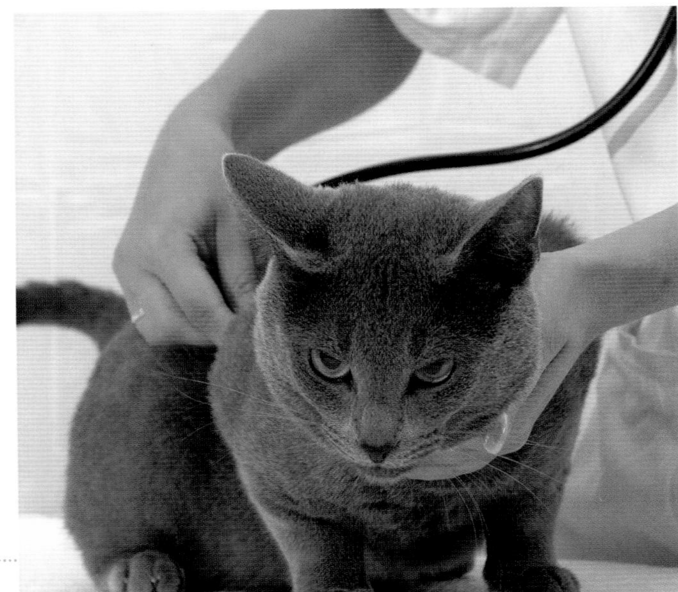

LEFT

Vets check a cat's heartbeat using a stethoscope, but there are ways in which you can check this yourself.

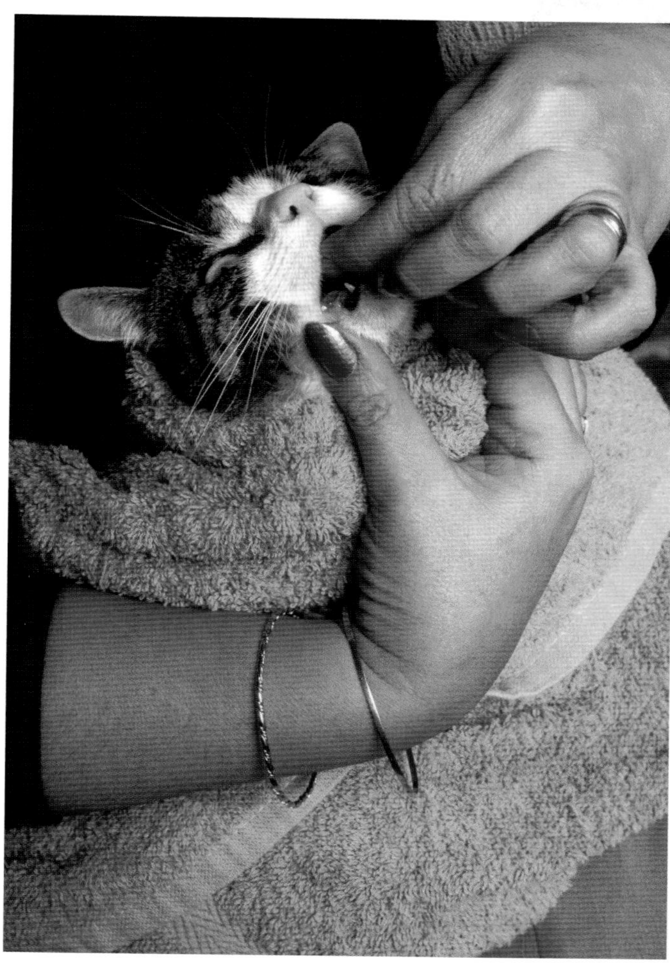

Giving Your Cat a Pill

Place the cat on the kitchen counter or have it sit on your lap. If uncooperative, wrap the cat tightly in a towel, leaving only his head visible. Hold the cat's head from the top using your left hand if you are right-handed. The cat's cheekbones provide a convenient handle by which to hold the head firmly without causing the cat any discomfort. Tilt the head back and the cat will often drop its lower jaw open. Force the mouth open by squeezing your thumb and finger together and applying gentle pressure at the corners of the cat's mouth. Hold the pill or capsule in your right hand between your index finger and thumb. You can place one of the remaining fingers of your right hand on the lower incisors to keep the lower jaw open. Drop the pill or capsule as far back on the tongue as possible. You can also use your forefinger to poke the pill gently down the throat. Close the mouth and blow on the cat's face to encourage it to swallow. Stroke the neck and throat while holding the mouth closed. Give the cat a small quick toss in the air. The cat gulps, and the pill goes down.

It is recommended that whenever giving your cat a pill or capsule, you always follow it immediately by syringing several doses of water into the cat's mouth to help the medication "go down." Giving your cat a drink of water after giving it a medication in either pill or capsule form helps the pill reach the stomach faster.

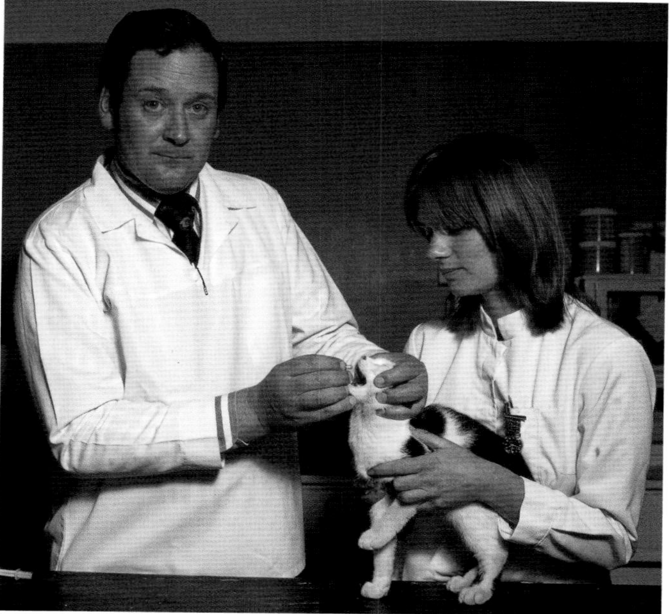

ABOVE
If your cat is not amenable to taking pills, it may help to have someone else hold it still.

Also, give him a favorite treat—baby food or fresh meat—so that he associates pill taking with a pleasant experience.

Pill Poppers The pill popper (or "piller") is used to administer pills and capsules safely, quickly, and easily. It is a syringe-type plastic instrument that consists of a long, plastic barrel with a plastic plunger, plus a rubber flexible tip. The rubber tip is split to hold pills better. The soft rubber is gentle to the inside of the cat's mouth and holds the tablet firmly.

Place the medication in the rubber tip of the piller. Tip the cat's head back, and open the mouth slightly. In one quick motion place the rubber tip of the piller as far as possible behind the root of the tongue. In the same motion push the plunger to empty the piller. Withdraw the piller, and close the cat's mouth. Rub the throat until you see the cat swallow.

The rubber tip wears down over time. This can create a risk of it actually falling off in the cat's mouth and being accidentally swallowed. Check the rubber tip for cracks or a slight color change.

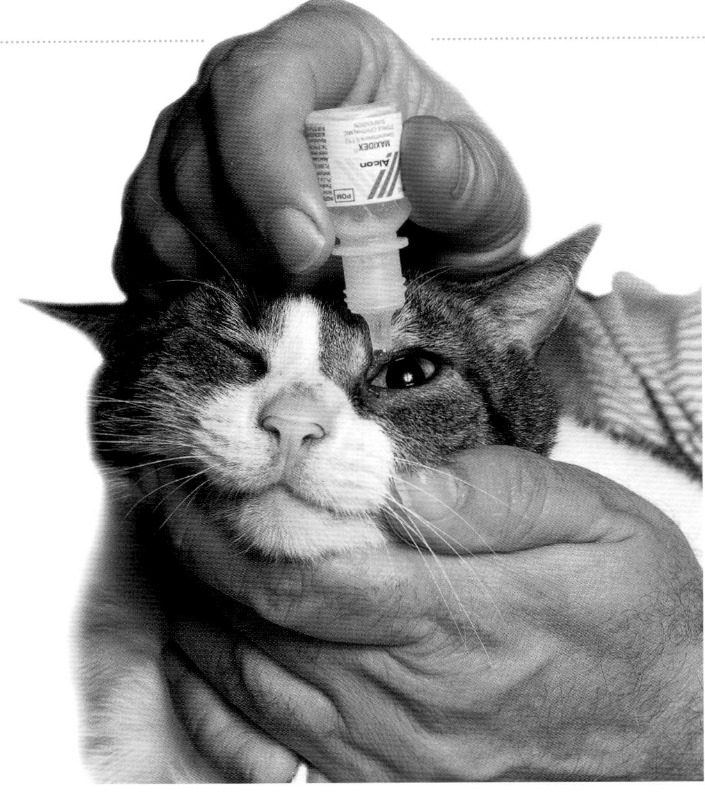

BELOW

An experienced vet can apply eye ointment straight from the tube, but it may be safer to use a clean finger.

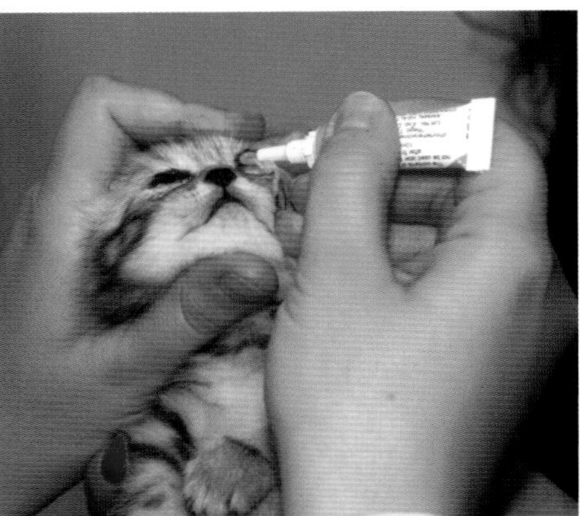

Administering Eyedrops

If the cat is difficult to handle, wrap it tightly in a towel. Place the cat on a table or counter. If you are right-handed, hold the cat's head with the nose pointed slightly up with your left hand. Your right hand holds the dropper bottle. Place the outer edge of your hand on top of the cat's head, with the tip of the dropper bottle aimed for the correct eye, and pull back to open up the eyelid fully. Putting your hand on top of the animal's head will help prevent accidentally poking the eye with the bottle. One or two drops are enough. Repeat with the other eye if needed. Never hold the eye dropper so that the tip can touch the eye, as the medication may become contaminated. Also if the animal moves suddenly, the tip may poke into the pet's eye and cause significant damage.

Administering Eye Ointment

The safest way to administer ointment into the eye is by using your finger. The tube tips are usually pointy and can cause a lot of damage if accidentally touched to the eye, or the ointment may become contaminated from contact with an infected eye. Wash your hands, and try not to touch anything with your right index finger. With the animal restrained, place a short strip (around ⅜ in. (1 cm)) of ointment on the tip of your right index finger. With your other hand and fingers, open up the eyelid and scrape the ointment from your finger onto the inside surface of the lower lid. Then close the lids and rub them around to distribute the ointment.

Administering Eardrops

Tip the cat's head slightly and insert the drops as far down the ear canal as possible. Gently massage for several minutes. If the drops need to be refrigerated, allow them to reach room temperature before using.

BELOW

If you have any concerns about the condition of your cat's ears, it is a good idea to consult a vet.

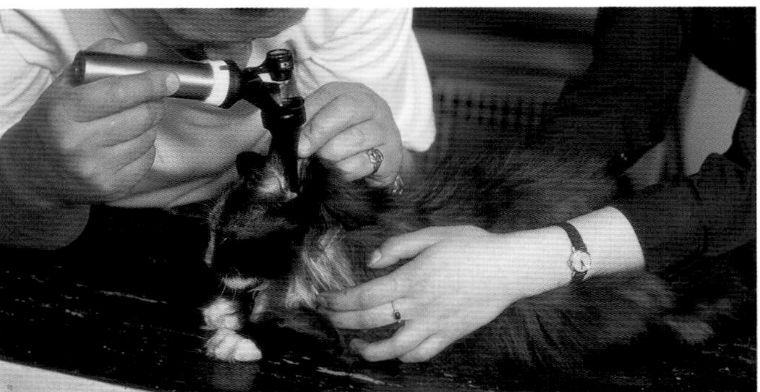

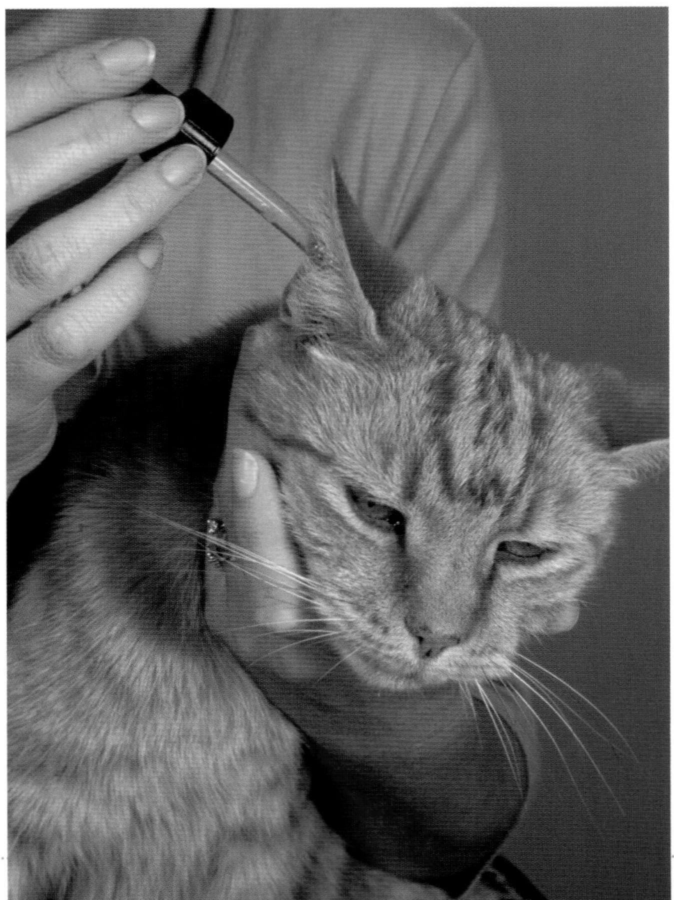

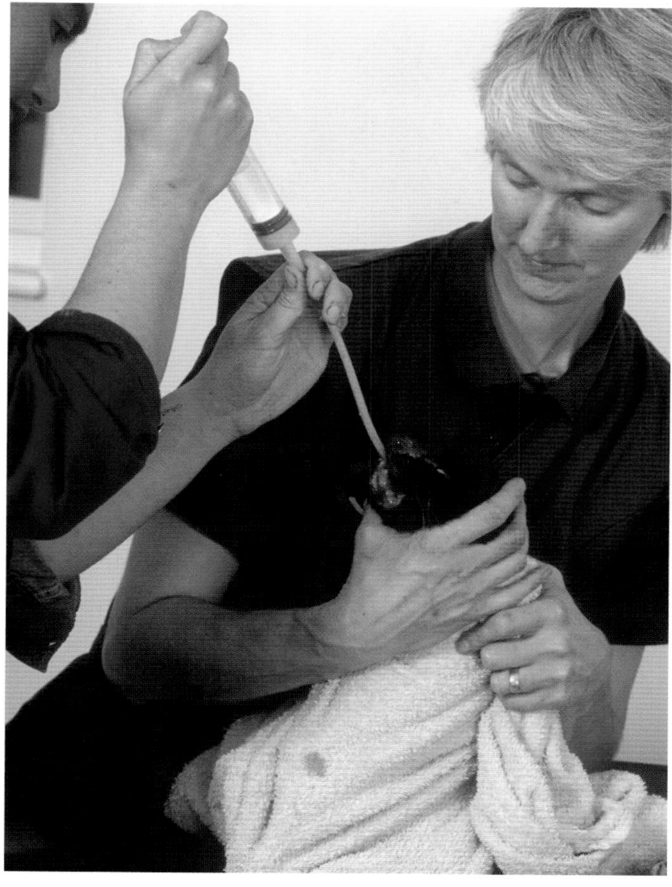

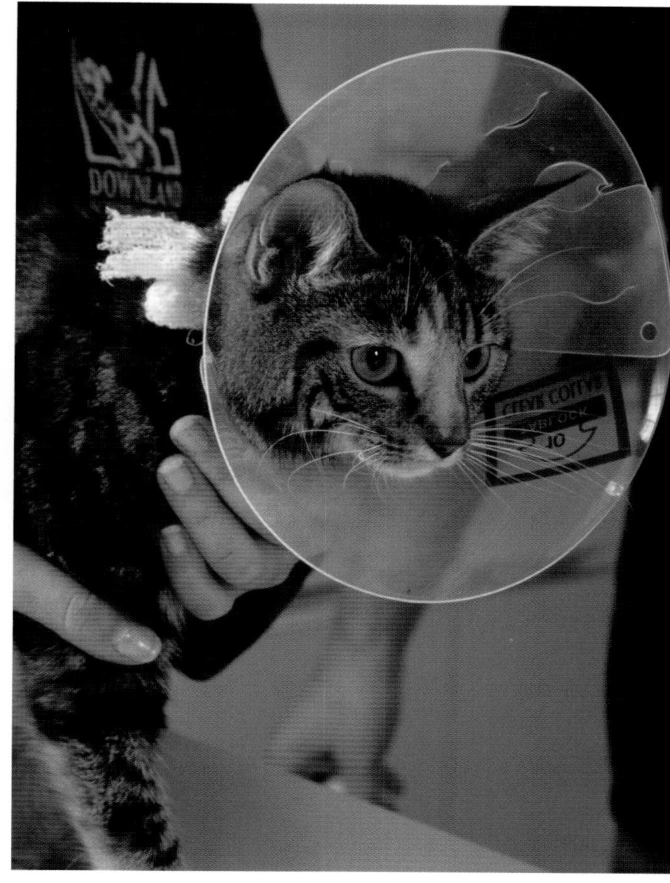

Force Feeding

A sick cat may stop eating. If the cat stops eating for more than a day, it is critical that it be forced to eat. High-calorie supplements are available in tubes. Place an inch on your finger and then force the cat's mouth open, place far back on the tongue, and hold the cat's mouth closed until it swallows. Liquefied food can be placed in a large syringe and force fed by placing the tip in the side of the mouth. Keep the cat hydrated by syringing unflavored rehydration formula or water.

ABOVE
If a cat refuses to eat for more than one day, it becomes necessary to try force-feeding.

ABOVE
Cats with wounds that need to heal without being licked or scratched may wear an Elizabethan collar.

The Elizabethan Collar

An Elizabethan collar is a truncated cone-shaped device that fits over the head of the cat to prevent the animal from biting or licking at its body or scratching at its head or neck while wounds or injuries heal. It is attached to the cat's collar with strings or tabs passed through holes punched in the plastic. The neck of the collar should be short enough to allow the cat to eat and drink. Collars can be bought from vets or pet stores.

Caring For the Elderly Cat

Advances in modern veterinary medicine and nutrition have extended the average life expectancy of a cat to almost 15 years, with many reaching 20 years and beyond. With increased longevity come concerns regarding the special needs of the senior citizen feline.

Although the common belief is one cat year equals seven years in human terms, cats actually age fastest in their first year. A 12–18-month-old cat is roughly equivalent to a 20-year-old human. By two years of age, the rate of maturing slows until each year is equivalent to four human years. A ten-year-old cat is equivalent to a person in their mid-50s. Some cats encounter age-related problems as young as seven years of age, while most felines show definite signs of aging by 12 years of age.

BELOW

Older cats usually groom themselves less, and bathing them may become increasingly necessary.

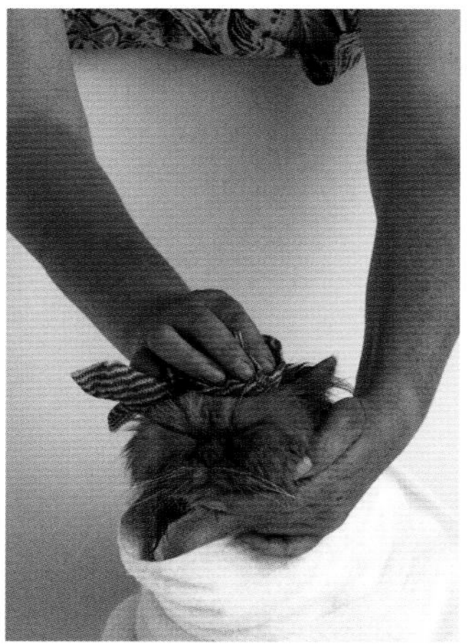

Special Needs of the Older Cat

A cat sleeps more as it ages. Because it grooms itself less, its coat may begin to look greasy, tangled, and have an odor. The claws may become thick and brittle. The skin grows thinner and less elastic. More frequent bathing, combing, and nail trimming may help prevent hairballs, matting, and skin problems, especially in longhaired cats.

The older cat often feels cold more easily. A heating pad or a cat sweater may make it more comfortable. Arthritis is common. Signs include a cat that moves more slowly, seems reluctant to climb, or hesitates when jumping down. It may have difficulty climbing into the litter tray or using stairs, so add extra litter trays, food, and water in various locations in the home, especially on each level of a multi-story home.

RIGHT

Older cats in multi-level houses should be provided with food and water in a variety of locations.

Some loss of hearing or vision is not uncommon in an older cat; however, neither seems to bother most cats as long as they are in familiar surroundings. Loss of ability to smell may result in poor appetite, so a more smelly, appetizing food may need to be offered. If the cat is too thin, it needs a diet with higher calorie count per cup. If gaining weight, consider a low-fat, high-protein diet.

Bad breath, drooling, or reluctance to eat may signal dental problems such as tartar, gingivitis, or tooth decay. Don't be too concerned if the cat must have teeth removed, as most cats manage fine with missing teeth. Soft foods and more frequent, smaller meals may help. The older cat may develop problems with incontinence, diarrhea, or constipation, possibly related to kidney problems or diabetes. Commercial diets are available, formulated for the special nutritional needs of the older cat or the cat with medical issues.

never simply assume that changes you see in your older cat are due to old age and therefore untreatable.

Euthanasia

There may come a time in a cat owner's life when there is a need for great love and perhaps greater courage. When injury, illness, or old age makes a cat's life too painful to continue, the option of euthanasia must be considered. Euthanasia is accomplished by injecting a large overdose of a very powerful anesthetic. The cat slips into a quiet, irreversible, deep unconsciousness. Death comes quickly and painlessly. The sense of loss after the death of a pet can be as profound as the loss of a human family member. If you feel overwhelmed by a sense of guilt or sadness, there are online grief counseling websites to help you deal with the loss of a pet.

Elderly cats can develop symptoms similar to human Alzheimer's. Behaviors can include wandering, excessive meowing, staring at walls, and disorientation. Medications are available that may help. Stress should be kept at a minimum for the elderly cat. If a senior cat displays signs of illness, it should be addressed immediately, as any problem is more likely to have a detrimental effect on the aging pet. While many vets no longer recommend yearly booster vaccinations for their older clients, a physical and dental checkup should be performed annually. Some signs of aging are also signs of poor health, so

RIGHT

Placing a memorial in a pet cemetery can help some people overcome the death of a beloved pet.

GROWTH AND BREEDING

It is hard to believe, but within one year your cute little bundle of fur will become a mature cat, and you may miss the kitten it once was. However, if you have given it a good start in life and take care of it throughout its time with you, you have many years of its company to look forward to. In fact, some owners love having cats around so much and especially love the qualities of one breed that they decide to start breeding them. However, this is a time-consuming and weighty responsibility and must not be entered into lightly.

A Cat's Life Cycle

The average life span of the indoor cat is 15–19 years, with many reaching into their twenties and some even making it to their thirties. The average life span of the feral cat living in the wild is only two years. If the cat is part of a feral colony with a caretaker, the average life span doubles.

One pair of cats and their kittens can produce 420,000 kittens in just seven years.

LEFT

Kittens soon learn to interact with the other members of the litter, playing stalking and hunting games.

Kittens are born blind, deaf, and virtually helpless. They sleep almost constantly, an instinctive behavior that protects them in the wild. By sleeping all the time, there is less opportunity for the babies to wander or make noise that might attract a predator. When not sleeping, they are nursing and staying warm and are completely dependent on their mothers for all their needs for the first few weeks of their lives.

Kittens open their eyes around ten days after birth. They develop very quickly from around two weeks of age until their seventh week. Their coordination and strength improve, they play-fight with their littermates and begin exploring the world outside the nest. They learn to wash themselves and others, as well as playing hunting and stalking games, showing their inborn ability as predators. As they reach three to four weeks old, the kittens begin eating solid food, with weaning usually complete by six to eight weeks. The weaned kitten becomes progressively more independent.

Coming of Age

The cat reaches puberty around nine or ten months of age, although some cats come into season or mate much earlier. As the young male approaches sexual maturity, he develops prominent jowls and a broader head. His urine acquires a strong, distinctive odor. He may begin territorial urine spraying and become aggressive. He will practice mounting behavior on both male and female cats, regardless of whether they are neutered or spayed or if the female is in season or not. A sexually mature female cat goes into heat and is both receptive to and attractive to male cats. She will mate with more than one male if given the opportunity.

LEFT

Once weaned, a kitten will begin to become more independent, and its skills will develop more and more.

The gestation period of the cat is around 65 days. The average litter consists of four kittens. The fertility of cats is phenomenal. She can produce two to three litters of kittens yearly and can continue to produce kittens for ten years or more.

Fascinating Facts

Of breeders who rear one litter of kittens, less than 40 percent breed a second. Of breeders who register their first litter, only around 20 percent are still breeding three years later.

LEFT

The decision to begin breeding cats should not be taken lightly, as there is a lot of work involved.

Breeding: Points to Consider

Some people just drift into cat breeding. Perhaps they have a single female and want to enjoy having a litter or two. Other people start breeding to make money selling kittens (not a very realistic expectation). Some others fall in love with a certain breed and want to become more involved. But cat breeding is not easy . . . and not for the faint-hearted. While there are many fulfilling rewards involved in breeding and showing cats, before deciding to take up the hobby, consider these questions:

- Do you have the finances to be a cat breeder? Quality breeding stock is expensive, and an emergency C-section is expensive.
- Do you have the appropriate temperament to be a cat breeder? It requires a lot of emotional strength to nurse a failing kitten for weeks and then watch it die.
- Do you have the time to devote to the maintenance of a cattery? Depending on the number of cats, routine care takes hours out of every day.
- Can you always be there for your cats? Breeders seldom take vacations, and family plans are often interrupted by illness or births.
- Can you market your kittens? Are you prepared to take responsibility for the kittens you produce for their entire lives?
- Are you ready to learn? The new breeder must become knowledgeable in every facet of their cats, their health issues, and genetics.

The cat lover breeds to improve his own cats, the bloodlines, and the overall breed. The path of a cat breeder is not an easy one but can lead to success in the show ring, the establishment of your own bloodlines with a distinctive look, pride, and a lasting sense of achievement.

Breeding: Preparation and Conception

Before being bred, a cat should receive a general health checkup. Vaccinations should be up-to-date. Available DNA tests for specific health problems should be performed.

The Male

A male cat used for breeding purposes is called a stud or tom. While both the female and the male cat contribute equally to the genetic makeup of their kittens, as a stud cat produces many more kittens in his lifetime than a female, his influence on a breeding program is more significant. The stud should be an excellent example of his breed, with a good temperament, robust health, and no significant genetic problems. Ideally he should have proven his qualities in the show ring.

The Female

A female used for breeding is called a queen. Although female cats generally mature sexually anywhere from five to nine months of age, ideally she should be at least ten months old before being bred. She should be of a good body weight, receive a complete veterinary checkup, and because she imparts her immunity to her kittens, her vaccinations should be up-to-date throughout her pregnancy and weaning.

Fascinating Facts

Unlike other animal breeders such as with dogs and horses, few catteries offer stud service. The difference in cat biology makes it necessary to quarantine a new cat entering a cattery situation, making stud service impractical or risky.

LEFT

The female and male cats in a breeding partnership contribute equally to the genetic makeup of the kittens.

Coming Into Heat

When a female cat is ready to be bred, she is said to be in season, in heat, or in estrus. A female cat exhibits no external physical signs of being in heat. She indicates readiness to be bred entirely through her behavior. The female starts to "call"—a loud, long, mournful cry that is repeated and repeated. She will be restless. She may be very affectionate, rubbing her head against her owner or objects. She will roll on the floor or tread with her hind feet, alternately lifting her rear feet in quick succession while raising her hindquarters in the air, holding her tail to one side and crouching low on her front legs. A person unfamiliar with the signs of a cat in heat will often mistake this behavior for illness or pain.

LEFT

A female cat in heat will let out mournful cries and may roll around on the floor.

ABOVE
Female cats in heat often adopt this posture: crouching low on the front legs with the hindquarters held high.

The amount of exposure to natural sunlight, the breed of the cat, and individual variations influence the pattern of heat cycles. Most queens (an adult female cat used for breeding) start to cycle in the late winter and continue through the summer.

Female cats are induced ovulators, which mean that ovulation does not take place until mating. If the female cat does not mate during her heat, hormonal levels drop off, and she comes out of season until it repeats itself in another two to three weeks.

BELOW
During mating, the male cat approaches the female from behind and grips her neck between his teeth.

Pyometra is an infection of the uterus in unsprayed females characterized by a yellow or bloody discharge from the vagina, fever, loss of appetite, and lethargy. It is the result of hormonal stimulation of repeated cycling with no pregnancy. Treatment for breeding cats is a series of prostaglandin injections and antibiotics. Cats not used in a breeding program should be spayed.

The Breeding
The male cat mounts the female from the side or rear, grasping her by the back of the neck with his teeth. This biting behavior controls the female but may also stimulate a part of the female's brain that induces ovulation. He scrapes his hind legs along her sides in a peddling motion. The female raises her rear and moves her tail out of the way. Sexual intercourse is brief, often lasting only a few seconds. As the male withdraws, the female emits a loud scream and turns on the male, hissing and lashing out with a front paw. The experienced stud cat quickly leaps out of the way. Immediately following breeding, the female rolls vigorously and licks her vulva for several minutes. Breeding will be repeated unless the cats are separated. Breeding four times a day over a three-day period is the usual suggested schedule for a controlled mating. When a virgin female is first mated, an experienced stud cat is best. Similarly, when a male is just learning to breed, it is wise to put him with an experienced female. The normal gestation period is 64 to 69 days. The due date is calculated from the first breeding.

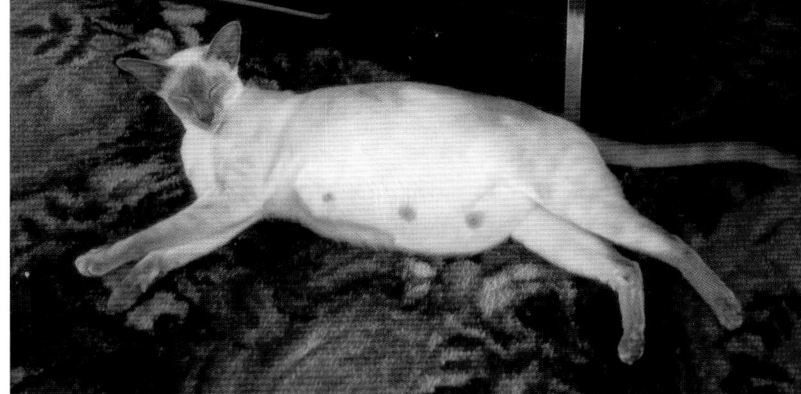

BELOW
A pregnant Oriental Shorthair Cat; the normal gestation period for a cat is between 64 and 69 days.

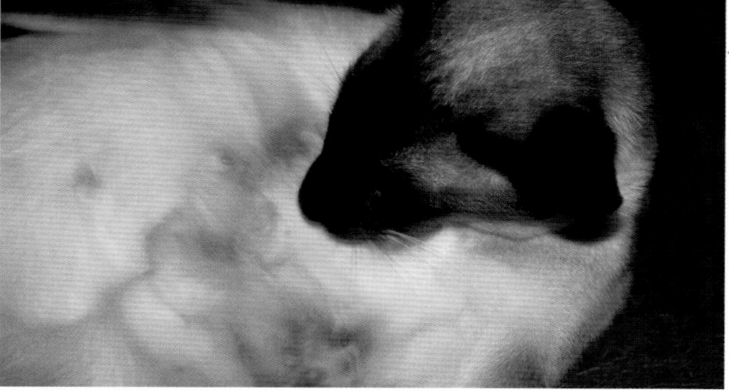

ABOVE
Around 21 days after breeding, the female cat's nipples will become enlarged and turn a rosy-pink color.

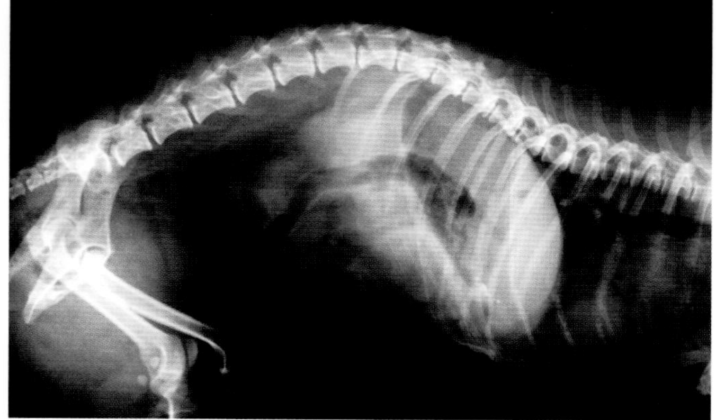

RIGHT
An X-ray scan can be taken of a pregnant cat after 38 days to determine the number of kittens.

Pregnancy and Birth

Signs of Pregnancy

The female will "pink up" around 21 days after being bred. The nipples increase in size and turn a rosy-pink color that deepens in shade as the pregnancy advances. Between 25–30 days the abdomen can be palpated to detect developing kittens. They each feel like a one-inch ball, and you should be able to count the number of kittens. By 35 days the individual kittens feel like one large mass. Ultrasound can detect kittens at 28 days and has the advantage of recording heartbeats to determine if the fetuses are viable. After 38 days an X-ray can be taken and the number of kittens counted, useful information to know during delivery. Most breeders attend the birth of the litter, taking on the role of the midwife.

Preparation for the Birth

The nutritional requirements of pregnant and nursing cats are double that of a non-breeding cat. Beginning in the last third of the pregnancy, feed the pregnant queen a high-quality diet formulated specifically for either breeding cats or kittens. Continue to feed the mother this food until the kittens are weaned.

As the female's stomach grows, she may be unable to groom under her tail and may need your help to stay clean. If she is a longhaired cat, around one week before her due date, clip the hair around her vulva and breeches. You may also clip her stomach hair. Place your finger over the nipple as you clip around it to prevent from nicking it. Clipping the stomach makes it easier for the newborns to find a nipple and prevents them from becoming entangled in the hair when nursing. Leave the hair long enough so that the kittens have traction when climbing over their mother's stomach and also enough to protect the mother cat from their nails.

LEFT
Pregnant cats have higher nutritional requirements and may need help with their grooming.

Fascinating Facts

The American writer Mark Twain, creator of Tom Sawyer and Huck Finn, is quoted as saying: "If a man could be crossed with a cat, it would improve the man but deteriorate the cat."

ABOVE

Newborn kittens should be placed on towels or blankets, with a heated pad on one side.

The Birthing Box

To avoid a cat from giving birth in an inappropriate place, she should be confined as she her due date approaches. Prepare a birthing box, and place it in a quiet, confined area. Layers of newspaper are adequate as bedding, although most breeders prefer towels or blankets. A lot of fluid accompanies the birth of each kitten, so have replacement bedding ready. Do not give the expectant queen clumping litter in case she delivers a kitten in the litter box. Clumping litter around a wet newborn's mouth can suffocate it. Use a wood pellet or newspaper.

Have another box ready to put the kittens in between births. Place a heating pad wrapped in a towel in one half of the box. Place the heating pad on only half the box, as this will allow the kitten to crawl away from the heat if it becomes too warm.

The Birthing Kit

Sterile gloves
An ear-bulb syringe
Iodine
5 in. (12 cm) hemostats
Scissors
Sterile gauze
Clean, dry, cotton rags or hand towels
A hairdryer
Sterile syringes

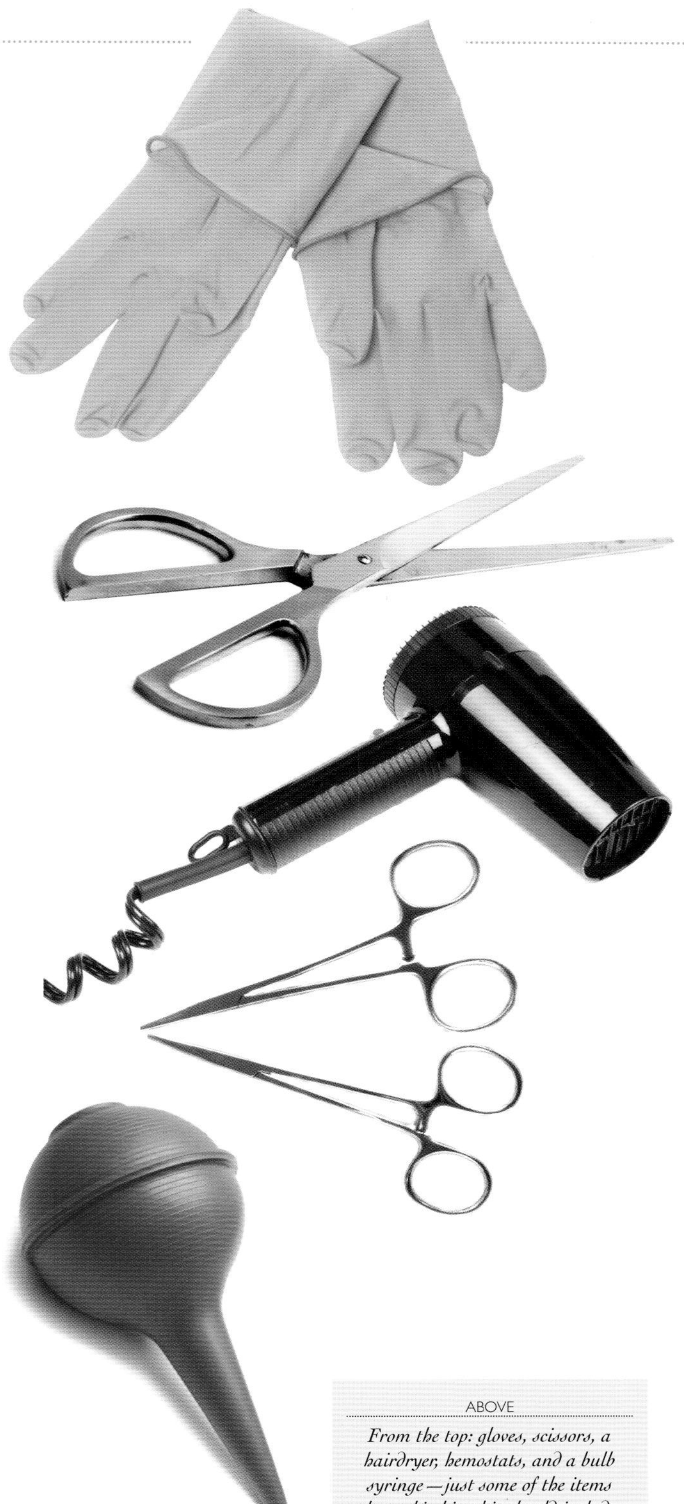

ABOVE

From the top: gloves, scissors, a hairdryer, hemostats, and a bulb syringe—just some of the items that a birthing kit should include.

Signs of Impending Birth

Twenty-four hours before delivery, the queen's rectal temperature should drop below 100° F (37.8° C). She may stop eating, be very affectionate, and meow for attention. Her nipples may have a milky discharge. She may dig repeatedly in the birthing and litter boxes, begin panting, and lick her genitals excessively.

ABOVE
A mother cat gives birth to the third kitten of her litter.

Delivery
Delivery of the kittens or "parturition" is generally divided into three stages:

The First Stage: Cervical Dilation The first stage of labor may last up to 36 hours, especially with first-time mothers. The mucous plug is lost. The cervix and vagina relax. The uterus begins invisible, intermittent contractions. The pelvic muscles loosen along with the area between the anus and the vulva (perineum). Movement of the fetuses may be seen and felt through the abdominal wall. The queen pants as a result of the oxygen debt incurred by the muscles moving the kittens into the birthing position.

Second Stage: Passage and Delivery of the Newborn The second stage of labor usually takes from five to 30 minutes per kitten. Uterine contractions increase in strength and frequency. As the kitten enters the pelvis, the outer layer of its amniotic sac may appear as a "bubble" out of the vulva. The sac usually breaks away from the mother cat. The pressure of the kitten's head as it passes into the pelvis causes the queen to "bear down" with strong, obvious contractions. In the womb the kitten lies on its back, but as it moves through the pelvis, it rotates along its length, extending its head, neck, and front legs forward. Once the head emerges from the vulva, the rest of the body is delivered by the next few contractions. Breech (tail first) births are not uncommon in cats.

BELOW
The mother cat will chew on the umbilical chords of the kittens as they are being born.

Third Stage: Passage of the Placenta and Associated Membranes

Labor enters stage three after the delivery of a kitten. The placenta is "delivered," often still attached to the kitten by the umbilical cord. If the kitten is delivered but the placenta remains inside of the queen, it may come out later. As each kitten is born, the mother chews the umbilical cord. She may eat the placenta, as it is rich in nutrients. However, if she eats too many it can cause diarrhea. If a second kitten is delivered directly behind the first, it may interfere with the passage of the first kitten's placenta. It is important to account for each placenta because a retained placenta can be a source of infection for the queen. The part of the uterus that the kitten came from contracts back into shape. After the delivery of the first kitten, the female will cycle through the second and third stages with the delivery of each kitten until her entire litter is delivered.

RIGHT
The afterbirth is rich in nutrients and is often eaten by the mother, as in this picture.

RIGHT
A female cat is left panting from the effort of giving birth to a litter of kittens.

ABOVE

Newborn kittens can inhale fluids and have trouble breathing, so it is important to check their airways.

Clearing the Airway

It is essential to clear the newborn's airway to keep the kitten from inhaling fluid into its lungs. If the kitten is born head first, break the membrane from around its mouth and nose and use an ear-bulb syringe to suck fluids from the mouth and throat. If the kitten makes gurgling sounds, fluid may be in the lungs. Wrapped in a cloth, hold the kitten on its back in both hands with the head of the kitten pointing toward your fingertips. Extend your arms above your head. Rapidly swing the kitten down in an arc several times and then aspirate the kitten's throat again with the bulb syringe. The centrifugal force should force fluid out of the mouth.

Stimulate Breathing

Once the airway is clear, stimulate the kitten by rubbing the body vigorously with a towel. If breathing does not begin right away, aspirate again, pull on the tongue, and stimulate by rubbing again. Keep up all stimulation efforts—rubbing, aspirating, and tongue pulling—until the kitten is breathing correctly. If a kitten seems slow to breathe, running hot water over its body may shock it into taking a breath.

Cutting the Cord

When the mother chews through the umbilical cord, there is a danger that she will bite it too short, so most breeders cut the umbilical themselves. Clamp the cord with the small hemostat around 1 in. (5 cm) from the belly and cut the cord with sterilized scissors. The tips of the hemostat crush the cord together. Wait a few minutes to remove the hemostat. Dip the entire umbilical stump in a 2 percent tincture of iodine to prevent infection.

Fascinating Facts

The largest litter recorded was produced by a Burmese\Siamese mother. There were 19 kittens. However, four of the kittens were stillborn.

Breech Birth

If a kitten is a breech birth (tail first), the head may become stuck in the birth canal although the body has been delivered. You can help complete the delivery by gripping the skin of the kitten's neck with gauze and pulling down with the next contraction. If a kitten is stuck, a gentle ¼ turn may help.

Birthing Problems

While most queens have uneventful deliveries, the most common problem is a kitten misaligned in the birth canal or a prolonged birth exhausting the mother. Either situation may require a Caesarean section. Some cats deliver part of the litter and then go out of labor for up to 24 hours before delivering the remaining kittens. Called interrupted labor, pauses in the delivery process are perfectly normal, however contact your veterinarian if:

- Labor is erratic or prolonged
- Your queen has strong, continuous contractions without producing a kitten
- Despite contractions, only one part or leg of a kitten is showing, indicating a kitten is stuck in the birth canal
- Abnormal bleeding occurs
- The queen is distressed and seems to be trying to tell you something
- Labor is not progressing as you expected
- Labor is finished but you have not accounted for all of the placentas

After Birth Care

Once all of the kittens are delivered and all of the placentas accounted for, an injection of Oxytocin is recommended to contract the uterus and limit bleeding. Some breeders give a preventative injection of long-acting penicillin to both mother and kittens to prevent a G-Strep infection. You may choose to have the mother and kittens examined by your veterinarian within 24 hours of birth.

Open the mouth of each kitten and check for cleft palette, a condition where the roof of the mouth is incomplete. If the mouth is cleft, take the kitten to a veterinarian, as this is a life-threatening condition.

BELOW

Once all of the kittens have been born, the mother cat cleans herself.

Determining the Sex

It can be difficult to tell the difference between a newborn male and female kitten. Lift the tail. The male's genital opening is a small circle. The female is more of a short slit. Using the circle opening of the anus as a reference point, the anus/genitals are sometimes described in a male as looking like a colon (:), while the female looks like an upside down exclamation mark. Usually there is a slightly greater space between the anus and genitals of a male kitten than in a female kitten. This "extra" space is the place where the testicles will eventually descend. It is easier if kittens of both sexes are available for comparison.

LEFT

It is easier to determine the sex of kittens once they are a little older; the left kitten is male and the right one female.

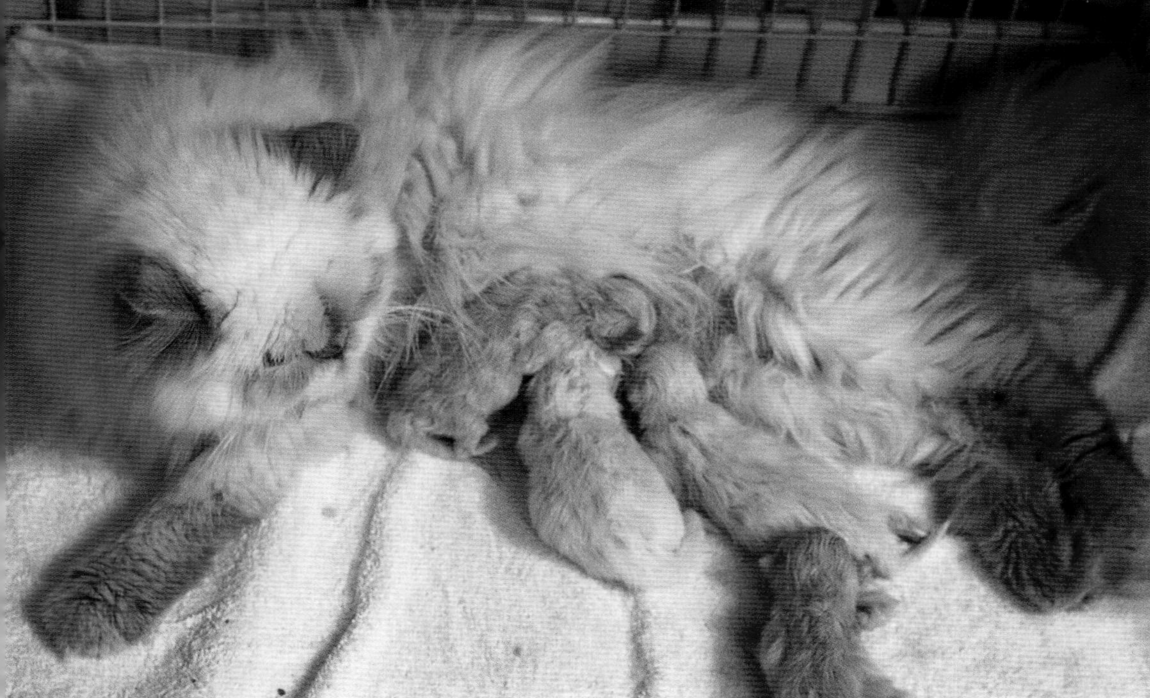

ABOVE
It is important for kittens to nurse from their mother within one day of being born.

to urinate and defecate by wiping the genitals with a warm, wet cloth.

Care of the Queen

Mother cats do not leave their kittens except to eat and eliminate. A new mother may neglect eating while caring for her newborns. If she starts losing weight, she will not be able to provide her kittens the nutrition they need to properly gain weight, so tempt her with tasty food close at hand. The lactating mother needs 125–150 calories per pound of her body weight. Female cats can come into heat as little as 48 hours after delivering a litter, and if bred will become pregnant.

There are several medical issues that require immediate veterinary care for the new mother. If the queen appears lethargic or feverish or inattentive to her kittens, she may be developing an infection from a retained placenta. Eclampsia is the result of low calcium levels in the blood resulting from the demands on her body due to milk production. Symptoms include restlessness, irritability, stiff gait, poor coordination, and/or vomiting. Eclampsia can be fatal if not treated in time. Mastitis is a condition that occurs when a lactating queen's mammary gland becomes inflamed, blocked, or infected. Symptoms include a swollen, hard, and hot teat. Mastitis can occur in cats having a false pregnancy.

Colostrum

It is important that the kittens nurse from their mother during the first 24 hours after birth to receive the first milk, called colostrum, which contains antibodies that protect the kittens against infections. The ability of the kitten to absorb these antibodies fades after 24–48 hours.

The Cold Kitten

Newborn kittens cannot maintain their own body temperature. The mother cat instinctively curls around her babies, snuggling them into her body to keep them warm. Keep the bedding dry and the room warm and draft-free.

Abandoned kittens lose body heat very quickly. Once the body temperature drops below 96° F (35.6° C), the kitten cannot digest the milk, and the undigested milk becomes a cold pack in the kitten's stomach. To warm up a cold kitten, immerse it in a pan of very warm water, keeping only its head above water. The water "engulfs" the kitten, conforming to its body shape and rapidly rewarming it. Once the kitten feels warm, towel dry it and keep warming it by drying it with a hairdryer on low.

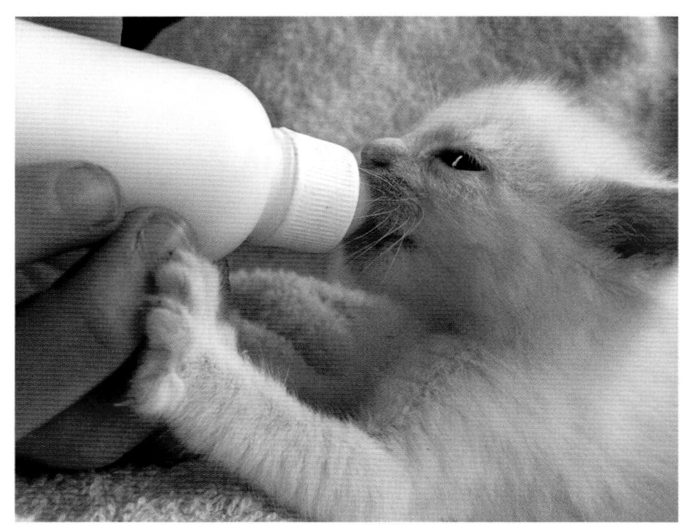

Hand Rearing Kittens

If the queen does not have enough milk or rejects the newborn, you may need to raise the kitten. You can hand feed a kitten using a kitten bottle and nipple or a syringe without the needle. Commercial kitten milk replacers are available, however goat's milk works well. Feed every 2–4 hours. If bubbles come out the nose when the kitten is sucking, it is either swallowing too quickly, is full, or has a cleft palette. Stimulate the kittens

Rearing Newborn Kittens

Week One

Mother cats instinctively know how to take care of their kittens. Do not disturb the queen and her kittens more than necessary but check on them frequently, especially if it is the queen's first litter. Once the newborn kittens are warm, they will begin nursing. Keep an eye on any newborn kitten that is not nursing, as it may need to be encouraged toward the mother's nipples. Newborns sleep continuously except to nurse. If a newborn cries, it is either cold, hungry, constipated, or its mother is laying on it.

BELOW

Kittens are born with their eyes closed, but they will begin opening after ten days.

Like a human baby, a kitten's growth can be monitored by measuring weight gain—it should gain ⅓ to 1 oz. (10 to 30 g) per day depending on the breed. Weigh kittens at least once a day. A kitten may lose weight on its first day, but it should gain after that. A kitten should double its birth weight in the first week.

The mother stimulates each kitten to urinate and defecate by licking the genitals and then consuming the feces and urine. Check the umbilicus for signs of inflammation or infection.

Week Two

Kittens are born with their ears and eyes closed. The kitten's eyes start opening around ten days. Watch for any bulging beneath the closed eyelids that indicate an accumulation of pus. If you see a bulge developing, you will need to open the eyelid to release the pressure. Take a warm, wet cloth and wipe any secretion from the eyelids. Gently pull the upper and lower lids apart. Once open, apply antibiotic drops for the ten days. Kittens are born with blue eyes. They are very near-sighted. Keep them away from bright lights. At this stage the umbilical cord dries up and drops off.

ABOVE

Even first-time mothers know instinctively how to take care of their kittens.

BELOW

A mother cat stimulates one of her kittens to urinate and defecate by licking its genitals.

Week Three

By now the ear canals are completely open. The kittens become more aware of their surroundings, attempting to stand and starting to explore and exhibit the start of play behavior. They urinate and defecate without stimulation. Socialization with people is especially important during this period, so handle the kittens frequently.

Week Four

Baby teeth start to appear, and some kittens may start to show an interest in their mother's food. Kittens begin to react to toys and similar stimuli. They progress from walking to running. They begin to dig or rake in any loose matter they encounter, behavior important to later use of the litter tray. The first signs of predatory behavior occur.

Week Five

The eyes begin to develop their true color. It is time to begin the weaning process. Introduce the babies to semi-solid food and drink. Provide a saucer of warm goat's milk, rice pabulum, or chicken baby food to begin the weaning process. Pay special attention to how well each kitten is adjusting to solid food, weight gain, and any incidents of vomiting or diarrhea as a result of the diet changes. Introduce the kittens to a miniature litter tray. Because some kittens try to eat the litter, do not use a clumping litter but provide a wood pellet or newspaper based litter that can be digested if eaten. Social play is an important component of kitten development, so play and exercise should be encouraged. Kittens can be safely wormed if necessary using a medication and dosage applicable for kittens of this age and weight. Never worm a sick kitten.

ABOVE

This four-week-old Siamese kitten takes some tentative steps — it will not be long before it is running.

BELOW

Social play is an essential part of a young kitten's development and should be encouraged.

ABOVE

From four weeks on kittens begin reacting to toys and display predatory behavior.

Weeks Six and Seven

The kittens are more confident on their feet. They will need a larger play area. Introduce them to a scratching post. By the end of the seventh week most kittens will be eating solid food and no longer relying on the mother for nourishment. The mother cat will spend less and less time with her kittens. Her milk will dry up.

Week Eight

At eight weeks the kittens receive their first vaccination. Typically they will be vaccinated against Rhinotracheitis virus (FVR), calicivirus (FCV), and Panleukopenia (Feline Infectious Enteritis). Never vaccinate a sick kitten. This is a good age to give a kitten its first bath, blow dry, and nail clipping.

Weeks Nine to Eleven

This is a very social time for all kittens. Expose them to as many new experiences as possible. Have new people cuddle the kittens so they become familiar with different people's scent and handling. Introduce the kitten to a carrier, a car ride, loud noises, and a grooming routine.

Week Twelve

At 12 weeks the kittens receive their second vaccination, a booster against Rhinotracheitis virus (FVR), calicivirus (FCV), and Panleukopenia (Feline Infectious Enteritis). Twelve weeks is the typical age at which a kitten is ready to leave its littermates behind and to go to its new home and family.

Fascinating Facts

A tabby named Dusty gave birth to 420 documented kittens in her lifetime.

BELOW

As the kitten grows it is important it becomes accustomed to being handled and meeting new people.

CAT SHOWS

"It would be well to hold cat shows, so that different breeds, colors, markings, etc. might be more carefully attended to, and the domestic cat sitting in front of the fire would possess a beauty and attractiveness unimagined," said Harrison Weir, the "Father of the Cat Fancy," in 1871. Cat shows provide breeders with the opportunity to showcase their cats. Exhibitors have the opportunity to earn titles on their cats, gain prestige and satisfaction, and enjoy the anticipation, drama, and excitement of a social and competitive occasion in their pursuit of feline perfection.

History and Development

Cat Registries

A cat registry is responsible for registering cats for exhibition and breeding purposes. It recognizes breeds, maintains a database of pedigrees, registers cattery names, and develops breed descriptions and written standards. The registry recognizes individual cat clubs, approves judges, and licenses cat shows. Registration and show procedures vary widely in different registries, and titles earned in one registry are not typically recognized by another. A cat may be registered in more than one registry.

The First Cat Show

In 1598 enthusiastic cat owners gathered in Winchester, England, and held a "show" to compare their cats. The winner was awarded Best of Mouser. Of course this exhibition at a local fair was nothing like our modern cat shows.

The first contemporary cat show was not recorded until almost 300 years later at the Crystal Palace in London, England, on July 13, 1871. The organizer of this milestone was Harrison Weir, a well-known writer, artist, and cat lover. Considered the father of cat lovers, it was Weir who first conceived of the idea and format of the benched cat show. Inspired, he quickly arranged classes, entry fees, prizes, and a judging schedule . . . and the modern cat show was born. Breeds exhibited included Persians, Angoras (called "longhairs"), Manx, Abyssinian, and Royal Cats of Siam (ancestors to Siamese and Havana Browns). Other classes included "gelded" cats, domestic cats crossed with wildcats, fat cats, and "Cats Owned by Working Men."

Fascinating Facts

One hundred and sixty felines attended the 1871 show at the Crystal Palace.

ABOVE

Persian cats have featured in cat shows since the early forms of such events.

BELOW

An illustration from Pets of the Family *by Harrison Weir, the founder of the modern cat show.*

BELOW

An engraving showing a variety of the feline entrants in the 1887 Crystal Palace Cat Show.

The Cat Fancy in Great Britain

Four years after the first cat show in England, a cat show in Scotland attracted 560 entries. Two years later, in 1887, the first cat registry, the National Cat Club, was created to register cats, maintain studbooks, and organize cat shows. As president, Weir developed the concept of the standard.

The Scottish Cat Club formed in 1894. The first official studbook was published in 1895. In 1898 another English registry, The Cat Club, was founded by Lady Beresford, disbanding in 1902 following five years of arguing with the National Cat Club. On March 8, 1910, 19 delegates representing ten cat clubs met in Westminster, London, and formed one registry, the Governing Council of the Cat Fancy, GCCF, which is now the main registry in the United Kingdom, the feline equivalent of the Kennel Club.

On February 20, 1983 an alternative association, the Cat Association of Britain (CA), was formed and run more along the lines of U.S. shows. In 2003 Felis Britannicus was created; accepting cats registered in CA and became the United Kingdom's affiliate with Fédération Internationale Féline (FIFe). By 2004 The International Cat Association (TICA), the second largest cat registry in the U.S., expanded to the United Kingdom, bringing with it an American-style judging format.

ABOVE

An 1870s illustration of a prize-winning Angora cat, owned by a Miss A. Armitage.

LEFT

Cat owners groom their blue Persians before a show in Trinity Hall in London, England, in 1937.

The First Cat Shows in America

Although informal shows had been held in New York City, Boston, and Philadelphia, the U.S.'s first official cat show was held in Madison Square Garden, in New York City on May 8, 1895. Organized by James T. Hyde, it attracted 176 entries, and the Best Cat was a brown tabby Maine Coon named "Cosie."

The following year exhibitors joined together at the show's end to form the American Cat Club, but it only lasted one year. Other groups of cat lovers gathered together to form clubs, including one in Chicago named the Beresford Club after the great English cat admirer. The Beresford Club created the first register and studbook in America in 1899. Its duties and registry were gradually assumed by the American Cat Association (ACA), incorporated on May 11, 1904, which remains the oldest cat registry and association in America today, although active mainly in the south.

More U.S. Cat Registries

Cat lovers are a feisty group, and dissention is not uncommon. Difference of opinion has led to the formation of several new cat registries in the U.S. over the years, as small groups split away from more established registries. In 1906 a group divided from ACA to form the Cat Fanciers' Association (CFA). By 1929 CFA was the largest registry in the U.S. and has maintained that position. CFA is a club-based organization. Cat clubs send delegates to semi-annual or annual meetings to vote on proposals, amendments, and other changes at the direction of the club members. A board of directors is elected annually by the clubs.

ABOVE

These two cream Persians, shown in the U.S., featured in Francis Simpson's The Book of the Cat *from 1903.*

BELOW

Cats await judgement at the CFA-Iams Cat Championships, held in Madison Square Gardens in 2006.

BELOW

Champion blue shorthair Brother Bump also appeared in Francis Simpson's The Book of the Cat.

In 1919 a disagreement within CFA caused several clubs to depart and form the United Cat Fanciers' Association, a name that was quickly changed to the Cat Fanciers' Federation (CFF), still active today, mainly in New England and the Midwest.

By 1955 The American Cat Fanciers Association (ACFA) was created when another group left CFA to form a registry where individuals rather than clubs voted to determine the policies of the association. Individuals cast votes by mail to elect officers or to implement changes in rules. Clubs were formed to organize shows or to promote animal welfare activities but do not have voting privileges.

In 1979 yet another group of fanciers split from ACFA to form The International Cat Association (TICA). The youngest American cat registry, TICA quickly grew to become second in size and is the fastest growing registry in the U.S. It is a phenotypic registry, meaning a cat is shown based on what it looks like, not what it may be genetically. Both TICA and CFA have membership outside of North America.

RIGHT

This 1900 lithograph indicates that cat shows were popular in France long before FIFe was established.

ABOVE

Le Chat, *by Theophile-Alexandre Steinien; cats have been popular in Europe since long before cat registries and organizations such as FIFe were set up.*

There are several more small registries in North America, including The Canadian Cat Association/Association Feline Canadienne (CCA /AFC), The United Feline Organization (UFO), and The American Association of Cat Enthusiasts (AACE).

FIFe

Established in 1949, the Fédération Internationale Féline (FIFe) is a worldwide federation of member cat registries. FIFe is an umbrella organization that allows individual cat registries of the member countries to follow the same rules regarding breed standards, cattery names, shows, and judges. In 2007 FIFe had 41 member registries from 39 countries, mainly in Europe.

BELOW
The short-legged Munchkin breed is banned by FIFe but is embraced by The Dwarf Cat Association.

Australia
The earliest cat show in Australia for which a catalogue exists is the 1912 Australia Cat Club show. In 1928 The Governing Council of the Cat Fancy Australia and Victoria became the third cat registry in the world, continuing to this day. As in other countries, different regions of Australia developed their own cat registries. There are separate cat associations in every state of Australia, equaling more than one dozen. Most are associated with two organizations—The Coordinating Cat Council of Australia (CCCA) or the Australian Cat Federation (ACF).

The Rest of the World
The major cat associations based in Europe and North America including FIFe, CFA, and TICA are international organizations with affiliate clubs around the world.

The World Cat Congress
In June 1994, Associazione Felina Italiana, an Italian cat club, organized the World Congress of Feline Associations (WCC) in Venice to promote better understanding and cooperation among the world's various cat associations regarding matters of mutual interest, including feline legislation and welfare. Their 1999 charter defined WCC's objectives, membership requirements, structure of its meetings, and funding. A full constitution followed in 2003. The WCC operates an "open door" policy by which cats registered with one registry can be shown under the rules of another registry.

Specialty Registries
Smaller independent cat registries exist that specialize in cat breeds ineligible for registration with some major registries. For example, The Dwarf Cat Association recognizes breeds derived from the short-legged Munchkin, which are banned by FIFe. The Rare and Exotic Feline Registry specializes in hybrid cat species developed by crossing domestic cats with wildcat species.

RIGHT
The Safari cat is a rare hybrid of Geoffroy's cat and a domestic breed—it is recognized by the Rare and Exotic Feline Registry.

Showing Your Cat

Showing your cat is an exciting and enjoyable hobby. Newbie is the affectionate term for a newcomer to the cat fancy. If you are considering showing your cat for the first time, the best way to begin is by attending a cat show without your cat so that you can gain an idea of what to expect. Find exhibitors of your breed and introduce yourself. When not busy going to the judging ring or grooming a cat, most exhibitors enjoy chatting with a newcomer.

Before you enter a cat show, confirm that your cat is of show quality. While it doesn't have to be a showstopper, you want to avoid the embarrassment of taking a pet-quality cat with a disqualifying fault to the show. Ideally, the breeder of your cat should be able to tell you if it is of show quality. If in doubt, take a few photographs of your cat to a show and ask for an opinion.

The Breed Standard

Each cat registry approves a written standard for each breed it recognizes. The breed standard is a description of the perfect specimen of that breed. A point system assigns values that reflect the relative importance of the various parts or characteristics of the breed. A judge uses the breed standard as a guide when evaluating cats. The standard of an individual breed is generally similar in different registries. There are exceptions, of course. For example, in Great Britain's GCCF, the nose leather of the Persian must not be higher than the bottom of the eye, while in American-based registries a higher nose leather is preferred.

Fascinating Facts

While there are more than 60 breeds of pedigreed cats, no one registry in the world recognizes every breed of cat. CFA, the largest cat registry, only recognizes 39 breeds for championship status (2007).

BELOW
Visiting cat shows prior to entering a competition is a great way to get advice from the experts.

ABOVE
This Oriental Shorhair is the proud owner of the Best in Show title.

Kittens, Championship, Premiership

In most cat registries, the cats are divided for show purposes into three main categories. "Kittens" are defined as cats from four months up to eight months of age. A kitten does not earn a title from the classes. "Championship" is for adult cats, whole males and females eight months of age or older. "Premiership" is for spayed females and neutered males eight months or older, and like the cats in Championship, they can earn titles in the classes. Kittens, Championship, and Premiership cats may be campaigned to win points toward earning international, national, regional, or breed titles.

Non-Pedigreed or Household Pets

One of the most admirable aspects of the cat fancy is how it embraces the virtues of the non-pedigreed cat. Many cat shows have classes for Non-Pedigreed cats or Household Pets (HHP). There is no written standard for these mixed-breed felines. Instead they are judged on their uniqueness, condition, vitality, grooming, overall health, and temperament. In some registries such as TICA, Household Pets receive a registration number, their wins are recorded, and they earn titles and awards. Generally all that is required to register a HHP is the cat's name, birth date, color, sex, and whether longhaired or shorthaired.

Before entering your family pet in a cat show, check with the show organization, as there are some differences in acceptability for show. You do not want to discover on the day that your cat is not able to be shown.

Different Registries—Different Styles

The style and format of a cat show can vary widely between registries. GCCF shows are conducted very differently from cat shows in America. The organization of a cat show in GCCF is conducted to try to insure that the judging is as objective as possible, with no outside influences. The cats are benched in pens in the show hall, grouped by breed in catalog order, longhairs in pen number 1, proceeding through the shorthairs, and ending with the non-pedigreed cats. Each cat's cage or pen contains only a white blanket, white water bowl, white litter tray, and the cat, so there are no identifying markings to suggest to the judge who the cat or owner might be. Once the exhibitors settle their cats into their pens, they are asked to leave the show hall so that the main judging is conducted in private. The white-coated judge and steward push a cart from pen to pen, removing each cat one at a time to be judged, disinfecting between the handling of each exhibit. The results are written into a book, and slips from the books appear on the result board later in the day for owners to view. The show committee places award ribbons on the pen.

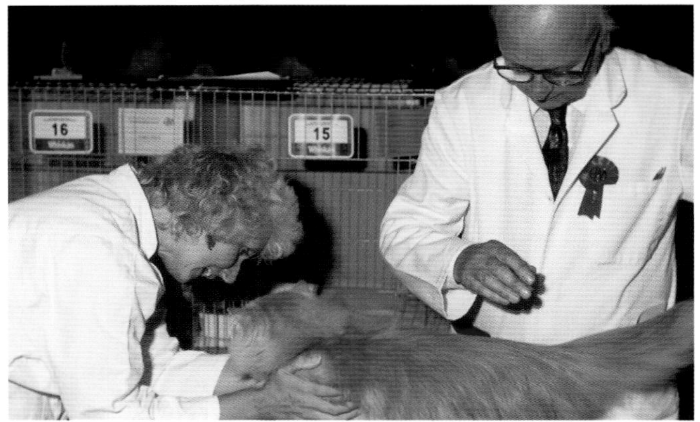

LEFT
Two judges at a cat show inspect one of the entrants in order to award it points.

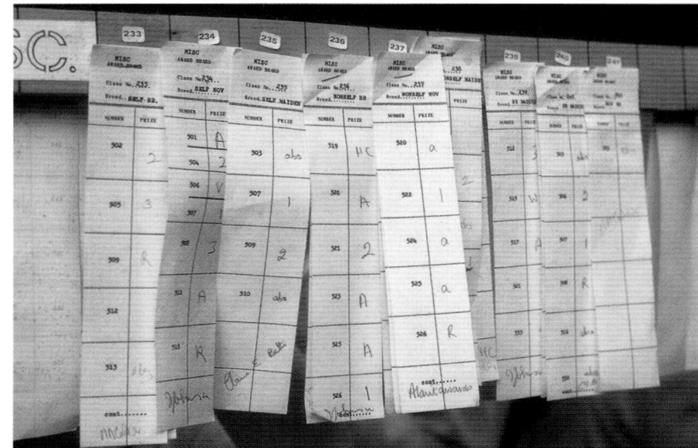

LEFT
The judges' results are written in a book and placed on a board at the end of the day for the owners to inspect.

LEFT
A busy cat show hall; the cats are arranged into sections according to their breed.

The GCCF Supreme Cat Show This show debuted in 1976 and has developed into a large and prestigious show held at the National Exhibition Center in Birmingham, England, every November. All cats qualify by winning open classes at other shows. A new method of judging was started—Ring Judging—where all cats are taken from their brilliantly decorated pens to the judging rings, where the judges sit facing the public to judge the cats and often give a commentary as their judge. This show produces Britain's top prize winners, the Supreme title holders.

USA In contrast to the U.K. (in general), in the United States each exhibitor brings colorful curtains to individually decorate their cat's benching cage. The benching assignments are not by breed but are determined by the show committee. Exhibitors can request who they would like to be benched next to, so friends are often grouped together. Judging is not conducted at the benching cage. Instead each judge has a "ring," with around 12 empty cages, a judging table, and chairs for an audience. During the show cats are called to the ring by their assigned number as needed. Exhibitors bring their cats from the benching area and place them in their judging cage, with their number on top. There are chairs arranged in front of each judging area where the exhibitors can sit and watch the cats be judged. Judges frequently make comments about the cats as they remove them one at a time from the judging cage and place them on the judging table.

LEFT

The GCCF Supreme Cat Show was first held in 1976 and takes place in Birmingham, England.

Once the judge is finished handling the cat, the cat is placed back into its judging cage. Ribbons and awards are hung on the cages as each class is completed. The owner of the cat then removes their cat from the judging cage and returns to their benching area until the next ring of judging. This style of show is more entertaining than the GCCF show, although the risk of politics influencing judging—the judge being aware of who owns the cat—is a factor.

ABOVE

A judge examines a Siamese kitten, looking for a long, muscular body without a noticeable taper.

LEFT

After judging, the cat is placed back into its pen and ribbons are awarded, while the cat waits for its owner.

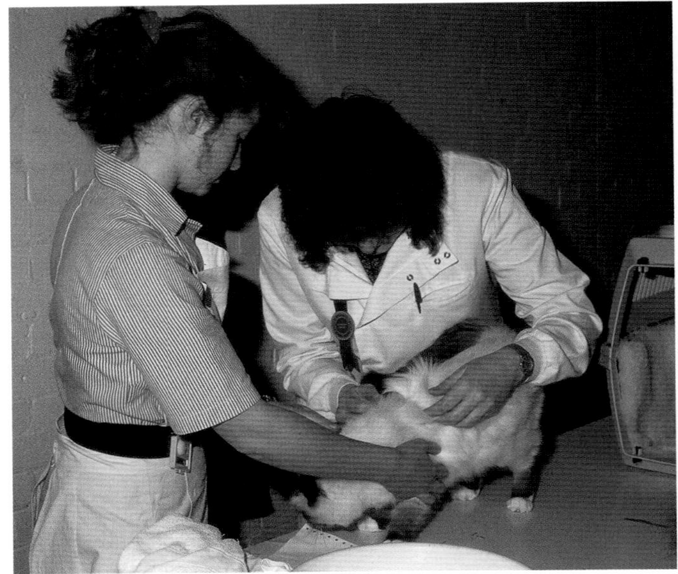

Other Countries and Organizations In other countries, a third style of cat show exists that is a hybrid of the GCCF and American style formats. Judges are lined up behind a row of tables facing the audience and benching area. A steward takes the cat from the owner and presents it to the judges one by one. The judge examines the cat and writes an evaluation on a preprinted form. Once all the judges have seen the cat, the steward returns it to the owner. After all the judging is completed, the judges nominate and vote on each group of cats, choosing the best.

ABOVE
A cat that is to be shown has to undergo a veterinary inspection before the show begins.

Procedures, Classes, and Awards in GCCF
Shows in GCCF are usually one day events, starting at 10:00 a.m., by which time the cat must have passed a veterinary inspection and be placed in its assigned pen. The cat may be entered in several classes. The open class is the only one that counts toward earning titles. The entry fee usually includes the Open Class and three Miscellaneous Classes.

Show catalogs are available after you leave the show hall and the open judging begins. The catalogs include information about the cats, their breeds and colors, and include breeder advertisements. Around 12:30 p.m. exhibitors are allowed back into the show hall. While open class judging (or grand or imperial class judging) is already complete, judging of the side classes continues throughout the afternoon. Challenge certificates are awarded for the open class winner (one for the best male and one for the best female), plus Best of Breed. The judge can withhold an award for lack of merit. All adult cats can enter the open class, regardless of title. When you return you may put one white toy and a white food bowl with food in the pen. The show usually finishes around 5:00 p.m.

ABOVE AND BELOW
Judges give a thorough examination of entrants on a table next to the cat's pen.

Once the cat has been awarded three challenge certificates by three different judges at three different shows, the cat is a champion and can start competing in the grand champion class. The grand champion class is for cats that have already championed. Three grand challenge certificates are needed from three different judges at three different shows to become a grand champion. Once the cat has become a grand champion, it can enter the imperial grand champion class. Five certificates from five different judges at five different shows are needed to become an imperial grand champion. This is the highest title, other than the U.K. grand awarded at the supreme show. The same system applies to neuters in the premier classes. You will not be allowed to remove your cat before the show closes or you risk forfeiting any prizes won.

Procedures, Classes, and Awards in CFA and TICA

American-style cat shows are one, two, or three day shows with four to six judgings each day. Each judge judges every cat in a separate show within a show format. Classes are divided by breed, color, and sex. Each judge awards a top 10 or 15 Best Kittens/Cats, depending on the total number of cats entered. There is no official Best in Show, although points earned from all rings are added up for the show, and the cat earning the most points is the highest scoring cat and is considered Best In Show unofficially.

BELOW

Cats' pens in the American-style cat shows allow much more decoration and personality than in other shows.

Fascinating Facts

Usually your cat must be individually registered before entering a show. In the U.S. some associations allow cats to be shown without a registration number for at least their first show, although their awards will not be officially recorded.

LEFT

Cali, a shorthaired Manx, wins the Best In Show award at the 2006 CFA-Iams Cat Championships.

Even within the U.S.-style format, there are distinct differences between registries. For instance, in CFA the judge's book includes the cats' titles, and the cats' numbers called to a final are announced over a loudspeaker system. In TICA the judges do not know the titles of the cats, and the numbers of the cats needed for a final are posted on a board. Both procedures are intended to remove factors that might influence a judge's decision.

In CFA adult cats in Championship classes compete to earn points toward the title of Champion (CH) and Grand Champion (GC). The cats in Premiership earn corresponding titles, Premier (PR) and Grand Premier (PR). In TICA the cats work toward titles progressive from Champion (CH), Grand Champion (GC), Double Grand Champion (DGC), Triple Grand Champion (TGC), Quadruple Grand Champion (QGC), and Supreme.

Finding a Cat Show

Each registry has a website with a show schedule listing upcoming shows and provides information to help the newcomer know how to enter their first cat show. GCCF requires that a cat is entered two months or more before the date of the show. In the U.S. the show is open for entries up to one week before the show date.

Preparing for the Show
It is important that your cat enjoys the showing. Begin by ensuring your cat is accustomed to traveling and being in a cage.

Naturally your cat must be healthy. No fleas, ticks, ringworm, or other parasites. Cats must not have been exposed to infectious disease for at least 21 days before the show. Shows in some countries, including Great Britain, require that cats pass a veterinary inspection as they enter the show hall. The U.S. does not require this.

A cat show is a beauty contest. Getting your cat in condition to be shown begins long before the day of competition. Longhaired breeds such as Persians need weekly bathing and daily combing to avoid matting and to promote a healthy coat. Coat conditioners and styling sprays are used to make their hair silky and shiny. Shorthaired breeds require less grooming.

Each breed will have its own grooming tips and tricks when preparing for a show. If possible, contact a breeder/exhibitor of your breed ahead of time to get some pointers on how your breed is usually groomed for a show.

Your Show Kit Except at a closed ring show such as GCCF, cage curtains are an essential item to line the inside of your cat's benching cage in American-style judging. They separate the cat from its neighbors in the other cages. The curtains fit the size of the cage. They can be bought premade in many different colors and styles, or you can sew your own. The material should be sturdy and easy to clean. In addition to cage curtains, remember to bring all necessary grooming supplies,

RIGHT

Some of the items that should be included in a show kit are a litter tray, water, bowls, and scissors.

food, water, bowls, bed, nail trimmers, tissue, litter tray, litter, scoop, and a bag for garbage. Bring a book, snacks for yourself, and a pen to write in your catalog.

Home from the Show
Whenever large numbers of cats congregate, there is an increased possibility to contract an infectious disease, fleas, mites, or ringworm. Some exhibitors keep their show cats separated from their breeding cats as a precaution. Upon returning from a show, it is a smart precaution to wash and disinfect everything you took to the show. Don't be surprised if your cat is tired following the show. Even though a cat spends most of its time in the benching cage asleep, its normal routine has been disturbed, and that can be exhausting.

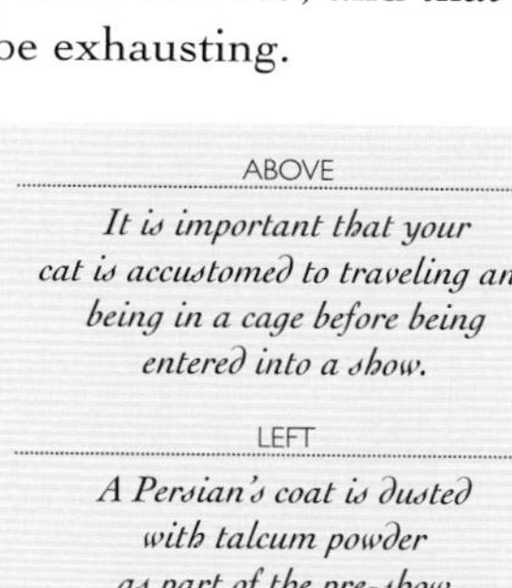

ABOVE

It is important that your cat is accustomed to traveling and being in a cage before being entered into a show.

LEFT

A Persian's coat is dusted with talcum powder as part of the pre-show grooming process.

The Breeds

EVOLUTION

When dinosaurs became extinct, all creatures weighing more than 50 pounds also disappeared. The surviving mammals, warm-blooded animals that suckled their young, were the small, tree-dwelling, insect-eaters who now found themselves with an abundance of food and very few predators. Over time some of these early mammals evolved into herbivores (plant-eaters), while others evolved into carnivores (meat-eaters). These first carnivorous mammals were called the creodonts. The creodonts were the ancestors of all modern carnivores—including domestic cats.

Eocene Era

Around 54 million years ago, a genus of forest dwelling mammals—the miacids—developed. These animals evolved into subgroups that were the predecessors of modern species of cats, bears, beavers, racoons, weasels, hyenas, and dogs.

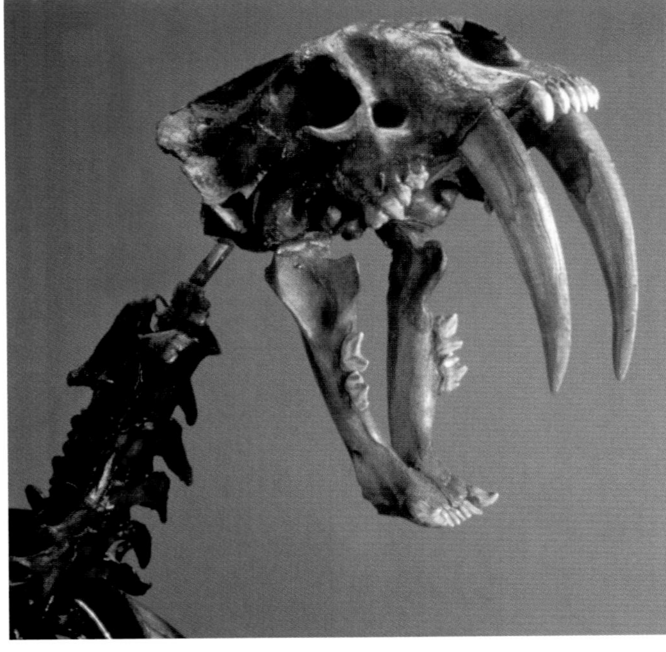

RIGHT

Felids, such as this saber-toothed cat, evolved from the carnivorous mammals of the subfamily feloidea.

All carnivorous mammals came from the miacids. These ancestors of present-day felines were long-bodied, short-legged, pea-brained, and looked more like a modern weasel than a cat. A common theory is that miacids survived over other evolving carnivorous mammals because of teeth that were specially developed to eat meat.

From the mid-Eocene to the early Oligocene (48–38 million years ago), carnivorous mammals evolved and diversified rapidly. Two distinct subfamilies developed: the *feloidea*, from which evolved the felids (cats), and the *canoidea* (all other carnivorous families).

Dinictis

Dinictis, a lynx-sized animal with a longer body, long legs and tail, and catlike teeth for stabbing prey, developed from the miacids. An important ancestor in the evolutionary line of the modern cat, Dinictis' brain was smaller than present-day cats', but its teeth were larger; and that was more important in ensuring its survival. Dinictis developed in Asia and from there spread to other continents. The single land mass (Pangea) from which the earth started was ripping apart, a process we now call the continental drift. As this was happening around 135 million years ago, the animals drifted as well. This is why no indigenous cats can be found in Australia or Antarctica, and cats only arrived in South America in the last two million years. South America had no mammals until the isthmus of Panama formed, joining the Southern and Northern Hemispheres, and cats migrated from North America.

RIGHT

The smilodon, also known as machaerodos, had well-developed teeth that extended beyond the jaw.

Miacids > > Dinictus > > > Saber-toothed cats > > Smilodons > > extinct
> Feloidea > > Wild Cats and Domestic Cat > > present day

Fascinating Facts

Hunting is not instinctive for cats. Kittens born to non-hunting mothers may never learn to hunt.

TOP

Domestic cats are part of the group known as the Small or Non-roaring Cats, or Felis.

ABOVE

Lions are one of the cats belonging to the genus Panthera, *the Big or Roaring Cats.*

Oligocene Era

Two separate lines developed from Dinictis: the true saber-toothed cats, in which the canine teeth become even larger, and the *Feloidea*, in which the canines become smaller. The early saber-toothed cats, which diverged in the Oligocene era (34–23 million years ago), could not use their fangs unless the mouth was wide open. The successors of these cats, the Smilodons, had more advanced teeth that extended beyond the jaw and could be used without gaping the mouth. However, all saber-toothed cats used their teeth as stabbing instruments, rather than biting, and this likely lead to their extinction as the more effective Feloidae grew in numbers.

Saber-toothed cats and their decedents are extinct today, although they were still around 3,000 years ago. Much of the evidence suggested that these cats came from the Rancho La Brea Tar Pits in Los Angeles. Here tar seeps out of the ground and has been trapping animals for thousands of years. Amongst the finds are the remains of around 2,000 individual saber-tooth cats.

The Cat Family

The felids evolved to increase their brain instead of teeth size. They became cunning, swift hunters who could kill their prey with a bite to the neck. Fossils dating back 12 million years are very similar to the bones of modern cats. Around three million years ago, the three existing cat genera were established: the Big or Roaring Cats (*Panthera*), the Small or Non-roaring Cats (*Felis*), and the Cheetah (*Acinonyx*). The cheetah is the lone member of the family and warrants a genus of its own—one difference is that its claws are not fully retractable.

Felis and *Panthera* are divided, not because of size but because of the difference in construction of the vocal equipment. The hyoid bone, found at the base of the tongue, is partially made out of cartilage in the Big Cats, which gives mobility to the vocal apparatus and allows it to produce roaring sounds.

BELOW

The cheetah (Acinonyx) *differs from the other cats in a number of ways and has its own genus.*

LEFT
Our domestic cats, including breeds such as the Siamese, have probably descended from the African wildcat.

Felis Silvestris

It is believed that our domestic cats most likely descended from *Felis silvestris*, the wildcat. This species has the same structure and number of chromosomes as today's cats. *Felis silvestris libyca*, the African wildcat, is tan-colored and tabby striped, with a flecked coat like the Abyssinian. It breeds easily with domestics and as a result is on the brink of distinction as a pure species. This genus is easily domesticated and often lives near humans.

The European wildcat (*Felis silvestris silvestris*) and the jungle cat (*Felis chaus*) probably played a role in the development of the domestic cat. *Felis silvestris* has well-defined, mackerel tabby markings and could have brought this pattern to the species, a pattern that all domestic cats share. A certain amount of crossbreeding with the stocky, European wildcat may have influenced the more sturdy breeds, such as the Persian and British Shorthairs, while slimmer, foreign, and Oriental breeds show the influence of the African wildcat. It is certainly possible that other types of wildcats contributed to the development of the domestic. Many species of wildcats inhabited southwest Asia, and they may have produced their own domestic cats.

Domestication

The earliest records of cats living within human colonies date back to around 7500 B.C. It started when humans began storing larger amounts of grain and other foodstuffs that were at the mercy of vermin. Felines were then seen as valuable rodent catchers, and cat and man became allies. But it is a relationship that cats have always accepted with reservations.

Domestication is a process that is not fully understood. Certainly it has a genetic basis, since the docile behavior and the dependency of domestic animals has developed after years of selective breeding. Cat domestication probably happened gradually, with the cats that were living around humans inter-breeding and passing on their "docile" genes. Wilder cats would move on to less inhabited areas.

BELOW
The familiar markings of the mackerel tabby were probably passed down from the African wildcat.

Fascinating Facts

Most deaf cats do not meow.

BELOW

Whether humans domesticated cats or vice versa, the two species benefit from each other's company.

We know that by 1500 B.C., when cats were immortalized in Egyptian artifacts, they were truly a part of human culture. However, in the 9,500 years of association with humans, the cat has never fully committed itself to domestication. Most breeds can return to a wild lifestyle

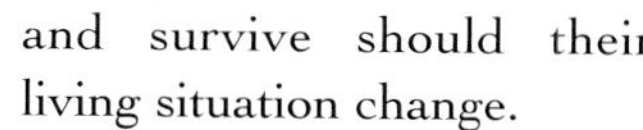

and survive should their living situation change.

Some experts believe that it is the cat that domesticated man instead of the other way around. At times it certainly seems that way because cats have such a huge influence on us. There are people who believe that when humans evolved from hunter-gatherers to an agricultural existence, humans provided a reliable food source in the vermin they attracted by storing grain. Humans soon learned that cats were invaluable in controlling the rodents that destroyed their crops. And somewhere along the way, they learned that cats and humans found comfort in each other.

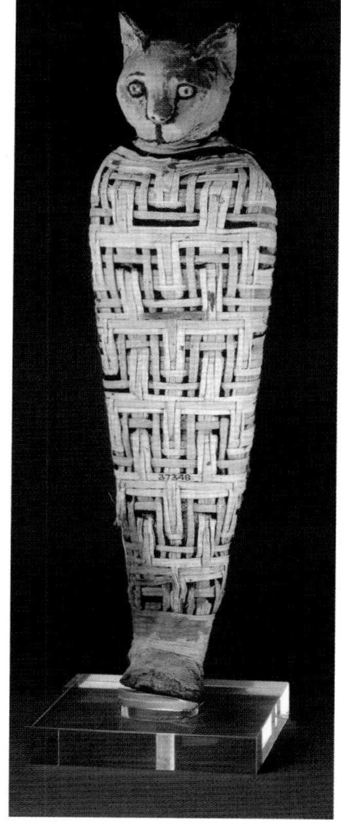

ABOVE

The mummified remains of cats from ancient Egypt show how cats had become a part of human culture.

The Future

Today's cats, both big and small, have large canine teeth in the upper jaw and a pair of near-matching "daggers" in the lower jaw. It is unclear how many species of modern cats exist, so where will cat evolution go from here? Cats are the world's most efficient predators, one reason why they have survived for so many years on so many continents. There is every reason to believe that they will meet future challenges.

FELINE GENETICS

Forty million years ago, cats came into existence. They have seen thousands of animals thrive and disappear. Their success is largely due to the ability to genetically adapt to the changing environment. Traits are passed from one generation to another by a system of genetic inheritance. The first person to develop an understanding of how traits are inherited was Gregor Mendel (1822–84). He did his experiments on pea plants, not felines, but his basic conclusions were grounded, and his laws of inheritance hold true today.

Definition

Genetics is defined as the part of biology dealing with heredity. It is responsible for the transmission of characteristics, via genes, through the generations, and it applies to all living things, including felines. The dominant and recessive genes controlling these traits cause the physical differences between cats.

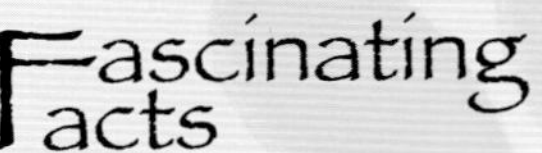

In relation to body size, cat's eyes are bigger than most mammals.

RIGHT

Gregor Mendel, the Austrian botanist who developed ideas about genetic inheritance.

Dominant and Recessive Genes
DNA has two copies of each gene within a cell. Sometimes both copies are exactly the same; however, when they are not and one gene is capable of suppressing the other, that gene is called a Dominant gene. The gene that is suppressed is called a Recessive gene. In order for a recessive gene to be "seen" it must be present in both copies of the DNA (all recessive, no dominant gene present).

One half of the genes come from the mother, one half from the father, each providing a different mixture that accounts for appearance, health, and temperament. Kittens that receive identical genes from both parents (donated by AA or aa symbols) are pure and are referred to as homozygotes. If one parent is dominant and the other recessive, mixed genotype (Aa) results, and they are heterozygotes. Two recessive genes must be present before a characteristic can express itself. A recessive gene can be carried for several generations without being declared.

LEFT

Coat color is determined by a cat's genes; coats of dominant genes absorb more light and appear to be darker.

Chromosomes
The domestic cat carries 38 chromosomes—19 from the mother and 19 from the father. When the ovum is fertilized, it carries 19 pairs of chromosomes, and each pair carries genes. Eighteen of these pairs are identical, but one pair, the sex chromosome, is different. It is this pair that decides the sex of the kitten.

Females carry two X chromosomes; males carry X and Y. Kittens inherit one from each parent: X from the mother and either X or Y from the father. Two X chromosomes and the kitten is female; XY and the kitten is male.

Color

Genes are also responsible for color. Some genes interact and alter each other's expression, resulting in strong influences on color and appearance and conformation. They cause the variations of pattern and shade in the cat's fur. Masking genes (epistatic) prevent the expression of other genes in the same cat. For example, the dominant white gene prevents the color cells from reaching the skin and masks the presence of pigments that appear as black, brown, red, orange, and yellow.

BELOW

The color and patterning of wildcats, such as this serval, is important to their survival.

Melanin is the pigment produced by cells spread throughout the top layer of skin and hair follicles. There are two types of melanin: spherical shapes that absorb most light; and longer and oval shapes that refract the light in the red/orange/yellow range. Color can be affected by an enzyme sensitive to heat and light. The less sensitive, the darker the color. For example, a black coat will be less sensitive to heat than a brown one.

LEFT

The genes for black and red are contained in X chromosomes, so cats with both colors are almost always female.

A pair of dominant genes or a pair of recessive genes determines pigmentation. Cats with fur coats of dominant genes absorb light across the entire surface. The result is a darker color: black, chocolate, cinnamon, and red. Those cats with recessive genes have scattered pigmentation; therefore absorbing less light, resulting in a lighter color: blue, lilac, fawn, and cream.

The Basics of Color Genetics

When the modifications, additions, and dilutions are removed, there are only two genes for color: black and red (sometimes referred to as orange). Genes for different things, such as eye color or hair length, are found in the chromosomes that are not sex chromosomes. The location for the gene for black or red is on the X chromosome. Since male cats only have one copy of the X chromosome, they can either be black or red but not both. Females, however, can have two copies of black, two copies of red, or one copy of each. This is the foundation for what is called the "third basic color"—tortoiseshell. In the case of black and red they are both dominant, so in female cats there is codominance; they have a copy of each gene. Some of the cat is black, some is red.

RIGHT

Cats with recessive genes have scattered pigmentation and appear pale, like this lilac Burmilla cat.

Modifying Genes

How do we get from black, red, tortoiseshell, to the variety of colors we find in Persian cats? This is explained by "modifier genes"—a gene that affects the phenotypic expression of another gene. There are genes on all other chromosomes, except the X and Y chromosomes, that can change or modify the black or red color: "recessive" leads to dilute, pointed, and chocolate, while "dominant" leads to tabby, bicolor, shaded/smoke/shell, silver/golden, and white.

on each hair, ending with a dark point. This is caused by the agouti (A) gene. The non-agouti (a) gene prevents the yellow band from being produced on the hair and allows an even distribution on the hair shaft, resulting in a solid-colored cat. Interestingly it is almost impossible to obtain a solid red or cream color. These cats have a degree of tabby patterns; even if it is so subtle that it appears invisible.

In the wild, color played an important part in feline survival. Not only did camouflage coloration protect the cat from its enemies, it supplied cover to increase its efficiency as a hunter. Tabby markings were predominant in the wildcat and the original domestic cats of Egypt.

There is a distinct tendency for bars and stripes to appear in all solid-colored cats, even black. Often with the loss of the kitten coat, these marks disappear. The fact that they are still evident proves that the "mark of the tabby" has followed, and will follow, all generations. Tabby pattern has bands of light and dark

The complex pigmentation of the Siamese, Himalayan, and Balinese, and colors such as silver and mink, is caused by genetic arrangement.

BELOW

Red or cream cats usually have a tabby pattern, as in this red-and-white van tabby American Shorthair.

Eye Color

Genes are responsible for eye coloration, as well as its unique structure and function. Eyes can be orange, blue, green, yellow, copper-colored, or hazel. Occasionally cats are born with odd-colored eyes—one blue, one green, for example. Survival in the wild required the eye to adapt to night vision, and hunting skills are tied to the cat's superior depth perception. Today the cat still has the three eyelids it was given centuries ago. The third eye, the haw, protects while sliding across the surface of the eye when the cat is sleeping, excited, or sick. When not in use, the haw rests in the corner of the eye next to the nose.

ABOVE

A seal tabby point Birman cat, showing the semi-cobby body shape that is typical of this breed.

Body Types

Body types are defined by genetics. There are seven recognized structures: cobby, semi-cobby, foreign, semi-foreign, oriental, long and substantial, and out-of-balance.

ABOVE

This orange Manx is a good example of a cat with a cobby body shape—short, compact, and sturdy.

Cobby

Short, compact, sturdy body with broad shoulders and rump. Includes: Burmese, Exotic Shorthair, Manx, Persian, Cymric, Himalayan.

Semi-cobby

The body is slightly longer and not as sturdy as the cobby. Includes: American Shorthair, American Wirehair, Birman, Bombay, Norwegian, British Shorthair, Korat, Scottish Fold.

Foreign

Body shape is long and elegant. Includes: Somali, Abyssinian, Russian Blue, Turkish Angora.

Semi-foreign

The body shape is still relatively long, but the bone structure is heavier than the foreign. Includes: Devon Rex, American Curl, Havana, Ocicat, Egyptian Mau, Singapura, Bengal, and Tonkinese. Of these the Bengal and the Ocicat are the sturdiest.

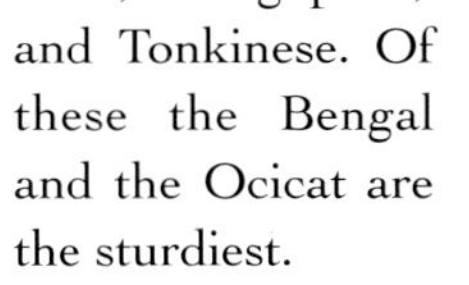

BELOW

Foreign cats, such as the Turkish Angora, have a long, elegant body shape.

Oriental
These breeds have long, lean, and elegant bodies. Includes Siamese, Cornish Rex, Balinese, Oriental.

Long and substantial Long body with strong bone structure. Includes: Maine Coon, Turkish Van, Ragdoll.

Out-of-balance
This group, which includes the Chartreux (semi-cobby with slender legs) and the Sphynx (semi-foreign with a full belly) has inconsistent characteristics of body types.

BELOW
Chartreux cats, which are semi-cobby with slender legs, are grouped with other out-of-balance cats.

Mutation

A mutation is a change that occurs within the genetic structure. A gene at a specific locus on the chromosome may have more than one form because genes occasionally mutate into alterative forms. These changes can sometimes be passed to future generations.

ABOVE
Siamese cats and other Oriental breeds have long, lean, elegant bodies.
LEFT
Breeds such as the Turkish Van cat tend to have a long body with a strong bone structure.

Original genes are "normal" or "wild-type" genes. Some mutations have positive effects; for example the gene that created the agouti camouflaging that helped the cat blend into its environment. Other mutations have negative effects. The Scottish Fold gene can cause crippling bone disorders. If the mutation is harmful enough that the offspring do not survive to reproduce, the mutation dies without influencing the gene pool. Some mutations do make it into the gene pool because they do not reduce the cat's chances of survival. Other genes survive because they are recessive, and they can be carried for several years without making themselves known or without anyone knowing they are there until they are paired with another copy of the gene.

New cat breeds, like the American Curl and the Scottish Fold, are examples of spontaneous mutations.

Breeds
Breeders have selected various recessive mutant genes to establish breeds. An example of true breeding is the Siamese. However, some breeds have been established by using dominant mutant genes. The American Curl carries a dominant gene that affects the ear shape, causing it to curl back toward the head. The tailless Manx also results from a dominant mutant gene.

Behavior

Behavior can also be genetic, and many of our pets' actions are brought over from their wild past. For example, a kitten will chase a flashlight beam, flinging itself recklessly at walls in an attempt to follow it. To the observer this is play, but the cat is using the hunting instincts it inherited.

Special Skills

Heredity has provided the cat with exceptional senses. Its hearing is better than most other carnivorous animals. The whiskers are sensitive feelers that register the slightest contact. Cats have the longest and sharpest canine teeth of all the flesh-eating mammals, and the tongue's upper surface is rasplike and able to draw blood by licking the surface of the skin.

Cats have the sharpest claws of all the mammals. They are perfect cutting tools, pressed together on each side and hooked. They can be withdrawn at will into sheaths in the paws, enabling the animal to pad along silently in search of prey.

All of this marvelous equipment is there because of genetic influence. Originally it enabled the cat to survive in the wild; today many of the same traits are visible in your pet. Understanding inherited behavior can go a long way in helping you deal with your pet. The next time he is trying to climb a wall or is swinging from the curtains, remember that this is the way of his ancestors.

ABOVE
The American Curl cat carries a dominant gene that results in its ears curling back toward its head.

BELOW
Cats are adapted to hunting by having long, sharp, canine teeth and fearsome claws.

TERMINOLOGY AND STANDARDS

Whether you are a cat owner or just thinking about getting your first cat, a new breeder, or are interested in showing your cat, understanding the terminology will help you better understand the feline world. If you are involved with cats in any way, it helps to be able to communicate clearly with breeders, researchers, veterinarians, and other cat lovers. Here we list some of the more frequently used terms and explain what breeders mean when they talk about a "standard." (*See also* pages 30–47 for further information on the anatomy of the cat.)

Terminology

Breed

The term "breed" is used to describe a group of cats that share common physical characteristics and a common registry that goes back several generations. However, this term is not precise because what may be seen as a breed in one country may not be in another. All cats within a breed will have some common physical features, such as body type, but they may vary in other ways, like coloring.

Points

A cat's points are the ears, nose, feet, and tail. In cats that have a pointed coat pattern, their basic coat color is confined to the points. The remainder of the cat's body is usually pale cream, fawn, or white that may have a bluish, creamy, or ivory hue. For show cats, the color-pointing must match the basic body color. For example, a blue point must have a bluish-white body.

ABOVE
The points of a cat, which are the only colored parts in some breeds, include the ears, nose, feet, and tail.

Body Types

There are two *basic* body types (but see page 155 for more specific subdivisions). The first one is *cobby*, the most common examples being the British Shorthair and the Persian. This type has a compact, sturdy body with a deep chest, broad shoulders and hindquarters, short legs and tail, and a short, round head. There is a considerable range for variation within this broad definition. For example, a round-headed cat may have a medium or short nose, small or medium ears, eyes set close or far from the nose. Most moggies are cobby cats.

ABOVE

This Oriental Shorthair is a typical example of a cat with the slender, foreign body shape.

The second basic body type is the *foreign* cat. The word foreign, in this context, has nothing to do with geography. It simply means, in terms of the cat fancy, non-cobby. The Siamese, an extreme example of the foreign type, is described as oriental. The foreign or oriental body is slender and lithe, with a narrow and wedge-shaped head and long legs. It gives the impression of sleekness and a relatively light weight.

Fur and Hair

All mammals have hair: humans, pigs, elephants, whales, monkeys, dogs, and cats, but depending on the development of the individual species, the hair has a different appearance, feel, and purpose. The term "fur" generally applies to mammals with very thick body hair. With cats, "hair" and "fur" are almost always interchangeable, although with "hairless" breeds, such as the Sphynx, the short, downy, almost invisible covering is usually referred to as hair. Hair is either straight (round shafts) or curly (flattened shafts).

Whiskers (Vibrissae) On cats, whiskers are long, thick, tactile hairs extending from the sides of the muzzle, above the eyes, the cheeks, and at the outside of the lower legs. They are more than twice the thickness of ordinary hair and are imbedded three times deeper. They are extremely sensitive and play an important roll in the cat's ability to judge openings and find their way around in the darkness. They may contain scent-sensing powers and also transmit information to the cat's brain about any changes in air pressure.

LEFT

With breeds that appear hairless, such as the Sphynx, the soft down is referred to as "hair" rather than "fur."

Guard Hairs These are the long, stiffer hairs that extend past the base coat. Guard hairs help in holding back water to keep the cat dry. They are also the hairs that usually determine the base color of the cat.

Undercoat (Down) This is the hair that usually mats if a cat is not well groomed. It is the softest, fluffiest part of the coat, and it is also the hair that provides warmth.

Awn Hairs The definition of awn hairs depends on the breed of cat, but they usually form the base coat. In some breeds the finer awn hairs may be the same length as the guard hairs, while in other breeds, like the Manx, the guard hairs are longer.

Vellus These are sparse, baby-fine hairs such as those found on the Sphynx cat.

Haw and Pupils

Cats have an inner, third eyelid called a "nictating membrane." This is commonly referred to as the haw. It serves to protect the eye from dryness or damage. The third eyelid will partially close when the cat is sick, but a very happy cat will show the nictating membrane. Cats' moods are reflected in the eyes; the size of the pupils is the clue. An angry cat will have narrow pupils; an excited or frightened cat will open their eyes wide and display large pupils; mellow, happy cat's eyes will often appear a shade darker than normal.

ABOVE

A cat will appear to smile as it brings air into the Jacobson's Organ, located behind the front teeth.

Jacobson's Organ

Cats have a magnificent structure called the "vomeronasal organ," or Jacobson's Organ. It is located just inside the mouth behind the front teeth, and it connects to the nasal cavity. Slightly opening the mouth enables the Jacobson's Organ to open the ducts connecting to the nasal cavity. The cat's appearance, as he brings air into the Jacobson's Organ, can look a lot like a smile, but it can also look like a grimace. This seems to play a large part in the sense of smell. There are three hypotheses on the exact function of this organ: to perceive the smell of food; as a "sixth sense" to help predict unusual occurrences, such as earthquakes; for sensing sexual odors (pheromones).

Nose Leather

A cat's nose leather, an area of colored skin not covered by hair, may be either black or pink depending on genetics and the cat's basic coloring. White or light-colored cats are susceptible to squamous cancer of the nose and ears, especially when exposed to sun over long periods of time.

Dewclaws

Dewclaws do not touch the ground nor do they have a practical function. They are located high on the inside of the leg above the foot, where they can brush the dew from the ground, which gave them their name. They are often removed from the rear legs because they can interfere with the movement of the animal. It is recommended that front and rear claws be removed as they can catch, even on each other, causing falls and tearing of the skin.

BELOW

Dewclaws are located on a cat's inner leg above the foot and do not have a practical function.

What is a standard?

A standard is defined as an abstract, aesthetic ideal. Artistic unity requires that individual parts be in harmony with one another; that they possess balance and proportion; that together they enhance each other and strengthen the whole. With a standard we aim for a satisfying visual shape that possesses a certain style.

Nothing grotesque, distorted, or ugly is connotative in the standard. Some winning cats look ugly or distorted because they violate, in some way, the basic concept. A cat can have individual "good" features and yet not fulfill the standard. Some parts clash. For example there can be plenty of strength coupled with profound weakness. Excessive exaggeration, distortion, or contradictory parts create a grotesque instead of a pleasing image. There is a delicate balance between what enhances the style and what distorts it. And this balance is the breeder's quest.

The standard, as set out by the cat fancy, does not describe a living animal. It is an ideal that is never completely accomplished in one cat. Breeders only try to approach the ideal, always aware that perfection lies beyond their grasp and in this way keeps them inspired.

The ideal cat is perfectly proportioned, of a pleasing appearance, and excellently bred; an elegant version of a domesticated feline. The whole presentation is pleasant to the eye, well groomed, friendly, and manageable; ready to compete. If the various parts of a cat are harmoniously balanced and complement each other well, the overall result will be a beautiful cat.

BELOW

Breeders try to accomplish an aesthetic ideal in cats in order to win prizes in competitive events.

Colors and Markings

Cats come in an amazing variety of colors and patterns, and it is not unusual to see many different colors in the same litter of kittens. There are two primary colors in cats—black and red. All others are variations of these, with the exception of solid white. White is a masking gene that hides the other colors. A solid white cat is either black or red, but the color is hidden by the white.

Patterns are the different markings on all colors. The three most common patterns are solid, tabby, and pointed. All colors and patterns can have some white. Referred to as "white spotting," this is also caused by a masking gene. However, white spotting only hides some of a cat's color instead of all of it. The white spotting or piebald spotting gene, S/s, has variable expression, so an SS cat often has more extensive white patching than an Ss cat. It is this gene that creates the familiar white blaze across the face, a white bib, a tuxedo pattern, or dappled paws. Some researchers believe that there are separate white spotting genes for distinct forms of white patterns, such as the white locket that some cats have around their necks.

Color and pattern have nothing to do with determining a cat's breed. This is established by the physical characteristics described in each breed's standard. Just as all pointed cats are not Siamese, all longhaired cats are not Persians, all tailless cats are not Manx, so all blue cats are not Russian Blues.

ABOVE

Tabby patterns seen in Maine Coon cats such as this one can also occur in many other breeds.

BELOW

The seal-point coloring is common to many breeds of cats, including the Snowshoe.

The same color and pattern can be seen in many different breeds. For example, there are brown classic tabby Maine Coons, American Shorthairs, Oriental Shorthairs, Devon Rex, Persians, Norwegian Forest Cats, Siberians, and Scottish Folds. There are seal point Siamese, Himalayans, Birmans, Snowshoes, Ragdolls, Balinese, and Tonkinese. Domestic cats have all the same colors and patterns that are seen in purebred cats.

LEFT

This gray tabby-point Balinese is another example of tabby patterning—a common pattern that can occur on many cats.

BELOW (LEFT & RIGHT)
A blue-and-cream Scottish Fold and a Colorpoint Longhair (Himalayan).

ABOVE
A modifying gene can change black into the blue shade seen in the paws and tail of this Ragdoll.

The color and pattern names referred to are the official names used by The International Cat Association (TICA). However, there are other names commonly used to describe the same color:

Official Color	Commonly Called
Red	Orange, rust, marmalade, yellow, ginger
Blue	Gray
Chocolate	Brown
Seal	Silver Gray
(Black) Tortie and White	Calico
Cream	Buff

The addition of different modifying genes changes the two basic colors. Red can change to cream. Black can change to blue, chocolate, cinnamon, lilac, or fawn. Chocolate, cinnamon, lilac, and fawn are rarely seen in the general cat population. The most common patterns and the four most commonly seen colors are: black, blue, red, and cream.

So there is more to the cat than you may have first believed; different breeds, shapes, a whole array of colors and markings. There is the technical terminology used in cat shows, terms used by breeders, and the terms we use with our pets. There are standards set out by the cat fancy for shows and breeders and the standard for a cattery. It may be confusing at first, but it can be a fascinating world for the cat lover.

BREED CLASSIFICATION

Breed definition varies throughout the world. Several breeds were considered the foundation of Cat Fancy because they were recognized prior to its development. Other breeds have evolved from within existing breeds or random-bred populations once a new structural mutation was identified. Some were developed as variations from a parental breed. For example the Persian family: Persians, Himalayans, and Exotics; the Siamese family: Siamese, Colorpoint Shorthairs, Oriental Shorthairs, Javanese, and Balinese. These breed demarcations account for the majority of classifications around the world.

Cats are classified in the phylum Chordata, subphylum Vertebrata, class Mammalia, order Carnivora, family Felidae. Some cat breeds are only available in a few countries, while others are worldwide.

Types of Cats

British and American Shorthair Cats

Like Persians, these cats look similar, although there are some differences between British and American cat breeds. The overall look for the British shorthair is a chunky, cobby cat. It is usually acceptable for the American Shorthair to be slightly heavier, and in general longer than its British counterpart. The colors are almost the same as those for the Persian, with more colors for the American Shorthair than for the British. Although the British Shorthair is the oldest British cat breed, it gained recognition in the United States only in the late 1900s. These cats are quieter than other shorthair breeds, but they will need extra grooming because of their thick coats. They can grow to be large and heavy, so if you are looking for a small cat, it is best to choose another type.

LEFT

An Exotic Shorthair cat; this breed is usually classed under Longhair for judging purposes.

BELOW

The Chartreux cat is considered by many to be a blue British Shorthair instead of a separate breed.

Other Shorthair Cats

These are grouped together for convenience, but some, like the Exotic Shorthair, are judged in the Longhair section. This group includes all shorthaired cats that do not fit into other groups. Included are Abyssinians, Cornish and Devon Rex, American Wirehair and Curl, and the newer types such as the Asian cats, including Burmillas and the spotted Bengals and Ocicats.

RIGHT

The Abyssinian cat is grouped together with other shorthair breeds, such as Cornish and Devon Rex.

Oriental Shorthair Cats
These cats look like Siamese. All the cats in this category will meet the Siamese standard of points. They do not show a restricted coat pattern, genetically called the Himalayan factor, but come in many colors and patterns. They usually have the Siamese cat temperament.

Fascinating Facts

The largest cat was an Australian cat named Himmy, who weighed 47 lbs (21.3 kg) and was 38 in. (96 cm) long. (Guinness Book of Records)

BOTTOM RIGHT
The long coat of the Norwegian Forest Cat determines which breed group it falls into.

Burmese Cats
Burmese cats are very distinctive and are all of the same type and character—only the colors differ. These cats are extremely active, need a lot of attention, and do not like being left alone. However, they are generally not as noisy as Siamese. They are one of the most popular breeds because of their loving disposition.

Siamese Cats
Siamese cats, one of the most popular, are sleek and elegant and have distinctive coat patterns. Siamese cats demand attention.

Longhair, Persian Cats
These cats have the same kind of shape, size, and fur length. They have short noses, small ears, and an abundance of fur. Generally they are quiet and do not demand attention; however, they do need daily grooming.

Longhair, Non-Persian Cats
The only thing these cats have in common is the length of their fur. Included in this group are Birmans, Turkish, Maine Coons, and Norwegian Forest Cats. They are all different, with no common characteristics.

Fascinating Facts

Cats have excellent vision, and in the dark their eyes become more like "ears," the reason being that their pupils can pick up acoustic vibrations.

Cat Registries and Classification

A cat registry is an organization that registers cats for exhibition and breeding purposes. It stores the pedigrees (genealogies) of cats, prefixes or affixes of catteries, studbooks (lists of authorized studs of recognized breeds), breed descriptions, and the standards of points (SoP). It keeps lists of judges qualified to adjudicate shows run by, or affiliated with, that registry. A cat registry is not the same as a cat club or breed society, although these may be connected with one or more registries with which they have lodged breed standards in order to be able to exhibit under the protection of that registry.

British Cat Registries

The first cat registry, National Cat Club, began in 1887 in England. Until the formation of the Governing Council of the Cat Fancy (GCCF) in 1910, the National Cat Club was also the Governing Body of the Cat Fancy. In 1898 a rival registry, the Cat Club, began. It failed in 1903 and was replaced by the Cat Fanciers Association. Cats could only be registered with one or the other. These two fancies merged in 1910 and became the GCCF.

American Cat Registries

In the U.S. the 1899 Chicago cat show resulted in the formation of the Chicago Cat Club. The more powerful Beresford Cat Club, named after noted British breeder Lady Marcus Beresford, followed it. In 1906 the American Cat Association became the main registry, changing in 1908 to the Cat Fanciers' Association Inc. (CFA).

Around the World

In the years that followed many cat registries have been formed worldwide. These range from international organizations or federations to national registries. In many countries, independent registries have also been formed that may or may not be recognized by the main registries. While some cat registries still forbid the practice, it is now common to allow a cat to be registered by more than one. The largest overall organization is the Fédération Internationale Féline (FIFe), which is a worldwide federation.

The World Cat Congress (WCC) is an international coordinating organization of the largest cat registries. The WCC operates under the belief that cats registered with one registry can be shown under the rules of another.

Breed Numbers, Acronyms, and Codes

Registries allot a breed number, acronym, or a code to the breeds they register. Most use a two- or three-letter acronym—for example MK (Munchkin), JBT (Japanese Bobtail). This may be followed by numbers or lowercase acronyms that indicate color and pattern. For historical reasons the British GCCF allocates numbers to breeds. These lists may be found on individual registry websites or in their newsletters, when they are not yet on the internet. All FIFe member cat registries use the Easy Memory System (EMS) breed and variety code, which consists of a breed abbreviation followed by pattern and color letters and digits that are consistent across all breeds.

International Compromise

Where a breed is already recognized by another registry, it is becoming increasingly common to adopt the existing acronym, with the possible addition or subtraction of a letter, in order to avoid confusion. Where two breeds with different characteristics have the same name, it is usual to prefix the name with the country/area of origin. For example in the U.S., "Burmese" and "European Burmese" are different breeds with different conformation. In the U.K. "Burmese" refers to the European form; "American Burmese" is not recognized.

RIGHT

A breed's acronym, such as the Japanese Bobtail's JBT, may be followed by numbers or lowercase acronyms.

International Confusion

A single breed may have two different breed names in different countries. In Britain, a cat of Persian type with the colorpoint pattern is called a Colorpoint Persian. In the U.S. it is called a Himalayan. The American-bred Serengeti was founded in 1992 by Karen Sausaman, from Oriental x Bengal crosses. It resembles the wildcats of the Serengeti plains but without the introduction of wildcat blood. In Britain a Bengal x Siamese cross was originally called the Savannah, but it was later renamed Serengeti because of an existing American breed called the Savannah.

Despite the large number of feline breeds, there is one similar trait; they are all considered either longhair or shorthair. Common breeds found in the shorthair classification include Abyssinian and the British Shorthair. Of the longhair classification, breeds such as the Norwegian Forest Cats and Turkish Angoras are examples.

ABOVE

Breeds of cats are allotted an acronym when registered; for example MK refers to Munchkin.

FERAL CATS

The living conditions of feral cats vary immensely. Some live short, dangerous lives in deplorable conditions. Others are welcomed as working cats around factories and farms, and these animals can live to be ten years or older. Because of the perceived dangers to humans, other species, and the cats themselves and out of compassion for the animals, many people campaign to encourage people to spay and neuter their pets and support the humane control of feral cats.

What Are Feral Cats?

Feral cats are free-roaming cats that have never lived with humans. They are the descendants of domesticated cats that were abandoned by their owners or that strayed into wild areas from their homes. When these cats mate, their offspring never associate with humans, therefore making the kittens feral. Any cat that has reverted back to the wild is feral.

Adult feral cats that were never raised with humans can rarely be socialized, but feral kittens can. The ideal time for capture is between six and eight weeks old. Taming at this age may only take a few days. While older kittens can be tamed, it takes longer. Also an older kitten may only bond with the person working with them, which can make adoption difficult.

BELOW

Kittens born in the wild have never associated with humans and are feral.

ABOVE

Though feral kittens can adapt to life with humans, adult feral cats cannot be tamed.

The average life span of a feral cat that survives beyond kittenhood is believed to be less than two years, as compared to a domestic house cat that lives an average of 12 to 16 years; however, these cats can live to be a good age when food and shelter are available.

Lifestyle

Feral cats are usually found in large groups called colonies. Cats are extremely adaptable, and ferals have been found in conditions of extreme cold and heat. Cats in urban colonies raid garbage containers, scavenge for food, or are fed by concerned people. Many feral cats also kill and eat small mammals such as mice, voles, and shrews. They may hunt birds and reptiles and can have a devastating effect on the wildlife population.

Feral cats can carry diseases, so if your pet comes in contact with one it has an increased risk of catching something, especially if your animal is not vaccinated. Possible risks to people who come into contact with feral cats or their feces include ringworm, rabies, and parasites such as hookworm. The risk of these conditions being transmitted to you is low, unless you have a disease like HIV/AIDS that affects the immune system.

Fascinating Facts

All cats need taurine in their diet to avoid blindness. Cats must also have fat in their diet, as they are unable to produce it on their own.

RIGHT

Feral cats hunting in rural areas can have a devastating effect on wildlife populations.

Colonies

Feral cat colonies arise from stray or abandoned unneutered cats, so all breeds and types are found in the colonies. The cats breed rapidly; a female can have up to 18 kittens a year, although relatively few survive to a breeding age. One pair of fertile cats can potentially produce thousands of offspring. A growing number of animal societies realize that feral cats are wild animals and should not be judged by pet standards. Where the cats perform a useful task, such as controlling rodents, or are not a threat to the local ecology, the approach is to trap, neuter, and return them to their own habitat, while removing any sick, injured, or tamable felines.

Controlling the Population

The only permanent solution is for owners to spay and neuter all pet cats. For years the control was to trap the animals and humanely euthanize them. Today the effectiveness and ethics of this method is being questioned. As long as there is a food source, more cats will move into the area.

Instead of reducing the numbers, it makes room for more to move in, and the breeding starts all over again. Nor can you simply trap cats and take them to a shelter. They are not adoptable, many carry diseases, and it is next to impossible to socialize them.

Feeding feral cats does not help the situation. While it does ease the hunger of the individual, the extra food brings more cats into the area and that leads to fighting, disease transmission, and more homeless kittens. The cat food may also attract rats, which are a source of rabies.

ABOVE
The lives of feral cats are fraught with danger.

Leaving these cats to fend for themselves is not an option either. They face death by starvation, disease, traffic, and predators. Experts estimate that 60–70 percent of kittens die in their first six months. Those that do survive spend their lives struggling to find food and repeatedly breeding, adding to the population.

BELOW
Feral cats breed rapidly, although mortality rates among kittens are high.

TNR: Trap, Neuter, Return Recent studies published in the *Journal of the American Veterinary Medical Association* have indicated that trap-neuter-release programs are not effective in reducing feral cat populations. Arguably, these programs cannot be effective unless they manage cats on a population instead of on a colony basis.

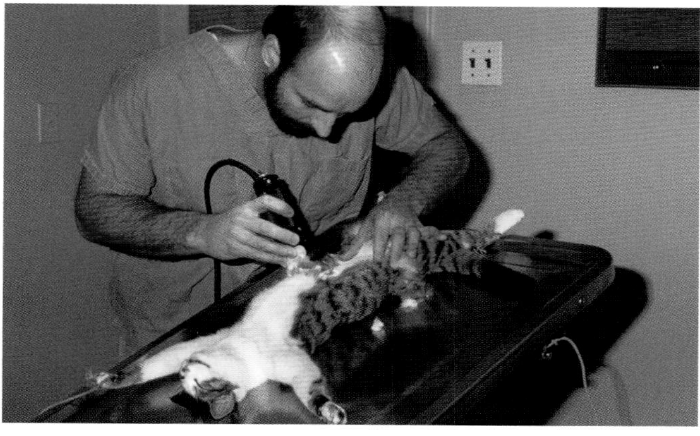

Fascinating Facts

Kittens, when they are born, have closed ear canals that do not begin to open for nine to ten days.

ABOVE

Trap, neuter, and release programs are one way of controlling feral cat populations.

However, to this day this still appears to be the most effective way of controlling feral colonies so they maintain the same manageable size until they live out their natural lives. They defend their territory, preventing more cats from moving in.

Of course you need willing volunteers to make a TNR program work. The first task is to set up a feeding and sleeping area. This should be a partially enclosed space where the cats can find shelter from cold and heat. Lay out old blankets, pillows, and mats to provide sleeping areas. Make sure there is plenty of food and fresh water. The area must be cleaned daily of food residue, and puddles must be emptied to discourage mosquitoes.

Trapping A trap may be obtained from an animal shelter or humane society. Before you trap, you must have everything in place.

- Make arrangements with a veterinarian for examination, altering, and immunization. This must be a vet who is experienced in working with feral cats. Often they will donate their time.
- You must have a pre-exposure rabies vaccination and an updated tetanus shot.
- Have a plan. If you trap a cat the wrong way, you will frighten it, and you probably won't get a second chance. Ferals learn quickly. Sometimes cats are injured or even killed when trapped incorrectly.
- Feed the cats at the same place and time every day so they get used to seeing you.
- Leave the unset trap in the area covered with a towel so that the cats will get used to seeing and smelling it.
- Don't feed the cats the day before trapping so that they will be hungry.

ABOVE

This feral cat was successfully trapped and is shown here at a rescue center in Rome, Italy.

The best time to trap is the night before the planned surgery at the cat's normal feeding time. To be sure of success, don't bait with cat food. Try tuna or sardines, anything with a strong scent. Keep the traps open and unset with food inside for a few days. When you begin the actual trapping, leave your traps set for an hour or two at most. Never leave them set overnight or all day long. A captured feral cat will be terrified and could seriously injure you in its panic, so always keep your hands and face away from the trap and wear protective clothing and gloves.

It may take several months for you to trap, neuter, and vaccinate all the feral cats in your colony. Your reward will be the knowledge that you are giving one group of cats a chance at a new life, as well as doing your part in controlling overpopulation.

NEW AND RARE BREEDS

A new breed or color must first be recognized for registration before it can become a provincial breed and enter a championship show competition. Registration does not guarantee eventual progression to provincial and championship status. In the fancy, four large groups are necessary to encompass, present, and feature breeds: natural, hybrid, established, and mutant breeds. People are always curious about new and unusual breeds, so the fancy's mission is to educate the public and to promote the well-being of all cats.

Recognition of New Breeds

What constitutes a new breed varies. The International Cat Association (TICA) is relatively progressive and will recognize breeds derived from crossing existing breeds; mutations of an existing breed; naturally occurring breeds indigenous to a geographical location; a breed already recognized by another registry; and experimental breeds that do not yet have a TICA-approved breed name. Fédération Internationale Féline (FIFe) will register some new breeds imported from other registries but have set procedures for these breeds to gain full recognition. The Governing Council of the Cat Fancy (GCCF) is a more conservative registry and recognizes new color variations of an existing breed, but it does not usually recognize other mutations of an existing breed, for example spontaneous rexed fur. (Rexed fur appears to be without guard hairs; in other words, wavy hair.)

BELOW

Some mutations are skeletal, such as the missing or greatly reduced tail of the Manx cat.

How New Breeds Occur

New breeds occur as either spontaneous mutations or the result of hybridization of two previously known breeds. When offspring are like neither parent, a mutation is suspected. However, when a different offspring occurs as a result of parents' dissimilar breeds and colors, those kittens are not mutations but a reflection of the ancestry. Mutations take the form of skeletal changes, such as those occurring in the Manx and Scottish Folds; in new coat forms as in the Devon Rex, Cornish Rex, American Wirehair; new colors such as Red Abyssinian. Examples of hybridization are the Exotic Shorthair, Himalayan, and Oriental Shorthair.

ABOVE

Rexed fur, such as that of this Cornish Rex, is wavy and seems to lack the sturdy guard hairs.

BELOW

Hybridization has resulted in breeds such as the Himalayan (Colorpoint Longhair).

Consequences

Breeders who contemplate hybridization to create a new breed are warned of the consequences of such an undertaking. The breeder must consider not only the validity of the program but also if the outcome of the suggested hybridization will enhance the fancy by its addition. Questions that must be addressed are whether or not there will be sufficient breeding stock available from those breeders who will be asked to participate in the program; is the proposal simply a whim?

Fascinating Facts

Over 300,000 mummified cats were found in an ancient Egyptian tomb.

ABOVE

The Burmilla cat is an example of a new breed and is proving to be very popular with cat lovers.

The future of the proposed breed depends upon its evolution. The purpose of a registry of purebred cats is to provide a continuing history that will be a service to the breeders.

Examples of New and Rare Breeds

Burmilla Also called the Silver Burmese, this delicately colored, beautiful cat has become one of the most popular new British breeds.

German Rex This cat has become almost unobtainable today. The type has remained the same for over 20 years: fairly heavy bone structure, roundish head, wide-set ears, thick tail, and dense fur.

Peke Face This Persian is a spontaneous mutation of the Red Persian. Controversy surrounds the breed, which usually has skin problems. Its facial features, that some see as deformities, also contribute to eating and breathing problems.

RIGHT

The Peke Face Persian is a spontaneous mutation of Red Persians, such as this one.

Munchkin Cat This cat is characterized by very short legs. It began with a spontaneous mutation; therefore, it is a product of nature that appeared without the help of man.

Ojos Azules Despite the Spanish name (Blue Eyes), this is an American cat. It is a rare breed that dates back to 1984 when Cornflower, a tortie female with remarkable blue eyes, was discovered in New Mexico.

Shorthair Cats

This section will discuss the various breeds of shorthair cats, their characteristics, habitat, diet, conservation status, and comments about the variations that set one cat apart from another. The breeds share some worldwide classifications, but there are also differences between the countries. For example, British and American Shorthair cats look similar. While the British Shorthair is a chunky, cobby cat, it is acceptable for the American Shorthair to be longer and slightly heavier than its British counterpart.

On the other hand, Oriental looks much like the Siamese and will meet the Siamese standard of points. They don't show the restricted coat pattern of the Siamese, known as the Himalayan factor, but come in many colors. Other shorthair cats are grouped together out of convenience and include those shorthairs that do not fit into other categories. These include Abyssians, Cornish and Devon Rex, American Wirehair, and Curl, and the newer types such as the Asian cats, including the Burmilla, Bengal, and Ocicat. Occasionally a breed may have a different name in a different country. If this is the case, both names are included in the description.

The breeds have been grouped according to body type, for example, cobby, foreign, or oriental. Cats with similar qualities are also arranged together: hybrid, hairless, semi-longhair, and those that have both longhair and shorthair versions. These include Russian Blue, Abyssinian, and Siamese. All cat registries do not recognize all breeds. There are also some classification differences. This section will address the classification and recognition of shorthairs in various countries and organizations.

Early Breed History

The first shorthair, the European, is believed to have been bred from the European wildcat and the early Egyptian cat. In the early 900s the Romans brought the European Shorthairs into the British Isles, where they were welcomed as the defenders of the meager British grain supply.

As more shorthaired cats were bred in England, people had additional choice regarding color and type. They began to prefer larger cats with rounder faces and sweeter expressions. Over the years a large, sturdy cat with a strong, well-proportioned legs and a rounded head became the ideal cat.

English artist Hogarth's 1742 painting, *The Hogarth Children*, shows a gold-eyed, silver tabby climbing over the back of a chair. Since Persians and other Longhairs were not imported to England until the 1860s, the Hogarth painting proves that the silver tabby color existed in purebred English Shorthairs long before Longhairs arrived.

Travel to America

The first domesticated cats in America came over with the early European explorers and settlers. There is documentation showing that several Shorthair cats were brought to America on the Mayflower. As more settlements were formed, more cats were imported to keep the rodent population under control. At first the early American cats were selected more for ruggedness and natural hunting talent than for beauty. As American cats became more plentiful, farmers and miners began choosing kittens they liked, especially those with showy colors and bold patterns, as well as the previously essential hunting talent. A broad genetic base for the Shorthair was supplied by cats of the same breed but with different countries of origin; therefore eliminating the problems usually associated with inbreeding. Pedigrees were unnecessary until other breeds were imported during the last 20 years of the 1800s.

When this breed was first accepted in the United States, there were so few recognized shorthaired breeds that the name Shorthair was considered sufficient identification for the breed now known as American Shorthair, just as Longhair was considered a name that could encompass a breed including Persians, Angoras, and Maine Coons for many decades.

LEFT

The Devon Rex is a gentle and playful cat with an unusual, curly coat of varying colors.

Fascinating Facts

Jake, an orange tabby from Bonfield, Ontario, Canada, holds the Guinness World Record for the cat with the most toes—he has 28.

LEFT

This seal-point Snowshoe cat shows the breed's characteristic V-shape face.

ABOVE

Sphynx cats appear hairless, although many have fine down or a puff of fur on the tip of their tail.

BRITISH SHORTHAIR

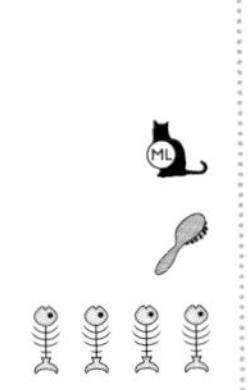

SIZE: Medium to large

COAT CARE: Low maintenance

DIET: High maintenance

BODY SHAPE: Cobby

COLOR VARIATIONS: All solid colors, dilutes, tabby patterns, bicolors, and colorpoints

LIFE EXPECTANCY: 14–20 years

British Shorthairs are even-tempered, undemanding cats, the essence of reserve, especially when they are first introduced to a person or situation. Once they overcome their initial shyness, they turn into dedicated companions who love to spend time with you. They will sit beside you while you are watching television or reading and will follow you around the kitchen as you cook. They usually are loyal to all members of the family, instead of just bonding with one person.

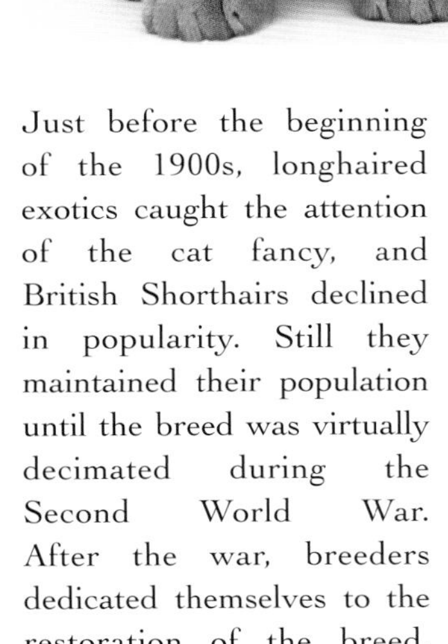

Just before the beginning of the 1900s, longhaired exotics caught the attention of the cat fancy, and British Shorthairs declined in popularity. Still they maintained their population until the breed was virtually decimated during the Second World War. After the war, breeders dedicated themselves to the restoration of the breed. They gained permission from the British Governing Council of the Cat Fancy to interbreed their Brits; therefore rebuilding the gene pool. Persians and shorthairs, such as the Chartreux, were introduced

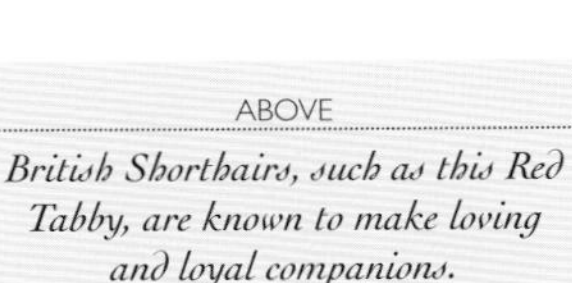

ABOVE

British Shorthairs, such as this Red Tabby, are known to make loving and loyal companions.

to the existing bloodlines. However, the GCCF objected to the use of Persian cats, and the offspring were not permitted to be shown or registered as British Shorthairs. The offspring were then mated back to British Shorthairs, and after three generations they were allowed to be registered as British Shorthairs. This program transformed the British Shorthair into the cat we know today: a large, powerful animal with a full, round face and a placid disposition.

Origins

The ancestors of the British Shorthair were brought to Northern Europe and later to Britain around 2,000 years ago by Roman soldiers, who had cats as pets and to control rodents. The British Shorthair's progenitor was a common street cat once called the European Shorthair, whose conformation was much different from the cat we know today. This English alley cat actually acquired its pedigree in the show ring.

For hundreds of years this strong and intelligent cat lived in Britain's alleys and barns, until cat lover Harrison Weir became interested in establishing the breed. Weir's devotion was shared by a Mr. Jung, who became one of the first cat show judges. They believed that if these beautiful felines were carefully bred, a race of cats with aristocratic pedigrees and the same inner goodness and quality would be developed. The breed produced was named the British Shorthair, and they were the only cats to be shown as pedigreed at the first cat shows. All others were simply shown as Longhair or Shorthair, divided by their various colors.

The Breed Progresses

Weir wrote the first standards of cat-show judging, and his favorites, the Shorthairs, were among the cats in the exhibition he organized at Crystal Palace in London in 1871. At Weir's instruction, a special category was established for British Blues. The Shorthaired Cat Society was formed in 1901 and was a Founding Member of the Governing Council of the Cat Fancy, catering for all the then known shorthair breeds. Still the cat was not recognized in North America until 1970, and then only blue cats of the breed were accepted under the name of British Blues. It was not until May 1980 that the CFA granted all colors of the British Shorthair championship status. Today it is a worldwide breed.

ABOVE

Championship status was only granted to British Shorthairs of all colors as recently as 1980.

Characteristics

Head

The head is round and huge and has a rounded underlying bone structure well-set on a short, thick neck. The forehead should be rounded with a slight, flat plane on top of the head. The forehead should not slope. The nose is medium broad, and in the profile there is a gentle dip. A well-developed chin is firm and aligned with the nose and upper lip. The muzzle is distinctive, with a definite stop beyond large, round whisker pads. The head design sets the cat apart from other breeds developed from domestic shorthairs.

One of the most endearing features is the built-in smile caused by the round, prominent, whisker pads.

This smile was used to depict Lewis Carroll's Cheshire cat in *Alice of Wonderland*. Illustrator Sir John Tenniel, along with the author, chose a tabby British Shorthair. These cats have been favorites in both advertising and on the big screen, as well as the choice of many illustrators because of their impressive body structure and appealing smile.

BELOW

This Blue-cream British Shorthair has the striking orange eyes sometimes found in solid-colored cats.

Ears and Eyes

In British Shorthairs, the ear set is important. They should be medium in size, broad at the base, and rounded at the tips. They are set far apart, fitting in with but not distorting the rounded contour of the head.

The eyes are large, round, and wide-open and are set to show breadth of nose. They are wide apart and level. Eye color must conform to requirement for coat color. Orange eyes are found in solid colors, tabbies, white, smoke, and bicolor. Blue eyes are found in white, bicolors, and colorpoints. The blue of a colorpoint is genetically different from the blue in a white cat. Green eyes are found in black/blue, silver-shaded, and silver tabbies.

Body and Legs

The British Shorthair is a medium to large, compact, well-balanced, and powerful cat, not reaching full body maturity until two to five years. Males weigh 9–17 lbs (4–7.7 kg); females weigh 7–12 lbs (3.1–5.4 kg). It has good depth of body, a broad chest, and level back. Females are smaller in all respects, with the adult males developing prominent cheek jowls that distinguish them from the females. This large cat prefers to be on the ground and sometimes stumbles, but then quickly recovers to give its owner its trademark Cheshire grin.

The legs are medium in length, well-boned, and strong. They are in proportion to the body. The forelegs are straight. Paws are round and firm, with five toes in front and four behind. The tail is medium length, plush but not fluffy, in proportion to the body but thicker at the base and tampering to a rounded tip.

Coat

The short, dense coat is resilient and firm to the touch. It is not double-coated or woolly. They are often described as crisp or cracking, which refers to the way the coat breaks over the cat's body contours. Blue is still the most popular coat color, but they range from black smoke to tabbies and bicolors. The term "blue" refers to the gray-blue color, also known as gray or Maltese. This neutral tone takes on various shades at different times, sometimes appearing almost lavender. This apparent tint is affected by fluctuations in coat shade and texture, as well as variations in lighting and background. Blue cats can be difficult to photograph correctly.

LEFT
The coat of this breed is short and dense, with gray-blue being the most popular color.

They want to be as close to you as they possibly can without actually having to touch you.

The British Longhair
This is a semi-longhair version of the British Shorthair. Apart from fur, it is identical to the British Shorthair. The British Longhair is also known as Lowlander in the United States and Britanica in Europe, but it is not recognized in the United Kingdom as a separate breed. The rationale for this breed is that the original longhaired British cat, through interbreeding with imported longhairs, was developed into the Persian. It became increasingly huge in size and extreme in type and with longer, thicker fur than the early Persians. During the late 1800s and early 1900s, the Persian was considered the longhaired parallel of the British Shorthair.

The Exotic Shorthair
In the later half of the 1900s, a shorthaired version of today's Persian was developed and named the Exotic Shorthair. This cat was very different from the British Shorthair. It was therefore proposed that a longhaired cat of the British type be reintroduced into the cat fancy.

Calico cats are almost always female. Technically, they are tortoiseshell, or orange and black, with the addition of white spots. The gene for the orange and black color is sex linked, carried only on the X chromosome. Male cats do not usually inherit the combination that produces black and orange. A cat with two X chromosomes is female; a cat with X and Y is male. Since two X chromosomes, one carrying orange and one carrying black, are necessary for the coloration, the cat is usually female. A gene that is not sex-linked codes for white.

The coat, developed to protect the cat from Britain's harsh weather, is extremely thick and lush. It is believed that the reason these cats are not lap cats are because their unusually heavy coat, together their owner's body heat, causes them to feel overheated. So while they may start out sitting in your lap, they may quickly end up next to you or on the arm of your chair.

Fascinating Facts

"Tabby" refers to the markings, not the cat's color.

Temperament

Breeders describe British Shorthairs as sweet and affectionate but not clingy; they are cats that keep a low profile. They are independent, yet very affectionate with their owners, following them around the house and inspecting everything they do.

For some reason, males are more people-oriented than females. They are like little teddy bears, extremely quiet and talk very little, but they are still very alert and can sometimes be quizzical. Everything is done cautiously; they are rarely in a hurry. They make ideal pets for less active owners as well as for busy households, as they do not need to be entertained.

The British Shorthair is an easygoing breed. It has a stable disposition and can easily live in an apartment. It is not very demanding of attention, although it will make its desire to play known if its owner looks available. Brits do not have the curious nature that gets many foreign breeds into trouble, and if they are allowed outside, they are unlikely to roam. However, they are often more than happy to be indoor cats.

They are not normally destructive or hyperactive, although they can be playful. British Shorthairs have become a favorite of animal trainers because of their nature and intelligence, and in recent years these cats have appeared in Hollywood movies and television commercials.

LEFT

British Shorthairs are easygoing and playful, making them a favorite among animal trainers.

Calm and Patient

British Shorthairs want nothing more than to be close to you. They will quietly follow you around the house or yard until they can settle down contentedly by your side. They are a cat of unparalleled patience and confidence, which makes them especially good with children and other types of pets. A moderately active cat, they are not destructive as a breed, adapting well to any size household. British Shorthairs are loving to all people they consider to be family.

As kittens, they are playful, but adult British Shorthairs are usually less active than other

breeds. They are a relatively independent breed of cat and are happy to entertain themselves, often just napping.

Words used to describe the British Shorthair include: calm, affable, intelligent, quiet, and independent.

Coat Color and Temperament Link

Is coat color linked to temperament? There are breeders and veterinarians who believe this is true. They claim that tortie cats are temperamental; however, the addition of white in the coat has a calming effect, making the tortie and white cats not as moody as the brindles. British Shorthair colors that have a link to temperament are: black = good-natured; white = streetwise and friendly; blue (gray) = quiet and affectionate; blue-cream = lively; tortoiseshell = quick-witted; black-and-white = even-tempered, friendly; tabby = good natured; spotted = affable; black smoke = good-natured. The color/temperament link is based only on observation and opinion; however, research suggests that color does have a strong influence on what cat people choose to be their pet.

ABOVE

Some vets and breeders consider tortoiseshell cats to be temperamental and quick-witted.

Grooming
The British Shorthair's care is the same as all cat's care. Begin grooming your kitten right from the start so they get used to being brushed. The hair is thick, so you need a comb with very sharp teeth, but their coat does not tangle and has no tendency to get filthy or knotted. They do not need to be bathed. Their coat should be combed or brushed once a week to get rid of old and dead hairs. They enjoy the closeness and handling of grooming and will allow you to brush them for long periods of time.

LEFT

Cats of this breed can become overweight and should be given controlled portions.

BOTTOM

Grooming a shorthaired cat from a young age will help keep its coat in good condition.

Care

Feeding
Most breeders recommend a high-quality dry food. You must be careful to not allow your British Shorthair to get fat or its life span will be shortened. Middle-aged cats, from 5–10 years, are most likely to have weight problems that can usually be controlled by switching to a low-calorie food. Feed controlled portions once or twice a day. If your cat seems to be overweight, ask your vet for more specific advice. These cats are prone to dental problems, so feeding them a tartar control food or dental stick is recommended.

Famous British Shorthairs

- Writer Lewis Carroll and illustrator Sir John Tenniel chose a British Shorthair as the model for the Cheshire cat in *Alice's Adventures in Wonderland*.
- In Terry Pratchett's *Discworld* Humor/Fantasy Novels, the Lancre Witch Nanny Ogg's cat Greebo, also known as The Terror of the Ramtops, is a British Blue.
- Winston Churchill (Church) from *Pet Sematary* was a British Blue.
- A British Shorthair silver tabby is the face of Whiskas and a British Blue is the face of Sheba cat food. The Bacardi Breezer commercials also featured a silver tabby British Shorthair.

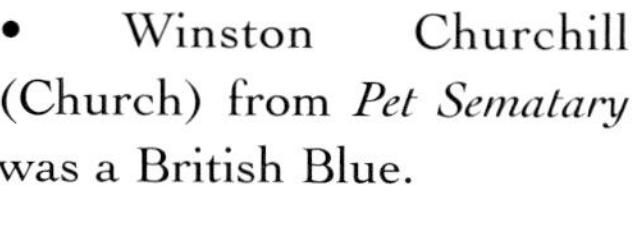

CHARTREUX

SIZE: Medium to large

COAT CARE: Low maintenance

DIET: High maintenance

BODY SHAPE: Primitive/semi-cobby

COLOR VARIATIONS: Any shade of blue-gray from ash to slate; tips lightly brushed with silver

LIFE EXPECTANCY: 14–17 years

The Chartreux, also known as the Monastery Cat, is steeped in legend. No one really knows where the cat originated, but folklore has it that the Chartreux was developed at Le Grand Chartreux Monastery in the French Alps by the Carthusian Monks who managed to find time between praying, weapon forging, and creating the world-famous Chartreuse liqueurs to breed these cats.

Origins

Although there were never many of them, natural colonies of these cats were known to exist in Paris and in isolated regions of France until the early 1900s. The modern history of the breed began in around 1920. The Legar sisters found a colony on the tiny Brittany island of Belle-Isle-sur-Mer, and they caught the sisters' interest because they matched the description of the Chartreux. They decided to work with the breed and in 1931 became the first to exhibit the cats in France. However, the Second World War wiped out most of the breed, so to keep the bloodlines going the remaining Chartreux were bred with blue British Shorthairs, Russian Blues, and Persians.

BELOW

This Chartreux kitten shows the breed's blue-gray coat, golden eyes, and alert nature.

In 1950 breeders outcrossed the Chartreux to Blue Persians to achieve a paler shade of blue, more intense golden eyes, and a sturdier bone structure. In European cat shows, the Chartreux is shown in the same breed category as the British Shorthair, and hybridization is allowed. American breeders didn't take an interest in the Chartreux until 1970. More purist than the Europeans, they maintain two distinctly different standards and never cross the Chartreux with British Blues. Recently French breeders have followed this lead.

Characteristics

Head

The head is relatively large but not broad, rounded but not spherical. The muzzle is narrow and proportional to the head, the jaw is powerful, especially in adult males, and the nose is medium and straight, with a slight stop permitted. Nose leather is slate gray, and the lips are blue.

ABOVE
Its characteristically stocky figure has led to the Chartreux being compared to a potato in appearance.

Ears and Eyes
The ears are small- to medium-sized, minimal flare at the base, with slightly rounded tips. They stand high and erect on the head. Rounded eyes must be alert and expressive. They are wide-set and large, open but not overpowering. They should be a clear, deep gold to copper color, with bright orange preferred.

Body and Legs
The stocky body and slender legs have earned this cat the description, "a potato on toothpicks." The body type is neither classic nor cobby but husky and robust. Males, 11–15 lbs (5–6.8 kg), are much larger than females, 6–10 lbs (2.7–4.5 kg), and slower to mature.

Coat Short, dense, and slightly woolly is the preferred texture, although a silkier, thinner coat is allowed for females. Color ranges from shades of blue-gray to ash and slate. Tips may be slightly touched with silver. The preferred tone is bright, unblemished blue that has a general iridescent color.

Temperament

The Chartreux is quiet and sweet, a playful, comical cat that makes a wonderful companion. Blessed with a well-developed sense of humor, these cats enjoy a game of fetch or a romp around with the family. They are extremely quiet, quick to learn their name, and come when called.

Care

Feeding
Chartreux can sometimes be sensitive to changes in diet or very rich food. Older Chartreux may need to be switched to a low-calorie cat food so that they do not become overweight.

Grooming
The short, thick coat does not require much maintenance; usually brushing once a week is enough. During shedding season, spend more time brushing out dead hairs so that they do not cover your clothes and furniture.

AMERICAN SHORTHAIR

SIZE: Medium to large

COAT CARE: Low maintenance

DIET: Moderate maintenance

BODY SHAPE: Cobby/muscular

COLOR VARIATIONS: Solid, parti-colors tortoiseshell, patched

LIFE EXPECTANCY: 15+ years

The American Shorthair is America's own breed. Its ancestors are the cats that came with the early pioneers from Europe, and records indicate several arrived on the Mayflower. It is believed that these cats were taken aboard to kill rats that ate the ships' food supplies and spread disease to the humans. Over the years they began to be appreciated for their beauty and loving nature. In 1896 they commanded a price of $2,500 at the second annual Cat Show at Madison Square Garden.

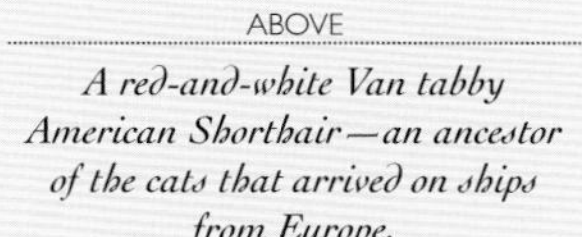

ABOVE

A red-and-white Van tabby American Shorthair—an ancestor of the cats that arrived on ships from Europe.

Because of their hardy constitutions, American Shorthairs usually live long, vital lives, generally 15 years or more, so be prepared for a long-term commitment. However, some American Shorthair lines are known to have the inherited heart disease, feline hypertrophic cardiomyopathy (HCM), and the inherited joint disorder, feline hip dysplasia. While hip dysplasia is not life threatening, hypertrophic cardiomyopathy is and can cause sudden death. Breeds most likely to have hip dysplasia, which can cause pain, stiffness, and lameness, are the larger, heavy-boned breeds such as the Maine Coon and the Persian, so it's possible the American Shorthair inherited the disorder from its Persian ancestors. Talk to your breeder about these and any other health concerns, and be sure to buy from a breeder who offers a written health guarantee.

To those who are not familiar with the wonderful variety of breeds available to today's cat lover, some of our modern cats might seem unusual. However, even the most beginner cat lover can relate to the comfortably familiar American Shorthair, with its sturdy, middle-of-the-road body style and average, all-American, good looks. But don't let looks deceive you, because the American Shorthair is a pedigreed breed with as long a history as many of the cat fancy's exotic feline members.

Origins

The Cat Fanciers' Association (CFA) officially recognized this cat as one of its first five registered breeds in 1906. It was originally known as the Domestic Shorthair, but the breed was renamed "American Shorthair" in 1965 to better represent its all-American status.

The name "American Shorthair" also reinforces the idea that the native, North American shorthaired cat is distinctly different from what may be found in neighborhoods and barnyards. A non-pedigreed shorthaired cat, or Domestic Shorthair, might resemble an American Shorthair, but the test is in whether the animal can consistently produce kittens of the same conformation, coat quality, and temperament. Years of selective breeding and the careful recording of many generations are what enable today's breeders to be certain that each litter will invariably carry specific qualities.

The first American Shorthair to be registered in the United States was an orange tabby male named Belle. Belle was imported from England in the early 1900s. It wasn't until 1904 that the first American-born American Shorthair named Buster Brown was registered under the breed name Shorthair. When in 1965 the name was changed to American Shorthair, the CFA named a silver tabby male, Shawnee Trademark, Best Cat, and the breed finally began to receive some respect in the cat fancy. Today American Shorthairs are accepted by all major cat associations, such as CFA and TICA, and earn their warranted share of admiration and awards. With the introduction of foreign breeds into the United States during the early part of the 1900s, the naturally pure bloodlines of the native shorthairs began to weaken. Longhairs and Siamese were running free, resulting in kittens with a variety of body types, coat lengths, colors, and temperaments.

BELOW

On average, healthy American Shorthair cats enjoy a long lifespan of 15 years or more.

LEFT
The American Shorthair was one of the first breeds to be recognized by the Cat Fancier's Association.

ABOVE
This breed has a well-balanced body shape and is strong and powerful, despite its medium size.

Those who admired the qualities of the American Shorthair began to selectively breed them, working to perfect the patterns and colors while retaining the strong conformation, lovely face, and gentle disposition.

Characteristics

Head
The head is large with a full-cheeked face that gives the impression of an oblong, just slightly longer than it is wide. When viewed from the front, the head can be divided into two equal parts: from the base of the ears to the middle of the eyes and from the middle of the eyes to the chin tip. The cat has a sweet, open expression. When viewed in profile, the forehead forms a smooth, moderately convex curve that flows over the top of the head into the neck. When viewed from the front, there is no dome between the ears.

The nose is medium length and uniform in width. When viewed in profile, there is a gentle, concavely curved rise from the bridge to the forehead. The muzzle is squared, with definite jowls in mature males. The jaws are strong and long enough to grasp prey. Both level and scissors bite is considered correct. The chin is firm and well developed, forming a perpendicular line with the upper lip.

Ears and Eyes
The ears are medium sized, slightly rounded at the tips, and not excessively open at the base. The distance between the ears, measured from the lower inner corners, is twice the distance as between the eyes.

The eyes are large and wide, with the upper lid shaped like half an almond and the lower

lid shaped in a fully rounded curve. There should be at least one eye width between the eyes. The outer corners are set slightly higher than the inner corners. The eyes are bright, clear, and alert, with the color conforming to the coat. Eye colors are brilliant gold, deep blue, green, or hazel.

Body and Legs

This breed is a true working-class cat. The general effect is that of a strongly built, well-balanced, symmetrical cat with conformation suggesting power, endurance, and agility. It has well developed shoulders, chest, and hindquarters. The back is broad, straight, and level. The cat is medium large but just as strong as larger cats. Females are smaller than males in all respects. Mature females weigh 8–10 lbs (3.6–4.5 kg) and mature males 11–15 lbs (5–6.8 kg). These cats achieve full growth at about three to four years old. The breed is slightly longer than it is tall.

When viewed from the side, the body can be divided into three equal parts: from the tip of the breastbone to the elbow, from the elbow to the front hind leg, from the front hind leg to the rear tip of the buttock.

The legs are medium in length and heavily muscled. All four legs are straight and parallel, with paws facing forward. The paws are full, firm, and rounded with heavy pads. There are five toes in front and four behind. The tail is medium long, heavy at the base, tapering to an abrupt, blunt end in appearance but with normal tapering final vertebrae.

Coat

The coat is short, thick, even, and hard in texture. The American Shorthair comes in 80 different colors and patterns, ranging from brown-patch tabby to blue-eyed white; from the beautifully shaded cameo to the stunning calico van. The most common color is the silver tabby, with dense black markings set on a silver background.

Coat colors are broken into four divisions: solid colors (black, white, blue, red, and cream); parti-colors —combinations of two or more colors—(tortoiseshell, calico, blue-cream, bicolored, shaded, and smoke colors); tabby patterns (classic, mackerel); and patched (brown, red, blue, cream, and cameo).

ABOVE RIGHT

Eye color in American Shorthairs ranges from brilliant gold to blue, green, and hazel.

Temperament

If you want a cat that will be a gentle companion, a playmate for children, and an active member of the family, then you have found it in this breed. American Shorthairs are known for their longevity,

good health, good nature with dogs and children, and their quiet disposition.

The American Shorthair sometimes behaves like a dog. It will greet you at the front door and follow you from room to room. Usually they prefer not to be picked up, but they love being on your lap or by your side. You probably will be able to train your cat to come when called, to fetch toys, to stay off counters and tables, and to use a scratching post. Most American Shorthair owners enjoy the fact that these are quiet cats; in fact, hearing such a robust cat approach with the quietest meows is a constant source of entertainment.

These cats not only tolerate children, but they actually look for them at playtime or when they want a nap. If you've ever watched them with small children, you know they have the ability to tolerate enthusiastic handling. They have been known to wear dolls' clothes while being pushed around in strollers. They have been involved in all types of children's play, and rarely do they attempt to scratch or bite. Generally these even-

LEFT

The thick coats of American Shorthairs can occur in 80 different patterns and colors.

tempered animals keep purring through it all. When something gets to be too much for them, they just leave and come back when things are quieter.

Adaptable Personality
Breeders note that the American Shorthair is the perfect breed for those who enjoy a cat sitting on their lap but also want one who is not always demanding your attention. This cat's adaptable personality and sociable nature makes it easy to train. One facet of their personality that is important to know is that they prefer to get around on their own. While some American Shorthairs may accept being carried, many will struggle to be put down if carried too far, too often. In fact if your pet becomes frightened while in your arms, it is usually safer to put the cat on the floor and restrain it there instead of in your arms. They usually calm down quicker if all four feet are standing on a solid surface.

American Shorthairs have a real desire to play, and they usually stay active and frisky far into old age. They enjoy romping around with their family but can just as easily entertain themselves with a ball or wad of paper. American Shorthairs have strong hunting instincts and enjoy catching and killing catnip mice and real ones, too. If you let your cat outside, expect it to proudly bring home gifts.

American Shorthairs enjoy high places, such as the tops of shelves and cat trees, but can also be trained to stay off of furniture. They are fascinated by water, as long as they aren't in it, and have been known to tip over unattended glasses or jump into a recently drained sink or bathtub to look around.

Care

Feeding
American Shorthairs require no special care or feeding; however, they tend to become overweight, so you should be careful not to overfeed them. Feed controlled portions once or twice daily. Later they may need a reduced-calorie diet.

Grooming
Begin grooming as soon as your kitten leaves the mother so it gets used to being brushed. The breed is extremely low maintenance, so a weekly brushing is all that is required.

Fascinating Facts

Cats are carnivores, meaning they are meat-eaters. They don't have the ability to manufacture proteins in their liver as dogs and humans do, and so they have to get their protein from food. Complete proteins come from meat sources. Incomplete proteins come from grains. Incomplete proteins do not have all the amino acids required to form what we call a complete protein.

EXOTIC SHORTHAIR

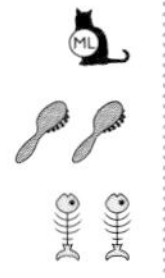

SIZE: Medium or large

COAT CARE: Moderate maintenance

DIET: Moderate maintenance

BODY SHAPE: Cobby

COLOR VARIATIONS: Solid, silver/gold, shaded/smoke, tabby, parti-color, bicolor, Himalayan

LIFE EXPECTANCY: 12+ years

The Exotic Shorthair has become a popular pet because it is happy in an apartment or a house. For busy people who like the look of a Persian but don't have time for the daily grooming, the Exotics are the answer. They are bred to meet the Persian standard with one exception—the coat.

Origins

In the late 1950s breeders, recognizing the popularity of the Persians, secretly began mixing it into their American Shorthairs bloodlines. The aim was to improve body type and to introduce the prized silver color into the Americans. Because of this hybridization, the American Shorthair conformation went through a period of remodeling during the 1960s. The Burmese was used to introduce the short coat. Other lines were developed using the British and American Shorthair, and Russian Blues were used by some. Today the only acceptable outcross is to the Persian.

The kittens from the American Shorthair and the Persian had a decidedly different appearance than the breeders were seeking. This caused an uproar between American Shorthair and Persian breeders. Finally, because the look was appealing, those working with the hybrid lines decided to develop a new breed—the Exotic Shorthair. American Shorthair breeders were given a choice of registering as Americans or Exotics, but once registered as Exotics they could not return to American. In 1967 CFA gave formal recognition to the Exotic Shorthair as a breed. The breed is now accepted by many registries, including the GCCF (Governing Council of the Cat Fancy)—the U.K.'s largest cat registry.

Characteristics

Head

The head is round and large, with great breadth of skull. The face is round, with round underlying bone structure. The nose is short, snubbed, and broad with a break centered between the eyes. The cheeks are full, jaws broad and powerful, and the chin is full, well-developed, and firmly rounded.

ABOVE
The Exotic Shorthair results from breeding the American Shorthair with the Persian.

ABOVE

Exotic Shorthairs are similar in temperament to Persians and make affectionate and loyal pets.

Ears and Eyes
The ears are small, round-tipped, and tilted forward. They are set far apart and are not overly open at the base.

Large, round, and full eyes are set level and far apart. Eye color can be copper, yellow, gold, amber, green, or blue green. The correct color depends on the coat color.

Body and Legs
The body should have heavy bone, with good muscle tone. The back should be short and level, with a well-rounded midsection. The shoulders and hips should be the same width. The weight is from 9–12 lbs (4–5.4 kg). The female may be smaller than the male. The tail should be short but in proportion to the body length, carried at an angle lower than the back.

Legs should be short, thick, and heavily boned, having a height at the shoulders and rump about equal to the length of the back. Feet should be large, round, and firm, with toes close together. There are five toes in front and four behind.

Coat
The coat is thick, dense, plush, and short. The Exotic coat is unique to the breed and gives them a soft, rounded look.

Temperament

Exotics do not have the laid-back personality of the Persian but will often play until exhausted. Still the personality is a lot like that of the Persian: quiet, loyal, sweet, and affectionate. They want to be involved in family life and will quietly follow from room to room.

Care

Feeding
Feed only good-quality cat food in controlled portions. Do not change diet abruptly.

Grooming
No combing is required unless your cat is in a shedding cycle. A good combing, followed by a thorough bath, followed by another combing once your cat is dry, will remove most of the shedding hair.

ABYSSINIAN

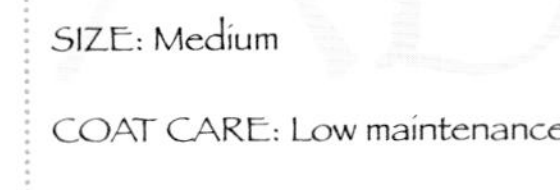

SIZE: Medium

COAT CARE: Low maintenance

DIET: High maintenance

BODY SHAPE: Moderate

COLOR VARIATIONS: Ruddy, sorrel, blue, fawn. In England, Australia, and New Zealand, silver has been added

LIFE EXPECTANCY: 10+ years

The source of the name is from the first Abyssinians exhibited in shows in England, apparently said to have been imported from Abyssinia. The initial mention of the cat is in *Harper's Weekly*, where in the 1871 Crystal Palace show, third prize was won by the Abyssinian cat. In the British book by Gordon Stables—*Cats, Their Points, and Characteristics*—published in 1874, there is also mention of an Abyssinian. The book shows a colored lithograph of a cat with a flecked coat and an absence of tabby markings on the paws, face, and neck.

Origins

The Abyssinian is a natural breed of domesticated cat. The origin is somewhat of a mystery, and there are many exotic stories about where these cats began. One belief is that it was developed from an Egyptian female kitten named Zula. She was taken from a port in Alexandria, Egypt, by a British soldier who brought her to England, where she was bred with an English tabby. The most "Abyssinian" looking kitten of her litter was bred with its mother to splice the Aby gene. It is believed that all Abyssinians in Europe, the Americas, and Australia are descended from Zula, but there has been at least one, and maybe as many as three, Abyssinians introduced from Libya into the existing Abyssinian gene pool in the U.S. The Abyssinian has become one of the most popular shorthair breeds in the U.S. It is said that there are still wild Abyssinians in some parts of North Africa.

Confusion

British troops left Abyssinia in May 1868, so that could have been the time when

cats with flecked coats first entered England. Unfortunately there are no written records tracing the early Abyssinians to those imported cats, and many British breeders believe that Abyssinians were actually created by crossing various existing silver and brown tabbies with native, British, flecked cats.

The first Abyssinians to be imported to North America from England arrived in the early 1900s, but it was not until the late 1930s that several top-quality Abys were exported from Britain to form the foundation of today's American breeding programs.

Recent studies by geneticists indicate that the most convincing origin of the Abyssinian breed is the coast of the Indian Ocean and parts of southeast Asia. The earliest identifiable Aby is a taxidermal exhibit still occupying a place in the Leiden Zoological Museum in Holland. This ruddy, flecked cat was purchased in around 1834–36 from a supplier of small wildcat exhibits and labeled by the museum founder as "Patrie, domestica India." Although the Abyssinian as a breed was refined in England, its introduction to that country and others may have been the result of colonists and merchants stopping in Calcutta, India.

Characteristics

Head

The head is a modified, slightly rounded wedge without flat planes. There is a slight rise from the bridge of the nose to the forehead; no break, muzzle not sharply pointed or square, and the chin is neither receding nor protruding.

ABOVE
The Abyssinian has large ears, bright, expressive eyes, and a gently rounded muzzle.

Ears and Eyes

The ears are alert, large, and moderately pointed. They are broad and cupped at the base.

The almond-shaped eyes are large, brilliant, and expressive. They are neither round nor Oriental and are accentuated by a dark line. Eye color is gold or green.

Body and Legs

The medium-sized body is long, lithe, and graceful, showing well-developed muscular strength. Conformation strikes a halfway point between the cobby and svelte types. The tail is thick at the base, fairly long, and tapering.

The legs are proportionately slim and fine-boned. The cat stands well off the ground, and this gives the impression that it is on its tiptoes.

Coat

The soft, silky coat is fine in texture. It is dense and resilient to the touch. It has a luxurious sheen. The coat is

ABOVE

The Abyssinian cat is a natural breed, and the earliest written references date back to the 1870s.

medium length and has two or three dark bands of flecking. There is a longhaired version of the Abyssinian called the Somali.

Temperament

Abyssinians are busy cats and can get bored and depressed without daily activity. Many enjoy heights and will explore their surroundings in three dimensions, from the floor to their owner's shoulders to the top of the highest bookcase. They seem to be inclined to use their paws in the same way that humans use their hands. They are highly intelligent and very independent. They are so intelligent, in fact, that they can quickly sense when we are feeling sad, and they rub and purr and cuddle to tell you things aren't really that bad as long as they are around. It's creepy how they can sense a mood change and respond to it.

Abys are not known for being especially loud cats but communicate their feelings and desires in many ways. These include vision/eye position, smell, touch, voice, body language, and effective actions. Although they are beautiful, they are not happy to just lie around and be admired; they want to be where the action is. They interact with their owners and often enjoy the company of another cat.

Doglike Behavior

It is said that Abys have a great love of the water. They seem to enjoy playing in a dripping tap, as well as drinking from one. Their habits have been compared to a dog's. They like to play a game of fetch, will bring you little things, meet you

at the door when you come home, and will become your best friend. They are loyal, and they make wonderful companions.

Abys can be very easily taught to do tricks and respond to their names. Many will come when they are called. Most learn by themselves and like to open doors and turn faucets off and on. If they want to play with you, they will get a toy, put it at your feet, and run away. These cats love playing hide-and-seek and outsmart their owners every time.

Be prepared for some high-energy fun. Abys love playing and consider it their job to remind us that play is an important part of living. Owning an Aby is one of life's great joys.

Care

Feeding

The diet must contain ample protein and balanced fatty acids to meet high-energy requirements and maintain the coat. They can usually be "free fed" because they are so active that they burn off extra calories. Hot milk before bed may help calm them down. Brewer's yeast will supply the B vitamins that can take the edge off of this active cat. Many Abyssinians are prone to gingivitis, so they need quality dry food at least three to five times a week to help prevent tartar buildup.

Grooming

Maintaining and grooming the Abyssinian cat is easy, as they do not demand a lot of attention. Occasional combing of the coat to reduce hairballs is all they need. Bathing once a year during the shedding season will make them more comfortable and will cut down on the amount of hair on the furniture. They are generally healthy, but since the Abys are prone to gingivitis, a weekly tooth cleaning is essential. This habit should be established during their kittenhood.

Fascinating Facts

The pupils of a cat's eyes may enlarge as much as four times as it approaches its food bowl.

ABOVE

Abyssinian cats are energetic and intelligent and can be easily taught to perform tricks.

BELOW

To avoid dental problems, it is advisable to accustom Abyssinian kittens to getting their teeth cleaned.

EGYPTIAN MAU

SIZE: Medium

COAT CARE: Moderate maintenance

DIET: High maintenance

BODY SHAPE: Moderate

COLOR VARIATIONS: Silver, bronze, smoke

LIFE EXPECTANCY: 15+ years

The Egyptian Mau (the Egyptian word for cat) is one of the oldest domestic cat breeds existing today. Experts believe that the Egyptian Mau is the cat the Egyptians domesticated from a spotted subspecies of the African wildcat. Evidence of the cats' pedigree can be found in ancient Egyptian art and architecture. For example, a papyrus painting from 1100 B.C. shows the Egyptian sun god Ra as a spotted cat, beheading an evil serpent.

These cats were not only treasured by the ancient Egyptians as pets and workers, but they were also worshipped as deities and were mummified at death. According to a translation from the Egyptian Book of the Dead in 240 B.C.: "The male cat is Ra himself, and he is called by reason of the speech of the god Sa, who said concerning him, 'He is like unto that which he hath made, thus his name became Mau.'"

Origins

The Egyptian Mau was developed in Europe in the 1900s by Italian, Swiss, and French cat fanciers. After the Second World War, the breed became almost extinct in Europe. Princess Nathalie Troubetskoy is credited with saving these cats. The princess had been exiled from Russia during the war, and while living in Rome, Italy, she was given a small, spotted kitten. Fascinated by this vulnerable animal, she decided to research its history. When she discovered the historical significance of the Egyptian Mau, she set out to rescue the species. Princess Troubetskoy moved to the United States in 1956 and took with her three Maus from stock that she had bred in Rome and one from Egypt via the Syrian Embassy. Troubetskoy started a cattery in the United States and worked to promote the breed. To publicize her campaign, she exhibited one of her cats, Liza, at the Empire Cat Club show in New York City in 1957. She attracted fellow fanciers of the Egyptian Mau, and they helped breed the cat. However, because of the small gene pool and the difficulty to obtain the Mau from Egypt, it was difficult to increase their numbers.

ABOVE LEFT

Cats were worshipped by the Egyptians as deities and occur frequently in their art and architecture.

BELOW

The spotted coat of the Egyptian Mau is unique in that it is natural and not the result of hybridization.

Some inbreeding and outcrossing was necessary to continue the line in the United States. The Maus were also selectively bred to eliminate temperament problems that were present in some bloodlines.

Rare Breed

Egyptian Maus are recognized by most of the major cat registries in the United States, Canada, Japan, and continental Europe. However, the Mau is still a rare breed, with the largest Mau registry—the Cat Fanciers' Association—only recording around 500 kitten births every year worldwide. Despite their small numbers, Maus are regularly seen at foreign cat shows and have been granted many high awards. The breed did not arrive in the U.K. until 1998, and the Egyptian Mau Club is currently seeking recognition of the breed from the Governing Council of the Cat Fancy (GCCF). They were recognized in Europe in 1953 and were first accepted in 1968 by the Cat Fanciers Federation (CFF).

This is the only breed of cat whose spotted coat is a natural occurrence and not a human-engineered hybridization. Over 3,000 years ago this pattern was documented in a painting on the wall of a temple in Thebes. Portrayed in paintings as well as sculptures, deified and placed in temples, the Egyptian Mau is one of the oldest breeds of cats.

Characteristics

Head

The medium-length head is a slightly rounded wedge without flat planes. It is not full cheeked. The profile shows a gentle contour, with a slight rise from the bridge of the nose to the forehand. The muzzle should flow into the existing head wedge and should be neither short nor point. The Mau should have a strong chin.

ABOVE
Egyptian Mau cats have gooseberry green eyes, a slender face shape, and a prominent chin..

BELOW
Maus are very intelligent cats and enjoy the company of humans, forming strong bonds with their owners.

Ears and Eyes
The ears are medium to large, alert, and moderately pointed. They are broad at the base and slightly flared, with ample width between them. They may be tufted.

The almond-shaped eyes are large and alert and are slightly slanted toward the ears. They are neither round nor Oriental. The color is light green, often referred to as gooseberry green.

Body and Legs
The medium-long body is graceful, showing well-developed muscular strength. A loose skin flap extends from the flank to the hind leg knee, which allows for greater length of stride and agility. The tail is medium long, thick at the base, with a slight taper.

The hind legs are proportionately longer, giving the Mau the appearance of being on its tiptoes when it is standing straight. The small, dainty paws should be slightly oval.

Egyptian Maus are the fastest breed of domestic cat. Maus have been clocked running over 30 mph (48 km/h).

Coat
The coat is medium length with a luxurious sheen. The smoke-colored hair is silky and fine, but the silver and bronze hair is dense and resilient and accommodates two or more bands of flecking.

Temperament

While most people are drawn to the Maus for their exotic looks, it is often their extraordinary personalities that prevail. The Mau is a gregarious and interactive cat that enjoys people and other animals. It wants to

be a part of everything that is going on. A Mau will follow you around the house, ride on your shoulders, and sit on your lap. They bond strongly with their owners, but some can be shy toward strangers. The Maus are very athletic, performing incredible leaps and stunts but are not as hyperactive as Abyssinians. They are often referred to as the "gentle cousin" of the Aby. They are relatively quiet cats, but they talk to you when they want something.

Possessive

Maus are very protective of their toys, carrying them around and growling at anyone who threatens to take them. Socialization of young kittens includes toy training; they must be taught that fun does not include aggression. They have a reputation for stealing judges' toys at cat shows and refusing to give them back. Maus are extremely intelligent and will learn to open cupboards and drawers, especially ones containing food and toys.

Many Maus will spend hours playing fetch without any special training.

They often express their happiness by chortling in a soft, melodious voice and quickly wiggling their tails. This elegant cat with a beautiful spotted coat attracts many admirers at cat shows.

Care

Feeding

Feed your Egyptian Mau a balanced diet as you would any cat, but you must be careful not to overfeed. Although the general health of the Maus is improving, some health problems persist. Some Maus are allergic to specific foods that cause itchy skin and hot spots. These allergies are usually not life threatening, but they can be difficult to identify and treat.

Grooming

Daily grooming with a fine-toothed comb, such as a flea comb, will help remove the dead and shedding hair. A soft or rubber brush may be used occasionally, but it should be used carefully to avoid pulling out or breaking healthy hairs. Stroking the cat with bare hands from head to tail, as in a petting motion, not only helps remove hair but is also therapeutic to the cat and the owner. You may then give the coat a final polish with a silk scarf or a piece of soft chamois.

OCICAT

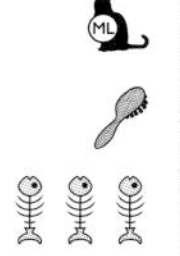

SIZE: Medium to large

COAT CARE: Low maintenance

DIET: High maintenance

BODY SHAPE: Moderate

COLOR VARIATIONS: Tawny, chocolate, and cinnamon, their dilutes, blue, lavender, and fawn, and all of them with silver, as well as black silver (ebony silver)

LIFE EXPECTANCY: 10+ years

The Ocicat, named after its resemblance to the ocelot, is a new and still-rare breed. It has spots resembling a wildcat and the temperament of a domestic animal. Despite its appearance, there is no wild DNA in the gene pool. The species is a mixture of Siamese and Abyssinian, and later American Shorthairs (silver tabbies) were added to give the breed their silver color, bone structure, and distinct markings.

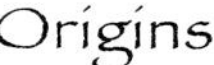

Origins

The first breeder of Ocicats was Virginia Daly of Berkley, Michigan, who attempted to breed an Abyssinian-pointed Siamese in 1964. The first generation of kittens appeared Abyssinian, but the surprising result in the second generation was a spotted kitten, Tonga, nicknamed an "ocicat" by the breeder's daughter. Tonga was neutered and sold as a pet, but breeding of his parents produced more spotted kittens and became the base of a Ocicat breeding program. Other breeders used the same recipe: Siamese + Aby and offspring + Siamese. Today the Ocicat is found worldwide, popular for its temperament and wild appearance. In 1984 Ocicats International was organized. In 1986 in Florida, CFA provisional status was granted; championship status followed in TICA in 1987. Ocicats first came to the U.K. in the mid-1980s. Championship status in GCCF was reached in June 2005. Within FIFe the Ocicat received full championship status in 1992.

BELOW

Ocicats, a rare breed, are a cross between Siamese, Abyssinian, and American Shorthairs.

Characteristics

Head
The head is a modified wedge showing a slight curve from muzzle to cheek. There is a visible but gentle rise from the bridge of the nose to the brow. The muzzle is broad and well defined, with a suggestion of squareness. The chin is strong, the jaw firm, and there is a moderate whisker pinch.

Ears and Eyes
The moderately large ears are set at a 45-degree angle, neither too high nor too low. Ear tufts are desirable. Large, almond-shaped eyes angle slightly up toward the ears. All eye colors, except blue, are acceptable. There is no correspondence between eye and coat color.

Body and Legs
The Ocicat is a solid, hard, long-bodied cat with depth and fullness, but it is never coarse. There is substantial bone and muscle development and still the cat has an athletic appearance. It is surprisingly heavy for its size. The tail is fairly long, medium slim, with a slight taper.

The legs are medium long and well-muscled, powerful, and substantial. The paws are oval and compact.

Coat
The coat is short and smooth, with a lustrous sheen. It is tight, close-lying, and sleek but long enough to hold agouti bands of color. All hairs except the tip of the tail are banded.

Temperament

Ocicats are a friendly, outgoing breed. Most can be trained to fetch, walk on a leash and harness, come when called, speak, sit, and lie down on command. Some take readily to water. They will typically march straight up to strangers and announce that they'd like to be pet. This makes them great family pets, and most can also get along well with animals of other species. Ocicats require more attention than cats who aren't as people-oriented. Their sociable nature may make them less able than some other breeds to be left alone for long periods of time, but it does make them a good choice for a household with other cats or dogs.

BELOW
A Chocolate Ocicat, showing the characteristic athletic appearance of this attractive breed.

Care

Feeding
Feed 1 oz. (28 g) of canned food daily, or ⅓ oz. (9 g) of dry food per pound of body weight. Give your cat at least two meals a day or leave food out.

Grooming
Their sleek, short coats need to be brushed occasionally to remove dead hair.

SCOTTISH FOLD

SIZE: Medium

COAT CARE: Shorthair low; longhair high

DIET: Moderate maintenance

BODY SHAPE: Cobby

COLOR VARIATIONS: All colors and patterns, except those that include hybridization

LIFE EXPECTANCY: 12+ years

The Scottish Fold's ear cartilage contains a fold that bends the ears forward and down toward the front of the head. This is a spontaneous mutation. The original cats only had one fold, but due to selective breeding they can now have a double or triple crease that causes the ear to lay flat against the head.

LEFT

The unusual ear shape of the Scottish Fold is a spontaneous mutation caused by a dominant gene.

Origins

The original Scottish Fold was a longhaired, white, barn cat named Susie. She was found at a farm near Coupar Angus in Perthshire, Scotland, in 1961. When Susie had kittens, two of them were born with folded ears. William Ross, a cat fancier, acquired one of the cats. Ross registered the breed with the Governing Council of the Cat Fancy in Great Britain and started to breed Scottish Fold kittens, with the help of geneticist Pat Turner.

The breeding program produced 76 kittens in the first three years—42 with folded ears and 34 with straight ears. The conclusion was that a simple dominant gene causes the ear mutation. If one parent provides the gene for straight ears and one has the gene for folded ears, the kittens will be Folds.

The gene for a folded ear is linked to a thickened tail and hind limbs; therefore the cat must not be bred fold-to-fold. It holds championship status in all associations.

Characteristics

Head

The head is well rounded, with a firm chin and jaw. The muzzle has well-rounded whisker pads.

The cheeks are prominent, and the nose is short with a gentle curve. There should be no definite nose break.

Ears and Eyes
The ears are small and fold forward and down. The smaller, tightly folded ears are preferred over larger, loosely folded ears. The ear tips are rounded, and the ears should be set in a caplike manner. The large, well-rounded eyes are wide open, with a sweet expression. Color is brilliant gold, deep blue, green, blue-green, hazel, brilliant copper, or odd-eyed. Odd-eyed Folds will have one blue and one gold eye.

Body and Legs
The rounded body is medium and even from shoulder to pelvic girdle. The tail is medium to long but is in proportion to the body. It should be flexible and tapering.

There should be no thickness or lack of mobility due to short, course legs. The toes are neat and well rounded.

Coat
The longhair coat is medium to long. Breeches, tail plume, toe tufts, and ear furnishings should be clearly visible. A ruff is desirable. The shorthair (medium-short) coat is dense, soft, plush, and full of life. It stands out from the body because of the density. It is not flat or tight to the body. These may have any coat color combination except for Siamese-style points.

Temperament

The Scottish Fold is a sweet-natured, quiet-voiced cat who loves to be a part of everything. They have a medium activity level, but they do love to play and usually expect you to be involved. While not every Fold will want to be on your lap, they do want to be close to you.

Care

Feeding
Feed a good-balanced, premium, cat food diet of high biological protein and fat. They may have a tendency to become obese, so feed controlled portions.

ABOVE
A blue-cream and white Scottish Fold; longhaired varieties require regular grooming with a steel comb.

Grooming
Scottish Fold is especially susceptible to ear mites, so the ears should be cleaned once a week with a cotton swab dampened in a mild hydrogen peroxide solution. The shorthaired Fold is easy to take care of and requires no special grooming. Longhaired Folds need to be combed with a steel comb two or three times a week.

MANX

SIZE: Medium

COAT CARE: Moderate maintenance

DIET: Moderate maintenance

BODY SHAPE: Cobby

COLOR VARIATIONS: Any color, except those that indicate hybridization

LIFE EXPECTANCY: 12+ years

The Manx is a breed with a naturally occurring mutation of the spine that shortens the tail, resulting in a range of lengths from normal to tailless. Many have a small "stub," but those Manx that are most desirable are entirely tailless, a distinguishing characteristic of the breed. Some believe that the Manx gene, because it was discovered in naturally occurring populations of cats, is a gene conferring some kind of selective advantage to the cats. However, the most likely reason for this gene's natural occurrence is a genetic drift.

Briefly, the genetics are the following: M = Manx gene (dominant). Cats with the homozygous genotype (MM) die before birth, and stillborn kittens show gross abnormalities of the central nervous system. Cats with the heterozygous genotype (Mm) show severely shortened tail length, ranging from taillessness to a partial, stumpy tail. Some Manx cats die before they are 12 months old and exhibit skeletal and organ defects.

RIGHT

Manx cats originated on the Isle of Man but crossed over to America at least 100 years ago.

Origins

The Manx breed originated on the Isle of Man. They are an old breed, called "stibbin" in the Manx language, and common on the island for as long as 300 years. Since the Isle did not have an indigenous feline species from which the Manx could develop, it is believed that domestic cats were introduced by settlers and explorers, but who and when is unknown.

One story states that the resourceful cats swam ashore when one of the ships in the Spanish Armada was wrecked off the Isle of Man in 1588. Another story has the cats coming with Phoenician traders, who transported them from Japan. No matter how they arrived, it is presumed that they did with their tails intact.

Inhabitants of the island, unimpressed by the scientific theory of mutation, came up with their own: that the Manx is a cross

between a cat and rabbit. This was supported, not only by the lack of a tail but also by the longer hind legs, which give the cat a hop when it moves.

The Manx Outside the Isle of Man

Today the Manx is a well-established and popular breed. King Edward VIII was reportedly a Manx fancier and often attended cat shows featuring the breed. British fanciers formed the first Manx club in 1901. The cat arrived in America at least 100 years ago, and they are noted in early American cat registries. CFA has recognized the Manx as a breed for many years. The oldest studbook available, Vol. 19, lists Manx as one of the breeds that CFA recognized in the 1920s. By 1991 the Manx had gained worldwide recognition and now holds championship status in all associations.

RIGHT

A natural spinal mutation causes the Manx cat to have a short, stumpy tail or even no tail at all.

Characteristics

Head

The Manx has a round head, with round, prominent cheeks. In profile it is medium in length, with a gentle dip from forehead to nose. It has a well-developed muzzle, a strong chin, and a definite whisker break with large, round, whisker pads.

Ears and Eyes

The medium-sized ears are widely spaced and wide at the base, tapering to rounded tips.

The large, round, and full eyes are set at a slight angle toward the nose. Eye colors are deep blue, brilliant copper, green, blue-green, or hazel. Odd-eyed white cats have one blue and one copper eye, with equal color depth.

Body and Legs

The Manx is a medium-sized, compact cat, with solid muscles and well balanced, with substantial bone structure. It has a stout appearance with a broad chest. The repetition of curves and circles give the Manx the appearance of great substance and durability. It is powerful without a hint of coarseness. The flank has greater depth than in other breeds. The short back forms a smooth, continuous arch from shoulders to rump, curving at the rump to form a desirable, round look. The Manx legs are heavily boned. The forelegs are short and set apart. The hind legs are much longer than the forelegs, with heavy, muscular thighs. The paws are neat and round.

This cat appears entirely tailless in a perfect specimen. Manx kittens are classified according to tail length (breeders have reported all varying tail lengths even within the same litter):

- Dimple rumpy or rumpy—no tail at all

- Riser or rumpy riser—stub of cartilage or several vertebrae under the fur, most noticeable when the kitten is happy and is raising its "tail"

• Stumpy—partial tail, more than a "riser" but less than "tailed." In rare cases, kittens are born with kinked tails because of incomplete growth of the tail during development.

• Tailed or longy—complete or almost complete tail

Coat
The double coat is short and dense, with a well-padded quality due to the longer, open, outer coat and close, cottony undercoat. The texture of guard hairs is partially hard, but the appearance is glossy. A softer coat may occur in whites and dilute colors.

There are two types of Manx coats: shorthair and longhair. The coat length is the only difference between the two.

Temperament

The Manx is a very playful cat. They have extremely powerful hindquarters and can jump higher than anyone could imagine. It is not unusual to find them perching on the highest point in any room. Manx exhibit many doglike characteristics, such as retrieving and burying their toys. Once these cats bond with someone, it is difficult for many Manx to be happy in a different home. The Manx is a mellow, even-tempered cat, friendly and affectionate. Its origins as a "working" cat are still

RIGHT

Though the Manx cat has a very quiet voice, females can use a "trill" when talking to their kittens.

strongly seen in the breed, and any Manx that has access to outdoor life is a fierce, dedicated hunter. Many people call the Manx the "dog cat" because of its strong desire to be with people. The Manx voice is usually very quiet, but it has a distinct "trill" that you can often hear when females are talking to their kittens.

Many Manx are very protective of their home, and any unusual noise will cause a low growl and even an attack from a "watch Manx." Strange dogs are especially at risk. Manx make good pets for younger children if they grow up with them, because of their even-temperedness. An older Manx may have some difficulty adjusting to the activity of children, however, since Manx generally prefer a quiet, settled environment.

Care

Feeding

Adult cats need a balanced maintenance diet. Check the contents of the food and avoid those with high ash/magnesium/potassium content. The diet should be divided between dry and moist food—1/4 moist to 3/4 dry. A source of fresh water should be provided at all times and changed daily. Don't change the cat's diet drastically or suddenly—gradually introduce new foods, and watch for any reaction to them.

Grooming

The shorthair Manx only needs to be combed with a wire comb to get out loose hair. Longhair Manx should be combed daily. Because rumpy Manx have no tails, sometimes feces will cling to the close-lying hairs around the anus. This in turn may be smeared on the floor or whatever the cat climbs after visiting the litter box. If the cat's diet causes it to produce very soft stools, this can happen on a fairly regular basis.

Fascinating Facts

A two-year-old cat named Mr. Peebles is the world's smallest fully-grown cat, weighing in at only 3 lbs (0.4 kg). The cat has a genetic defect and is expected to hold this title for a while. His record has been verified by the Guinness World Records

JAPANESE BOBTAIL

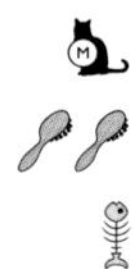

SIZE: Medium

COAT CARE: Moderate maintenance

DIET: Low maintenance

BODY SHAPE: Moderate/slender

COLOR VARIATIONS: All colors and patterns, except point-restricted (Siamese) or agouti patterns

LIFE EXPECTANCY: 12+ years

The Japanese Bobtail has an unusual "bobbed" tail more closely resembling that of a rabbit's. The short tail is a genetic mutation caused by the expression of a recessive gene. As long as both parents are bobtails, all kittens born to a litter will have bobtails as well. Unlike the Manx and other cat breeds, where genetic disorders are common to tailless or stumpy tails, none of these problems exist with the Japanese Bobtail.

Origins

The earliest written evidence of cats in Japan indicates that they arrived from China or Korea at least 1,000 years ago. In 1602 Japanese authorities decreed that all cats should be set free to help with rodents threatening the silkworms. Buying or selling cats became illegal, so bobtailed cats lived on farms and in the streets. Japanese Bobtails became known as the "street cats" of Japan.

The Japanese Bobtail is mentioned in *Kaempfer's Japan*, published in London in 1701–02. Kaempfer, a German doctor, wrote: "There is only one breed of cat that is kept. It has large patches of yellow, black, and white fur; its short tail looks like it has been bent and broken. It has no mind to hunt for rats and mice but just wants to be carried and stroked by women."

In 1968 the late Elizabeth Freret imported the first three Japanese Bobtails to the United States. Japanese Bobtails were accepted for championship status in CFA in 1976. The cats hold championship status in all associations except FIFe. FIFe only accepts the shorthaired variety.

Characteristics

Head

The head forms an almost perfect equilateral triangle, with gentle, curving lines, high cheekbones, and a noticeable whisker break. The long nose is well defined, the muzzle fairly broad and rounding into the whisker break.

Ears and Eyes

The large ears are upright and set wide apart but at right angles instead of flaring out. The large, oval, wide eyes are set at a

LEFT

Japanese Bobtail cats were originally used to control rats in the streets and farms of Japan.

Fascinating Facts

Kittens are not affected when their whiskers are cut, but adult cats become disoriented.

ABOVE
The tail hair of Bobtail cats, especially the longhaired varieties, fans out to create a pom-pom.

pronounced slant. Eye color may be blue, copper, green, or odd-eyed. Blue eyes and odd-eyes are acceptable in bicolors, tricolors, and parti-colors, as well as in solid white. Copper and green eyes are acceptable with all coat colors. Preference should be given to deep, vivid shades.

Body and Legs
The cat has a medium-sized body with a long, lean torso. It is elegant, not tubular, showing well-developed muscular strength without coarseness. The cat is not flabby or cobby.

The legs are long, slender, but not dainty. Hind legs are longer than forelegs; paws are oval.

The tail is unique to each cat. It is clearly visible and composed of one or more curves, angles, or kinks. It should harmonize with the cat. The hair fans out to create a pom-pom effect that hides the bone structure of the tail.

Coat
The shorthair is medium length, soft, and silky with no noticeable undercoat. The longhair is medium-long to long, soft, and silky with no noticeable undercoat. A frontal ruff and ear and toe tufts are desirable. The coat should lay to accent the bodylines.

Temperament

These are active, intelligent, talkative cats. Their soft voices are capable of almost an entire scale of tones; some say they sing. Since they love human companionship, they almost always speak when spoken to. They like to carry things in their mouths and enjoy playing fetch. These cats are masters of the pounce, and they love to ride on shoulders. They adjust well to dogs and other animals and are especially good with children.

Care

Feeding
Easy to care for, the Bob only needs a quality, balanced diet of premium cat food and a daily antioxidant supplement. Food can be left out all day long.

Grooming
A light, daily combing is necessary.

AMERICAN WIREHAIR

SIZE: Medium to large

COAT CARE: Low maintenance

DIET: Moderate maintenance

BODY SHAPE: Cobby

COLOR VARIATIONS: All colors and patterns, except those that indicate hybridization

LIFE EXPECTANCY: 15+ years

The American Wirehair is rare, but it is being successfully bred and shown in Japan and France, so it may someday be found all over the world. The breed is a natural mutation that occurred in a litter of upstate New York farm cats in 1966. Wirehairs are the third breed in the original Native American threesome: American Shorthair, the Maine Coon, and the American Wirehair. Another mutation has been added since then—the American Curl.

Origins

The breed is a uniquely American, spontaneous mutation, where two ordinary cats came together and a kitten was born that was unlike its parents or the rest of the litter. What is interesting about this individual mutation is that it has not been reported in any other country.

It was felt that since this mutation had occurred in the domestic American cat, the standard for it should conform to that of the American Shorthair. However, there were unique Wirehair qualities besides the coat, and they were worth keeping. The first Wirehair litter contained five kittens, but unfortunately only one male and one female survived. The owner was fascinated by the strange coat on the male, so he showed his neighbor, Joan O'Shea. Joan felt the coat had merit and decided to try and reproduce it. The original male was bred to his sister, and more "kinkies" arrived.

ABOVE

American Wirehairs originated in New Jersey in the 1960s; the mutation is unique to the U.S.

The Route to Recognition

The process of establishing the breed was long and arduous, involving plenty of close-line breeding. The original breeders realized that it would be best to use an outcross to inject hybrid vigor. The closest body type was the American Shorthair, and it has remained the only available outcross.

Fascinating Facts

The oldest living cat is a 31-year-old Burmese named Kataleena Lady who lives in Melbourne, Australia. Kataleena Lady was born on March 11, 1977. (Guinness Book of Records)

Wirehairs were first recognized by the Cat Fanciers' Association (CFA) in 1967 and accepted for championship competition in 1978. The cat has been denied recognition by the international registry FIFe and by Britain's GCCF. It holds championship status in CFA, ACA, TICA, ACFA, CCA, UFO, and NCFA.

Characteristics

Head

The underlying bone structure is round, with prominent cheekbones and a well-developed muzzle and chin. There is a slight whisker break. In profile, the nose shows a gentle, concave curve.

Ears and Eyes

The medium-sized ears are slightly rounded at the tips. They are set wide and are not overly open at the base. The large, round eyes are bright and clear. They are set apart. The aperture has a slight upward tilt. Eye colors include: hazel, green, deep blue, brilliant gold, or odd-eyed (one blue and one gold).

Body and Legs

The body is medium to large, the back level and the shoulders and hips the same width. The torso is well rounded. The tail tapers to a rounded tip.

The legs are medium length and well-muscled. The paws are firm, full, and rounded, with heavy pads.

Coat

The medium-length coat has a springy, tight curl. The overall appearance of wiring, coarseness, and resilience of the coat is more important than the crimping of each hair. Whiskers should be curly.

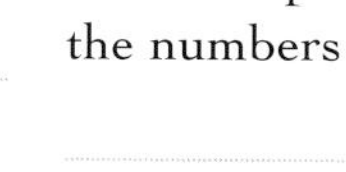

Temperament

Wirehairs are extremely sweet and are people-oriented. They adapt well to all members of the family, including children and other pets. They can be inquisitive and playful but are also quiet and reserved. It is difficult to make generalizations on their temperament because the numbers are so small.

Care

Feeding

Feed a good-quality cat food. Add a vegetable enzyme for insurance.

Grooming

The skin is sensitive to outside influences, so should be kept thoroughly clean through regular bathing. The coat is often greasy due to the oily skin. American Wirehairs tend to get excess waxy buildup in their ears.

ABOVE

The coat of the American Wirehair is always coarse and curly but has many varieties of pattern and color.

CORNISH REX

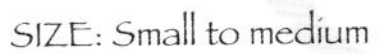

SIZE: Small to medium

COAT CARE: High maintenance

DIET: Moderate maintenance

BODY SHAPE: Slender

COLOR VARIATIONS: All colors and patterns

LIFE EXPECTANCY: 12+ years

LEFT

The Cornish Rex has large ears, high cheekbones, a long nose, and a very dense, wavy coat.

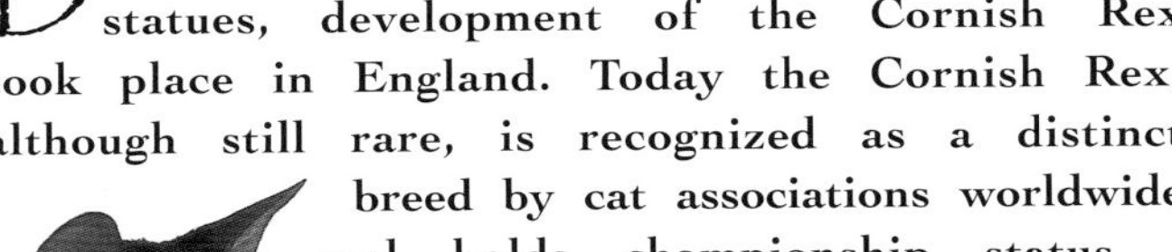

Despite its resemblance to ancient Egyptian statues, development of the Cornish Rex took place in England. Today the Cornish Rex, although still rare, is recognized as a distinct breed by cat associations worldwide and holds championship status in all associations.

Origins

The oldest of the Rex breeds resulted from a mutation in a kitten born of an ordinary farm cat in 1950. The first mutated cat was mated to its mother, and more curly-coated kittens were born.

Characteristics

Head

The head is small and egg-shaped; length one-third greater than width; definite whisker break; muzzle narrowing slightly to a rounded end. It has high cheekbones and a Roman nose with a prominent bridge.

Ears and Eyes

The ears are large and full from base, erect and alert, and sit high on the head. The eyes are medium to large and a full eye-width apart, an oval shape, and slant slightly up. The color should be clear, intense, and appropriate to coat color.

Body and Legs

The Cornish Rex has a small to medium torso, long but not tubular. Its back is naturally arched, and the rump is well muscled and rounded. The tail is long, slender, tapering toward the end, and flexible. Legs are long and slender; thighs well muscled; paws are dainty and slightly oval.

Coat

Its short, soft, silky coat is free from guard hairs. The fur is dense, and the size of waves varies.

Temperament

They are athletic and agile, love to jump and play, enjoying games like fetch and catch. The Cornish Rex is affectionate and good with children, dogs, and other cats.

Care

Feeding

Give a preservative-free diet, with a fatty vitamin such as cod-liver oil or fish oil.

Grooming

Daily hand grooming is needed.

DEVON REX

BODY SHAPE: Slender

COLOR VARIATIONS: All colors and patterns

LIFE EXPECTANCY: 12+ years

SIZE: Medium

COAT CARE: High maintenance

DIET: Moderate maintenance

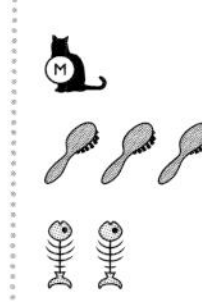

Lots of things to play with and climb on should be provided for this cat. If you have the time to give the cat the attention it deserves, then a Devon Rex may be just the cat for you.

Origins

In 1959 Beryl Cox, in Devon, England, saw a stray tomcat with an unusual, curly coat. Miss Cox's straight-coated tortoiseshell delivered four kittens, one of which had the same curly coat as the tomcat. She named the kitten Kirlee. All Devon Rexes trace their ancestry back to Kirlee. Championship status is given by all associations.

RIGHT

All Devon Rex cats can be traced back to a single ancestor, born in Devon, England, in the 1950s.

Characteristics

Head
The face is full-cheeked with high cheekbones; a prominent whisker break and strong chin.

Ears and Eyes
Ears are large and set very low; weak at base; tapering to rounded tops. Eyes are large, oval, and wide-set. Color depends on coat color.

Body and Legs
The Devon Rex is slender, with a broad chest and medium-fine boning. The tail is long, fine, and tapering, and well covered with short fur.

Legs are long and slim; paws small and oval.

Coat
Well covered with fur; greatest density on back, sides, tail, legs, face, and ears. Texture soft and fine, short to very short; rippled wave when coat smoothed with the hand.

Temperament

Devons are lovingly called "monkeys in cats' clothing." Antics include swinging from curtains and climbing up the walls. They have several doglike qualities: fetching toys, walking on a harness and leash. They are very gentle and loving and hate to be bored or alone.

Care

Feeding
This active cat is usually hungry and requires good-quality food. Special attention must be given to not let this breed get obese.

Grooming
After bathing, towel dry using a soft motion and patting the cat, and then smooth the coat with the hand into a natural flatness, allowing the Devon to lick itself dry.

Fascinating Facts

Unlike the other Rex breeds—Devon and Cornish—the Selkirk Rex (see page 298) is not a good alternative for someone with cat allergies. They have the shedding undercoats typical of their parent breeds.

SIAMESE

SIZE: Small to medium

COAT CARE: Moderate maintenance

DIET: Moderate maintenance

BODY SHAPE: Foreign/oriental

COLOR VARIATIONS: Pointed: seal, blue, chocolate, and lilac; if colorpoint shorthair, all color and pattern point variations permitted, including lynx and tortie

LIFE EXPECTANCY: 15+ years

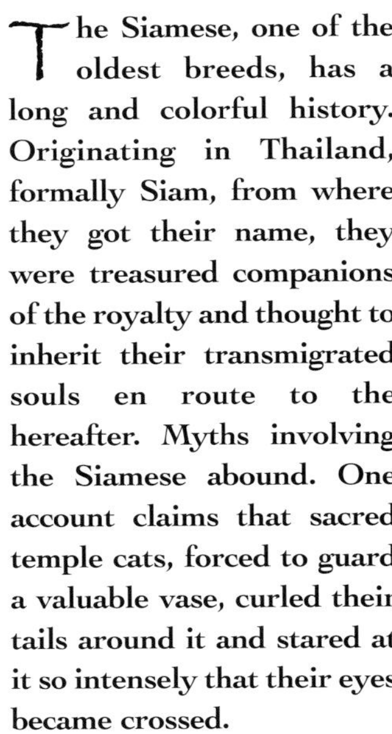

The Siamese, one of the oldest breeds, has a long and colorful history. Originating in Thailand, formally Siam, from where they got their name, they were treasured companions of the royalty and thought to inherit their transmigrated souls en route to the hereafter. Myths involving the Siamese abound. One account claims that sacred temple cats, forced to guard a valuable vase, curled their tails around it and stared at it so intensely that their eyes became crossed.

ABOVE

Siamese cats (a seal point Siamese is shown here) originated in Thailand, where they frequently featured in mythology and were highly valued.

Another story tells of the Siamese selected to guard princesses' rings. Holding the rings on their tails caused kinks to develop, preventing the rings from sliding off. The *Cat-Book Poems*, written in Ayuda sometime between 1350 and 1776, describes the Siamese and includes illustrations of cats with slim bodies and legs, pale-colored coats with dark pigmentation on the ears, tails, and feet. The book claims these cats had red eyes, probably caused by the reflection of light.

Origins

The Siamese is one of the first distinctly recognized breeds of Oriental cats. The exact origins of the breed are unknown, but it is believed to be from southeast Asia and is said to descend from the sacred temple cats of Siam, now Thailand. In Thailand, where they are one of several native

By the mid-1980s cats of the original style had disappeared from cat shows, but a few breeders, especially in the U.K., continued to breed and register them, resulting in today's two types of Siamese —the modern "show-style" and the "traditional," both having descended from the same distant ancestors.

The first Siamese to reach America lived in the White House. While not documented, this well-known story tells of a Siamese given to Mrs. Rutherford Hayes by U.S. Consul David Stickles in 1878. Another story says that the Siamese arrived in 1890, a gift from the King of Siam to an American friend.

breeds, they are called Wichien-maat, a name meaning "Moon diamond."

The earliest documented account of the Siamese cat in Britain is a pair that was given to the sister of the consul general in Bangkok in 1884. She exhibited them and their three offspring in London at the Crystal Palace Show in 1885, where they made a huge impression because of their unique appearance and distinct behavior. Unfortunately, all three of the kittens died soon after the show. The reason for their deaths is not documented.

There is some indication that Siamese were shown in the first modern-style cat show in England in 1871. They were described as "an unnatural, nightmare of a cat." Despite the bad press, they quickly became popular. At the time they were celebrated for their crossed eyes and kinked tails. These were not considered faults until later.

Change of Standards

In the 1950s–1960s, as the Siamese was increasing in popularity, many breeders and cat show judges began to favor the more slender look, and as a result of generations of selective breeding they created long, fine-boned, narrow-headed cats. Eventually the modern show Siamese was created. The major cat organizations altered the language and/or interpretation of their official breed standards to favor this newer type of Siamese, and the minority of breeders who stayed with the original style found that their cats were no longer competitive in the show ring.

RIGHT

Over the years the Siamese's desirable characteristics have changed, and selective breeding has shifted to meet these needs.

LEFT
Siamese cats have become extremely popular and are used in the matrix of many other modern breeds.

By the early 1900s the cats were appearing in American shows. Because of its popularity, the Siamese has been used in the matrix of scores of modern breeds: Ocicat, Himalayan, Burmese, Tonkinese, Snowshoe, and many oriental breeds. Siamese hold championship status in all associations.

Characteristics

Head
The medium-sized head is a long, tapering wedge with no break at the whiskers, which are smooth and black. The skull is flat, muzzle fine, and wedge-shaped. The chin and jaw are medium. There is no break, no bulge over the eyes, and no dip in the nose, which is long and straight. Allowance must be made for jowls in the stud cat.

Eyes and Ears
The medium-sized eyes are almond shaped and slanted toward the nose in harmony with the lines of the wedge and the ears. They should not be crossed. The color is a deep, vivid blue.

The ears are strikingly large, pointed, and wide at the base, continuing the lines of the wedge.

Body and Legs
The Siamese body is long, svelte, and graceful, a distinctive combination of fine bones and firm muscles. The shoulders and hips continue the same sleek lines of the tubular body. The tail is long, thin, and tapering to a fine point.

The legs are long and slim, with the hind legs higher than the front legs. The oval-shaped paws are small and dainty. Males are usually larger than females.

Coat
The glossy coat is short and fine textured. Color, a prominent feature of this breed, includes: seal point, chocolate point, blue point, lilac point. Seal points, still the best known, were the first to arrive. Their seal-brown extremities and pale fawn bodies are spectacular. Chocolate points, with creamy white bodies and milk-chocolate

Fascinating Facts

The color of the points in Siamese cats is heat related. Cool areas are darker. Siamese kittens are born white because of the heat inside the mother's uterus before birth. This heat keeps the kittens' hair from darkening on the points.

legs, tail, mask, and ears, appear from time to time. The blue point has a bluish white body with slate blue points. The lilac point has a white body with pinkish gray points.

Temperament

Siamese are known for communicating their needs clearly. No gentle purring or a rub against the leg for this cat. If you cannot be drawn into a conversation, they are happy to keep a running monologue for hours. Determinedly social and very dependant on humans, these cats crave active involvement in life. They follow their owners everywhere and will whine if left alone too long. While they may appear aloof and unpredictable, it's all an act. They need to be with you, to be treated with respect and patience, and they require a lot of affection if you are to develop a close and caring relationship with them.

Care

Feeding
Always feed your Siamese the highest quality food you can afford. They are a highly muscled, athletic cat and need a high-quality, high-protein cat food.

Grooming
Siamese cats require subtle grooming and not intensive efforts. Bathing is done as needed. Many Siamese cats never need a bath. Others, especially unneutered males, may need to be washed once a week.

Colorpoint Shorthair

Colorpoint Shorthairs are the first cousins of the Siamese. This breed is distinguished by its sixteen different point colors beyond the four Siamese colors. They are half-siblings to the Siamese by the fact of their foundation and breeding with the Siamese. The Colorpoint Shorthair is a hybrid breed of the Siamese.

Origins
The Colorpoint of 1947–48 is a distant relative from its angular, leggy descendant of today. The effort to produce a Siamese-style pointed cat in colors other than the traditional four began in Britain and North America in the 1940s. Modern day Colorpoints are the same structural standard as the Siamese, the only difference being its unique point colors.

Early in the program, breeders concentrated on cats with red or cream confined to the points: face, legs, ears, and tails. Early hybridizations with domestic shorthairs and refinement by concentrating the Siamese gene with the red gene produced the first colors to eventually be called Colorpoint Shorthair. To distinguish the new breed from the Siamese, CFA breeders adopted the name Colorpoint Shorthair for registration purposes. The breed won recognition in 1964. The early cats that helped become the new breed were given the first color class of the Colorpoints and had red and cream points.

Colorpoint Shorthairs hold championship status in

CFA, UFO, TCA, and CCA. Also in ACFA, TICA, ACA, CFF, NCFA, and AACE, but as Siamese.

Characteristics

Head The medium-sized head is a long, tapering wedge with no break at the whiskers. The skull is flat, the muzzle fine and wedge shaped. The chin and jaw is medium; nose long and straight with no break.

Ears and Eyes The ears are strikingly large, pointed, and wide at the base, continuing the lines of the wedge. The medium-sized eyes are almond shaped and slanted toward the nose in harmony with the lines of the wedge and the ears. They should not be crossed. The color is a deep, vivid blue.

Body and Legs The Siamese body is long, svelte, and graceful, a distinctive combination of fine bones and firm muscles. The shoulders and hips continue the same sleek lines of the tubular body. The tail is long, thin, and tapering to a fine point.

The legs are long and slim, with the hind legs higher than the front legs. The oval-shaped paws are small and dainty. Males are usually larger than females.

Coat The coat is short, fine textured, and glossy. It lies close to the body.

Temperament
This breed is not for everyone, but for those who love people-oriented, habitually climbing, always-in-motion cats who simply won't accept being ignored, this is the perfect choice. Colorpoints make great companions for people with a good sense of humor. Natural acrobats, they will keep you entertained with their stunts. Bring out any toy and watch as they race around to pounce on it. But their favorite games are those with you; they want you to share in the fun.

Curious and intelligent, the Colorpoint is always busy climbing their cat trees, bringing you their ball for a

ABOVE LEFT
The muscular, streamlined body of the Siamese, together with its long tail, gives it a graceful and elegant appearance. A tabby Siamese is shown here.

BELOW LEFT
Siamese cats are very vocal and highly sociable, although to the uninitiated they can appear aloof. This is a red point Siamese—or Colorpoint Shorthair.

RIGHT

This Siamese cat clearly illustrates the breed's large, pointed ears and deep, vivid, blue eyes. This is an apricot point Siamese—or Colorpoint Shorthair.

long game of fetch, getting into things that they shouldn't. And of course, talking. While not as vocal as Siamese, they are still very chatty. Their distinctive yowl leaves no doubt about their Siamese heritage. Temperament is what attracts most fanciers to this breed. Very interactive, Colorpoints are constant companions who give you all of their loyalty and love. They want to be with you every waking hour and curled up on the bed with you when you are asleep, so expect an above-average time commitment.

Care

Feeding Always feed your Colorpoint the highest quality food you can afford.

Grooming Daily grooming to remove dead hairs, especially during shedding periods. Like their Siamese cousins, Colorpoint Shorthairs require little grooming and are especially good in households with allergies to cats, since both breeds have little dandruff. Occasional bathing is recommended.

KORAT

SIZE: Medium

COAT CARE: Low maintenance

DIET: Low maintenance

BODY SHAPE: Foreign/oriental

COLOR VARIATIONS: Any shade of blue tipped with silver

LIFE EXPECTANCY: 12+ years

The Korat cat is considered a symbol of good fortune by the people of Thailand. Many good luck stories are attached to this cat: they are silver, signifying wealth; they are the color of rain clouds, with eyes the shade of young rice, implying good crops. The gift of a pair of Korats to a bride ensures a prosperous marriage. Rare and highly prized, every modern Korat is believed to trace its ancestry back to the original cats.

Origins

The earliest known picture of a Korat, or Si-Sawat, cat is to be found in the ancient book of paintings and verses, The *Cat-Book Poems* in Bangkok's National Library. The Fine Arts Department, a division of Thailand's Ministry of Education, believes it to have been produced some time during the Ayudhya period of Siamese History (1350–1767).

In 1959 the first known pair of Korats was imported into the United States. They arrived in Great Britain from the U.S. in 1972. The Korats were accepted for competition in CFA in 1966 and approved by GCCF in 1976. After many tries, in 1983 the Korat was awarded champion status in FIFe. Today it holds championship status in all associations.

Characteristics

Head

The head is heart-shaped, with breadth between and across the eyes. The sides of the face gently curve down toward the chin to complete a heart. There is a slight stop between the forehead and nose. The chin and jaw are strong and well developed, not overly squared or overly pointed.

Ears and Eyes

The ears are large, with rounded tips and a large flare at the base. They are set high on the head. The eyes are large and luminous, wide open, and oversized for the face. There is an Asian slant to the aperture when closed.

ABOVE LEFT

Korats, with their distinctive silver coats, are revered as good omens in their country of origin.

The preferred color is luminous green, but an amber cast is acceptable.

Body and Legs
The body is semi-cobby, with a distinctive broad-chested torso and good space between forelegs. This is a muscular cat with unexpected weight. The back is carried in a curve.

Coat
The fine coat is single, short, and glossy. It lies close to the body.

Temperament

The Korat is an active, territorial cat, with strong likes and dislikes. They consider their "human" to be a part of their territory, so they make great companions, always close and faithful but never "in your face." Korats are intelligent and grasp most training, such as playing games of fetch and walking on a leash. Korats bond with their owner, usually some time in the first few weeks in its new home. After bonding, the cat will want to be with their owner and will follow them from room to room to be close. The true Korat temperament is a mild cat with a very strong will. It is not afraid of anything. Despite its independent characteristics, a Korat is easy to train with love and firmness. Humans are very important to these cats, but Korats usually prefer their own kind and thrive best in homes without too many different breeds living together.

Fascinating Facts

The world's longest cat, named Verismo's Leonetti Reserve Red, measured 48 in. (121.9 cm) from nose to tip of tail on March 10, 2002. (Guinness Book of Records).

ABOVE

The Korat has a heart-shaped head and strikingly large eyes in relation to the size of its face.

Care

Feeding
Feed good-quality cat food. Korats are not prone to obesity and usually eat only what is necessary to maintain their weight.

Grooming
The Korat's short coat does not require special grooming, although they do enjoy soft brushing for the attention it brings from their human companion.

RUSSIAN BLUE

SIZE: Small to medium

COAT CARE: Low maintenance

DIET: Moderate maintenance

BODY SHAPE: Foreign/oriental

COLOR VARIATIONS: Even, bright blue throughout

LIFE EXPECTANCY: 16+ years

While little is known about the true origin of the Russian Blue, it is believed to be a natural breed with beginnings in the Archangel Isles in Northern Russia. Originally known as the Archangel Cat or Foreign Blue, it is said sailors brought it from Russia to England and Northern Europe in the 1860s. Rumor also has it that these cats were the descendants of the Royal Cat of the Russian Czars and were a favorite pet of Queen Victoria.

Origins

Unlike so many modern cat breeds, the Russian Blue is a naturally occurring breed. Some breeders crossbred it with the Siamese, but the Siamese traits have now been largely bred out. Russian Blues should not be confused with British Blues, which are not a distinct breed but are actually a British Shorthair with a blue coat, nor the Chartreux or Korat, which are two other naturally occurring breeds of blue cats.

Russian Blues were first shown at the Crystal Palace in London, England, as the Archangel Cat; the original Russian Blue competed in a class for all blue cats. In 1912 the Russian Blue was given a class of its own. Although they were imported to the United States as early as 1900, there is little recorded work with the breed in America until after the Second World War, when breeders combined the English bloodlines, with their plush, silvery coats, and the Scandinavian bloodlines, with their emerald-green eyes and flat profiles, to produce the Russian Blue we know today.

Distinctive characteristics include green eyes, white patches on the underside, and dark banding on the

BELOW

The Russian Blue is a naturally occurring breed believed to have originated in northern Russia.

tail. The Russian Blue holds championship status in all associations.

Characteristics

Head
The head is a smooth, medium wedge, neither long and tapering nor short and massive. The muzzle is blunt, without an exaggerated pinch or whisker break. The nose is medium in length.

Ears and Eyes
The ears are large and wide at the base. The tips are more pointed than rounded. They are set far apart, as much on the side as on the top of the head.

The eyes are set wide apart, the aperture rounded. They are a vivid green.

Body and Legs
The body is fine-boned, long, firm, and muscular. The cat is lithe and graceful in outline and carriage and is not tubular in appearance.

Coat
The coat is short, dense, fine, and plush. The double coat strands out from the body because of the density. It has a noticeable soft and silky feel.

Temperament

These gentle, affectionate cats will entertain themselves when left alone and be a contented companion when you return. They are quiet, clean cats that are loving and playful. Despite their shy nature, Russians are devoted to their loved ones. Sensitive to the mood of the household, Russians will "clown around" to calm down a crying baby or pat at your face to chase away the blues. They prefer consistent attention, making them ideal companions for the older cat lover.

Care

Feeding
Russians are not picky eaters. Breeders recommend a diet of dry, canned, and fresh food. Russians need access to fresh grass, especially if kept indoors.

ABOVE
This Russian Blue shows the characteristic pointed ears, vivid green eyes, and short, dense coat.

Grooming
Russians shed hair with the changing of seasons. To remove loose hair, wet your hands and stroke the cat. Russians can be gently groomed with a soft brush once or twice a week. It is important not to overbrush Russians because it can damage the coat.

ORIENTAL SHORTHAIR

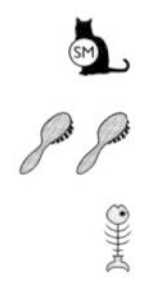

SIZE: Small to medium

COAT CARE: Moderate maintenance

DIET: Low maintenance

BODY SHAPE: Foreign/oriental

COLOR VARIATIONS: Solid, smoke, shaded, bicolor, parti-color, and tabby classes, allowing over 300 colors and patterns

LIFE EXPECTANCY: 12+ years

Oriental Shorthairs represent a diverse group of cats that have their foundation in the Siamese breed. The Oriental was created in the 1970s to establish a Siamese-type cat with a wider variety of colors and patterns not restricted to colorpoint patterns. However, some Oriental Shorthairs come in pointed varieties. These pointed cats cannot be shown in all associations; in some, pointed Orientals are shown as Siamese.

The Angora is the original name of the Oriental Longhair (European Javanese, Dutch Mandarin) British breed of cat. The Angora name was dropped from British Cat Registries in 2002 because of confusion with the Turkish Angora and also to align it with other Oriental Longhairs. The British Angora should not be confused with the Turkish Angora, one of the most ancient breeds of longhaired cats.

ABOVE

The Oriental Shorthair was accepted by the Cat Fanciers Association for competition in 1977.

Origins

The Siamese cat, both pointed and solid colors, was imported to Britain from Siam (Thailand) in the later half of the 1800s. The gene that causes the color to be restricted to the points is a recessive gene; therefore, the general population of the cats of Siam were mainly solid colored. When the cats from Siam were bred, the pointed cats were eventually registered as Siamese, while the others were referred to as "non blue-eyed Siamese" or Foreign Shorthair. Other breeds that were developed from the moggies of Siam include the Havana Brown and the Korat.

In 1920 the British Siamese Cat Club passed a ruling excluding all colors except the blue-eyed pointed cat that is the Siamese we know today. The Oriental Shorthair was developed to explore all the possibilities of color and pattern. It was not until 1977 that the Oriental Shorthair was accepted for competition into the CFA.

Fascinating Facts

The most expensive cat wedding was between two cats named Phat & Ploy. The marriage took place at a disco in Thailand. The cost paid by owner Jaratarcha was 410,979 thai bhat ($12,960).

BELOW
The Oriental Longhair has been known as British Angora, Javanese, Foreign Longhair, and Manadarin.

In 1985 the CFA recognized the bicolor Oriental Shorthair. The bicolor is any one of the accepted Oriental Shorthair color patterns with the addition of white to the stomach, face, and legs and/or paws. The Oriental has the personality to match its colorful coat.

Oriental Longhair

In 2002 the British Angora was renamed Oriental Longhair by British cat fancies. This avoided confusion with the Turkish Angora. This breed features a tubular, Siamese-style body but with a longer coat than its shorthaired cousin. The coat can also come in a variety of colors and patterns, including tabby, tortie, and solid. With no globally recognized naming convention, other cat fancies refer to this type as Javanese, Foreign Longhair, or Mandarin.

In 1995 Orientals added the bicolor pattern to their repertoire. With the clear white underside, legs, chest, and inverted V on the face, these distinctly marked members of the breed have already acquired a following of devoted fans.

Breeders dedicated to developing another major addition to the breed added the Oriental Longhair variety, paralleling their Balinese and Javanese counterparts. These beautiful felines carry the same graceful bodies with the addition of a silky long coat, goatee, and long plumed tail.

If an Oriental Longhair is bred to a Shorthaired Oriental or a Siamese, the kittens will all be shorthaired. However, if these kittens are reintroduced into a breeding program as adults, approximately half of their kittens will have long coats.

The Oriental Longhair is related to the CFA Balinese and Javanese and the TICA Oriental Longhair breeds in the United States. The Orientals hold championship status in all associations.

Characteristics

Head
The head is a long, tapering wedge with no break at the whiskers. The skull is flat, the muzzle fine and wedge-shaped. The chin and jaw are medium-sized, the nose is long and straight. There is no break.

Ears and Eyes
The ears are strikingly large, pointed, and wide at the base. They continue the lines of the wedge. The medium-sized eyes are almond shaped and slanted toward the nose in harmony with the lines of the wedge and ears. The eyes are uncrossed, and the accepted color is green, except for white Orientals that may have blue, green, or odd eyes.

Body and Legs
The body is long and svelte, a distinct combination of fine bones and firm muscles. The shoulders and hips continue in the same sleek lines of the tubular body. The tail is long and thin at the base, tapering to a fine point.

The legs are long and slim, with the hind legs higher than the front. The paws are small, dainty, and oval.

Coat
The Shorthair is short, fine-textured, glossy, or satinlike. It lies close to the body and gives the impression of being painted on. The Longhair is medium length, fine and silky, without a downy undercoat. The hair lies close to the body and is longest on the tail.

Temperament

Oriental Shorthairs are intelligent, social animals that bond closely to their owners. They are curious, friendly, demanding, and often vocal. Oriental Shorthairs have been compared to a greyhound in appearance, and some say they are doglike in personality, one reason being that they become so attached to people.

These cats eagerly greet you at the door, anxious to tell you all about the events of the day. If you're late, they will complain and tell you how worried they were. Hide a toy on top of the bookcase, and it will quickly be found. They have been known to open a drawer or empty out your purse to discover their favorite toy. It might be a

crumpled-up piece of paper that they can chase around the kitchen floor; it really doesn't matter. Give

them the attention and affection they desperately need, and they will do anything to please you. Ignore them, and they will be filled with despair. These elegant cats remain playful, spirited, and loyal long after kittenhood.

Oriental Longhairs equally love their owners and demand attention and affection. They enjoy riding high on their shoulders or curling up in their lap. Crawl into bed, and they will cuddle under a warm blanket.

Constant Friend

These extremely intelligent cats make very good companions for people who like constant companionship. Oriental Longhairs will follow you wherever you go. If you sit down, they will sit on your lap; if you eat, they will sit next to you on the chair without being demanding or begging for food; if you go to bed, they will sleep with you. With Oriental Longhairs, you will have a very attractive companion, faithful for a lifetime. Orientals can suffer from inherited heart problems, but they have long lives, contradicting their reputation as a delicate breed.

Care

Feeding

Feed the cat at least two meals a day, or leave food out. Feed 1 ounce of canned food daily or ⅓ ounce of dry food per pound of body weight.

Grooming

The Oriental Shorthair coat has some of the lowest level of grooming needs in the cat world. The cat and its coat will benefit from occasional brushing and grooming. Oriental Longhairs require little grooming because of their thin coat. Brushing their coat and combing it gently will remove dead hairs and will produce a silklike, glistening coat.

ABOVE

A chocolate-tipped tabby Oriental Shorthair, showing the short, fine coat that seems to be almost painted on.

HAVANA

SIZE: Medium

COAT CARE: Low maintenance

DIET: Low maintenance

BODY SHAPE: Foreign/oriental

COLOR VARIATIONS: Warm red-brown

LIFE EXPECTANCY: 12+ years

The beautiful turquoise-eyed Havana originated in Siam. The *Cat-Book Poems*, written in Ayudhya, Siam, describe these cats. They appear alongside the Siamese and silver-blue Korats. The people of Siam believed the burnished-brown felines protected them from evil. Solid brown cats were among the first to arrive in England from Siam in the late 1800s. It is believed that they were not all of the same genetic background but were a mix of Burmese, chocolate point Siamese, Tonkinese, and Havanas.

Origins

At a 1928 cat show, a special award to "the cat with the best chocolate-brown body" was given by the British Siamese Cat Club, but soon after the cat fell from grace. The Siamese Cat Club announced that they would no longer accept the breeding of any but blue-eyed Siamese. These solid brown cats with their turquoise-green eyes were banned from competition and disappeared from the cat fancy.

In the early 1950s a handful of British breeders studied chocolate-brown gene inheritance, subsequently starting a breeding program. They used Siamese, domestic Shorthairs, and Russian Blues. The aim was to produce a solid color in the range of the chocolate point Siamese instead of the sable of the Russian Blue. In 1952 the first solid chocolate kitten to be registered in England was born and became the foundation for the new breed. The kitten was produced by mating a seal point Siamese that carried the chocolate gene with a solid black cat also carrying the gene.

In 1958 the Governing Council of the Cat Fancy accepted the breed for championship competition under the name Chestnut Brown Foreign, later renaming it Havana. The first Havanas came to America in the mid-1950s. In 1959 the breed was finally recognized under the name Havana Brown. It was granted full championship status in 1964. They now hold championship status in all associations.

Characteristics

Head

The head is longer than it is wide, narrowing to a rounded muzzle with a pronounced break on both sides behind the whisker pads. The end of the muzzle appears almost square, with a distinct stop at the eyes and a well-developed chin.

ABOVE

The Havana originates from Siam and sports a chocolate-brown coat and intense, turquoise-green eyes. Elegant, intelligent, and considerably less vocal than their Siamese cousins, Havanas make affectionate pets.

Ears and Eyes

The ears are large, with rounded tips and cupped at the base. They are wide set but not flaring. They tilt forward, giving the cat an alert expression. The medium-sized, oval eyes are set wide apart. Color is any vivid, even shade of green, the deeper the better.

Body and Legs

The torso is medium in length, firm, and muscular. The general conformation is mid-range, between the thickset and svelte breeds. The cat stands relatively high on its legs. The tail is medium length, slender, and tapering at the end.

The legs are straight, with the hind legs slightly longer than the front. The paws are oval and compact.

Coat

The coat is short to medium in length. It is smooth and lustrous, an even shade of warm brown throughout.

Temperament

These beautiful cats are affectionate, intelligent, and unlike the Siamese, quiet. They are gentle and agreeable cats, adapting easily to different situations. In order to be happy and healthy, they rely on human interaction, so they will constantly be at your side. They often stretch out a paw and nudge their human companions, as if asking for affection. They enjoy games; fetch is a favorite. Havanas also enjoy carrying and hiding small objects, often bringing them to their beds.

Care

Feeding

The Havana is a hearty breed that has no special dietary needs. It is able to digest milk.

Grooming

The Havana is an easy-care cat. Brushing once a week to remove any loose hair is all that is needed.

Fascinating Facts

Cats use over 100 sounds to "talk."

BURMESE

BODY SHAPE: Foreign/oriental

SIZE: Medium

COLOR VARIATIONS: Brown, blue, chocolate, lilac, red, cream, seal tortie, blue tortie, chocolate tortie, lilac tortie

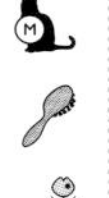

COAT CARE: Low maintenance

DIET: Low maintenance

LIFE EXPECTANCY: 15+ years

For the past 30 years, there has been controversy surrounding the appearance of the Burmese. The Burmese is now divided into subgroups: the American Burmese and the British Burmese. The British build is usually more Oriental, with a more triangular face, while the American Burmese is stockier and rounder in the body, head, eyes, and feet.

Most cat registries do not recognize a split between the two groups, but those that do formally refer to the type developed by British cat breeders as the European Burmese.

In 1936 the Cat Fanciers' Association granted recognition to the Burmese breed but withdrew it in 1947 because it was mixed with Siamese, and hybrid kittens were being sold as pure. The breed was recognized by the U.K. Governing Council of the Cat Fancy in 1952. After years of selective breeding, Burmese cats in America once again conformed to type and were recognized in 1953.

ABOVE

Burmese cats originated in Thailand and now fall into two main subgroups: the American and British varieties.

Origins

The earliest records of the Burmese come from Thailand (then Siam). The *Cat Book Poems* mention three types of cats that appear to represent known breeds: the Vichien Mat (Siamese), the Si-Sawat (Korat), and the Thong Daeng (Copper, now known as Burmese). These cats are believed to have remained in Thailand until it was invaded by the Burmese in the 1700s. Returning soldiers may have taken the temple cats back to Burma.

Fascinating Facts

Left-handedness is more common in cats than it is in human beings. One British study showed that 58 percent of cats favored one paw over the other, with twice as many favoring the left over the right.

In 1871 Harrison Weir organized a cat show at the Crystal Palace in London. A pair of Siamese, closely resembling modern American Burmese, were on display. They were Burmese in build but Siamese in marking. After this, cat fancy began with cat clubs and cat shows, but it took many years for breeds to be developed. The first Burmese in Britain, during the late 1800s, were considered Chocolate Siamese instead of their own separate breed, and this view persisted for many years.

This encouraged cross-breeding between Burmese and Siamese and attempts to breed Burmese to fit more closely to the Siamese build. The breed slowly died out in Great Britain.

Dr. Joseph Cressman Thompson imported Wong Mau, a brown female cat, into San Francisco in 1930. As had previously taken place, many breeders considered the cat to be a color variant of the Siamese, but Dr. Thompson considered the build to be different enough to be classified as a new breed. Without any similar type male, Wong Mau was bred with Tai Mei, a seal point Siamese from Thailand. Wong Mau was then bred with her son to produce dark brown kittens that were called Burmese cats.

Resurrection in Britain

In 1945 soldiers returning to Britain from Burma brought cats with them, and from 1949 to 1956 the British Burmese breeding program was being enriched with a variety of cats imported from America. By 1952 three generations had been produced, and official recognition was granted by the Governing Council of the Cat Fancy. Until the late 1960s the gene pool in Britain was very small. Most Burmese had descended from six initial imports and a Burmese/Chinese hybrid from Singapore. In 1969 more cats were brought over from Canada, and the gene pool was increased.

TOP RIGHT

Although Burmese cats were originally brown, other colors followed, including blue, lilac, and champagne.

In 1955 the first blue Burmese was born in England, and over the next 20 years red, cream, and tortoiseshell kittens followed. Champagne-colored cats, known as "chocolate" in the U.K., appeared in America, but breeding was hampered by the refusal of breed clubs to acknowledge that Burmese could be anything except brown.

In 1971 the first lilac kitten was born, being the latest solid color introduced in Burmese. During the 1970s brown, chocolate (champagne), blue, and lilac tortoiseshell cats were developed in England, but the Cat Fanciers' Association in America still does not accept them. Cinnamon, fawn, caramel, and apricot Burmese were developed in New Zealand from a breeding program started by geneticist Dr. Rod Hitchmough. The first cinnamon Burmese was Arsenios Cinnamon Dream Boy. From the 1950s on, countries in the Commonwealth and

ABOVE
Burmese cats have a tapered head, large eyes, a short, fine coat, muscular body, and slender legs.

Europe started importing Burmese cats from Britain, resulting in most countries basing their Standard of Points on the British model and not on the American one.

Characteristics

Head

The top of the head is slightly rounded, with good breadth between the ears. The cheekbones are wide, tapering to a short, blunt wedge. In profile, the head should show good depth between the top of the skull and the lower jaw. The brow should be slightly rounded. There should be a distinct nose break followed by a straight nose ending. The tip of the nose is on the same vertical plane as the chin. The lower jaw should show good depth of chin.

Ears and Eyes

The medium-sized ears are set far apart. They are broad at the base, with slightly rounded tips and a slightly forward tilt. The eyes are large and lustrous and set wide apart. The top line of the eyes shows a straight, Oriental slant toward the nose. Colors for all varieties: any shade of yellow, from chartreuse to amber, with golden yellow preferred.

Body and Legs

The body is medium in length and size. It is hard and muscular and heavier than it appears. The chest is strong and rounded; the back is straight from shoulder to rump. The tail is medium length, not thick at the base. It tapers slightly to a rounded tip.

The legs are slender and in proportion to the body, with paws that are small and oval.

Coat

The short, fine coat lies close to the body. It is satinlike in texture and very glossy. Originally, Burmese cats were exclusively brown, but years of selective breeding have produced a wide variety of colors. Different

associations have different rules about which count as Burmese.

Temperament

The Burmese cat is friendly and affectionate, needing attention from their human companions to be happy when kept in a family environment. They are extremely playful and can be taught to fetch pieces of paper in the same way a dog fetches a stick. They are good with children and make wonderful family pets. They are also sensitive to their owner's feelings. If the owner is going to be out all day, it is usually a good idea to have two Burmese, as they can quickly become bored and lonely. They are very demanding and will follow you around, crying for attention. If you stop, they will climb up your leg, begging to be picked up and cuddled. Burmese are very vocal cats but have softer, sweeter voices than the Siamese. They will often greet you when you return home or speak to you when they want something. Burmese maintain kitten interests and energy throughout their adulthood and are very athletic. The curiosity and friendliness of the Burmese can sometimes lead them to wander off into neighbors' cars or delivery vans, and they can disappear.

BELOW

Burmese cats crave company, and it is a good idea to have more than one if they are likely to be left alone all day.

Care

Feeding

Burmese cats rarely overeat, and over time it will become obvious how much your cat requires every day. Many Burmese demand to be fed dry food.

Grooming

Burmese cats do not require a lot of grooming because they take care of this themselves. However, they do enjoy the attention that comes with brushing.

BOMBAY

SIZE: Medium

COAT CARE: Low maintenance

DIET: Moderate maintenance

BODY SHAPE: Foreign/oriental

COLOR VARIATIONS: Black to the roots

LIFE EXPECTANCY: 12+ years

While many recognized breeds have been around for years or are the result of naturally occurring genetic mutations, the Bombay is an outcome of years of selective breeding in an effort to develop a "Parlor Panther." With its muscular body and shiny black coat, the Bombay resembles the black leopard of India. However, since it is the descendant of two domestic cat breeds, it does not have the personality of a panther. In fact this breed is known for being very sociable and extremely intelligent.

Origins

Nikki Horner of Shawnee Cattery in Louisville, Kentucky, deliberately bred an American Shorthair with a Sable Burmese in order to create a domesticated cat that resembled a wild panther. Her first attempts were disappointing; however, in 1958, when working with different breeding stock, she began to get the results that she was looking for: a cat with good muscular development and a very short, close-lying, black coat. The offspring of this breeding did resemble the black leopard of India. The American breed—the Bombay—was created. The name came from the Indian city of Bombay (now Mumbai). The Bombay holds championship status in all associations.

Characteristics

Head

The head is nicely rounded, with no sharp angles. The face is full, with breadth between the eyes, blending gently into a rounded, well-developed muzzle. In profile, a moderate stop is visible; no pugged or snubbed look. The chin is firm.

Ears and Eyes

The medium ears are set far apart and tilted slightly forward. They are broad at the base, with slightly rounded tips. The eyes are

BELOW

The Bombay cat, with its jet-black coat and lithe body, has been carefully bred to resemble the panther.

set far apart, with rounded aperture. Eye color ranges from gold to copper; however, cats that do not develop the copper eye color or have eye color that fades as they age are automatically disqualified from competition.

Body and Legs
The medium-sized body is compact, neither muscular nor rangy. The cat is of a heavy weight for its size. The tail is straight and medium length. The legs are in proportion to the body and tail. The paws are round.

Coat
The fine, short coat is satinlike in texture. It is close lying.

Temperament

The Bombay also shares many of the behavioral characteristics of the Burmese. They are adaptable to living in apartments and are generally calm. This cat will often accept dogs in the household more quickly than it will adapt to other cats, and it usually wants to be the dominant cat in the household.

They are intelligent, actively seek interaction with humans, and love to play games. Many fetch and do tricks. Some have been successfully leash-trained. Like Burmese, Bombays adore the heat and like to sleep under the covers.

They have a distinctive voice but not as harsh as the Siamese. Some are talkative, but others rarely vocalize. Bombays reach sexual maturity relatively quickly, so owners should plan on spaying females and neutering males between six and nine months of age. A Bombay male may not reach his full muscular development until he is almost two years old. An adult Bombay male will typically weigh between 8 –11 lbs (3.6–5.6 kg); females between 6–9 lbs (2.7–4 kg).

Care

Feeding
Bombays generally have large appetites. While most can freely feed without becoming overweight, some owners find that they must ration the food or switch to a low-calorie diet.

Grooming
The tight, short coat sheds very little and requires practically no maintenance. The Bombay is completely capable of grooming itself, but rubbing it with the palm of your hand or a rubber brush is always a welcome activity. There is very little seasonal variation in the coat.

RIGHT
Bombays are intelligent cats and can be trained to perform tricks but tend to dominate over other animals.

TONKINESE

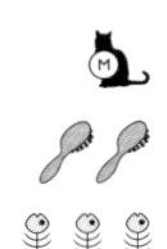

SIZE: Medium

COAT CARE: Moderate maintenance

DIET: High maintenance

BODY SHAPE: Neither cobby nor svelte; foreign/oriental

COLOR VARIATIONS: Platinum, champagne, natural, blue; pointed, mink, solid

LIFE EXPECTANCY: 15+ years

Tonkinese are known as the cats with the sense of humor, convinced humans were put on earth to love and serve them. They charmed their way through seven years and four presentations to the Cat Fanciers' Association in pursuit of championship status, which they achieved in 1984. The crossbreeding combines the best features of the Burmese and Siamese, carrying the coat patterns and the sparkling gold-green eyes of the Burmese or the pointed patterns and twinkling blue eyes of the Siamese.

Origins

The first known Tonkinese was Wong Mau, who was brought to the United States in 1930 from Rangoon, Burma. Wong Mau was bred with a Siamese and was the only known cat of her kind. From the 1950s to 1970s some breeders started to crossbreed Siamese and Burmese.

While still considered a new breed, the Tonkinese is not a hybrid as some people mistakenly assume. Being of the same bloodlines as Siamese and Burmese breeds, today's Tonkinese are believed to be a reconstruction of the chocolate Siamese cat imported to England in the early 1900s. It was recognized in 1974 by the Canadian Cat Association and in 1978 by the CFA. Popular in the United States, the Tonkinese remains rare in Europe.

Characteristics

Head

The head is a modified wedge, with high, gently planed cheekbones. The muzzle is blunt, with a slight whisker break, gently curved and following the line of the wedge. There is a slight stop at eye level. In profile, the tip of the chin is in line with the tip of the nose in the same vertical plane. There is a soft rise from the tip of the nose to the stop, a gentle contour with a slight rise from the nose stop to the forehead, and a slight convex curve to the forehead.

Ears and Eyes

The ears are medium-sized, alert, with oval tips and broad at the base. They are set as much on the side of the head as on top. Hair on

RIGHT
Tonkinese cats originated in Burma in the 1930s and combine features of Burmese and Siamese cats.

the ears is very short and close lying so that leather may show.

The eyes, proportionate in size to the face, are almond-shaped and slanted along the cheekbones. The eye color is aqua, which is a definitive characteristic of the breed.

Body and Legs
The medium-length torso should demonstrate well-developed muscular strength without coarseness. Body and proportion are more important than size. The abdomen should be taut, well muscled, and firm.

The legs and feet are firm, slim, and proportionate in length and bone to the body. The hind legs are slightly longer than the front, with paws more oval than round. There are five toes in front and four behind.

Coat
A medium-short coat, close-lying, fine with a lustrous sheen, is ideal. The mature cat should be a rich, even, unmarked color, with almost unnoticeable shading but moving to a slightly lighter hue on the underparts. Point color—mask, ears, feet, and tail should all be densely marked but gently merging into the body color. Allowance is made for slight barring in young cats.

Temperament

The colorful personality of the Tonkinese makes it an ideal companion. Highly intelligent, with an incredible memory and strongly developed senses, the stubborn Tonkinese can be difficult to train.

Care

Caring for a Tonkinese is as simple as feeding a well-balanced diet, clipping nails weekly, grooming with a rubber brush, and visits to the vet for checkups and shots. As these are indoor only cats, the home must be cat-proofed. A cat tree and a variety of toys will keep your Tonk busy when you want to do something else besides play with him.

BELOW
The beautiful aqua color of the Tonkinese cat's eyes is a defining characteristic of the breed.

BURMILLA

SIZE: Medium

COAT CARE: Low maintenance

DIET: Moderate maintenance

BODY SHAPE: Foreign/oriental

COLOR VARIATIONS: Black, blue, brown, chocolate, and lilac

LIFE EXPECTANCY: 15+ years

The Burmilla was created accidentally in the U.K. A Chinchilla Persian and a lilac Burmese were in different rooms awaiting a same-breed partner. The cleaner left the door open accidentally, and the result was four kittens born in 1981. They were so adorable that a new breed was created.

Origins

The Burmilla Cat Club was founded on January 21, 1984. In GCCF, the Burmilla is considered part of the Asian cat breed. It is accepted in FIFe as the Burmilla. However, there is not international acceptance for this breed.

Characteristics

Head

Gently rounded top of head; medium width between ears; wide at eyebrow level and jaw hinge, tapering to a short, blunt wedge. The profile shows a gentle nose break. Tip of nose and chin should be in line. Chin is firm, with good depth.

Ears and Eyes

Medium to large, broad at base with slightly rounded tips. Ear set with slight forward tilt in profile. Eye shape is large; placed well apart at slight oblique setting; curved upper, line angled toward the nose, with a fuller curved lower line. Eye color luminous, any shade of green.

Body, Legs, and Coat

Rounded chest, medium width; straight back. Legs are slender, with strong bones; hind legs slightly longer than forelegs. Tail is medium to long, with a medium thickness at base, tapering slightly to rounded tip. Paws neat and oval. There are three coat types: the standard coat is the shorthair, and then there are longhair and plush.

LEFT

The affectionate Burmilla is a relatively new breed created in the 1980s and is not internationally recognized.

Temperament and Care

The Burmilla adores its owner and displays many kittenlike characteristics. They are sociable, playful, affectionate, and good with children and animals.

Feed your Burmilla a balanced diet of raw meat, canned food, and dry food. Brush their coat once a week.

SINGAPURA

BODY SHAPE: Foreign/oriental

COLOR VARIATIONS: Sepia agouti

LIFE EXPECTANCY: 9+ years

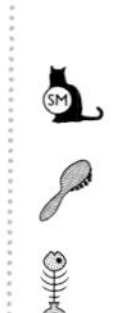

SIZE: Small to medium

COAT CARE: Low maintenance

DIET: Low maintenance

The Singapura is believed to have existed for approximately 300 years. It is thought they are descendents from ships' cats that arrived in Singapore. Once ashore, they bred with the local, feral cats. The Singapura has the look of an Abyssinian or an Asian but is much smaller. They are a tough, sturdy breed, perhaps because of their roots.

Origins

The Singapura is officially the world's smallest cat, though many individuals may reach the size of a Burmese. The modern Singapura stems from four cats brought back to America from Singapore in 1975 by Tommy Meadow. Others suspect that the breed may have originated from a cross between Burmese and Abyssinians. The first Singapura was imported into Britain in 1989, and they are now rapidly increasing in popularity as both show cats and pets.

Characteristics

Head
Rounded skull; whisker break; medium short, broad muzzle with blunt nose; very slight stop far below eye level; well-developed chin.

Ears and Eyes
Large, slightly pointed; wide open at base; medium set. Eyes large, almond shaped; showing slant. Colors: hazel, green, yellow.

Body, Legs, and Coat
Small to medium body that is stocky and muscular. Tail is slender but not "whippy" and has a blunt tip. Legs heavy and muscled at body; tapers to small, oval feet. The coat is fine, very short, and close to the body.

LEFT

A sepia agouti Singapura cat, showing the breed's large, almond-shaped eyes and very short, fine coat.

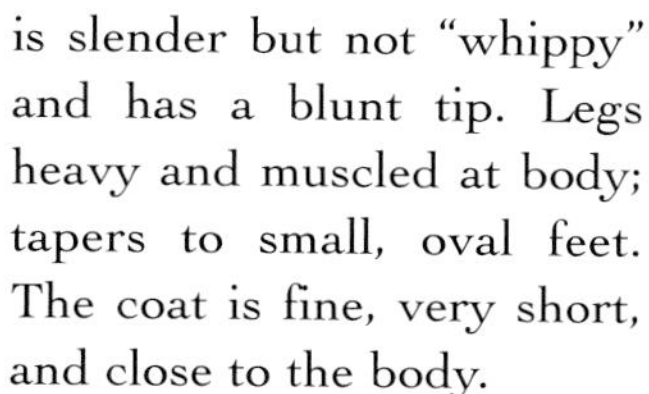

Temperament and Care

The Singapura craves attention. They dislike cold and damp and love living indoors in the warmth. They are naturally a friendly cat and are very curious, which makes them high-risk outdoor cats. The Singapura is an active cat and needs high-quality cat food. Its short, dense, and glossy coat does not require a lot of care, but they enjoy being groomed.

SNOWSHOE

SIZE: Medium

COAT CARE: Low maintenance

DIET: Low maintenance

BODY SHAPE: Foreign/oriental

COLOR VARIATIONS: Blue point, seal point

LIFE EXPECTANCY: 9+ years

LEFT
The questioning tail of this Seal and White Point Snowshoe indicates the breed's inquisitive nature.

The Snowshoe is a rare breed and combines the stocky, robust appearance of the American Shorthair with the length of the Siamese. It is a hybrid cat that originated as a random variable from Siamese parents.

Origins

The origin can be traced back to 1960, when Dorothy Hinds Daugherty from Philadelphia, Pennsylvania, found three kittens in a litter of Siamese, each with four white feet. She developed the first Snowshoe by crossing her Siamese with a bicolor American Shorthair. Continued breeding produced the "V" face of the current Snowshoe. Championship status in CFF, AACE, ACFA, ACA, NCFA, and UFO.

Characteristics

Head
Broad, modified wedge; slight stop at bridge of nose creating two distinct planes; muzzle, good length, with high cheekbones.

Ears and Eyes
Medium to medium large ears in proportion to body; broad base with slightly rounded tips. The eyes are oval, slanted toward base of ears, and are bright blue.

Body and Legs
The body should be long and firm; boning and musculature medium; powerful but not bulky. Tail is medium at base, slightly tapering to end. Legs are a good length in proportion to body. Boning, medium; paws, medium.

Coat
Short to medium short; no noticeable undercoat; smooth and close lying; seasonal changes. All Snowshoe kittens are born white, and the colors and markings become visible within one to three weeks. Every Snowshoe will have a unique pattern.

Temperament and Care

An amiable and loving cat, the Snowshoe is inquisitive and active. Although not as vocal as a Siamese, the Snowshoe is quite the talker but with a softer, more melodic voice. As it is an active cat, it is not prone to obesity, so freely feeding is acceptable. The Snowshoe requires minimal grooming.

Fascinating Facts

A cat cannot see directly under its nose. This is why the cat cannot seem to find crumbs on the floor.

OJOS AZULES

BODY SHAPE: Foreign/oriental

COLOR VARIATIONS: All colors

LIFE EXPECTANCY: 10+ years

SIZE: Medium

COAT CARE: Low maintenance

DIET: Low maintenance

Ojos Azules are known for their deep blue eyes. Development of the controversial breed is still experimental, so it is not widely recognized.

Origins and Characteristics
This new and very rare breed has descended from a tortie female discovered in New Mexico in 1984. She had dark blue eyes, normally found only in white or colorpoint cats. The breed's Spanish name means "blue eyes."

Ojos Azules is a sweet-looking cat of medium build, with a short, fine coat that comes in all colors. The tail is proportionate to the body, and an indicator of the Ojos gene is a flattened tail tip. Hind legs are slightly longer than forelegs. The head is an equilateral triangle, with a slightly rounded forehead. The blue eyes are round, and the ears are slightly rounded on the tips.

Temperament and Care
Ojos Azules is an active, friendly, and affectionate cat. It is not prone to obesity, so it can be freely fed, and it is very easy to groom.

LEFT

An Ojos Azules cat, with the distinctive blue eyes that give this new and rare breed its name.

MUNCHKIN

BODY SHAPE: Semi-foreign

COLOR VARIATIONS: All colors; white locket

LIFE EXPECTANCY: 9+ years

SIZE: Small to medium

COAT CARE: Moderate maintenance

DIET: Moderate maintenance

The Munchkin is a relatively new breed created by a mutation that causes achondroplasia, resulting in cats with abnormally short legs.

Origins and Characteristics
The breed originated in North American in 1983, when a very short-legged, pregnant cat was found. Sometimes referred to as the feline version of the Dachshund. New Breed status in TICA.

Its head is an equilateral triangle, with rounded corners and triangular shaped ears. Eyes are walnut shaped in vivid colors. The Munchkin body is broad and medium length, with a medium-thick, tapered tail. Legs are short, with rounded paws. The shorthair's coat is dense and luxurious. Longhair is semi-long with a ruff longer than body hair.

Temperament and Care
The Munchkin is gentle, loving, and playful, with a kittenlike personality. Munchkins are prone to obesity, so control feeding. Weekly brushing is needed.

SPHYNX

SIZE: Medium

COAT CARE: High maintenance

DIET: Low maintenance

BODY SHAPE: Foreign; hairless

COLOR VARIATIONS: All colors

LIFE EXPECTANCY: 15+ years

LEFT

While Sphynxes are strong and healthy cats, they can be prone to sunburn, and their ears need to be cleaned regularly.

The Sphynx is one of the most extraordinary cats to occur naturally—it appears completely hairless. It is a robust breed with few health or genetic problems, but as pale-skinned cats they are susceptible to sunburns and must be protected from the sun and extremes of cold.

Origins

In 1966 a domestic cat in Toronto, Canada, gave birth to a hairless kitten that was discovered to be a natural mutation. Breeders in Europe and North America have bred the Sphynx to normal coated cats and then back to hairless for more than 30 years. It holds championship status in TICA, ACA, ACFA, AACE, UFO, NCFA, and CCA.

Characteristics

Head
Medium-sized, moderate wedge with rounded contours; flat head; prominent cheekbones, and a strong, rounded muzzle with distinct whisker break.

Ears and Eyes
Very large ears that are broad at base; open, set upright, interior hairless. Eyes are large and a rounded oval shape. Color: vivid blue; green and hazel acceptable.

Body and Legs
Medium in size and length; chest broad; abdomen well rounded; hard and muscular, not delicate. Tail is whippy, tapering from body to tip. Legs are in proportion to the body. Hind legs slightly longer than front. Paws are oval, with long toes.

Coat
Appears hairless; texture is chamoislike. May have fine down; may have puff of hair on tail tip. Whiskers, thin.

Temperament and Care

These cats are agile, playful, inquisitive, and highly intelligent. They learn how to open up cupboards and fetch toys. They are outgoing and affectionate. Often described as monkeylike.

They are not prone to obesity and limit their own dietary requirements. The Sphynx must be bathed on a regular basis to remove oil from the skin. As the ears lack hairs to filter out dust and dirt, they need to be cleaned weekly.

DONSKOY

BODY SHAPE: Hairless

COLOR VARIATIONS: All colors

LIFE EXPECTANCY: 12+ years

SIZE: Medium

COAT CARE: Moderate maintenance

DIET: Low maintenance

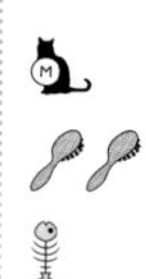

Unlike most kittens, the Donskoy can be born with its eyes open, while others will open their eyes within the first three days of life.

Origins

In 1987 a female brush-coated kitten was found in a small town in Russia. She was a blue tortie named Varya and the foundation female of the two Russian Hairless breeds known as the Donskoy/Don Sphynx/Don Hairless and the Petersburg Sphynx/Peterbald. At the time it was believed that Varya was sick, as she appeared to have lost most of her coat. Despite otherwise good health, Varya continued losing her hair, and eventually it became obvious that the loss was the result of a new, genetic, hairless gene.

Characteristics

Head

Short wedge, almost V-shaped, with a flat face and sharp features. Muzzle slightly rounded, with a short break. Profile has a definite curve to medium-length, straight nose. Chin and jaw are strong and well developed.

Ears and Eyes

Very large ears; broad at the base; open and set upright. Almond-shaped eyes have numerous vertical wrinkles spreading in horizontal lines above them. Color immaterial.

Body, Legs, and Coat

Compact bodies, strong boning. Back level; broad rump. Skin wrinkled on head, neck, and under the legs. Tail is long, straight, and strong. Legs are medium-strong. Hind legs are longer than forelegs. Front paws, oval with long toes and opposable thumbs. Back paws, slim with long webbed toes. Kittens' muzzle may have short thin hair, longer on cheeks and at the base of ears. Because of their lack of hair, they are good pets for those allergic to cat hair.

Temperament and Care

Donskoys are softhearted, friendly, and highly intelligent. Outgoing personality; loves attention. Many enjoy playing with and being in the water. Soft-voiced. Donskoys need a well-balanced, commercial diet. They need to be bathed regularly to remove oily buildup and have ears cleaned weekly.

ABOVE

Donskoy cats originated in Russia and are bred to be hairless, although there are many different colors.

PETERBALD

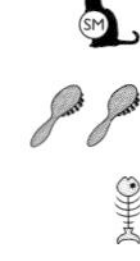

SIZE: Small to medium

COAT CARE: Moderate maintenance

DIET: Low maintenance

BODY SHAPE: Hairless

COLOR VARIATIONS: All colors

LIFE EXPECTANCY: 10+ years

The Peterbald is the newest hairless breed and originates from Russia.

Origins and Characteristics

Peterbalds are descended from the Russian Don Hairless breed, with outcrosses to Oriental and Siamese cats. They are accepted under New Breed and Color status in TICA. They are graceful, muscular, foreign-bodied cats, with long legs and fine to medium boning, with a long, whippy tail and oval feet. The Peterbald has a wedge-shaped head, with very large ears that are broad at the base and open and set upright.

Fascinating Facts

Cats have AB blood groups, just like people.

Eye color generally conforms to coat (skin) color. The coat comes in a wide range of colors and patterns, including colorpoint.

Temperament and Care

Peterbalds make lively, intelligent companions. They should be fed a well-balanced, commercial diet. Needs regular bathing to remove oil. Ears should be cleaned weekly.

PIXIEBOB

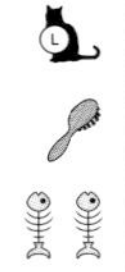

SIZE: Large

COAT CARE: Low maintenance

DIET: Moderate maintenance

BODY SHAPE: Stocky

COLOR VARIATIONS: Brown spotted tabby

LIFE EXPECTANCY: 12+ years

Legend has it that the Pixiebob originated from mating between wild bobcats and domestic cats.

Origins and Characteristics

Carol Ann Brewer founded the Pixiebob breed in 1985. It originates from a polydactyl male, with a short tail and spotted coat, and another male, with a bobcat-like tail. Registered as a domestic by TICA.

The head is gently rounded, with a blunt muzzle. Nose is wide; whisker break; deep chin. Pixiebobs have medium to large cupped ears that are deep at the base, with lynx tufting. Eyes are wild; soft triangle; gold, brown, light green. The body is substantial, with large boning and a primordial pouch. Tail, at least two inches. Long legs, heavy boning. Paws rounded; fleshy toes. The coat is short and woolly; stomach hair longer. Agouti hair has several color bands.

Temperament and Care

Pixiebobs are doglike; trainable and devoted. A low maintenance cat that needs little grooming, the Pixiebob prefers a raw diet.

CALIFORNIA SPANGLED

BODY SHAPE: Stocky

COLOR VARIATIONS: Eight classic varieties: black, brown, blue, bronze, charcoal, red, gold, and silver

LIFE EXPECTANCY: 12+ years

SIZE: Medium

COAT CARE: Moderate maintenance

DIET: Low maintenance

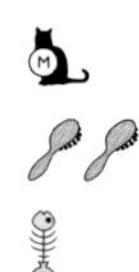

The California Spangled is claimed to be the world's rarest cat. Californian Paul Casey bred a domestic cat resembling a small leopard, to highlight the importance of preserving the leopard. The Snow Leopard has a white coat, with black markings and blue eyes.

Origins

Casey began a long breeding and selection program in the 1970s. He crossed Siamese, British Shorthairs, American Shorthairs, Manx, Abyssinians, and a line of Egyptian and Asian street cats. It took eleven generations before the type was fixed. The breed was formally introduced in 1986 and has New Breed and Color status in ACA and TICA.

ABOVE

A gold California Spangled cat, bred to resemble the leopard and believed to be the world's rarest breed.

Characteristics

Head, Ears, and Eyes

Sculpted; medium length and width; slightly domed forehead. Slight nose break; prominent cheekbones; well-developed muzzle; strong chin and powerful jaws.

Ear base and height approximately equal; rounded tip; high and back from face. Almond-shaped eyes, slight slant, and far apart. Color: gold to brown, appropriate to coat color; Snow Leopard, blue.

Body, Legs, and Coat

Muscular, moderately long; solid thighs; strong bone structure. Well-developed musculature. Moderately long tail; thickness at base equal to tip; dark rings and a dark tip on ground color. Well clad. Legs long and strong. Hind legs form almost 90 degrees. Feet, medium.

Short coat, except longer on stomach and tail. Pattern: spotted tabby. Spots are round, square, or triangular in shape and must be well defined and separate. Stripes on the head, throat, legs, and tail. Colors, eight varieties.

Temperament and Care

Lively, energetic, and extremely active but not aggressive. Though wild in appearance, the cat is social, affectionate, and gentle. It has strong hunting instincts and is easily intrigued by anything that moves. Feed the California Spangled good-quality cat food and brush them weekly.

Fascinating Facts

Whiskers also appear on the backs of the forelegs.

BENGAL

SIZE: Medium

COAT CARE: Moderate maintenance

DIET: Low maintenance

BODY SHAPE: Hybrid

COLOR VARIATIONS: Brown tabby; seal lynx point; seal sepia tabby/seal mink tabby

LIFE EXPECTANCY: 12+ years

The Bengal is a relatively new hybrid breed developed to have a gentle and friendly temperament, while displaying the markings and body structure of the wild Asian Leopard cat.

ABOVE

Despite being originally bred from the Asian Leopard, Bengal cats make affectionate and child-friendly pets.

Origins

Jean Sudgen from the U.S. is credited with this breed. In 1963 Sudgen crossed a black, shorthaired domestic with a female Asian Leopard cat. Offspring were produced, proving that a second generation was possible. She carried further crossing, and in 1984 the Bengal cat was recognized by TICA. The Bengal has championship status in TICA, CCA, UFO, and TCA.

Characteristics

Head, Ears, and Eyes
Broad, modified wedge, with rounded contours. Full muzzle, with prominent whisker pads, high cheekbones, and a wide, large nose. Ears are medium small, with a wide base and rounded tips. Eyes are oval, large, and wide apart. Color, blue or aqua.

Body, Legs, and Coat
Long but not oriental or foreign; boning robust; very muscular. The tail is thick, tapered at the end, with a rounded tip. Legs are medium; slightly longer in back; boning large and very muscular. Paws large and round. Coat length short to medium; thick texture; luxurious and usually soft.

Temperament and Care

The Bengals are mischievous and rowdy. They are also vocal, intelligent, and love to play with water. They are affectionate and mix well with children and other animals. Buyers should ask how many generations removed Bengal kittens are from wild blood; the best companion cats are at least four generations removed. Choose a high-quality food, and the Bengal's smooth, rich coat needs to be brushed only once a week.

SERENGETI

BODY SHAPE: Hybrid

COLOR VARIATIONS: Brown spotted, silver spotted, black smoke, and solid black

LIFE EXPECTANCY: 10+ years

SIZE: Medium

COAT CARE: Moderate maintenance

DIET: Low maintenance

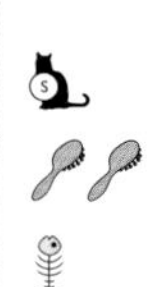

The Serengeti is a cross between the Bengal and an Oriental cat.

Origins and Charactersitics
This breed is still under development in the U.K. and U.S. It was created by Karen Sausman in California in 1994, and it is accepted in TICA. It has a broad head with a modified wedge, with a full muzzle, high cheekbones, and a wide nose. Its ears are large, with black backs and "eye spot." Eyes are expressive; gold to amber; green acceptable. This sturdy cat has long, muscular legs, with a clear yellow to gold coat; pattern distinct, widely spaced black spots; short, thick, and moderately soft.

Temperament and Care
The Serengeti is self-assured, friendly, active, and playful. Give it a good-quality cat food, high in meat. It needs to be brushed once a week.

LEFT
The Serengeti, combining traits from Bengal and Oriental cats, is a breed that is still being developed.

TOYGER

BODY SHAPE: Hybrid

COLOR VARIATIONS: Brown mackerel tabby

LIFE EXPECTANCY: 12+ years

SIZE: Medium to large

COAT CARE: Low maintenance

DIET: Low maintenance

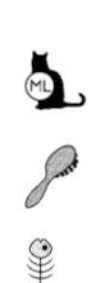

The Toyger, "toy tiger," is a domestic cat that looks like a miniature tiger.

Origins and Characteristics
In 1980 breeder Judy Sudgen noticed distinctive head markings in two of her cats, and by 1995 she had created the distinctive Toyger. It has a medium-sized oval head with rounded, muscular contours; a well-defined muzzle with a long, broad nose. The ears are small and rounded and wide-set to the back of the head. The eyes are medium, almond-shaped, and deep in color.

Its body is long, muscular; rounded contours; chest broad. Tail is long and slim. Legs are equal in length front and back; boning very large. Paws are well knuckled; large but neat. It has a short, thick, and luxurious coat; must be at least slightly glittered.

Temperament and Care
Intelligent, trainable, dependent; enjoys companionship but not demanding. Feed with a good-quality pet food, and brush weekly.

CHEETOH

SIZE: Large

COAT CARE: Low maintenance

DIET: Moderate maintenance

BODY SHAPE: Hybrid

COLOR VARIATIONS: Black/brown spotted sienna, black/brown spotted gold, black spotted smoke, black spotted silver, lynx pointed gold spotted snow, brown spotted/cinnamon

LIFE EXPECTANCY: 12+ years

The Cheetoh has a distinctive, low-shouldered, wildcat walk.

Origins and Characteristics

The Cheetoh is a hybrid, blending the Ocicat and Bengal cats with the Asian Leopard cat. The breed was recognized by the UFO in 2004. It is muscular, athletic, and graceful. The spotted appearance, with the large eyes and ears, enhances this wild look. Its sleek coat is short and thick, yet soft and velvety, similar to the fur of the Jungle Cats.

RIGHT

The Cheetoh is a large, elegant cat, with a sleek, velvety coat reminiscent of its wild ancestors.

Temperament and Care

Although they look fierce, Cheetohs are affectionate, loving cats. They are highly intelligent, curious, and active. Cheetohs are fed quality dry pet foods and raw meat. Minimum grooming required.

SAFARI

SIZE: Large

COAT CARE: Moderate maintenance

DIET: Moderate maintenance

BODY SHAPE: Hybrid

COLOR VARIATIONS: Bronze, silver, and black smoke

LIFE EXPECTANCY: 14+ years

The Safari cat is the "Rolls Royce" of the exotic hybrids.

Origins and Characteristics

The Safari is the product of breeding a Geoffroy's cat to a domestic. The Geoffroy's cat carries 36 chromosomes; the domestic carries 38. Because of this genetic difference, these cats are difficult to produce, so they are extremely rare. Their coats vary from black to silver-gray to orange. The Safari cat is wild looking and is relatively large for a domestic.

Temperament and Care

The Safari is intelligent and the most affectionate of all the hybrid cats. Safaris are known for their gentle temperaments, as well as for being very active. They love to climb and jump up to high places in the home. Feed them a good quality cat food with some raw meat. Regular grooming is needed, as coats can become matted.

CHAUSIE

BODY SHAPE: Hybrid

COLOR VARIATIONS: Black, brown ticked tabby, and silver tipped colors

LIFE EXPECTANCY: 14+ years

SIZE: Large

COAT CARE: Low maintenance

DIET: Moderate maintenance

This large, graceful cat is a domestic and Jungle Cat hybrid.

Origins and Characteristics
The Chausie was first bred in the late 1960s and early 1970s, and it was granted Advanced New Breed status in TICA in 2003. Chausies should be long and lean, with sufficient boning without making them seem chunky. Gold or yellow eye color preferred; hazel to light green allowed. Coat has enough length to accommodate at least two bands of flecking.

Temperament and Care
Chausie is a sweet-natured cat, extremely active, intelligent, and curious. They need plenty of playtime and toys to keep their minds and paws busy or they can become destructive. Chausies may be gluten-intolerant and have trouble digesting commercial cat food. The short coat requires an occasional bath and brushing.

RIGHT

A Chausie cat displaying this breed's highly active, curious, intelligent, and playful nature.

SAVANNAH

BODY SHAPE: Hybrid

COLOR VARIATIONS: Black, brown spotted tabby, silver spotted tabby, and black smoke

LIFE EXPECTANCY: 14+ years

SIZE: Large

COAT CARE: Low maintenance

DIET: Moderate maintenance

The Savannah is a cross between a Serval and a domestic cat.

Origins and Characteristics
Patrick Kelley and Joyce Sroufe developed the Savannah breed. Most breeders use a Bengal cat for the domestic parentage. The Savannah's wild look, color markings, and erect ears come from the Serval. Savannahs are long and leggy. The short tail has black rings, with a solid black tip. The eyes are usually green. Black, "tear-streak" markings run cheetahlike, from the corner of the eyes down the sides of the nose.

Temperament and Care
Savannahs have been described as friendly, assertive, active, playful, and good with dogs and children. They often greet people with head butts or a sudden pounce. Feed them premium cat foods and a partial raw food diet. They are shorthaired, so they do not require much grooming.

Longhair Cats

There is no questioning the beauty of a longhaired cat. If you are willing to devote the time necessary to groom these exceptional animals, you will gain years of pleasure from these living works of art. Originally the coat length and texture of longhair cats served as protection from the elements and provided camouflage, enabling a cat to easily blend into its environment. This section of the book will take you through the longhair cats, introducing you to the breeds and their individual characteristics, behavior, and care.

Hybrid Origins

In the 1800s Peter Simon Pallas, a German naturalist, suggested that Angora and Persian cats had descended from *Felis manul*, a cat that he discovered and named. The Pallas cat, also known as a Manul, is a small wildcat of South America. It is around the size of a large domestic cat and is covered with long, coarse fur. There is anecdotal evidence that Pallas cats can interbreed with domestic cats to produce offspring; however, to introduce the gene, the hybrid cat would have to be fertile and bred back to domestic cats.

In 1907 Reginald Pocock, while working as a research volunteer at the British Museum, described the various English domestic cats for the Royal Zoological Society. He strongly refuted Pallas' theory, citing the skull of Pallas' cat, which differed from that of the Angora or Persian of Pocock's day.

Another theory claims that the Persian has descended from the Sand Cat, a small wildcat living in African and Asian deserts. The basis for this is that both cats have long hair covering their paws, forming a pad over their soles. Measurements of the length of the hair on the Persian and Sand Cats' feet disproved this claim. The long hair on today's Persian's feet is because of its long coat. In the Sand Cat, it is a feature that protects their feet from the hot sand. The cat is otherwise shorthaired.

ABOVE

The distinctive coats of LaPerm kittens like these can range from wavy to tight, ringlet-type curls.

Multiple Mutations

A more believable explanation is a genetic mutation in a group of cats with foreign conformation, where inbreeding would have allowed the trait to become fixed. It is claimed that the longhair mutation originally happened in Russia, with Russian Longhairs traveling to Turkey, where they became Angoras, and to Persia, where they became Persians. The gene would have then been introduced by land to southeast Asia's native cats, creating longhair Japanese Bobtails. Sea-trade routes resulted in cold-climate adaptations: a heavier body, dense undercoat, and coarser hair. If this theory is correct, all longhairs came from the Siberian cat. It is even more feasible that the longhair mutation has happened more than once and is still happening. We have seen identical mutations, bobbed tails and curly hair, for example, independently occurring in separate locations.

TOP RIGHT

This Turkish Van, with its cream and orange coat, is a good example of a bicolored longhair.

The Longhair Coat

A domestic, longhaired cat is the correct name for any cat with medium or long fur, if it is not a pedigreed member of a recognized breed. Domestic longhairs come in all of the standard cat colors, including tabby, tortie, and bicolored. If their fur combines several shades of the same color, they may be referred to as a smoke.

Some longhaired cats are not able to maintain their own coat, and matted fur becomes a problem. The cat must be groomed for at least half an hour every day and preferably bathed biweekly. If the cat is bathed and groomed regularly from kittenhood, it will accept it as a part of its routine. Many owners of longhaired cats attempt to cut away tangled and matted fur. This should only be done by a professional, as it can be difficult to distinguish between hard, matted fur and the skin of the cat. Cuts are a real danger.

ABOVE

Persian cats are believed to have resulted after the genetic mutation causing long hair traveled from Russia to Persia.

This section begins with what are referred to as the "semi-longhair" cats—the Maine Coon, Norwegian Forest, Siberian, Turkish Van, Birman, Ragdoll, and the Somali—before going on to the well-known Persian and a whole range of fascinating, longhair breeds.

MAINE COON

SIZE: Medium to large

COAT CARE: Low maintenance

DIET: Low maintenance

BODY SHAPE: Semi-longhair

COLOR VARIATIONS: All colors and patterns, except for pointed colors and patterns that would indicate hybridization

LIFE EXPECTANCY: 16+ years

To its fans, the Maine Coon is the big one—the boss cat. Myth, legend, and folklore surround it, some amusing, some fantastic, and some only credible stories. One story claims that the breed is a raccoon/domestic cat hybrid, from where it gets the name. Although both share lush, long tails and the tendency to dunk food in water, such a union is biologically impossible. Another tale, far-fetched but at least feasible, states that the Maine Coon was produced by bobcat/domestic cat trysts. This explains the ear and toe tufts and the imposing size of the breed.

Origins

The Maine Coon is a solid, rugged cat and North America's oldest, natural, longhaired breed. It is also America's first indigenous show cat. In Boston in January of 1878, one dozen were listed in the show's program. Often called the "gentle giants" of the cat fancy, the Maine Coon's origins are steeped in legend.

ABOVE LEFT

It seems likely that Maine Coons are the result of native, shorthaired cats mating with longhairs from overseas.

One imaginative story claims these cats are descendants of longhaired cats belonging to Marie Antoinette. They, with other breeds, were smuggled into America by a sea captain named Clough. He was preparing to rescue the Queen, but unfortunately she met the guillotine, and the cats stayed in Maine. The accepted story has the Maine Coon controlling rats on board sailing ships. Some cats went ashore when the ships reached the northeastern coast of North America and established themselves on the settlers' farms. Given Maine's severe climate, only the strongest and most adaptable survived, and the Maine Coon developed into a large, rugged cat with a dense, water-resistant coat and a robust constitution.

ABOVE

The Maine Coon's coat has adapted to the harsh local climate, with heavier fur at the ruff and stomach.

Most breeders today believe that the breed originated in mating between pre-existing, shorthaired, domestic cats and overseas longhairs, perhaps Angora types introduced by New England seamen or longhairs brought to America by the Vikings. Maine Coons are similar in appearance to both the Norwegian Forest Cat and the Siberian; however, this may be attributed to convergent evolution—the shaping of unrelated species by similar environments, selecting for similar characteristics and resulting in similar animals.

Development

The Maine Coon was an early favorite in the emerging American cat fancy in the late 1800s. In the early 1900s, however, cat fanciers of the era abandoned Maine Coons for Persians, Angoras, and other exotic imports. By 1950 the breed had almost vanished. Fortunately a small group of breeders kept the breed alive, and it has since then regained its popularity. Everything about the Maine Coon points to its adaptation to a harsh climate. Since the cat is the result of "survival of the fittest," its fur is like no other breed's, and it must be felt to be appreciated; it is longer on the ruff, stomach, and breeches to protect against damp and snow and shorter on the back and neck to guard against tangling in the undergrowth. The long, bushy tail that the cat wraps around himself when he curls up to sleep can protect him from cold winters. Big, round, tufted feet serve as snowshoes. It is an extraordinary cat that holds championship status in all registries.

Fascinating Facts

The Maine Coon is the official feline of the State of Maine.

Characteristics

Head
The head is medium width and length, with a square muzzle and high cheekbones. The chin is firm; the nose is medium long and slightly concave in profile.

Ears and Eyes
The large ears are well tufted, wide at the base, and tapering to appear pointed.

They are set high and far apart. The eyes are wide set and large, with a slightly oblique setting slanted toward the outer base of the ear. The eye color should be shades of green, gold, or copper, but blue and odd-colored eyes are acceptable in white cats. There is no relationship between coat and eye color.

Body and Legs, and Coat
The medium to large body is muscular and broad chested. The body should be long to create a well-balanced, rectangular look. It is one of the largest domestic breeds; a male weighs 12–18 lbs (5.4–8.1 kg) and females 10–14 lbs (4.5–6.3 kg). The long, bushy tail is wide at the base and tapers to the tip. The medium-length legs are wide set and substantial. The round paws are large and well tufted. While the Maine Coon may be polydactyl, having one or more extra toes on their paws, this trait is generally bred out, as it has been rejected by the standard.

The coat is heavy and shaggy but still silky. It falls smoothly, shorter on the shoulders and longer on the stomach and breeches. A frontal ruff is desirable.

Temperament

The Maine Coon cat is well known for its loving nature, kindly disposition, and great intelligence. Maines are especially good with children and dogs and have always been a popular and sought-after companion. Maine Coons develop slowly and don't achieve their full size until they are three to five years old. Their dispositions remain kittenish throughout their lives; they are big, gentle, good-natured clowns. Even their voices set them apart from other cats. They have a distinctive, chirping trill that they use for everything from courting to coaxing their owners into playing with them. Maine Coons love to play, and most will joyfully retrieve small items. They rarely meow, and when they do, that soft, tiny voice doesn't fit their size.

A Streak of Independence
While Maine Coons are highly sociable cats, they are not overly dependent. They do not constantly pester you for attention but prefer to "hang out" with their owners, investigating whatever activity you're involved in and helping when they can. They are

not, as a general rule, known to be lap cats, but as with any personality trait, there are a few Maine Coons that prefer to be held. Most Maine Coons will keep close, probably occupying the chair next to yours instead. A Maine Coon will be your companion and your friend, but hardly ever your baby. Maine Coons are relaxed and easygoing in just about everything they do. The males are more of the clowns, while the females retain more dignity, but both remain playful throughout their lives. They generally get along well with kids and dogs, as well as other cats. They do not like to climb up high, preferring to chase objects on the ground and grasping them in their large paws, no doubt instincts developed as professional mousers. Many Maine Coons will play fetch with their owners. While Maine Coons are loving, devoted, and playful with their owners, they can be reserved around strangers, but given time even the most cautious adapt.

Care

Feeding

Most breeders recommend a high-quality, dry food. Usually the cats can freely feed without becoming overweight. If weight should become a problem, switching to a low-calorie food can control it. Many Maine Coons love water. Keep a good supply of clean, fresh water available at all times.

Grooming

Maine Coons do not need much grooming. A weekly combing is all that is usually required to keep the coat in top condition.

ABOVE

Maine Coons are playful, gentle, and entertaining, retaining their kitten-like characters throughout their lives.

NORWEGIAN FOREST CAT

SIZE: Medium to large

COAT CARE: Moderate maintenance

DIET: Moderate maintenance

BODY SHAPE: Semi-longhair

COLOR VARIATIONS: All colors and patterns, except those indicating hybridization resulting in chocolate, lilac, the Himalayan pattern, or those combinations with white.

LIFE EXPECTANCY: 15+ years

The Norwegian Forest Cat, called the skogkatt in Norway, is a natural breed. Despite its feral appearance, it is not a descendant of any wildcat species. These are the cats that explored the world with the Vikings, protecting their grain stores on land and sea. It is believed that they left their progeny on the shores of North America as a legacy to the future.

Origins

Forest Cats have existed for many years, as they have been mentioned in Norse mythology. Most Norse myths were passed down orally until they were finally recorded in the Edda Poems, written some time between A.D. 800 and 1200. These stories suggest that domestic cats have been in Norway for thousands of years, but whether the cats of these myths are Forest Cats is open to debate.

When the cats arrived in the northern countries, most likely with traders, settlers, or crusaders, the breed's ancestors were probably shorthaired. The cats survived and in time adapted to the severe climate of northern Norway. Over the centuries these cats developed long, dense, water-resistant coats, hardy constitutions, and well-honed survival instincts. These beautiful cats are really two-in-one because they can differ greatly in looks from the summer to the winter. Some time in the spring they lose their downy undercoat that provides warmth, and the contrast can be radical.

The Forest Cat was presented to the CFA Board for registration acceptance in February 1987. In 1993 they were accepted for full championship status.

Characteristics

Head

The head forms an equilateral triangle. The nose is straight from brow ridge to tip without a break. The chin is firm and gently rounded in profile. The muzzle is part of the

RIGHT

Norwegian Forest cats can have coats of many different colors and patterns.

Fascinating Facts

It has been scientifically proven that owning cats is good for our health and can decrease the occurrence of high blood pressure and other illnesses. Stroking a cat can help relieve stress, and the sensation of a purring cat on your lap conveys a strong sense of security and comfort.

straight line extending toward the base of the ear, without pronounced whisker pads and without a pinch.

Ears and Eyes
The ears are medium to large, rounded at the tips, broad at the base, and set as much on the side of the head as on top. Heavily furnished lynx tips are desirable but not required.

The large eyes are almond shaped and wide opened and set at a slight angle, with the outer corner higher than the inner. The color is a shade of green, gold, or green-gold; however, white cats may have blue or odd eyes.

Body and Legs
This cat is solidly muscled, with a well-balanced body. It is of moderate length, substantial bone structure, and it has a powerful appearance. It has a wide chest and considerable girth, without being fat. The flank has great depth.

Coat
The double coat consists of a dense undercoat covered by long, glossy, water-resistant, guard hairs. There is a frontal ruff, a collar at the neck, side muttonchops, and breeches on the hind legs. Softer coats are permitted in shaded, solid, and bicolor cats.

Temperament

Norwegian Forest Cats love people and are demanding of their attention. They do not like to be left alone for any length of time. They are used to an outdoor life and are well adapted to roam outside. Still they can be happy as indoor cats, provided they have plenty of room. They are intelligent and can be entertaining companions, as they are extremely playful.

TOP RIGHT
This Norwegian Forest shows the typical lynxlike ear tufts and golden-green eyes of this breed.

Care

This is a large cat that requires a good amount of food; however, their diet should be monitored, as they tend to become obese. Little combing is required for non-show cats, but it is recommended during spring shedding.

SIBERIAN

SIZE: Medium to medium-large

COAT CARE: Moderate maintenance

DIET: Moderate maintenance

BODY SHAPE: Semi-longhair

COLOR VARIATIONS: All colors and patterns, except pointed colors

LIFE EXPECTANCY: 12+ years

LEFT

Siberian cats developed an ability to bond with humans, perhaps in order to help them survive in the harsh climate.

This strong cat hails from a very unforgiving climate: Siberia. Recorded history shows that the Siberian breed has been around for at least one thousand years. They were first mentioned in Harrison Weir's *Our Cats and all About Them*. However, finding written information about these cats in Russia is difficult, despite the fact that the Siberian is a natural breed and is the national cat of Russia.

Origins

The Siberian cat is found in St. Petersburg and Leningrad, and the breed can be found in Russian paintings and writings hundreds of years old. Oral tradition suggests that the Siberian started to migrate toward the animal herders, where they found warmth from a campfire and a few pieces of food scraps. Their ability to bond with humans became a genetically ingrained survival trait, cushioning them from the harsh winter climate. For a significant period of time, it was against the law in Russia to own and feed pets. The Siberian ran the streets and survived in the shadows. Many took refuge in monasteries, and this has become a part of the historical lore of the Siberian.

Development

Siberians were introduced to America in 1990, so they are relatively rare. There is an increasing interest in Siberians worldwide, and they are currently accepted in the major registries, such as AACE, ACFA, CFA, TICA, and ACF. The breed can take as long as five years to mature. Adult males are usually larger than the females, and allowances should be made for a size differential between males, females, and young cats. Type takes preference over size.

Characteristics

Head

The medium-sized head is a broad, modified wedge, with gentle, rounded contours. The muzzle is rounded and moderately long. The top of the head is flat with a slightly curved forehead. The cheeks are not pronounced. The whiskers are long.

Ears and Eyes

The ears are medium large and wide at the base, with rounded tips. They are wide set and tilted forward. Lynx tipping is desirable. The eyes are large, almost round and wide set. Color has no relationship to coat color; acceptable eye color may cover the entire green-gold spectrum.

Fascinating Facts

Cat nose pads are unique, like fingerprints.

Body, Legs, and Coat
The body shape is moderately long and substantial, with the back slightly curved or arched. This is a compact cat, with a tight stomach and convex torso that appears with age. The boning is large, the chest and musculature are well rounded. The general impression is one of roundness and circles, instead of the rectangles and triangles of similar breeds. The Siberian has a rich, full coat in the winter, while in summer it is shorter and less dense.

Temperament

The Siberian is doglike in temperament, greeting visitors when they come to the door. They are exceptionally intelligent and very quick learners. Siberians have a triple purr and a chirping sound they use when they come to greet you. They are affectionate with their owners and good with children and other pets. When they are around water, they appear to be fascinated, and they will drop toys into it. The Siberian makes the ideal lap cat and will live happily indoors with you.

Care

Feed a Siberian any premium cat food. Weight can become a problem, so free feeding needs to be monitored. Siberian cats are self-grooming and can usually avoid tangles in their fur, so they do not require frequent brushing. However, regular brushing of the Siberian can reduce hairballs.

RIGHT
Siberians are intelligent, affectionate, and doglike in nature and do not need excessive grooming.

TURKISH VAN

SIZE: Large

COAT CARE: Moderate maintenance

DIET: Moderate maintenance

BODY SHAPE: Semi-longhair

COLOR VARIATIONS: Solids and whites, tabby and whites, parti-colors and whites

LIFE EXPECTANCY: 9+ years

LEFT

The Turkish Van is an ancient breed from Asia that has been known by various other names over the centuries.

The Turkish Van is a rare and ancient breed that was developed in central and southwest Asia. Today this area includes Iran, Iraq, southwest Russia, and eastern Turkey. Van is a common name in the region and is given to a number of towns, villages, and even a lake—Lake Van—so Van was the obvious choice for the name of this uniquely patterned cat native to the area.

Origins

These cats were first brought to England as the Turkish Cats, but this was later changed to Turkish Van to avoid confusion with the Turkish Angora. Despite its ancient lineage, the Turkish Van is a relative newcomer to the U.S., arriving in 1982. Because they are considered to be regional treasures in their homeland, they are not readily available for export.

The breed, known over the centuries by such names as the White Ringtail and the Russian Longhair, was first brought into Europe by crusaders returning from the Middle East. A common misconception is that the Turkish Van is simply a color variation of the Turkish Angora, but when they are seen together, the differences are clearly apparent.

In the 1950s a pair of Turkish Vans were brought to Britain by a couple on vacation, and they began breeding these distinctively marked cats. The cats bred true, so more Turkish stock was introduced and a breeding program started. They gained official recognition, and cats were exported to the U.S. and Australia, where they have also gained in popularity.

Important and Unique

Many believe that the breed was the first to carry the piebald gene. Other piebald cats that have been selectively bred to achieve similar markings are said to be van-patterned. Another interesting feature of the Turkish Van is that they love water, and in their native region they have been called the Swimming Cats.

Fascinating Facts

A falling cat always balances itself in the same way. First it rotates its head. Second it twists its spine. Third it aligns its rear legs, and finally it arches its back to lessen the impact on landing.

Characteristics

Head
The head is a broad wedge, with gentle contours. The medium-length nose and prominent cheekbones harmonize with the large, muscular body. The ears are not included in the wedge. In profile, the nose has a slight dip below eye level and is marked by a change of direction in the way the hair lies. The muzzle is rounded, the chin is firm and in a straight line with the nose and upper lip. Allowances are made for jowling in males.

Ears and Eyes
The ears are moderately large to large and are set fairly high and far apart, with the inside edge of the ear slightly angled to the outside. The outside edge is fairly straight but not necessarily aligned with the side of the face. They are wide at the base, tips are slightly rounded, and the inside should be well feathered.

The eyes are moderately large, rounded but slightly drawn out at the corners and set in a slant. They are equidistant from the outside base of the ear to the tip of the nose. Eyes should be clear, alert, and expressive. The colors are amber, blue, and odd-eyed.

ABOVE
Turkish Van cats have been bred in the U.K. since the 1950s and were introduced to America in 1982.

Body and Legs
The body is moderately long, sturdy, muscular, and deep chested. Mature males should exhibit marked muscular development in the neck and shoulders. The shoulders should be at least as broad as the head and flow into a well-rounded rib cage and then into a muscular hip and pelvic area. Turkish Van males are substantially bigger than females. The tail is long but in proportion to the body. It has a brushed appearance.

The legs are long and moderately muscular, set wide apart and taper to rounded, moderately large feet. The legs and feet should be proportionate to the body. There are five toes in front and four behind.

Coat
The coat is semi-long, with a cashmere-like texture. It is soft to the roots, with no trace of undercoat. As a result of the climatic extremes in their native region, the breed carries two distinct coat lengths, so allowances must be made for the seasonal coat: summer is short, conveying the appearance of a shorthair; winter coat is longer and thicker. There is feathering on the ears, feet, legs, and stomach. The frontal neck ruff and full-brush tail become more pronounced with age. Facial fur is short.

RIGHT
The coat of the Turkish Van is semi-long and soft to the roots, with a ruff at the neck and shorter fur on the face.

There are generally two distinct coat types found in the breed. Both can occur within a single litter and are dependent upon the lineage of the parents. One coat type is sometimes called the Dutch coat. This coat is generally relatively short and even. It is very plush, like a rabbit, and extremely soft. It is sometimes called the "wash and wear" coat. The other coat is called the English coat. This is longer than the Dutch coat and much thicker. Kittens sporting the English coat will look much furrier than those with the Dutch coat. Neither should have evidence of a woolly undercoat.

Temperament

The Turkish Van is a loyal, loving, and very intelligent cat. Its temperament depends greatly on its upbringing; the amount of human contact and handling it receives as a kitten and the temperament of the mother herself. They are very affectionate, giving head butts and love bites. To the uninitiated this could be slightly alarming, but when you get to know your cat you will begin to understand. They tend to bond strongly with one or two people in a family. They are social and remain active long into old age.

They are great climbers, so don't be surprised to find them sitting on top of

doors, kitchen cupboards, or bookshelves, and some wouldn't think twice about climbing your curtains and sitting on the curtain rail. A great game is retrieving rolled-up paper; some catching the ball of paper in mid-flight, others making great somersaults.

Wary
In general the Turkish Van does not like to be picked up and carried. This does not mean that they are not affectionate, but they are more like dogs in their loyalty, devotion, and interactions with their owners. They usually enjoy being wherever you are and into whatever you are doing: watching TV or sleeping with you. Some Vans enjoy riding around the house on your shoulder.

Where water is concerned, some are not interested, where others may love dripping taps, especially drinking from them and then flicking the water with their paws or dropping toys into their water bowl. It has been known for Turks to swim in the bath, swimming pool, or even the ocean. So be warned—they may come and join you in the shower.

Care

Feeding
The Turkish Van is an active cat and will require a good-quality cat food. Although not especially prone to obesity, it is wise to keep an eye on their diet.

Grooming
Turkish Vans require regular grooming to keep their beautiful, silky coat tangle free. It is best to do this on a daily basis, as this avoids major tangles. If grooming with a comb and brush is introduced at an early age, the cat will soon become used to it, and many potential problems will be avoided.

BELOW
Turkish Vans are very active and enjoy climbing, acrobatics, and in many cases, games involving water.

TURKISH ANGORA

BODY SHAPE: Semi-longhair

SIZE: Medium

COAT CARE: Low maintenance

DIET: Low maintenance

COLOR VARIATIONS: Any, except those showing hybridization (chocolate, lavender, Himalayan pattern, or those with white)

LIFE EXPECTANCY: 14+ years

Elegant and finely boned, Turkish Angoras are graceful creatures, energetic and usually the first to welcome visitors into the home. No wonder these cats are so treasured. Cat fanciers are enjoying a resurgence of a breed once believed to be extinct. In recent years new cats were brought to North America from Turkey, the breeds' country of origin, and the Turkish Angora has again joined the ranks of the cats in the pedigreed world.

Origins

The Turkish Angora is a pure, natural breed of cat, likely originating from the Manul cat domesticated by the Tartars. Turkish Angoras eventually migrated to Turkey, where they are regarded today with great reverence as one of their national treasures. Turkish Angoras, virtually unchanged over hundreds of years, still roam the villages and countryside. Today they are adapting well to living with people instead of living free, but they still maintain their own strong personality traits.

Over the years the Angora was used indiscriminately in breeding with Persians, resulting in it finally disappearing from the scene. They were known for a while simply as Longhairs. Fortunately controlled breeding programs had been set up in the Ankara Zoo in Turkey, where they continue today.

ABOVE LEFT

This black tortie smoke Turkish Angora shows just one of the many possible variations in coat color.

Although the first import on record arrived in America in 1954, it was not until the mid-1960s that the breed became numerous enough to seek recognition from CFA. White Turkish Angoras were accepted for registration in 1968, for Provisional Breed competition in 1970, and for championship competition in 1972. The first CFA grand champion came in 1976. However, it took another two years before colored Turkish Angoras were allowed to compete in championship with their all-white siblings.

Current Development

Whites are still popular today, but Turkish Angora breeders have focused increasingly on colored cats. Greater numbers of people are realizing how endearing and beautiful these elegant creatures look in colors other than white. These days, at a CFA show you might see these cats in colors such as black, blue, red, and cream; in tortoiseshell or blue-cream; in classic, mackerel, and spotted tabbies of many colors; bicolored cats in any of these colors with white. Breeders have recently begun working

with smoke and shaded colors. Any shade and pattern, except those that denote hybridization, is accepted for CFA registration. Many people have used the term Angora to signify any longhaired cat. However, the only pedigreed cat to carry that name is the Turkish Angora. CFA accepts for registration only those Turkish Angoras whose ancestry can be traced back to Turkey.

Characteristics

Head
The head is small to medium, in balance with the length of the body. It forms a medium to long, smooth wedge without a break. The muzzle is a continuation of the smooth lines of the wedge, with neither a pronounced whisker pad nor pinch.

Ears and Eyes
The ears are large, wide at the base, pointed, and tufted. They are set close together and high up on the head. They are vertical and erect. The large eyes are almond shaped, slanting upward with an open expression. There is no relationship between the eye color and the coat color. Eyes can be any shade of green, gold, green-gold, copper, blue, or odd-eyed.

Body and Legs
The body is medium-sized but is in balance. Grace and fineness of boning are more important than size. The torso is long and slender, with shoulders the same width as the hips. The rump is slightly higher than the shoulders. This is a finely boned cat, with firm musculature. The tail is long and tapering from a wide base to a narrow end, with a full brush. The legs are long and finely boned. The dainty pads are small and round. Tufts are preferred.

Coat
The silky, fine coat of the Angora changes according to the season. It moves from a short coat, with only slight breeches and fluffy tail in the summer, to the full winter coat, with medium long, silky hair complete with mane, breeches, and lush, plumy

tail. The coat must be silky, fine, and single with no hint of shagginess. The best coats, however, are seen on mature animals over the age of three.

Temperament

These cats will reward you with high-spirited affection. They love to show off and seem to become even more animated once they have your attention. And once an Angora makes up its mind about something, not even the most ingenious of us can change it. Perhaps one of the best Turkish words to describe the breed is "yaman," which means strong, smart, and capable. They do everything with an unparalleled skill and agility, from leaping to the top of the refrigerator, to following you while you work, to finding ingenious ways to avoid you when it's time to cut their nails. They are wonderful breeders, both male and female, producing healthy, robust kittens with little difficulty and plenty of enjoyment during both the courtship and the raising of their litters.

The Turkish Angora has an unsatisfied appetite for play. They love to race through the house chasing imaginary prey, their long, slender bodies and legs evolved for the hunt, still needing the chase. They can be found in very unlikely places: making an open door swing back and forth while playing on it or batting at an empty spool around the kitchen in the middle of the night. If there's a strange noise, you can bet your Turkish Angora is behind it.

Devoted

An Angora finds it necessary to be involved in every aspect of your life. It will love you with complete devotion and refuse to accept anything less in return; your Angora is interested in everything that you do. Whether you are working at your computer or making your bed, your Angora feels it must be there to oversee the work.

A Turkish Angora makes a wonderful pet. They are extremely intelligent, spirited, and devoted to their owners and have an athletic grace

BELOW
The Turkish Angora is bred under controlled conditions in its native country and is considered a national treasure.

Fascinating Facts

Cats almost never meow at another cat. They use this sound to communicate with humans.

RIGHT

Turkish Angora cats have long, slender, muscular bodies, with a fine, silky coat and a tapering tail.

around the house, with no shelf being too high up for them and no door too secure. Turkish Angoras are friendly and playful but are generally well behaved, unlike their Turkish Van cousins, who can be difficult. Neither do they have the same love of water that Vans have, although this isn't surprising given their different geographical origins.

Turkish Angora kittens are precocious, very active, and start to play from an early age. They don't develop a full angora coat until they're at least two years old.

BELOW

White Turkish Angoras were recognized by the Cat Fanciers Association years before their colored counterparts.

Care

This breed requires no special diet. It prefers meat, but it is not picky. The Turkish Angora's soft, silky coat rarely mats and requires only minimal grooming. Most breeders recommend combing once or twice a week with a fine-toothed comb or slicker brush to remove excess hair and keep the coat looking and feeling its best. Like all longhaired breeds, they lose some of their coat during the summer months, when more frequent combing may be needed to prevent hairballs.

BIRMAN

SIZE: Large

COAT CARE: Low maintenance

DIET: Moderate maintenance

BODY SHAPE: Semi-longhair

COLOR VARIATIONS: Original colors: seal point, blue point, chocolate point, lilac point

LIFE EXPECTANCY: 15+ years

The Birman cat is believed to have originated in Burma, where it was the companion cat of the Kittah priests and considered sacred. There is a legend as to how the Birmans developed the colors they are today. Originally, the guardians of the Temple of LaoTsun were yellow-eyed, white cats with long hair. The golden goddess of the temple, Tsun-Kyan-Kse, had deep blue eyes.

The head priest, Mun-Ha, had as his companion a beautiful cat named Sinh. One day the temple was attacked, and Mun-Ha was killed. At the moment of his death, Sinh placed his feet on his master and faced the goddess. The cat's white fur took on a golden cast; his eyes turned as blue as the eyes of the goddess, and his face, legs, and tail became the color of the earth. However, his paws, where they were touching the priest, remained white as a symbol of purity. All the other temple cats became similarly colored. Seven days later Sinh died, taking the soul of Mun-Ha to paradise.

Origins

The modern history of the Birman is almost as cloaked in mystery as its legendary origin. What is known for certain is that in around 1919, a pair of Birman cats was secretly shipped from Burma to France. The male cat did not survive the grueling conditions of the long voyage, but the female, Sita, did, and she was found to be pregnant.

From this base the Birman was established in the western world. The French cat registry recognized the Birman as a separate breed in 1925. By the end of the Second World War, only two Birmans were left alive in

LEFT

The reasons behind the Birman's coat and eye coloration are the subject of a legend in its native Burma.

Europe, and a program of outcrossing was necessary to reestablish the breed. Most cat registries require at least five generations of pure breeding after outcrossings to fully accredit a breed for championship competition. Birmans were recognized by England in 1966 and by the Cat Fanciers' Association in 1967.

Characteristics

Head

The head is strong, broad, and rounded, with a slight flat spot just in front of the ears. The cheeks are full, with a moderately rounded muzzle. The chin is strong, the jaws heavy, and the nose is of medium length and width. The head is Roman-shaped in profile.

Ears and Eyes

The medium length ears are almost as wide at the base as they are tall. They are set as much to the side of the head as they are to the top. There is a rounded point at the tip. The eyes are almost round, with a sweet expression. They are set wide apart, with the outer corner tilted slightly up. The color is blue, the deeper and more violet the better.

Body, Legs, and Coat

The Birman is long and stocky, neither svelte nor cobby. The tail is medium in length. The legs are medium length and heavy, with large and firm rounded paws. In the ideal Birman, the matching white gloves on the front paws should end at or between the second and third joint of the paws. On

ABOVE

The Birman is a stocky cat, with rounded, expressive eyes and large paws sporting white "gloves."

TOP RIGHT

Birmans are sociable, easygoing cats and retain their curious, playful nature into old age.

the back paws, the gloves should cover the toes. The coat is medium-long to long. It has a silky texture, with a heavy ruff around the neck. The coat does not mat.

Temperament

Birmans are people-oriented cats. They are always pleased to see you, and wherever you are, your Birman will be close behind. If you are in one room and the cat has been in another, it will wander in, softly waving its tail to say that it is happy to see you. Although kittens are excited by your presence, adults are more subject to their inherited dignity. They may demand your attention, but if you let them know that they are the most beautiful cat in the whole world, they will settle close by and allow you to continue your activity.

BELOW

Birmese kittens are excited in the presence of people,; the adults express themselves in a more dignified manner.

They have soft voices, sometimes described as "bell-like," and they often carry on conversations with you. Almost all Birmans have wonderful purring mechanisms, so picking up your cat or simply giving him a pat on the head will start the purr going. Some Birmans like to sit beside you and will purr softly for hours. It has been said that the Birman is intelligent, intuitive, inquisitive, charming, curious, playful, and dignified. Birman cats are generally easygoing and relaxed but remain playful into old age. Anything new catches their attention and needs to be explored, and they enjoy hours of fun with simple toys like bottle corks, paper bags, and are ecstatic when offered felt mice and tinsel balls. They love to help with all household chores, and it is not unusual to find them asleep in the laundry basket or playing in your wastepaper basket when you are working at the computer. Birmans love life, and their life revolves around the family. If you go to work,

Fascinating Facts

Ailurophile" is the word cat lovers are officially called.

they are there to greet you when you come home. If you are at home, they follow you around the house and are content just to be near you.

Friendly Nature

Birmans can live happily as the only pet, but some people who work for long hours recommend keeping two because they are such sociable cats. Their nature is gentle and friendly, and for this reason it is best that they don't live outdoors, where they are in danger of being attacked by other cats, dogs, or may run the risk of being hit by a car. An outdoor enclosed area of the yard, so that cats can enjoy the best of both worlds, is a way of keeping them safe.

Birmans make wonderful pets for children. They are tolerant and also playfully join in games. If allowed, they will sleep on the child's bed. Obviously small kittens and small children need supervision so that neither gets hurt while they are learning.

Birmans can adapt to a cat-friendly dog if introductions are made nicely and can also adapt to a current resident cat—again if introductions are careful and respect the "rights" of the resident cat. Like all cats they need to be supervised with pets such as hamsters, mice, guinea pigs, and rabbits—never forget that all cats are carnivores.

Care

Feeding

Birman cats are prone to hairballs, so you may want to feed a diet that is formulated to aid in hairball prevention. If he becomes lethargic and does not eat as much as he normally does, you should consult your veterinarian about treating him for hairballs. Since this breed is not as active as some, you may also need to ask your veterinarian about feeding your cat a calorie-controlled diet if he becomes overweight.

Grooming

The Birman has an easy-care angora coat that requires little grooming. Regular weekly grooming with a brush is all that is required for most of the year, although your cat will enjoy it if you decide to groom more regularly. Once-a-week brushing also helps control the hairball problem.

RAGDOLL

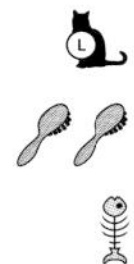

SIZE: Large

COAT CARE: Moderate maintenance

DIET: Low maintenance

BODY SHAPE: Semi-longhair

COLOR VARIATIONS: Solid, parti-colored mitted; parti-color, bicolor divisions

LIFE EXPECTANCY: 15+ years

The Ragdoll is surrounded by myth. One states that the foundation cat, Josephine, produced unremarkable kittens until she was struck by a car in the early 1960s. After her recovery, all succeeding litters displayed the Ragdoll characteristics: the propensity to lie limp and relax, like a child's rag doll, in the owner's arms; the large size, non-matting fur, and calm disposition. Geneticists dismissed the accident theory and attributed the breed's gentle, even temper to selective breeding.

Another Ragdoll myth is its insensitivity to pain. Breeders state that the cats' pain tolerance is the same as any other, but injuries often go unnoticed because of the animals' uncomplaining nature. One account claims that Josephine was taken to a laboratory after the accident. According to myth, she was genetically altered as part of a secret government experiment that resulted in the changes responsible for the Ragdoll's unique temperament. There is no scientific evidence to support this. In fact this type of genetic alteration did not exist in the 1960s.

ABOVE

There are various myths surrounding Ragdolls, but the breed is probably of Birman or Persian origin.

Origins

The accepted explanation says that Josephine was a feral, white, Turkish Angora-type cat that lived on a Mrs. Pennels' property in Riverside, California. After the car accident, Josephine mated with a feral black and white, longhaired tom and produced a solid black male named Daddy Warbucks and a seal pointed, bicolor female named Fugianna. Another litter followed, sired by a longhaired, solid brown tom. This produced a seal point female, Tiki, and a black and white-mitted male, Buckwheat. The breed's founder, Ann Baker, acquired these cats, and all generations can be traced back to them. The Ragdoll is of Birman/Persian origin.

In 1971 Anne Baker created her own registry for Ragdolls—the International Ragdoll Association (IRCA)—and

franchised and registered the name. Championship status is held in ACFA, ACA, CFF, TICA, AACA, CCA, NCFA, UFO; accepted in the miscellaneous class in CFA.

Characteristics

Head
The medium-sized head is a broad, modified wedge with slightly rounded contours. The muzzle is round and medium length, the chin is well developed, and there is a break between the eyes.

Ears and Eyes
The medium-sized ears are broad at the base, with a slightly forward tilt. The tips are rounded. The large eyes are oval and moderately wide set. They are not oriental. Color is blue.

Body and Legs
The large body is long, powerful, and muscular. The chest is full, and the bone structure is strong and substantial. The rump is slightly higher than the shoulders; however, the hindquarters are heavier. The cat has a surprising weight for its size.

Coat
The semi-long coat is silky and plush, with a medium undercoat. The coat lies with the body and breaks as the cat moves. The Ragdoll is a pointed breed, which means the body is lighter in color than the points (the face, legs, tail, and ears).

Temperament

One of the best features of these cats is their sweet, laid-back personality that makes them ideal indoor companions. Playful but not overactive, affectionate without being demanding, they make perfect pets for children. They adapt easily to their environment and can be trained to stay off of countertops and tables.

Care

Feeding
Use a variety of premium canned or dry foods. Using a variety will prevent a picky eater. Always leave a bowl of dry food around as a free-for-all and a fresh bowl of water.

Grooming
Although Ragdolls require less grooming than other longhair cats, it is important to groom them at least once a week. Not only will your cat have a beautifully groomed coat, but it will also prevent your Ragdoll from developing hairballs.

ABOVE LEFT
A seal point Ragdoll; the breed is renowned for its sweet nature and propensity to lie limp in its owners arms.

RAGAMUFFIN

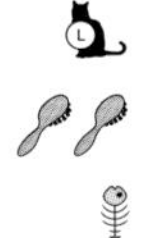

SIZE: Large

COAT CARE: Moderate maintenance

DIET: Low maintenance

BODY SHAPE: Semi-long hair

COLOR VARIATIONS: Solid, parti-colored mitted; parti-color, bicolor divisions; all variations of pointed color, including tortie point, red point, and lynx point

LIFE EXPECTANCY: 15+ years

The Ragamuffin is one of the newest breeds and was created in 1994. Although it's very similar to the Ragdoll, they are not exactly alike. For example, the Ragdoll has a flat plane between the ears, while the skull of the Ragamuffin is gently rounded. The Ragamuffin is a bit chubbier in the face, and the ears tip slightly forward. Ragamuffin breeders stress the sweet expression and walnut-shaped eyes.

Origins

Ann Baker founded the breed in the 1960s with a Ragdoll named Josephine and a regular, non-pedigree cat. The kittens were so special that Mrs. Baker wanted to preserve their qualities by breeding Josephine's offspring. She also wanted to be the only person to breed and sell Ragamuffins. Mrs. Baker's restrictions created dissension between her and other breeders. Finally they broke away and pushed for the new registry with the CFA. The Ragamuffin was accepted in the miscellaneous class in 2003.

Characteristics

Head

The head is a broad modified wedge with a rounded appearance. The muzzle is round, slightly shorter than moderate in length. The chin is firmly rounded. Puffiness in the whisker pad gives the cat its characteristic sweet look. In profile there is an obvious nose dip, giving the impression of a scoop and not a break. An allowance is made for jowliness in mature adult males.

Ears and Eyes

The ears are medium in size, set as much on the side of the head as on the top. There is a slight flaring, tilted slightly forward. They are rounded with moderate furnishings. The large eyes are walnut shaped and expressive, moderately wide set. Eye color: minks—green, blue-green, turquoise, blue, odd-eyed. Solids—all colors, including odd-eyed. The more intense the eye color, the better. Lighter color in dilutes is allowed.

Body and Legs

The body is rectangular, with a broad chest and powerful shoulders supporting a short neck. It is heavily boned, with a tendency toward a fatty pad on the lower abdomen. The tail is long, medium at the base, with a slight taper, and it is in proportion to the body. It is fully furred, similar in looks to a plume.

The legs are heavily boned, medium in length, with the back legs slightly longer than the front. The paws are large and round, able to support the weight of the cat without splaying, and with tufts beneath and between the toes. Allowance is made for finer boning in females.

Coat

The Ragamuffin's dense coat is long and silky. The hair grows longer around the face and neck, forming a ruff. It increases in length toward the stomach, with a wispy frill on the hind legs. Ragamuffins come in all coat colors and patterns.

Temperament

The cuddly Ragamuffin loves people and is very affectionate; it has a tendency to go limp when held. They love playing, fetching toys and climbing scratching posts. They greet family members at the door and will follow their owners around the house. Ragamuffins are wonderful with children; however, being left alone can make them very unhappy. Because of their gentle nature, Ragamuffins are generally kept indoors for their own protection.

Care

The Ragamuffin is one of the largest breeds and has a tendency to put on weight. Ask your veterinarian about feeding your cat a weight-management cat food. Although the coat is thick and plush, it does not readily mat or clump and is easy to take care of. Occasional brushing is usually all that is required.

RIGHT

Ragamuffins are heavily boned cats and have a tendency to put on weight, so their diet must be controlled.

BELOW

Ragamuffin cats are bred from Ragdolls and are one of the newest breeds, accepted by the CFA in 2003.

SOMALI

SIZE: Medium to large

COAT CARE: Moderate maintenance

DIET: Low maintenance

BODY SHAPE: Semi-longhair

COLOR VARIATIONS: Ruddy, red (sorrel), blue, and fawn

LIFE EXPECTANCY: 12+ years

The Somali, with its large ears, masked face, full ruff, and bushy tail, bears an amazing resemblance to a little fox. Quiet, intelligent cats, they get bursts of energy several times a day, when they will tear through the house. Tail and back arched, the Somali will run sideways, holding objects and food the way a monkey does.

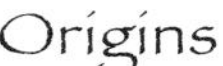

Origins

While the lineage of the Somali remains unclear, some believe that the long coat was a spontaneous, natural mutation in the Abyssinian; however, genetic studies suggest that the breed probably originated in England around the 1900s. Breeders low on stock began using longhaired cats in their Abyssinian breeding programs in the 1910s and again in the late 1940s. A consequence of the First and Second World Wars, many breeds had declined to near extinction, forcing breeders to mix their Abyssinian bloodlines.

Breed is Established in U.S.

In 1953 Raby Chuffa of Selene, a male Abyssinian whose name appears on many pedigrees, arrived in the U.S. from Britain. He is considered to be the father of the Somali breed in North America. Raby Chuffa's pedigree can be traced back to Roverdale Purrkins, an English Abyssinian female whose mother, Mrs. Mews, was of unknown ancestry and likely carried the longhair gene. Mrs. Mews produced two kittens: Roverdale Purrkins, registered as an Abyssinian, and a black, unregistered male. Roverdale Purrkins was used to start Robertson's Roverdale Cattery. When longhaired kittens began to appear in Abyssinian litters, they were disposed of quietly. No breeder wanted to be thought to have Abyssinian lines that were not pure.

In the 1960s breeders began to see the appeal of these cats. They seriously began trying to turn these rejects into

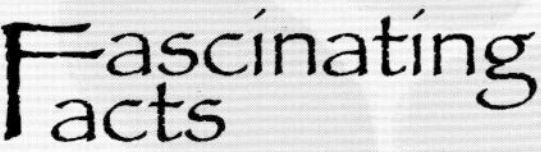

Somalis will hide in a cupboard and wait for you to open it. They turn on faucets and play in the water.

LEFT

The neck ruff, bushy tail, and large ears of the Somali cat can cause the red varieties to resemble a fox.

a breed of their own. At the same time, breeders in Canada, Australia, New Zealand, and Europe also began working with this breed. Evelyn Mague from the U.S. gave the longhaired cat the name Somali. Today the breed has championship status in all associations.

Characteristics

Head

The head is a modified wedge without flat planes. There is a slight rise, from the bridge of the nose to the forehead, and no break. The muzzle is not sharply pointed, and there is no evidence of foxiness or whisker pinch. The chin is full and rounded.

Ears and Eyes

The ears are large and cupped at the base. Horizontal tufts are located at the inner ear. Eyes are almond-shaped and accentuated by a fine, dark, line. They are large, brilliant, and expressive. Eye color is gold or green.

Body and Legs

The medium-long body is graceful but with well-developed musculature. Conformation strikes a balance between cobby and svelte. The tail, a full brush, is thick at the base and slightly tapering. The legs are in proportion to the torso. The feet are oval and compact.

Coat

The Somali has a distinctly flecked coat that is medium length, except over the shoulders, where a slightly shorter length is permitted. A double-coated ruff and breeches are desirable. Colors are ruddy, sorrel, blue, and fawn.

RIGHT

Somali cats were originally bred from Abyssinians, and like their ancestors, they will explore every part of the house.

Temperament

Like the Abyssinian, the Somali is high-spirited and curious, not a cat to follow orders. He demands the freedom of the house, exploring and getting into trouble. With their soft voices and active minds, these determined cats are a constant source of entertainment. While they are affectionate, they are not lap cats. They want to be near you, not on you.

Care

This breed has no special feeding requirements, although it especially enjoys eating meat. Since the coat is of a medium length, it only requires weekly grooming most of the year and daily grooming during shedding season.

PERSIAN

SIZE: Medium to large

COAT CARE: very high maintenance

DIET: High maintenance

BODY SHAPE: Cobby

COLOR VARIATIONS: Solid, silver, and golden, shaded and smoke, tabby, parti-colored, bicolor, and Himalayan

LIFE EXPECTANCY: 15+ years

LEFT

It is believed that the longhaired gene appeared in cats living in the cold, mountainous regions of Persia.

Persians, the most plentiful and prized of all pedigree cats, have descended from breeds brought to Europe from Afghanistan, Turkey, Persia, and Iran. It is believed that the gene for long hair appeared spontaneously in cats populating the cold, mountainous regions of Persia. Both Angora and Persian cats are mentioned in the manuscript of explorer Pietro della Valle (1586–1652)—*Voyages de Pietro della Valle*. He described Persian cats as gray, with very long and silky, glossy fur. He stated that these cats, found living in Persia, came from India with the Portuguese.

Origins and Development

The Persian is one of the oldest known breeds of cat. In the mid 1800s traveling diplomats began bringing longhaired kittens back from Middle Eastern countries to their families in England and continental Europe. Some travelers brought longhaired cats to France, inspiring them to be called "French Cats." They were generally called by a name reflecting their country of origin: Persians from Persia (Iran); Angoras from Ankara (Turkey), and though much less common, the Russian cats. They were an instant success, mainly in England, France, and Italy, and were in high demand, overshadowing the shorthaired, native, domestic cats. Then, as now, the beautiful long hair might have created the initial interest in the breed, but the gentle nature cemented the relationship of people with the Persian. The history of the modern Persian would begin with these cats, although their origins extend further back in time.

British cat owners began selectively breeding various strains by the late 1800s, and two distinct breeds

ABOVE
In the U.K. a Persian's color determines its breed, while in the U.S. all colors are varieties of the same breed.

emerged in the early 1900s. The more impressive of the two became known as the Persian. Its immense popularity eclipsed the lighter-framed and lighter-colored breed that was named the Turkish Angora.

Color and Breed Classification

For competition, Persians are divided into seven color divisions: solid, silver and golden, shaded and smoked, parti-color, tabby, calico and bicolor, Himalayan. These divisions are established on the basis of color patterns. Red peke-faced Persians, with more extreme facial conformation, appear in both the solid and the tabby division.

Owners of Persians formed clubs based on color, blue being one of the most popular. Queen Victoria had a blue pair, and 100 blues were exhibited at the 1899 London Cat Show. When Britain's Governing Council of Cat Fancy (GCCF) was formed in 1910, it decreed that Persians would be called Longhairs, and each color type would be a different breed. This new Longhair became equally popular in the United States, where it is known as the Persian and where the color is a variety and not a breed.

Persian cats may be any colors or markings, including tortoiseshell, blue, and tabby. Tipped varieties are known as Chinchilla. Pointed varieties are often categorized as a separate breed (*see* pages 286–87), called Himalayan in the United States and Colorpoint Longhair or Persian in Europe.

In the U.S. there was an attempt to establish the silver Persian as a separate breed called the Sterling, but it was not accepted, and silver and golden longhaired cats, recognized by CFA as Chinchilla Silvers, Shaded Silvers, Chinchilla Goldens, or Shaded Goldens, are judged in the Persian category of cat shows. In South Africa the attempt to separate the breed was more successful. The South American Cat Council (SACC) registers cats with five generations of purebred Chinchilla as a Chinchilla Longhair. The Chinchilla Longhair has a slightly longer nose than the Persian, resulting in healthy breathing and no tearing of the eyes. Its hair is translucent, with only the

tips carrying black pigment, a feature that gets lost when outcrossed to other colored Persians. Outcrossing may also result in losing nose and lip liner, which is a fault in the Chinchilla Longhair breed standard. One of the distinctions of this breed is the blue-green or green eye color, with kittens having blue or bluish-purple eye color.

Show Trends

The show trend, over the last few years, has been toward a fatter, more extreme facial type. Some breeders are against this, believing that the

LEFT
When Persians were first brought to England in the mid-1800s, their exotic appearance ensured their instant popularity.

exaggerated features can present problems in the breed. These include weepy eyes, upper respiratory weaknesses, malocclusions, and birthing difficulties. For those who prefer a less extreme face, the Traditional Cat Association (TCA) promotes the Traditional Persian, or Doll Face Persian.

Photographic records indicate that Persians, up until the 1960s, had a different appearance to cats from the early 1980s on; for example, from the traditional Doll Face to the "extreme," "ultra," "flat-faced," or "snubby" face of today. However, the Persian Breed Council's standard for the Persian had remained basically unchanged over this period. The Persian Breed Standard is somewhat open-ended and focused on a rounded head. Persians hold championship status in all associations.

Fascinating Facts

The average total length of hair on a Persian cat is 230 mi. (370 km), making skin and coat health a top priority.

Characteristics

Head

The head is round and huge, with great breadth of skull. The face is round, with round underlying bone structure. Skull structure should be smooth and round to the touch and not unduly exaggerated from where the forehead begins at the top of the break to the back of the head, as well as across the breadth between the ears. The nose is short, snubbed, and broad, with a break centered between the eyes. The cheeks are full, jaws broad and powerful, and the chin is full, well developed, and firmly rounded. When viewed in profile, the prominence of the eyes is apparent, and the forehead, nose, and chin appear to be in vertical alignment. The breed was originally established with a short, but not non-existent, muzzle. Over time this feature has become extremely exaggerated, especially in North America, and Persians with the more extreme flat head type are susceptible to a number of health problems, specifically affecting their sinuses and breathing.

Ears and Eyes

The ears are small, tilted forward, and rounded at the tip. They are not overly open at the base, and they are set far apart and low on the head.

The eyes are large and rounded and are set level and far apart. Eye color, deep blue or brilliant copper, depends on the coat color. Their eyes need to be checked for problems on a

RIGHT
These Brown Classic Tabby kittens demonstrate one of the seven color groups into which Persians are divided.

regular basis because some animals have trouble keeping them clean.

Body and Legs
The ideal Persian is heavily boned and well balanced. It has soft, round lines. It is large to medium-sized and cobby. It is broad and deep through the chest, equally massive across the shoulders and rump. It has a well-rounded midsection, a level back, and good muscle tone. The tail is short when compared to the body length, but it is in proportion. It is carried without a curve and at an angle lower than the back.

The cat has low legs that are short, thick, and strong. Forelegs are straight. Hind legs are straight when viewed from behind. The paws are large, rounded, and firm. Toes are close, five in front and four behind.

Coat
The coat is long and thick, standing off of the body. It is fine textured, glossy, and long over the entire body, including the shoulders. This cat has an immense ruff, a deep frill between the front legs, and ear and toe tufts that are long and full. The brush is very full.

Persians come in many colors and patterns, adding up to more than 80 varieties. The most common are:

White This coat is pure, glistening white. The nose leather and paw pads are pink; eye color is a deep blue or brilliant copper. Odd-eyed whites have one blue and one copper eye, with equal color depth.

Blue In the blue coat, a lighter shade is preferred, one level tone from nose to tip of tail and sound to the roots. A sound, darker

ABOVE
White Persians have a pure white coat and a pink nose; their eyes are either deep blue or brilliant copper.

LEFT
Persians are ideally heavily boned, with a broad chest and shoulders and short, thick legs with large paws.

shade is more acceptable than an unsound, lighter shade. Nose leather and paw pads are blue. Eye color is a brilliant copper.

Black The coal-black coat is dense, sound from roots to the tip of the fur. It is free from any tinge of rust on the tips or smoke undercoat. The nose leather is black. Paw pads are black or brown. Eye color is brilliant copper.

Red The coat should be a deep, rich, clear, brilliant red without shading, markings, or flecking. Lips and chin are the same color as the coat. The nose leather and paw pads are brick red. Eye color is brilliant copper.

Cream There is one level shade of buff cream, without markings, and it is sound to the roots. Lighter shades are preferred. The nose leather and paw pads are pink. Eye color is a brilliant copper.

Chocolate The coat is a rich, warm, chocolate-brown, sound from roots to tip of fur. Nose leather is brown, and paw pads are cinnamon-pink. The eye color is brilliant copper.

Fascinating Facts

Male tortoiseshell Persians exist, but they are very rare. There are only around one out of 3,000, and they are invariably sterile.

Lilac The coat should be a rich, warm lavender with a pinkish tone, sound and even throughout. Nose leather is lavender, and paw pads are pink. Eye color is a brilliant copper.

Temperament

Persians are placid and even-tempered, but they do love to play between spells of regal lounging around. They are devoted to their owners but can be selective; you have to earn their affection. While they love to be petted and coddled, they will not harass you for attention as other breeds will. Persians are very sweet cats. Their gentle temperament is one of the distinguishing features of the breed. The Persian is "a noble" in the cats' world. They are very adaptable to different places and make charming pets.

Persian's have a gentle temperament that works with almost any family, although those with young children should seek advice from Persian breeders before purchasing this cat. Because they require daily grooming, it is important that the family has time to make this commitment.

Care

Feeding

Cats with flat facial features will generally use the lower side of their tongue to pick up dry food. Studies have shown that almond-shaped food is easier for them to eat. Persian cats are two and a half times more likely to develop calcium oxalate urinary stones than other breeds; therefore, their diets should promote an alkaline urinary pH.

Grooming

The Persian's fur is too long and dense for them to maintain themselves. To keep the fur in its best condition, the Persian requires extensive daily grooming. They should be bathed regularly, dried carefully after, and brushed thoroughly every day.

If the coat becomes knotted or matted, a professional will be required to groom the coat. Not only is a matted coat unattractive, but it is also extremely uncomfortable for the cat. It cannot be emphasized enough that proper attention is essential for the coat. If done daily, it will only require 10–15 minutes of your time.

HIMALAYAN (Colorpoint Longhair)

SIZE: Medium to large

COAT CARE: very high maintenance

DIET: Moderate maintenance

BODY SHAPE: Cobby

COLOR VARIATIONS: All colors, pointed pattern only

LIFE EXPECTANCY: 15+ years

A Swedish geneticist first crossed a Siamese and a Persian in 1924, but it wasn't until 1935 that the first pointed pattern longhair was born. Today the Himalayan Persian is one of the most beloved of all pedigreed cats. Physically, the cat retains the Persian characteristics. Its hair is as magnificently long and thick as the Persian's, yet it has the broad range of colors of the Siamese. In Britain they are called Colorpoint Longhairs.

Origins

In the early 1930s two Harvard medical employees crossed a Siamese female with a black Persian male. This was not to create a new breed but to establish how certain characteristics were inherited. This produced all black, short-haired kittens. Next they bred a black Persian female with a Siamese male, and the outcome was the same. Both the gene for Colorpoint and long hair are recessive. The crossing of a male from the first litter with a female from the second produced a cat that had the long hair of the Persian and the color markings and the body shape of the Siamese.

The Harvard employees, having learned what they wanted to know about genetics, lost interest in breeding. During the same year British fanciers formed a breeders' club. Their aim was to produce a pointed pattern breed with the Persian body type and long hair. Around the same time, breeders in America were showing interest in the same goal, but the Second World War interfered with both programs.

In 1950 American breeder Marguerita Goforth succeeded in creating a Persian-like Colorpoint. Britain's Brian Stirling-Webb and Canada's Ben and Ann Borrett were among the pioneers who produced the Himalayan as we know it today. The CFA and the ACFA recognized the breed in 1957 under the name Himalayan. All major U.S. cat associations had by 1961 recognized the breed. Today the Himalayan has championship status in all associations.

ABOVE

The Himalayan is a cross between a Siamese and a Persian and is one of the most popular longhaired cats.

Characteristics

Head

The head is round and huge, with great breadth of skull. The face is round, and the nose is snubbed. There is a break centered between the eyes. The cheeks are full, the jaws powerful, and the chin is full, well developed, and firmly rounded.

Ears and Eyes

The ears are small, round tipped, and tilted forward. They are set low and far apart. The large eyes are round and full, set level and far apart. The color is deep, vivid blue.

Body and Legs

The body is broad and deep chested and equally large across the shoulders and rump. The midsection is well

rounded and the back level. It has good muscle tone. The legs are short, thick, and strong. Forelegs are straight. The paws are large, round, and firm.

BELOW

A lilac colorpoint with the breed's characteristic round face, small, rounded ears, snubbed nose, and blue eyes.

Coat

The coat is long and thick and stands off from the body. It is long all over the body, including the shoulders. The ruff is immense, and there is a deep frill between the front legs. The ear and toe tufts are long, and the brush is very full.

Temperament

Himalayans are the perfect indoor companion. They are gentle and sweet-tempered, but they still possess a playful side that reflects the Siamese. Although they love to be petted and groomed, they do not demand attention. They are more vocal and active than the Persian but are much quieter than the Siamese.

Care

Cats with flat facial features generally use the lower side of their tongue to pick up dry food. Studies have shown that almond-shaped food is easier for them to eat. Their coats mat easily, so daily grooming is needed.

NEBELUNG

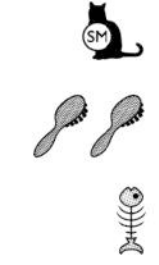

SIZE: Small to medium

COAT CARE: Moderate maintenance

DIET: Low maintenance

BODY SHAPE: Foreign

COLOR VARIATIONS: Even, bright blue

LIFE EXPECTANCY: 15+ years

The Nebelung's name in German means creature of the mist. Its coat is shiny and soft, which gives a luminous, misty effect around the body.

Origins

Although the Russian Longhair ceased to exist as a separate breed with the modern cat fancy, individual unrelated cats with its traits have appeared in the U.S. and Russia. Siegfried (born 1984) and Brunhilde (born 1985) were the first registered Nebelungs. They produced their first litter in 1986. Shortly after the kittens were born, application was made to The International Cat Association (TICA) for new breed status for the Nebelung. The breed standard was based on the Russian Blue, with the exception of coat length. In 1987 TICA accepted the Nebelungs as longhaired Russian Blues.

Characteristics

The Nebelung's most outstanding feature is its medium long, bright-blue coat. The guard hairs are silver tipped, giving the coat a lustrous quality. These guard hairs should contrast against the solid blue ground color when the coat is stroked against the grain. Eye color is a vivid green. Nebelung kittens' eyes change color rapidly, from yellow to green. The head is a modified wedge consisting of seven planes.

Temperament and Care

The Nebelung is highly intelligent, gentle, and loving to its owners and family members, but it may be shy with strangers, especially young children. A kitten may take time to adjust to its new home. If allowed to come forward on its own, it should become a devoted companion. Many Nebelungs like to sit in your lap and be petted.

Breeders recommend a mix of dry, canned, and fresh food. Nebelungs need access to fresh grass, especially if kept indoors. The coat resists matting and only requires a weekly brushing.

RIGHT

The soft coat of the Nebelung gives the impression of a mist, lending it the name "creature of the mist."

BALINESE

BODY SHAPE: Oriental

COLOR VARIATIONS: Seal point, blue point, chocolate point, and lilac point

LIFE EXPECTANCY: 15+ years

SIZE: Small to medium

COAT CARE: Moderate maintenance

DIET: Moderate maintenance

Balinese cats got their name because the way they move is reminiscent of the grace and elegance of Balinese dancers. The breed originated as a spontaneous mutation of the Siamese cat, and they were originally known as Longhaired Siamese. Although occasional long-haired kittens had been occurring in pedigreed Siamese litters, they were seen as an idiosyncrasy and sold as household pets instead of show cats.

ABOVE

Only Balinese cats in one of the traditional Siamese point colors, such as this chocolate point, are accepted by the CFA.

Origins

Little is known about the early history of the Balinese. Some say that at least one Chinese tapestry depicts pointed longhairs. The Cat Fanciers' Federation (CFF) had a Longhair Siamese registered in 1928. However, the real history starts later, in the 1950s, when true breeding programs were established.

Two breeders, Marion Dorsey of Rai-Mar Cattery in California and Helen Smith of MerryMews Cattery in New York decided that they would start a breeding program for the longhaired cats. Helen Smith named the cats "Balinese" because she felt they showed the grace and beauty of Balinese dancers and because Longhaired Siamese seemed to be a cumbersome name for such a graceful cat. She was the first to exhibit Balinese in CFA. Helen and Marion worked together during the 1950s and 1960s to develop breeding stock and to gain recognition as a new mutation breed. Mrs. Dorsey showed in a CFF show in Glendale, California, as early as 1956. It is due to these two women and their foresight that we have the Balinese today. The breed became popular after this, and a number of breeders began working on perfecting the Balinese appearance. This led to the development of two entirely separate strands of Balinese cats. Some owners prefer a traditional, "apple-headed" Balinese, while breeders and judges prefer a more contemporary appearance.

Variations in Standards

Like the Siamese, there are now two different varieties of Balinese being bred and shown: traditional Balinese and contemporary Balinese. The traditional Balinese cat has a coat approximately two inches long over its entire body, and it is a sturdy cat, with a semi-rounded muzzle and ears. The traditional Balinese closely resembles a Ragdoll

LEFT
This Balinese would be categorized as a Javanese (see page 292) by the CFA due to its red tabby coloring.

cat, although they do not share any of the same genes or breeding other than having a partial Siamese ancestry. A contemporary Balinese has a much shorter coat and is virtually identical to a standard show Siamese except for its tail, which is a graceful plume.

In most associations the Balinese is accepted in a full range of colors, including the four traditional Siamese point colors of seal, blue, chocolate, and lilac, as well as less traditional colors, such as red and cream, and patterns such as lynx (tabby) point and tortie point. However, in CFA the Balinese is only accepted in the four traditional Siamese colors; all other colors and patterns are considered Javanese (*see* page 292). The Balinese holds championship status in all associations.

Characteristics

Head
The medium-sized head is a long, tapering wedge in good proportion to the body. The skull is flat, the muzzle fine and wedge-shaped. The chin and jaw are medium sized. The nose is long and straight, a continuation of the forehead. There is no break.

Ears and Eyes
The ears are strikingly large and pointed. They are wide at the base, continuing the lines of the wedge. The medium-sized eyes are almond shaped. They slant toward the nose, keeping in line with the wedge and ears. They are uncrossed. The color is a deep and vivid blue.

Body, Legs, and Coat
The medium-sized body is long and graceful. The shoulders and hips continue the same sleek lines of the tubular body. The neck is long and slender. The bone structure of the tail is long and thin, tapering to a point. The legs are long and slim, with fine bone structure. The hind legs are higher than the front legs. The oval paws are small and dainty.

The medium-length coat is fine and silky, without a downy undercoat. It lies close to the body. The tail hair spreads out like a plume.

Temperament

Balinese adore their owners and need to be involved with everything they do. They have extraordinarily loving temperaments and bond closely with their owners. They make excellent pets and want to enjoy fun and games with the family. If you are sad, they will be sad with you; if you are sick, they will comfort you;

RIGHT

Balinese cats originated from a mutation in the Siamese; the breed's grace and elegance inspired its name.

if you are happy, they will play with you—with great energy and enthusiasm.

Balinese have the same outgoing personalities as their Siamese cousins. They are very vocal and will chat to you on just about any subject. They are highly intelligent cats, and just like Siamese, they can get in trouble when they are bored. They love toys and will turn anything into one. They love to play fetch and will carry a piece of crumpled-up paper back to you for hours. They also love furry mice, little balls, and any catnip toy.

Kittens are born with both eyes and ears closed. When the eyes open, they are always blue at first. They change color over a period of months to the final eye color.

Care

A good diet and plenty of exercise are essential to maintain the Balinese's firm, tubular body and silky coat. These cats are not picky eaters and require no special diet. Grooming is simple because the coat does not mat like the double coat of most longhaired breeds.

JAVANESE (Colorpoint Balinese)

SIZE: Medium

COAT CARE: Low maintenance

DIET: Low maintenance

BODY SHAPE: Svelte

COLOR VARIATIONS: Red, cream, blue-cream, and lilac-cream; tortie point in seal and chocolate; lynx point in seal, chocolate, blue, lilac, red, chocolate tortie, blue-cream, lilac-cream, and seal tortie

LIFE EXPECTANCY: 15+ years

Javanese, like their Siamese relatives, are known for being very intelligent and talkative. They are very sociable cats that can become depressed if they are left alone too often.

Origins

The original Javanese were heavier, shorter-headed cats, and to improve their type most breeders have bred back to Siamese and Colorpoint lines. This produces a variant generation: shorthair cats that carry the recessive longhair gene. Hopefully these variants produce a better longhair type when they are bred to a longhair or another variant. Frequent outcrosses to shorthair have contributed to the improvement in type that has been seen over the past ten years. It is a testament to years of work that the Javanese are beginning to hold their own in competition with their parent breeds. They have championship status in CFA, categorized as Javanese; in ACA, ACFA, CFF, TICA, CCA, UFO, AACE they are categorized as Balinese, and in TCA as Colorpoint Balinese.

Name Confusion

There has been and still is confusion surrounding the name "Javanese"—some organizations and countries refer to what is usually known as the "Oriental Longhair" (*see* page 227) as "Javanese" (also known as British Angora, Foreign Longhair, or Mandarin).

LEFT

This cat is a Javanese to some—but it is really an Oriental Longhair, with its solid cinnamon coat color and green eyes.

RIGHT

This Balinese is a Javanese by virtue of its red tabby coloring, which is outside the traditional seal, chocolate, lilac, and blue points.

Characteristics

The Javanese coat is one of their most distinguishing features—a soft, silky, single coat that lies close to the body. The fur should be two to three inches long on the body, longer and fuller on the tail. They are a study of contradictions; refined, sometimes fragile in appearance. In reality they are hard and muscular, with surprising strength. They have vivid blue eyes and strikingly large, pointed ears.

Temperament and Care

Highly intelligent, they become familiar with their owners' routines. They will talk, reminding you when you are late with their meals and greeting you whenever you have been away. In general the Javanese voice is softer and gentler than the Siamese.

Javanese have a tendency to become overweight if they do not get enough exercise. As there is no undercoat, they require little grooming and usually keep themselves immaculate.

Fascinating Facts

Javanese use their paws like little hands to open cupboards and drawers in search of a favorite toy they saw you hide. Many "fetch," but never convince yourself that you taught them this game. In reality, they have cleverly taught you how to throw.

TIFFANIE

BODY SHAPE: Semi-foreign

COLOR VARIATIONS: Chocolate, blue, cinnamon, lilac, and fawn; the accepted patterns are solid, mackerel, flecked, spotted tabby

LIFE EXPECTANCY: 12+ years

SIZE: Medium

COAT CARE: Moderate maintenance

DIET: Low maintenance

The Tiffanie is the longhaired version of the Burmilla, the offspring of Chinchilla and Burmese cats. Tiffanies are an endearing blend of the two original breeds. This delightfully pretty cat with an incredible personality quickly becomes a favorite of all who come to know it.

Origins

The semi-longhaired variety first made an appearance in the mid-1980s as a result of Britain's experimental breeding program for the Burmilla. Since the Burmilla carries a recessive longhaired gene from the Chinchilla Persian ancestry, some of the resulting kittens were semi-longhaired, with silky, medium-length coats. At first these kittens were not taken seriously, as they did not characterize the purpose of breeding silver-shaded shorthairs.

Characteristics

Tiffanies have sweet expressions, but the eyes, with their incredible apple-green color and black mascara-type lining, take the cake. Their luxurious silver coat is tipped in an ethereal mantle of black, blue, brown, chocolate, or lilac, complemented by a magnificent plumed tail.

Temperament and Care

For families, city dwellers, young couples, and single people, this is the ideal cat. Like their Persian ancestors, Tiffanies are content to sit on a bed and contemplate their beauty. Then their Burmese ancestry surfaces, and they will bounce around non-stop, playing with a little ball. Highly intelligent, they seem to know when someone is coming, and it's not unusual to find them sitting at the door waiting to be cuddled or hoping to play. They also adapt well to other pets. Tiffanies' feeding is simple to control, as they are not prone to obesity and regulate their diets well. Their coat is easy to care for and just needs to be brushed every three or four days.

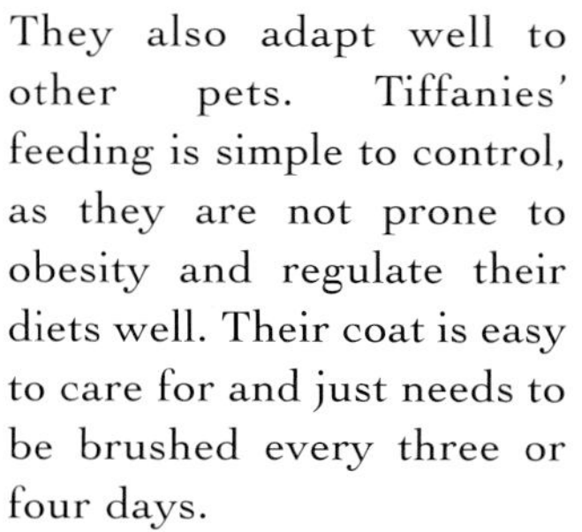

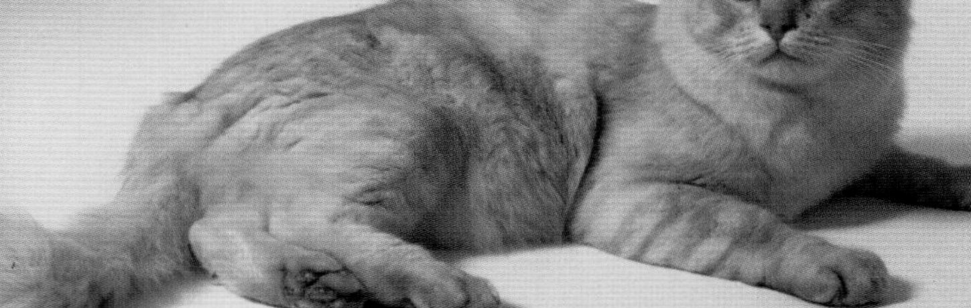

The most outstanding feature of this breed is its wonderful temperament. Tiffanies are gentle, loving, beautiful cats that make excellent pets. They are extremely devoted to their humans and most are real lap cats.

ABOVE

A Brown Tiffanie showing the breed's typical apple-green eyes, distinct neck ruff, and impressive bushy tail.

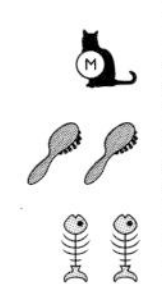

CYMRIC

SIZE: Medium

COAT CARE: Moderate maintenance

DIET: Moderate maintenance

BODY SHAPE: Cobby

COLOR VARIATIONS: Any color, except those indicating hybridization resulting in the colors chocolate, lavender, the Himalayan pattern, or those combined with white

LIFE EXPECTANCY: 12+ years

The Cymric is a longhaired version of the shorthaired, tailless Manx. It originated on the Isle of Man, where it is believed to have been introduced to the Isle by settlers and explorers. Originally it was named Longhaired Manx, but the name was changed to Cymric in the 1970s. Except for the length of the fur, the two breeds are identical.

Origins

The Manx, a natural breed, appeared on the Isle of Man from a mutation of the island's domestic cats. Over the years the interbreeding of these tailless cats has led to this factor being a dominant gene. The name Cymric—the Gaelic word for Wales—was chosen, as many longhaired Manx were seen in Wales.

Initially this name was used within all associations; now in some the breed is called Longhair Manx. Both breeds allow each other as outcrosses in ACFA, and kittens are individually registered by hair length as to the breed.

The Cymric holds championship status in the CFA under Longhaired Manx; championship status in ACA, ACFA, TICA, CCA, AACE, and UFO under the name Cymaric; provisional status in GCCF.

Characteristics

Head

The Cymric has a round head with round, prominent cheeks. In profile it is medium in length, with a gentle dip from forehead to nose. It has a well-developed muzzle, a strong chin, and a definite whisker break, with large, round whisker pads.

Ears and Eyes

The medium-sized ears are widely spaced and wide at the base, tapering to rounded tips.

The large, round eyes are set at a slight angle toward the nose. Eye colors are deep blue, brilliant copper,

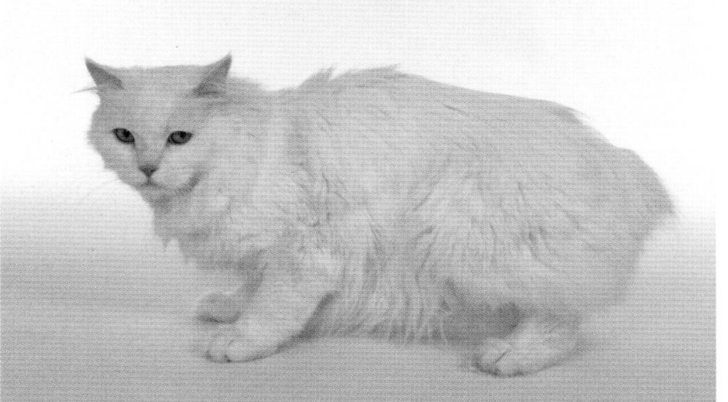

RIGHT

The Cymric is a longhaired version of the tailless Manx cat, and its name was inspired after it frequently occurred in Wales.

RIGHT

Cymric cats are said to be doglike in nature and are attracted to shiny objects, such as jewelry and keys.

green, blue-green, or hazel. The eye color depends on the coat color.

Body and Legs

The Cymric is a medium-sized, compact cat, solidly muscled and well balanced, with substantial bone structure. It has a stout appearance, with a broad chest. The repetition of curves and circles gives the cat the appearance of great substance and durability. It is powerful without a hint of coarseness. The flank has greater depth than in other breeds. The short back forms a smooth, continuous arch from shoulders to rump, curving at the rump to form a desirable round look. This cat appears entirely tailless in a perfect specimen.

Coat

The double coat is medium length, soft and silky, glossy, dense, and well padded over the main body. It lengthens from shoulders to rump. The breeches, abdomen, and neck ruff are usually longer than the coat on the main body. The cheek coat is thick and full. The neck ruff extends from the shoulders around the chest. Toe and ear tufts are desirable.

Temperament

The tailless Cymric, whose name is derived from the Gaelic word for Wales, is a friendly, affectionate, relaxed companion, an easy feline with which to share a home. According to some sources, the Cymric is somewhat doglike in its habits; it will play fetch and even growl at a sudden disturbance. This cat is also known for its love of shiny objects, so keep an eye on your jewelry and car keys. It accepts children, dogs, and other cats. As pets, these cats are excellent. They

usually gravitate toward one person in the household, and it's not unusual to find a Cymric in the lap of its owner or resting close by. Often they will emit little trills of joy when they are with you.

Fascinating Facts

You can tell a cat's mood by looking into its eyes. A frightened or excited cat will have large, round pupils. An angry cat will have narrow pupils. The pupil size is related as much to the cat's emotions as to the degree of light.

Care

Feed a premium cat food regularly, and give a hairball treatment twice a week between meals. Brush and comb your Cymric two or three times a week.

AMERICAN BOBTAIL

SIZE: Medium

COAT CARE: Moderate maintenance

DIET: Moderate maintenance

BODY SHAPE: Semi-cobby

COLOR VARIATIONS: All categories, divisions, and colors

LIFE EXPECTANCY: 13+ years

The American Bobtail is a naturally occurring short-tailed cat, which was first recognized in its longhair form. It originated around 40 years ago, when feral cats with natural bobtails were found. Its wildcat look combined with its full domesticity and pleasing personality is a credit to the breeders.

Origins

Little is known about the American Bobtail, as the breed is still in development, but it is believed to be a variant of the Manx gene. The Manx gene is dominant, which is lethal in the homozygous form. Since all living Manx are heterozygous, any Manx litter can produce tailless (rumpy), partly tailed (stumpy), or fully tailed kittens. It is a hearty, intelligent breed.

RIGHT

The American Bobtail has a wild and powerful appearance; its coat can be either shorthair or a medium-length longhair.

Characteristics

The Bobtail is well muscled, having the appearance of power. It has a noticeably wild look. The tail should be clearly visible above the back and is not to exceed the hock in length. The head is a broad modified wedge, with a distinctive brow above large, almost almond-shaped eyes. Its unique coat comes in a medium, semi-dense shorthair or a medium-length longhair that is resilient and resistant to water.

Temperament and Care

American Bobtails are a loving and incredibly intelligent cat. They easily adapt to a busy or quiet environment. In this breed no two tails are exactly the same. American Bobtails bond easily with their family. They get along well with most dogs and have a welcome spot in their hearts for newcomers, whether they are two-legged or four-legged. Psychotherapists have used them in treatment programs because they have been found to be very well behaved and sensitive to people in distress.

The cat generally eats too much, so you may have to stop offering unlimited amounts of dry food and consult your veterinarian about feeding a weight-control diet. Longhaired American Bobtails need to be brushed a couple of times a week.

AMERICAN CURL

BODY SHAPE: Semi-foreign

COLOR VARIATIONS: All colors and patterns, including Himalayan pattern, shaded, smoke, chinchilla, and bicolors

LIFE EXPECTANCY: 12+ years

SIZE: Medium

COAT CARE: Low maintenance

DIET: Low maintenance

The American Curl is different from any other breed, with its innocent look and devilish, curled-backed ears. They retain their playfulness long into maturity, giving them a reputation for never growing up.

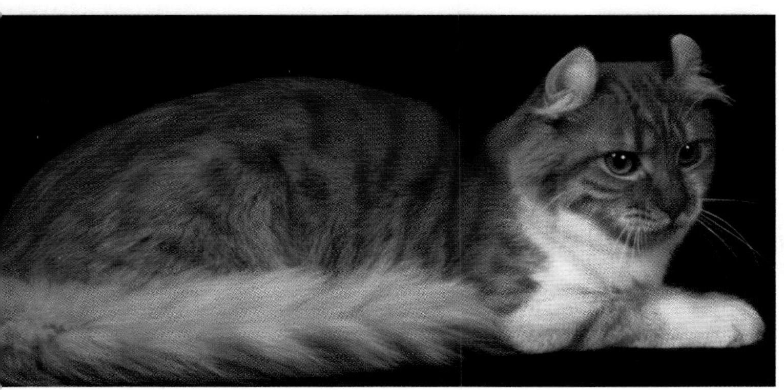

Origins

This breed has been hand-built from the beginning. It started with a mutation in the domestic cat population in 1981. A stray, longhaired black, female cat named Shulamith had ears that were not straight but were curled back, and when she had kittens they were distributed for careful breeding. The cartilage in the base of the ears is firm, even stiff to the touch. Once seen and felt, this trademark cannot be mistaken. The American Curl was first exhibited in 1983 and given championship recognition in 1987 by the International Cat Association. It now holds championship status in all associations.

Characteristics

The head is a modified wedge, with rounded contours. The firm ears are set on the corners of the head, curving in a gentle curl back from the face. The walnut-shaped eyes are large and expressive. The body should not be cobby or coarse, nor should it have fine or slender boning or musculature. The Curls' ears and expressive eyes make this breed a unique cat; a delight to look at and a pleasure to own.

LEFT

American Curl cats have a unique appearance, with their large, expressive eyes and gently curled-back ears.

Temperament and Care

American Curls are hearty cats. They are intelligent and playful yet gentle, very much a people cat. They like to rub their owner's chin and sit on their shoulders. They even like rough play and enjoy being with young children. They may be quiet, almost pensive in attitude and not overly active, but they remain extremely curious about their surroundings. They can be easily trained, even to walk on a leash or to fetch and retrieve. The American Curl has no special dietary needs, and they require very little grooming since their coat rarely mats.

SELKIRK REX

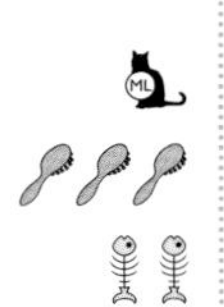

SIZE: Medium to large

COAT CARE: High maintenance

DIET: Moderate maintenance

BODY SHAPE: Semi-cobby

COLOR VARIATIONS: All categories, all divisions, all colors; white locket permitted

LIFE EXPECTANCY: 15+ years

The Selkirk Rex is one of the newest recognized breeds. It has a distinctive curly coat and whiskers that are barely there.

Origins

The Selkirk Rex originated in Montana in 1987, with a litter born to a rescued cat. The only unusually coated kitten in the litter was placed with a Persian breeder, Jeri Newman, who named her Miss DePesto. This foundation cat was bred to a black Persian male. The litter resulted in three curly kittens out of six—proving that, unlike the Devon Rex and the Cornish Rex, this mutation was dominant. Because it is dominant, curly kittens can be born in the same litter as straight-haired kittens. Allowable outcrosses for this breed are Persian, Exotic Shorthair, British Shorthair, and American Shorthair.

The Selkirk Rex is recognized in the miscellaneous class in CFA; championship status in TICA, ACA, and UFO; new breed and color in CAA and ACFA.

Characteristics

The Selkirk Rex has a rounded, stocky body type and comes in both longhair and shorthair varieties. The head is round, with large rounded eyes, medium-sized ears, and a distinct muzzle, with a length that is equal to half its width. The coat is dense, with loose, individual curls.

Temperament and Care

The Selkirk Rex is incredibly patient, loving, and tolerant. They have a sweet and endearing personality and make wonderful, affectionate pets. They can be a welcome addition to a home, where proper behavior and good manners are important. These cats are happy alone.

The breed is prone to hairballs, so choose a quality cat food that includes a hairball preventative. This cat needs to be groomed several times a week to avoid tangles and to remove loose hair. Be careful not to overcomb the coat, as too much grooming can straighten the hair.

LEFT

A blue-cream Selkirk Rex cat with the breed's distinctive curly coat, round eyes, and barely visible whiskers.

Fascinating Facts

The founder of the Selkirk Rex originally claimed that she had named the breed after the Selkirk Mountains, close to where the kittens were born in Montana. However, when it was pointed out to her that the Selkirk Mountains were located in British Columbia, she admitted that she had actually named the breed after her stepfather. This makes the Selkirk Rex the only cat breed today named after an individual.

LAPERM

BODY SHAPE: Semi-cobby

COLOR VARIATIONS: Comes in every recognized color and coat pattern

LIFE EXPECTANCY: 12+ years

SIZE: Small to medium

COAT CARE: Moderate maintenance

DIET: Low maintenance

RIGHT

LaPerm cats come in all colors and have curly whiskers as well as coats; the breed is still being developed.

LaPerm means wavy or curly in many different languages. With its distinctive coat, striking appearance, and affectionate personality, LaPerm stands out from many other breeds of cats.

Origins

The LaPerm breed started from a mutation in one individual cat, Curly, in 1982. As with the other Rex breeds, in order for the breed to develop, outcross matings had to take place. Curly chose her own mates from amongst the barn cats on the farm where she lived. This led to the natural development of a small colony of LaPerms that were then used as the basis for a formal breeding program. The breed is still being developed worldwide, and to widen the gene pool, an outcross program is underway. It is only a matter of time before this unique breed will be recognized worldwide.

Characteristics

The LaPerm can have anything from a wavy coat to ringlet-type curls. The tightest curls occur on the underside of the cat, on the throat area, and at the base of the ears. The face and head of the LaPerm are triangular in shape, with wide-set ears and large, expressive eyes. They have curly whiskers. As well as medium to medium-long, LaPerm coats can also come in shorthaired versions.

Temperament and Care

LaPerms are inquisitive, gentle, and affectionate but also very active. The LaPerm will often follow your lead. If they are busy playing and you want to relax, simply pick up your cat and it will stay on your lap, enjoying the attention. LaPerms seek human contact and will purr as soon as they become aware of your presence. They will reach for your face with their paws and rub their faces against your head, neck, and face. Choose a quality, balanced cat food for your LaPerm. As for grooming, the LaPerm is low maintenance because the coat does not easily mat. A bath and towel drying is all that is required to maintain the curliness.

Wildcats

When we look at the domestic cat, we can still see many of the features of their wild ancestry. Cats today, from the domestic cat to the big cats, are descendants of the miacids, some of which became cheetahs, lions, and tigers. The wildcat (that is, the smaller type of wildcat) can be categorized into subsections: the European wildcat, the Asiatic desert cat, and the African wildcat. Our domestic cat is believed to be a descendant of the African wildcat.

Wildcats are found in every continent, except Australia and Antarctica, but the majority are in Africa, Asia, Europe, and South America. They come in every size—from the very small to the huge cats of the African plains. Many have vibrant patterns and are exotic colors; all of them are exciting, exotic animals. There are many different species, from the tiny black-footed cat of southern Africa to the majestic cat of Africa. This section of the book will give you an overview of these wondrous creatures.

RIGHT

The majority of cat species, such as this Pallas cat, live in forested areas and are agile climbers.

Grouping

Felidae is the biological family of the cats; a member of this family is called a felid. They are the most strictly carnivorous mammals of the nine families in the order *Carnivora*. The first felids emerged during the Oligocene era, around 30 million years ago. A wild relative of the domestic cat, the desert wildcat still lives in the Middle East and Africa. Other well-known members of the felid family include big cats such as the lion, the tiger, the leopard, the jaguar, the cougar, and the cheetah and smaller wildcats, such as the lynxes and the caracal.

Characteristics

The many species of felids vary greatly in size. One of the smallest is the black-footed cat; the largest is the tiger. The fur of felids takes many different forms, being much thicker in those species that live in cold environments, such as the snow leopard. The color also varies, although brown to golden fur is common in most species. They are often marked with distinguishing spots, stripes, or rosettes, and many species also have a "tear stripe," a black stripe running from the corner of each eye down the side of the nose.

The tongue is covered with horny papillae, which help to rip meat from their prey. With the exception of the cheetah, almost all felids have fully retractable claws.

BELOW

The margay, like most of the wildcats, is a solitary and secretive animal, hunting mainly at night.

Wildcat vs. Domestic Cat

Since domestics often breed with wildcats, confusing the bloodlines, the key difference between the two is behavior. Domestic cats can live in groups and are generally not afraid of people. Since behavioral analyses of a large and diverse group of cats would be almost impossible, an international research team turned to genetics.

Carlos Driscoll of the National Cancer Institute and his colleagues analyzed genetic material from almost 1,000 cats, including domestic cats and the wildcat subspecies: the European wildcat, Middle Eastern wildcat, Central Asian wildcat, southern African wildcat, and Chinese desert cat. They found that each wild group represents a subspecies of the wildcat *Felis silvestris*. The DNA from domestic cats matched with that of the Middle Eastern wildcat subspecies *Felis silvestris lybica*, which lives in the remote deserts of Israel and Saudi Arabia.

BELOW

The caracal, shown here hunting for food, lives in the grassy savannah plains of Africa.

Fascinating Facts

A tiger's head often carries the Chinese mark of Wang or king on the forehead.

Habitat

Felids are purely carnivorous animals, subsisting almost entirely on other vertebrates. Aside from the lion, they are solitary, and most are secretive animals, often nocturnal, and live in relatively inaccessible habitats. Around three-quarters of cat species live in forested terrain, and they are generally agile climbers. However, felids may be found in almost any environment, with some species being native to mountainous terrain or to deserts.

THE BIG CATS

The Big Cats are the most well known and well loved of wildcats, inspiring us with their powerful, majestic, and graceful demeanor. In its most specific definition, the term "big cats" only encompasses the lion, tiger, jaguar, and leopard, as these are the "roaring cats" of the genus Panthera. However, the other leopards, such as the Snow Leopard and the Clouded Leopard, and the Cheetah, though different, are generally grouped with the big cats, as they are equally impressive in size and character.

Lion (Panthera leo)

The Lion has always held man's respect and stirred his imagination. Man has credited the magnificent beast with the character traits he treasures the most: nobility, courage, loyalty, and assertiveness. The full-grown male, whose splendid mane ranges in color from a rich golden brown to a deep blackish-brown, marks him as the authentic monarch of the plains. The legacy of the lion, king of the beasts, is shown throughout history by its appearance in the earliest drawings made by man—over 15,000 years ago.

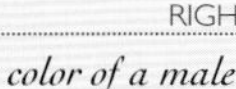

RIGHT

The color of a male lion's mane can vary from one animal to another and usually darkens with age.

Characteristics

Males range from 5 ft., 6 in.–8 ft. (172–250 cm) in body length, females from 5–6 ft. (158–192 cm). Tail length varies from 2–3 ft. (60–100 cm). Females are 99–150 lbs (45–68 kg) lighter than the average-size male but have an equal muscle mass. Males weigh between 330–572 lbs (150–260 kg), while females weigh between 268–400 lbs (122–182 kg).

Lions have a broad face, rounded ears, and a proportionally short neck. Male lions have a mane, which varies in color, usually being silver-grey or a yellow-red. The darker the mane is, the older the lion. Captive lions are known to have fuller manes than wild lions. The underside of the male is a buff color, while the female's underside is off-white. Both sexes have sharp retractable claws on each paw and powerful shoulders that they use to bring down

ABOVE

The female lion does the majority of the hunting, although the male will assist in killing larger prey.

prey. Hingelike jaws containing 2 in. (5 cm) canines also aid the lion in hunting. The lion's life span is 25–30 years.

Habitat

The lion was once found from northern Africa through southwest Asia, but it has become extinct in most countries within the last 150 years. Moving west into Europe, it became extinct 2,000 years ago, and east into India there is a relict population only in Gir Forest. Today the majority of Africa's lions can be found in eastern and southern Africa, with a small number in western Africa. Most of the lions today exist inside protected areas. No accurate number of how many live in the wild exists.

Lion prides are often found in the open plains but occupy almost all habitats, except deep desert and rainforest. Lions climb trees to relax and cool off or sometimes to escape stampedes. During the day they rest by water holes or salt licks, but at night these places are usually reserved for hunting.

Diet

Lions are opportunistic eaters, and they will take almost any prey, ranging from small rodents to young rhinos, hippos, and elephants. The majority of their prey, however, are medium- to large-hoofed mammals, mainly zebra, wildebeest, impala, wart-hog, hartebeest, and waterbuck. They will stay away from adult rhinos, hippos, elephants, and giraffes. The female does most of the hunting, with the male joining his mate after the kill is made. Males will participate on a hunt only when the prey is especially large, for example, a water buffalo. Then his size and strength is required to bring down the animal; however, enough females can do it successfully on their own. Males must also hunt before they are partnered with a mate, when there is no female to feed him.

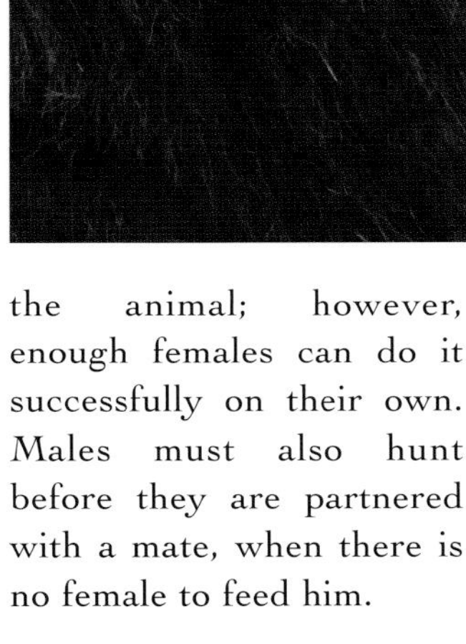

Conservation Status

Lions are generally considered problem animals, whose existence is at odds with human settlements and their herds of cattle. Their scavenging makes them highly susceptible to poisoned carcasses put out to eliminate predators. Where the wild prey is migratory, lions will feed on captive stock during the lean season, making them easy targets for humans.

Fascinating Facts

The heaviest lion in captivity today is an African lion called "Ruteledge" at the Oaklawn Farm Zoo, Nova Scotia, Canada. Ruteledge weighs in at 807 lbs (366 kg), has a shoulder height of 3 ft., 3 in. (1 m), a girth of 6 ft. (1.7 m). (Guinness Book of Records).

Tiger (Panthera tigris tigris)

Regardless of the culture or language, the tiger is considered to be the undisputed ruler of its domain. Over the centuries it has had a profound influence on village life in Asia. The popular belief is that the tiger is the oldest resident of the jungle, living there long before humans arrived. Locals working in their yards or in the forest have too much respect for, and fear of, the big cat to call it by its common name. Instead they use courteous titles like "grandfather or grandmother in the forest," "old man of the forest," "general," or "king of the forest." The tiger is feared, respected, admired, or distrusted, depending on the situation. The beliefs center around its power to help or harm and save or destroy. In Sumatra the final analysis is that the tiger is a good and just animal and a friend rather than an enemy, who can be called on in times of sickness or difficulty.

Characteristics
The majority of tigers are tawny brown in color, with dark stripes and whitish tones on its underside. Records indicate, however, that a few wild tigers have been seen in unusual colors, including all white and all black.

Vital Statistics The weight of Siberian tigers, the heaviest of the subspecies, is 500 lbs (225 kg) or more, with males heavier than females. The lightest subspecies is the Sumatran. The males weigh around 250 lbs (110 kg) and females around 200 lbs (90 kg). Depending on the subspecies, the head-body length of a tiger is around 4½–9 ft. (140–280 cm). The length of the tail is 3–4 ft. (90–120 cm). The foot pads vary in size with age, resulting in inaccurate estimates when used to census wild populations.

Tigers have round pupils and yellow irises, except for the blue eyes of white tigers. Due to a retinal adaptation that reflects light back to the retina, the night vision of tigers is six times better than that of humans.

ABOVE
It is believed that the tiger's striped coat, unusual among felids, provides camouflage when hunting.

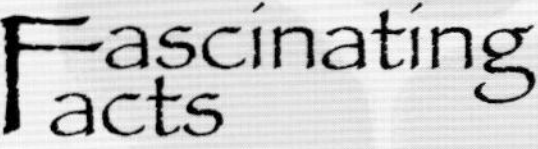

Everyone recognizes the tiger by its striped coat, but few people know these stripes extend through to the skin. Zoo veterinarians noticed this when they shaved off sections of the coat to perform surgery.

RIGHT
Tigers live in a range of habitats, including forested areas, grasslands, and the borders of swamps.

The claws, like those of domestic cats, are retractable. A tiger scratches on trees to mark its territory.

Stripes Tigers are the only striped felid. Many scientists believe that the stripes act as camouflage and help tigers hide from their prey. The Sumatran tiger has the most stripes of all the tiger subspecies, and the Siberian tiger has the fewest, but on average there are 100–150 stripes per animal. The Siberian tiger's stripes are wider and lighter in color than those of the other subspecies. The stripes continue through to the skin. The hide of the white tiger is a bluish color, also complete with stripes. Tiger stripes are like human fingerprints; no two are alike.

The head of the tiger often carries the Chinese mark of Wang, or king, on the forehead. The life span is thought to be about 10 years.

Habitat
Tigers range from India to Siberia and southeast Asia. They prefer to live in a forest, although they can be found in grassland and swamp borders. They require sufficient cover, a population of large prey, and a constant water supply.

Diet
The tiger's main prey are large animals such as deer, buffalo, and wild pigs, but they will also hunt fish, monkeys, birds, reptiles, and sometimes even baby elephants. Occasionally tigers kill leopards, bears, and other tigers.

Conservation Status
Tigers are listed as endangered. They are illegally poached for their fur and other body parts and suffer from habitat loss. The Chinese tiger (*P.t.amoyensis*) and the Siberian tiger (*P.t.altaica*) are under extreme threat of extinction.

Jaguar (Panthera onca)

Jaguars are the biggest feline species in the New World and the only member of the genus *Panthera*, the roaring cats, that occurs in the Americas. They are the third largest cat, being outsized only by lions (*P. leo*) and tigers (*P. trigris*). Although they are not the largest, jaguars have the strongest jaws in relation to head size of any of the cats.

Jaguars are worshipped in many indigenous American cultures. The Maya believed that Jaguar, god of the underworld, helped the sun travel under the earth at night, ensuring its new rising every morning.

Characteristics

Jaguars are muscular cats, with relatively short, large limbs and a deep-chested body. They weigh 180–264 lbs (90–120 kg) for males and 132–180 lbs (60–90 kg) for females, with a large variation in body size. They have a broad, heavy head and comparatively short legs and tail. The background of the jaguar's coat is a tawny yellow, like many of the Asiatic leopards, and lightens to off-white on the throat and stomach. It is marked with small isolated spots on the head and neck, with dark open ring structures—rosettes—on the sides and flank. Generally the pattern contains one to four dark spots inside of the rings. Interestingly the rosettes of the leopard and Jaguar are almost identical, with the exception of the Jaguar having spots inside the rosettes where the leopard has none. Along the middle of the Jaguar's back, a row of black spots may merge into a solid line. According to one Indian myth, the Jaguar got its spotted coat by patting mud on its body with its paws. The life span of the jaguar is 20–22 years.

Habitat

Jaguars live in a wide variety of tropical habitats, ranging from mountain forests and wet savannah to tropical rainforests and deciduous tropical forests. The largest recorded jaguars occur in wet savannahs, while jaguars that live in more forested regions are generally smaller in size.

Diet

The eating habits of these cats are not well known. They probably prey on deer and large ground-dwelling birds. Jaguars have the reputation of being so destructive to cattle and horses that the larger Mexican ranches hire a tiger hunter to kill them or at least to drive them away. Jaguars also enjoy sea turtle eggs, and they roam the

beaches to dig up and eat the eggs that are buried in the sand.

Conservation status

Deforestation rates are high in Latin America, and loss of forest habitat separates jaguar populations, making them more vulnerable to the predations of man. People compete with jaguars for prey, and they are frequently shot on sight, despite protective legislation. Jaguars are also known to kill cattle and are often killed by ranchers as pests.

The vulnerability of the jaguar to persecution is demonstrated by its disappearance by the mid-1900s from the southwestern United States and northern Mexico. Commercial hunting and trapping of jaguars for their pelts has declined drastically since the mid-1970s, when anti-fur campaigns and controls shut down international markets.

The jaguar is fully protected at the national level across most of its range, with hunting prohibited in Argentina, Brazil, Colombia, French Guiana, Honduras, Nicaragua, Panama, Paraguay, Suriname, the United States, Uruguay, and Venezuela, and hunting restrictions are in place in Brazil, Costa Rica, Guatemala, Mexico, and Peru. The species also occurs within protected areas in some of its habitat. Jaguars have a reputation for being human eaters; however, there is little evidence to back this up.

RIGHT

Jaguars are under threat from loss of habitat, ranchers who perceive them as pests, and the fur trade.

Fascinating Facts

Cats are great contortionists. Their forelegs can turn in almost any direction, and both halves of their bodies can move in opposite directions.

LEFT

The pattern of spots on a leopard's coat is unique to the animal, like a human's fingerprints.

Leopard (Panthera pardus)

The leopard is a member of the pantherine lineage, which also includes the lion, tiger, jaguar, clouded leopard, and snow leopard. Fossils from their most recent common ancestor have yet to be identified, but mitochondrial gene sequence data suggest that species deviation began six million years ago. Phylogenetic analyses of the subspecies of *P. pardus* indicate an African origin, which validates the paleontological evidence. The earliest record is from Tanzania, approximately 3.8 million years ago.

Characteristics

The background color of the leopard's very short and sleek coat is pale, cream-yellow on its underside. This darkens to orange-brown on its back. Solid black spots adorn its limbs and head, smaller and denser than the golden, umber-centered rosettes that cover its back and sides. The tail has irregular patches that, at the tip, become dark-ringed bands. Leopards can also be all black, a condition known as *melanism*. Black leopards, also known as panthers, are not a separate species. The spots can still be seen as black rosettes on a dark-brown background. Melanistic leopards and normal leopards have been known to occur in the same litter. Black leopards are more common in areas with denser trees. The dark rosettes help it blend into the foliage while stalking its prey. Like human fingerprints, each individual leopard's spots are unique. The life span is 12–17 years.

The Snow Leopard (*Uncia uncia*) is a large cat native to the mountain ranges of central and southern Asia. Along with the clouded leopard, it cannot roar despite possessing a cartilaginous hyoid apparatus. The snow leopard has a whitish tan coat, with ringed spots of dark, ash-brown, and rosettes of black. The fur turns white in the winter. Its tail is heavy with fur, and the bottom of its paws is covered with fur for protection against snow and cold. The life span of a snow leopard is normally 15–18 years.

ABOVE

The snow leopard's thick coat enables it to survive in the snowy mountainous regions of Asia.

The Clouded Leopard (*Neofelis nebulosa*) is a medium-sized cat. It has a tawny coat and is distinctively marked with large, irregularly shaped, dark-edged ellipses that are said to be shaped like clouds. It seems to be a cross between a big cat and a small cat. *Neo* means "new" and *felis* means "small cat," so its scientific name literally means a new kind of small cat.

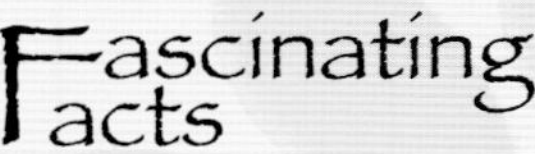

Fascinating Facts

Leopards are capable of carrying animals up to twice their own weight into the trees to eat them.

RIGHT

The cloudlike shapes that give the clouded leopard its name can be clearly seen on this cub.

Habitat

Leopards could originally be found from the British Isles to Japan and throughout most of Asia. Today they can still be found in Africa, except for the true deserts of Sahara and Kalahari, and some parts of Asia such as Sri Lanka. Leopards are more common in Eastern and Central Africa. Conversely they are rare in western and northern Africa and most of Asia.

Diet

Leopards are opportunistic hunters. Their diet consists of monkeys, rodents, reptiles, amphibians, birds, fish, wild pigs, and ungulates. They hunt during the day to avoid contact with lions and hyenas, which are night hunters. When it kills an animal such as a gazelle, it carries it into the trees to eat it.

Conservation Status

Extensive hunting for their beautiful fur and habitat encroachment has taken its toll on leopard numbers. Farmers kill them because they pose a threat to their livestock, and they can be easily poisoned because they feed on carrion. The status ranges from threatened to endangered to critically endangered, depending on the geographic region. Illegal hunting of leopards for their fur became so common in the 1960s that as many as 50,000 skins were marked annually. They are listed as critically endangered.

Cheetah (Acinonyx jubatus)

The Cheetah is famous for its speed. It is the world's fastest land animal, having been known to reach speeds of up to 70 mph. However, it is unable to keep this pace for any length of time and rarely pursues prey farther than 500 yards. Adaptations that enable the cheetah to run as fast as it does include large nostrils, allowing for increased oxygen intake, and an enlarged heart and lungs, working together to circulate oxygen efficiently. While running, the cheetah uses its tail for rudderlike steering. The cheetah is distinctly different from all other felids in both anatomy and behavior, and yet in many ways it is the epitome of feline grace.

ABOVE
The black marks that run from the cheetah's eyes to its mouth help shield its eyes from the sun.

Characteristics

The cheetah has a slender, long-legged body, with blunt, semi-retractable claws that give the cat extra grip in its high-speed pursuits. Its coat is tan with small, round, black spots, and the fur is coarse and short. Some cheetahs also have a rare fur pattern caused by a mutation. These cheetahs have larger, blotchy, spots, and they are known as "king cheetahs." They were once believed to be a separate subspecies, but that proved to be untrue. They became a part of a breeding program to develop genetic mutations, such as fur patterns, size, and rare and unusual color forms, with no regard to the genetic integrity of the species. The king cheetah has only been seen in the wild a few times, but it has been bred successfully in captivity.

The cheetah has a small head with high-set eyes. Black "tear marks," which run from the corner of the eyes down the sides of the nose to the mouth, keep the sun out of the eyes and aid in hunting.

RIGHT

A cheetah scans the plains for suitable prey, which it will stalk before breaking into a high-speed chase.

Vital Statistics The adult body length is 3½–4½ ft. (112–135 cm); tail length 2–2½ ft. (66–84cm); shoulder height starts at 29 in. (73 cm); weight varies from 75–119 lbs (34–54 kg). The male is only slightly larger than the female, so it is difficult to tell males and females apart by appearance alone.

Unlike true Big Cats, the cheetah can purr as it inhales, but it cannot roar. By contrast the big cats can roar but cannot purr, except while exhaling. The cheetah is not considered one of the Big Cats because it does not have the floating hyoid bone in its neck that would enable it to roar. Its life span is 10–15 years.

Habitat

The cheetah was once widely distributed throughout Africa, the Arabian Peninsula, Asia Minor, and even east of India. Records show that fossils were found from China, northern India, southern Europe, and as far as the western United States. Sadly now the species is dying out and can be found sparsely scattered in Namibia, Kenya, Asia, as well as a few other small countries.

Cheetahs thrive in areas with vast expanses of land, where prey is abundant. In Namibia they have been found in a variety of habitats, including grasslands, savannahs, dense vegetation, and mountainous terrain. The African cheetah can only be found naturally in Zimbabwe and South Africa Transvaal Province. Ninety-five percent live on commercial farms.

Diet

The cheetah eats gazelles, young antelope, young calves, warthogs, hares, and game birds. They typically stalk their prey until they are only 30 to 90 feet away. They then burst into a chase that lasts around 20 seconds. The cheetah successfully catches its prey in around half of the chases.

Fascinating Facts

A cat retracts its claws by flexing its toes. This protects their sharpness and lets the cat walk quietly when stalking prey.

Conservation Status

Population estimates vary from 2,000 to 15,000. The World Conservation Union classifies the cheetah as vulnerable, with the African subspecies as endangered and the Asiatic subspecies as critically endangered. The cheetah is listed as endangered.

SMALL CATS OF EUROPE

Europe was once host to many more wildcats than the three that now remain, sometimes only to be found in obscure mountainous regions. Anything from the saber-toothed cat millions of years ago, to lions and leopards in more recent times, existed on this continent. However, due to inevitable climactic change and regrettable depletion due to hunting, most have been driven to extinction or have moved out of the area, leaving only the Eurasian (or Northern) Lynx, the Spanish (or Iberian) Lynx, and the more widespread European Wildcat.

Eurasian Lynx (Lynx lynx)

While all of the lynx species are alike in appearance, preference for different prey has led to a variance in life history and social organization. Only in the extreme northern parts of the Eurasian cats' range are there ecological similarities with the smaller Canada lynx. The Eurasian cat generally has more dark, distinct spotting on its coat than the Canadian cats.

Characteristics

The Eurasian lynx is the largest of the lynxes. Adult males weigh on average 47 lbs (21.6 kg), while females are slightly smaller at 40 lbs (18.1 kg). The lynxes of eastern Siberia consistently reach the greatest size. The Eurasian lynx has relatively long legs and large feet that provide a snowshoe effect, allowing for more effective travel through deep snow. In the winter the fur grows heavily and protects the bottom of the feet. The coat is grayish, with tints varying from shades of rust to yellow. The life span of the Eurasian lynx is more than 20 years.

Fascinating Facts

The name lynx comes from the Greek word "to shine" and may be in reference to the reflective ability of the cat's eyes.

BELOW

The Eurasian lynx's preferred habitat is deciduous or mixed woodland, with dense undergrowth.

Habitat

With one of the widest ranges of all cat species, Eurasian lynx prefer deciduous forests or old growth taiga and mixed woodlands, with plenty of undergrowth for cover. They are also found throughout the northern slopes of the Himalayas to an elevation of 8,200 ft. (2,500 m), alpine tundra, rocky areas above the tree line, the mountains of the central Asian desert region, and the Tibetan Plateau.

Diet

In some parts of their range, lynx prey mainly on large, ungulate species, mostly females or the young, including red deer, reindeer, and argali. Lynx are capable of killing prey three to four times their own size.

Conservation Status

As a species, this lynx is not endangered, but in some parts it has become extremely rare and may not survive unless steps are taken to conserve it.

LEFT
The Spanish lynx is one of the world's most endangered cats, and it is being carefully monitored.

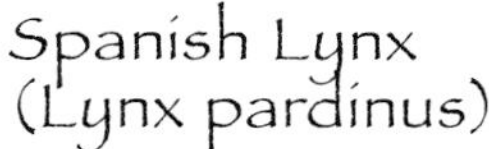

Spanish Lynx (Lynx pardinus)

The Spanish lynx (Lynx pardinus), or Iberian lynx, is sometimes classified as a subspecies of the Eurasian lynx, but most authorities agree that it is a separate species.

Characteristics

Spanish/Iberian lynx are similar in appearance to Eurasian lynx but smaller. Spanish lynx have the characteristically bobbed tail, tufted ears and jaws, spotted coat, muscular body, long legs,, and quick reflexes. Males weigh, on average, 28 lbs (12.8 kg) but can reach 59 lbs (26.8 kg). Females reach a weight of around 20 lbs (9.3 kg).

Habitat

The majority of Spanish lynx populations are restricted to the Iberian Peninsula in Spain, an area of around 540 sq. mi. (14,000 sq km), with a few small populations in the Algarve Mountains and Serra da Malcata Nature Reserve in Portugal. The Spanish populations live in controlled hunting zones called "cotos." Although critically endangered, these animals are still on the offensive animal list and may be shot on sight, except for when they range within national parks and reserves. The lynx living in Portugal are believed to number only around 50 animals.

Diet

The main diet for this Lynx is small ungulates such as roe deer, chamois, and musk deer, and in other parts pikas, large rodents, and hares. In some of their range they will hunt larger ungulates as much as three to four times their own size, most notably reindeer.

Conservation Status

Due to low numbers, habitat fragmentation, and limited habitat, Spanish lynx is considered one of the world's most endangered cat species. Currently the Spanish government is attempting to set up a permanent and protected area for this lynx. Studies of these animals, with the help of radio collars, are giving researchers an idea of the total ranges of the lynx.

European Wildcat (Felis silvestris silvestris)

The European wildcat evolved approximately 650,000 years ago. It is in the direct ancestral line of the domestic cat and is the parent species for several related small cats. The European or Forest wildcat, as it is often called, was once found throughout Europe and is considered by some to be the oldest form of the species. During the past 300 years, the range of the European wildcat, through pressures brought about by hunting and the spread of human population, has been substantially reduced.

Characteristics

The physical appearance of the European wildcat is much bulkier than that of the African wildcat and the domestic cat. Its distinguishing traits are its large size, along with its thick fur. It is around one-third larger than a feral cat but resembles it in both build and coat. Its coat is long and thick to protect it from harsh European winters, and it is colored and marked identically to a basic brown-striped, tabby alley cat. The weight of the cat is 10–30 lbs (4.5–13.6 kg). The head/body length is 22–28 in. (55.9–71.1 cm), and the tail length is 12 in. (30.5 cm). The life span of the European wildcat is around 15 years.

Habitat

The European wildcat inhabits the forests of Western, Central, and Eastern Europe, as well as Scotland and Turkey. It no longer lives in Scandinavia, Iceland, England, Wales, or Ireland.

Two forms coexisted in large numbers in the Iberian Peninsula: the common European form, north of the Douro and Ebro rivers, and the giant Iberian form, previously considered to be a different subspecies. The last is one of the heaviest subspecies of *Felis silvestris*. In his book, *Pleistocene Mammals of Europe* (1963), paleontologist Dr. Björn Kurtén noted that this subspecies is approximately the same size and form that lived in all of Europe during the Pleistocene. Although Spain and Portugal are the West European countries with the greatest population of wildcats, the animals in those regions are threatened by breeding with feral cats and loss of habitat.

Diet

The staple diet for the majority of European wildcats is that of small

Fascinating Facts

Cats are able to hear sounds that move faster than 45,000 hertz. They could hear the sound of a bat.

RIGHT

The European wildcat is an ancient form of felid and is a direct ancestor of our domestic cats.

rodents such as wood mouse, pine vole, water vole, and shrew, while the wildcats studied in Scotland hunted rabbit and hare, species more abundant in open terrain. With the European wildcat as a whole, birds feature as a secondary source of food, and small mammals, small reptiles, and insects supplement the diet. Interestingly, while domesticated cats love fish, wildcats rarely eat them.

Conservation Status

Although legally protected, these cats are still shot by hunters mistaking them for domestic cats.

LEFT

A European wildcat climbs a tree in a Scottish pine forest, demonstrating the agility of this species.

Unfortunately, it hybridizes freely with domestic cats, and this represents a major threat to its survival as a pure species. Formerly persecuted because it was believed to steal the chicks of game birds and poultry, it is now recognized as a friend because it controls rodents. Today the cat is only to be found in scattered populations in parts of France, Germany, Belgium, Spain, Portugal, Italy, the United Kingdom, Greece, parts of Eastern Europe, and countries around the Black Sea to the west of the Caspian Sea. Several island populations, such as those found on Sardinia, Crete, and other Mediterranean islands, are also recognized as part of the European group. Others maintain a closer link to the African wildcat. The greatest threat to the European wildcat is hybridization. Although many wildcat subspecies live in remote areas, many live in relative close proximity to human habitation and domestic and feral cat populations. In these areas wildcats are in danger of becoming extinct.

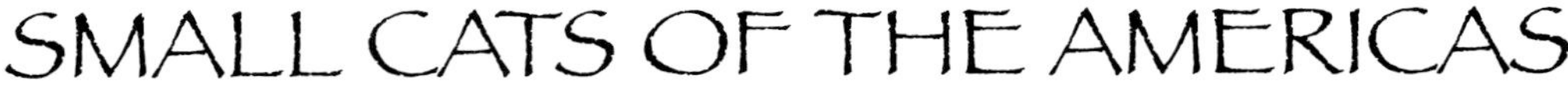

SMALL CATS OF THE AMERICAS

Wildcats are believed to have existed in the Americas for millions of years, with big cats like the jaguar and lion crossing over from Eurasia via the Bering land bridge around two million years ago. Early forms of the cheetah are also thought to have inhabited North America as long ago as two and half million years. Unfortunately climactic change forced the extinction of such cats. However, many small cats still roam the land, from the forests of eastern Canada to the scrublands of Mexico, but in far restricted numbers and areas than before.

Puma (Felis concolor Linnaeus)

Pumas were once cited as good examples of Bergman's rule, which states that animals in cooler climates are expected to have a large body size to reduce heat loss. Studies showed that pumas from the equator were almost half the size of the Canadian and Patagonian pumas. However, this has been shown to be the result of differences in seasonal food availability, not climate conditions.

Usually classified in the genus *Felis*, the puma was placed by Wozencraft (1993) in its own genus, *Puma*. Despite looking like a big cat, pumas have many of the characteristics of a small cat. They can purr continuously, which the Panthera cats are unable to do. Pumas lack a thick pad of fibrous tissue in their larynxes. They can produce high-pitched screams because the supporting bones of the tongue are completely ossified.

Characteristics

The puma is a slender animal, with strong, muscular limbs and an elongated body. The hind legs are longer than the front, an adaptation that is believed to be for jumping. They have relatively small heads, with short faces. The rounded, dark ears are not tufted. A long, heavy, cylindrical tail is used as a counterbalance. In tropical regions the puma's coat is short and bristly, but in the higher latitudes it is longer and softer. There seems to be two color phases, a red and a gray. Red-phased cats that live in tropical regions are buff, cinnamon, and tawny. Gray-phased pumas are generally silvery gray to bluish and slate gray. Darker animals are found in the humid forests of the north Pacific coast, and all-black pumas have been recorded from South and Central America but never from North America. The life span of the puma is 10–15 years.

Habitat

Pumas can survive in altitudes as high as 2.8 mi. (4,500 m). They can live in almost all possible habitats: coniferous forests, tropical rainforests, swamp, grassland, brush country, rugged snow country, and desert regions.

Diet

Pumas are opportunistic hunters and will kill anything they can eat, deer being the primary food. They supplement their seasonal diet with small animals, reptiles, and

ABOVE

Pumas primarily predate upon deer, but they will also eat many other animals, including insects and reptiles.

Fascinating Facts

As hunters, cats have a good ability to detect motion. They can see movements that are too fast for our eyes, yet find it hard to focus on very slow movement.

ABOVE

Puma populations have dwindled, and they continue to be persecuted due to their penchant for livestock.

insects. Vegetable matter, usually grass, is eaten to aid digestion and to stimulate vomiting to help eliminate fur balls.

Pumas have been reported to prey on livestock. A study in Idaho revealed that on average a puma will kill one deer every ten or 11 days.

Conservation Status
Pumas in North America have a long history of persecution by white settlers. They have been practically eradicated in the eastern United States. The Florida panther is only a remnant of the population. Native Americans have a long history of interaction with the puma. Cochiti tribes who lived in present-day New Mexico carved a pair of life-sized pumas into the bedrock of a mesa. It was a shrine that some still visit today. The ancient Peruvian city of Cuzco was laid out in the shape of a puma, and the Inca feared and respected them as deities.

Pumas regard livestock as food, especially when their natural prey has been overhunted by people. This fact has been used as an excuse for persecution, and social attitudes dictate that on ranch lands an unknown moving animal must be shot. Hunting is a major threat to the puma in Latin America. A puma in Patagonia was killed by a cow after it had killed the cow's calf. Rabies in pumas has been recorded, a fact which humans have used as an excuse to decimate their populations.

Canadian Lynx (Lynx canadensis)

The debate continues over whether or not the Canadian lynx is a separate species from the Eurasian lynx or merely a subspecies. Experts are evenly divided, but for now it remains a separate species based on its marked adaptive differences for prey capture.

Characteristics

Canadian lynx are easily recognizable, with their black ear tufts, flared facial ruff, and short tail. They can only be confused with the closely related bobcat *Lynx rufus* in the southern part of their range; however, a close look reveals a number of differences. The lynx has longer legs and broader foot pads for walking in deep snow. Their ear tufts are longer, and the facial ruff is more developed. Their tail has a black tip, while the bobcat's is more striped and white underneath. These two seem to have divided the continent between them, with the lynx in the northern forests and the bobcat being limited by snow depth to southern Canada through to central Mexico.

Habitat

Major populations of Canadian lynx are found throughout Canada, in western Montana, and in nearby parts of Idaho and Washington. There are small populations in New England and Utah.

Diet

Canadian lynx feed almost exclusively on snowshoe hares and have adapted to the cyclic availability of their prey. Snowshoe hare numbers peak every ten years. As they start to decline, so do lynx numbers after a two-year lag. When the hare population decreases, fewer lynx reproduce, and litter size decreases.

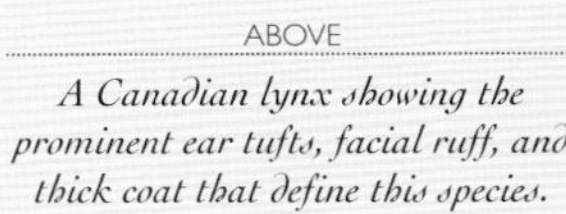

ABOVE

A Canadian lynx showing the prominent ear tufts, facial ruff, and thick coat that define this species.

Conservation Status

Trapping continues to be one of the greatest threats for the lynx, and recovery is difficult. They also face habitat loss because of destruction caused by humans. However, the outlook for the Canadian lynx is more promising than it is for many of the other feline species. It was listed as threatened in 2000.

Bobcat (Felis rufus)

Bobcats are indigenous to the U.S., and there are probably close to one million bobcats living there in total. This cat, when bottle-raised, makes a good pet, but if it is caged the bobcat will revert back to the wild.

Characteristics

The bobcat is a medium-sized, short-tailed cat. Its general color is reddish brown or gray, with the upper part reddish-brown and streaked with black. The underparts are whitish, spotted with black. The back of the ears is black-rimmed, with white centers and slight tufts. Hair on the sides of the head is long, producing a ruff. Elsewhere, the coat is medium short. The legs are relatively long, with large feet. There are five toes in front, four behind. Its life span is around 15–20 years.

BELOW

Bobcats are extremely versatile when it comes to their environment; they can adapt to cold or hot conditions.

Habitat

The bobcat is historically present in all bordering 48 U.S. states. The range extends south into Mexico to the Mescale River at 18-degree north latitude, and north to 50-degree north latitude in Canada. In the Rockies they range slightly farther north.

Bobcats are found in pine forests, mountainous regions, semi-deserts and scrubland, and subtropical swamps. They are unable to survive on the treeless Canadian prairies or at altitudes higher than 11,800 ft. (3,600 m). They climb trees and rocky areas as refuges.

Fascinating Facts

The bobcat can run very fast, up to 30 mph (48 km/h), but it prefers to walk. The bobcat has a special technique for running fast to catch its prey. It puts its back feet into the front feet's spot. If the bobcat is walking on leaves and twigs that would make noise, this technique also prevents it from making any sound and makes it a very quiet hunter.

Diet

Their food consists mainly of small mammals and birds. Among the mammals, wood rats, ground squirrels, mice, and rabbits supply the bulk of the diet. Although deer are occasionally killed and eaten, most of the deer meat found in bobcat stomachs has been carrion. They also prey upon domestic sheep, goats, and poultry, but the damage done is rarely great.

Conservation Status

In some areas they are rare, while in others they have stable and sometimes dense populations. For this reason some states allow regulated hunting, while in others they are protected.

Jaguarondi (Herpailurus yaguarondi)

Jaguarondis move in a quick, weasellike manner. Historical accounts from Mexico suggest that they are also good swimmers and willingly enter water. They are believed to be solitary in the wild, but there is evidence that they form groups when kept in captivity.

Characteristics

Their fur is short and smooth, either rusty brown or charcoal gray. The jaguarondi is a small cat, with a long tail, short legs, small round ears, and a slender body. It is a plain color with no patterning, although it is slightly lighter on the underside. The darker colors are more likely to be found in rainforest regions and the paler colors in drier regions.

Habitat

Jaguarondis live in dense shrubbery and thickets and on the edge of forests. They are rarely found on open land. There, these cats live a life of relative safety because such thickets are almost impenetrable to both dogs and man. They are expert climbers, however, and catch part of their food in the trees. They are largely active at night but move around a good deal in the daytime, often going to water to drink in the afternoon.

Diet

Jaguarondis hunt during the early morning and evening and have been seen springing into the air to capture prey. Their food consists of rats, mice, birds, and rabbits. They have also been known to capture poultry. An analysis of stomach contents from 13 Venezuelan jaguarondis revealed the remains of lizards, rodents, small birds, cottontail rabbits, and grass.

Fascinating Facts

Most felids are able to land on their feet after a fall, an ability that relies on vision and the sense of balance acting together.

Conservation Status

Although the fur of the jaguarondi is not highly sought after by fur traders, the cat is at risk through general deforestation and loss of its natural habitat. In the United States, where sightings of the cat are very rare, it is classified as an endangered species.

BELOW

The jaguarondi lives in dense shrubbery and forest edges and hunts rodents, reptiles, and small birds.

Ocelot (Leopardus pardalis)

As recently as the 1980s this distinctive-looking cat was hunted for its fur and even kept as a pet. Other common names for the ocelot include "painted leopard" and "tigrillo."

Characteristics

The fur color may vary from cream reddish gray marked with open-centered dark spots. The underside is white. The dappled camouflage allows the animal to blend in perfectly with its surroundings. The backs of the ears are black, with a central yellow spot.

Habitat

Once found in much of southern North America, Central America, and South America, today the ocelot has almost disappeared from its range in the southern states, and some subspecies are threatened by the conversion of large areas of plains into arable farmland.

Diet

The ocelot is a land hunter and active during the night. The mainstays of its diet are nocturnal rodents, such as cane mice, rice rats, opossums, and armadillos. They will also take larger prey, such as lesser anteaters, deer, squirrel monkeys, and land tortoises. Seasonal changes and the abundance of fish and land crabs during the wet season supplement the diet. Occasionally they will take birds and reptiles.

Conservation Status

Ocelots are protected by the Lacey Act, which makes it illegal to transport, import, export, sell, receive, acquire, or purchase any wild animal that was taken in violation of the law. Ocelots do relatively well living close to humans, as long as hunting is restricted and they have the appropriate habitats available to them. Habitat destruction is the primary threat to ocelots throughout some areas of their range. In the United States they are protected by the Recovery Plan for the Listed Cats of Arizona and Texas, the primary objective of which is to maintain the ocelot populations in Texas. Today many ocelots are of hybrid ancestry.

ABOVE
The ocelot has long been hunted for its beautiful coat, but the species is now protected by law.

ABOVE LEFT

Margays are well adapted to tree life, with the ability to hang from branches and run down trunks headfirst.

ABOVE RIGHT

Andean mountain cats are an elusive species, and very little is known about their diet or habits.

Margay (Leopardus wiedii)

Of all of the felines, the margay is most adapted to a true arboreal life. It is the only cat with the ability to rotate its hind legs 180 degrees, enabling it to run headfirst down trees. It can hang from a branch by one hind foot.

Margays are similar to ocelots but smaller. They have golden ground color, covered in large spots. They eat small mammals, birds, eggs, lizards, and tree frogs. This cat is extremely rare and endangered throughout its range. The life span is 18 years.

Andean Mountain Cat (Oreailurus jacobita)

Andean mountain cats were first scientifically described in 1865, but it was not until 1980 that a positive sighting was made. In 1999 a second set of pictures was finally taken of this elusive cat by a biologist in Chile.

A separate generic status (*Oreailurus*) has now been proposed for this species. No subspecies have been accepted. Only found in a rocky, arid to semi-arid range, the mountain cat habitat is specialized. Nothing specific is known about the diet of this species, but it probably preys on small mammals. The life span is 16 years.

Pampas Cat (Oncifelis colocolo)

The taxonomic evaluation of 96 museum specimens concluded that the Pampas Cat might be three distinct species. These cats look like heavy-set domestic cats, with fur that varies from thick and soft in colder areas to thin and strawlike in warmer climates. The color can vary from shades of yellow, brown, gray, and silver. They prey on small mammals and birds. Pampas cats are known to take poultry in populated areas.

Habitat destruction is the major threat to this species. The pampas regions of Argentina and Uruguay have been heavily settled, encroaching upon the cat's natural habitat. The life span is 16 years.

RIGHT

The fur of the pampas cat varies in texture and color depending on the climate in which it lives.

Geoffroy's Cat (Oncifelas geoffroyi)

Geoffroy's Cat, named after the naturalist Geoffroy St. Hilaire, is found throughout southern South America, east of the Andes. Males weigh around 10 lbs (4.5 kg) and females 8 lbs (3.6 kg). In the northern range the coat is an ocher color, with uniformly patterned, small, black spots. Gray and black are common colors in the south.

Geoffroy's cats hunt small birds, lizards, insects, and rodents. They will eat eggs, and in captivity they have been observed chewing green hay stems. Coveted for its fur, Geoffrey's cats are one of the most hunted of the wildcat species. The life span is 14 years.

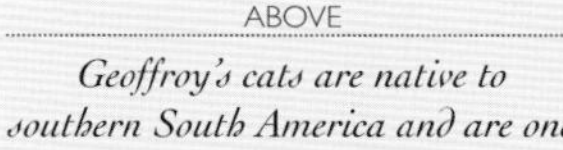

ABOVE
Geoffroy's cats are native to southern South America and are one of the world's most hunted wildcats.

Kodkod (Oncifelis guigna)

The kodkod is the smallest South American cat, around half the size of a large domestic cat. Gray-brown or buff in color, the kodkod is marked with round black spots, with some streaking on the head and shoulders and blackish spots on upper and lower parts.

Little is known about their prey, but kodkods are known to eat small mammals and birds. Kodkod are very rare in the wild and currently threatened by extensive habitat destruction. This species are faced with extinction unless trade is strictly regulated. The life span is 11 years.

Tiger Cat (Leopardus tigrinus)

The Tiger Cat, also known as "Oncilla," is similar to other small cats of South America, but it is found at higher elevations. They have a yellowish red to grayish yellow coat, with rows of large, dark rosettes and a pale underside that is less spotted than the rest of the body.

Tiger Cats prefer humid evergreen and montane cloud forests 130–9,850 ft. (40–3,000 m) above sea level. They feed on small mammals and birds. It is difficult to assess threats when so little is known; however, its cloud forest habitat is being lost to coffee plantations. The life span is 15–20 years.

BELOW
The kodkod is threatened with extinction due to the destruction of its South American habitat.

BELOW
The tiger cat (Leopardus tigrinus) *was previously known as Felis tigrinus until revision of this branch of Felidae in recent years.*

SMALL CATS OF ASIA

Being such a vast continent, with landscapes ranging from arctic tundra through to plateaus, mountains, monsoon areas, and rainforests, the variety of cats in Asia is equally broad—some are found throughout the land, some are confined to specific locations. Like most wildcats, they can often be hard to spot—such as the elusive Marbled Cat, and many are endangered to varying degrees—the Chinese Desert Cat is in danger of extinction. Some are fascinating for their "uncatlike" behavior—the Fishing Cat being one of these examples.

Jungle Cat (Felis chaus)

This cat, contrary to its name, is not typically found in jungles. Like the African wildcats and domestic cats, the jungle cat has been mummified and placed in tombs in ancient Egypt.

Characteristics

The jungle cat has long legs and a slender body. The fur is sandy brown, reddish, or gray, and it is unpatterned except for some brown striping on the legs. The ears are tall and rounded and are reddish, with small lynxlike tufts on the tips. The tail is short, faintly ringed, and has a black tip. Adults weigh 9–35 lbs (4–16 kg); height, 14–16 in. (35–38 cm). The life span is up to 15 years.

Habitat

These cats live in a great range of habitats that include marsh and swampland on forest margins and tropical deciduous and evergreen forests. However, the jungle cat is not found in the denser tropical rainforests, as its name might suggest. This cat is not an especially shy creature and can often be found close to human habitation, hunting in crop fields and plantations for small rodents. In India it has been reported to inhabit vacant buildings.

Diet

Jungle cats prey on small mammals, birds, reptiles, and amphibians and hunt subterranean bandicoot rats. In Uzbekistan they seem to rely more on birds in the winter and reptiles and insects in the summer. They are known to kill porcupines and will take fish, frogs, and snakes. They are potential predators on game birds, domestic poultry, and chital fawns. Tiger kills will also be scavenged. In addition they have been reported to eat the fruits of the Russian olive in Tadzhikistan.

Conservation Status

The greatest threat is reclamation and destruction of natural wetlands. They are killed by farmers because of their threat to domestic poultry.

LEFT

The jungle cat lives in a wide range of habitats but not in dense forests, as its name might suggest.

Temminck's Golden Cat (Catopuma temminckii)

Temminck's cat, also known as the Asian golden cat, ranges from the southern edge of the Himalayas south to Malaya and Sumatra. Although scientists know little about this cat, it figures prominently in Asian folklore.

Characteristics

The cat comes in a variety of colors, including red, gold, gray, or black. Temminck's golden cat is a medium-sized, well-proportioned cat, with short round ears. It is a beautiful cat, with a deep-golden coat fading to white on its undersides. There is a distinctive gray patch behind each ear, while a white line bordered in black runs from each eye to the top of its head. The life span is around 18 years.

Habitat

Found in southeast Asia from Nepal, Tibet, Sikkim, Assam, Sichuan, Yunnan, Thailand, and Malaysia down to Sumatra, Temminck's golden cat generally lives in dense tropical and subtropical forests. In the Himalayas the cat can be found at altitudes up to 10,000 ft. (3 km).

Diet

The golden cat feeds on small to medium-sized mammals, including rabbits, deer, sheep, and goats. It was also found that injured monkeys and scavenged eagle kills are an important part of this cat's diet. It is mainly nocturnal and hunts using the stalk and rush method.

Conservation Status

The Asiatic golden cat is listed as "near threatened." It is widely reported as uncommon and threatened by deforestation. Major threats also include hunting for its pelt and bones. Its meat is considered a delicacy, and the whole animal is often roasted on a spit. The bones are then ground into a powder to be given to children for fevers. Livestock predation, which usually leads to persecution, has also been reported. Although they are reported to be decreasing in India and Indonesia, no factual information is known of their status in the wild.

ABOVE

The Temminck's golden cat is hunted for its fur and meat as well as its bones, which are used in medicines.

Fascinating Facts

Temminck's cat has a legend connected with it, stating that a single hair from the golden cat will protect the bearer from tigers.

Fishing cat (Prionailurus viverrina)

The fishing cat is another feline that contradicts the belief that cats don't like water. Powerful swimmers, they push themselves along with their webbed hind feet. They have been seen wading in shallow water, hunting for a variety of aquatic prey.

Characteristics
The fishing cat has a long, sinuous body, with relatively short legs and a somewhat flattened tail. Its forepaws have long toes and claws that extend significantly from their sheaths even when fully retracted. All four feet are webbed. Its coat is light brown, with dark brown irregular spots fading to white underneath. The backs of its ears are black, with a central white spot. The life span is 15–20 years.

BELOW
Two young fishing cats hunt at the water's edge. Fishing cats have webbed feet and are strong swimmers.

Habitat
Geographically, fishing cats are found unevenly distributed throughout southern Asia, from Malaysia, parts of Indonesia and Sri Lanka, to the Himalayan foothills of Nepal. The fishing cat may be found in the marshes and swamps of southern and south-eastern Asia. It avoids human settlements. It hunts by day in the water and from the ground. It is the best swimmer of all the cats, catching fish by pursuit and using its long claws as fishhooks.

Diet
Fishing cats frequently enter the water to take fish, frogs, crabs, and even mollusks. They also prey on snakes, birds, and small mammals. They are said to have taken calves, goats, and dogs and will scavenge the carcasses of larger animals.

Conservation Status
Fifty percent of Asian wetlands are under threat and disappearing, making this the primary threat facing this species. Fishing cats are considered a food item in some areas, and skins sometimes turn up in Asian markets. They are protected over most of their range, with the exceptions of Bhutan, Malaysia, and Vietnam. Their wild status overall is basically unknown. They are listed as "near threatened."

Fascinating Facts

Cats lap up liquid from the underside of their tongue and not from the top when drinking.

Pallas Cat (Otocolobus manul)

The Pallas cat is named after German naturalist Peter Simon Pallas (1741–1811). The Pallas cat is accustomed to cold, dry surroundings.

Characteristics
This small-sized wildcat is known for its flattened face, stocky build, and long hair. The cats' coat is unique: black spots on the head and varying black stripes either on the back, tail, or both. The hair tips are white, producing a mystical, frosty appearance. The color varies from a light gray to a yellowish buff and russet. The large, owllike eyes are yellow, and the pupils contract into small circles instead of the usual vertical slits. The ears are short, rounded, and set low on the sides of the head. The legs are short and stout, and the tail is thickly furred. Its life span is around 12 years.

RIGHT
A Pallas cat, showing the species' characteristic flat face, stocky build, and long, white-tipped fur.

Habitat
It lives in rocky terrain and grasslands throughout central Asia and parts of Eastern Europe. The range of the Pallas cat extends from Iran through southern Asia to parts of western China. Its habitat varies from rocky desert through steppes to barren mountainous regions up to around 15,000 ft. (4,500 m).

Diet
Pika form the major part of their diet, with small rodents, birds, and insects. They not only catch their prey by chasing it but also by waiting outside of dens and ambushing the prey. If the holes are shallow, they have also been seen "fishing" for prey with their paws.

Conservation Status
Pallas cats are not covered by the U.S. Endangered Species Act but are protected by national legislation over most of their range. In the U.S. they are considered "insufficiently known;" this means that they occur widely but there is no one place where they are common. The species is vulnerable to rare and uncommon elsewhere, including in Afghanistan, Ladakh, northern India and Pakistan, and the small, isolated population in Baluchistan.

Leopard Cat (Prionailurus bengalensis)

The leopard cat, sometimes referred to as the Bengal cat, is a small wildcat of Asia. They are most active at twilight and night, but they also hunt during the day. They are excellent swimmers and have populated many offshore islands. Leopard cats make dens in hollow trees or small caves, and the male may help the female rear the young.

Characteristics

Leopard cats' color varies from yellowish brown in the tropics to grayish brown in the northern sections of their range. Usually they are pale tawny on the upper parts and white on the underparts. The body and tail are covered with dark spots, with stripes running down the back of the head. These break into short bands and elongated spots down the middle of the back. The eyes are outlined with white stripes that originate at the internal corners and streak across the cheeks. The life span is 10–13 years.

Habitat

This cat lives in coniferous forests, as well as tropical rainforests. It stays close to water and may be found in heights of up to 1.8 mi. (3,000 m). It can climb trees skillfully. It is able to swim but rarely does.

Diet

Leopard cats are, like most felids, opportunists, and they will prey on hares, rodents, reptiles, moles, insects, amphibians, game birds, fish, mouse deer, and the fawns of roe deer. Grass and eggs may supplement their diets. They have been known to raid poultry and to take on aquatic prey.

Fascinating Facts

Cats' brains are similar to the human brain. Cats and humans have identical regions in the brain responsible for emotion.

LEFT

The leopard cat is an opportunistic hunter and feeds on a wide range of prey animals.

Conservation Status

In recent years, mainly due to the high profile of conservation measures on "Big Cat" fur trading, emphasis of trading has moved to the smaller wildcat species, and the leopard cat is under continued threat from hunting in many parts of its range. The leopard cat is listed as "least concern" by the IUCN.

Marbled Cat (Pardofelis marmorata)

Marbled cats of Asia have been compared to small clouded leopards, as both bear the distinctive marbling pattern on their coats.

Characteristics

The ecology of the marbled cat and the clouded leopard is very similar. Although both are closely related to the large or Panthera cats, the face of the marbled cat is more like that of a small cat than it is of the clouded leopard. One characteristic that the marbled cat shares with the clouded leopard is very long canine teeth. The fur of the marbled cat is thick and soft and brownish yellow in color. It is covered in large blotches that are paler in their centers and outlined with black. There are black spots on the limbs and some black lines on the head and neck. Interrupted bands run from the inner corner of each eye over the head. The life span is around 12 years.

RIGHT & BELOW

Marbled cats are similar in appearance to clouded leopards, with patterned coats and long canine teeth.

Habitat and Diet

Marbled cats have been found in tropical forests, from Nepal through southeast Asia to Borneo and Sumatra, but its presence in parts of the area is known only from observations. It is believed to spend a lot of time in trees where it is difficult to see, so it may inhabit a larger area than is currently known. Its diet consists mainly of birds but also includes squirrels, rats, and other small rodents, lizards, insects, and frogs. Marbled cats hunt mostly in trees. In Borneo they may be more terrestrial and forage on the ground.

Conservation Status

The International Union for the Conservation of Nature and Natural Resources classifies the marbled cat as "intermediate." This is because it is seriously threatened, but the exact numbers are not known. All international commerce of the marbled cat is prohibited.

Flat-headed Cat (Prionailurus planiceps)

This very rare and elusive species occurs from southern Thailand through the Malay peninsula to Sumatra and Borneo.

Characteristics

Flat-headed cats are around the size of a domestic cat but are easily distinguished by their broad, flattened heads, small ears set far down on the sides of the skull, stumpy legs, and comparatively short tails. The width of the head seems to be increased by the large eyes. The thick, soft pelage is a reddish brown tipped with white. This gives the look of a silvery gray tinge to the coat. Two well-defined pale lines run from the eyes to the ears, and dark spots and stripes are sometimes described on the body. The underparts of this cat are white with brown spots. The inside of the limbs and underside of the tail are reddish brown. Its life span is around 14 years.

Habitat and Diet

No research has been done on this species in the wild, but reports of sightings indicate it prefers swampy areas, oxbow lakes, and riverine forests. It has also been seen hunting in palm oil plantations.

The diet appears to be primarily fish and sometimes frogs and shrimp. These cats have been known to like fruit and prey on rodents in the Malay palm oil plantations. They also take chickens. They are reportedly destructive in gardens, where they dig up sweet potatoes and fruits.

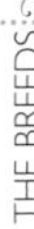

ABOVE
Flat-headed cats have a broad, flattened head, small, low-set ears, large eyes, stumpy legs, and a short tail.

Flat-headed cats discovered on the Malay peninsula were apparently feeding on the numerous rats on the plantations.

Conservation Status

Habitat devastation is probably a very important factor shaping their population sizes, but so little is known about the demography of this and so many of the other small cats that only very rough estimates can be made about their status. All trade has been restricted, and they have been listed as "vulnerable."

Chinese Desert Cat (Felis bieti)

The Chinese desert cat is very rare. It is also known, more appropriately, as the Chinese mountain cat and also as the pale cat, the grass cat, or the pale desert cat.

Characteristics

Chinese desert cats, larger than domestic cats, are thickset and robust, with a heavy coat. Colored a pale yellowish gray, they are darker on the back, with an orange-tinted underside. The coat is peppered with black guard hairs. There are few body markings, just two or three transverse, pale-brownish streaks on the legs and haunches. Two indistinct brownish streaks across the cheeks are usually present. The adult weight can range from 10–20 lbs (4.5–9 kg). The life span is unknown.

Habitat and Diet

This cat is distributed over these regions of China: Tibet, Qinghai, and Sichuan. It inhabits sparsely wooded forests and scrublands, but despite its name it is rarely found in true deserts. This cat is active at night, hunting for rodents, pikas, and birds.

Conservation Status

A restricted range and extensive habitat destruction have caused the Convention on International Trade in Endangered Species to list it as in danger of becoming extinct if trade is not strictly regulated.

BELOW
Despite its name, the Chinese desert cat usually inhabits sparsely wooded forests and scrublands.

ABOVE
The iriomote cat is similar in appearance to a domestic cat and is an endangered species.

gray on the back and flanks, but it is paler on the underparts, with some faint spots on the stomach and limbs. A pale flash marks the inside of each eye. This cat has an extra long tail, the first half conspicuously white underneath.

The habitat of the bay cat is being rapidly destroyed. There is estimated to be only 50 individuals left. The life span is unknown.

Iriomote Cat (Prionailurus bengalensis iriomotensis)

The Iriomote cat was first described in 1967 by Dr. Imaizumi of the National Science Museum in Tokyo, Japan. He believed it was a member of the extinct line genus Mayailurus. Fossil remains suggested that the Iriomote cat had been a separate species for at least two million years.

It is similar to a domestic cat but has shorter legs and tail. Its coloration is dark brown, with rows of darker brown spots running along its body. This cat is found near water; it avoids populated areas. It is listed as endangered. The life span is 12–16 years.

Bay Cat (Catopuma badia)

The bay cat is indigenous to the island of Borneo. It inhabits dense primary forests and areas of rocky limestone. The coat is mahogany red or blackish

Rusty Spotted Cat (Prionailurus rubiginosus)

The rusty spotted cat is extremely rare. It is found in southern India and Sri Lanka. As the name suggests, this feline is grayish brown, with a reddish permeation to the fur. The undersides are tawny white. Elongated rusty brown spots are layered over the background coloration in lines along the sides and back, turning into blotches on the undersides.

It is found in southern India, Gujarat, Jammu and Kashmir, and Sri Lanka, but recent sightings elsewhere in India suggest that it may be more widely distributed.

This cat is not considered threatened. The life span is 16 years.

ABOVE RIGHT
Rusted spotted cats are very rare and have a reddish coat, with elongated rusty brown spots.

LEFT
The bay cat is threatened, with extinction due to extensive deforestation in its native Borneo.

SMALL CATS OF AFRICA

Africa is the second largest continent but less varied in habitat than Asia—at least in terms of altitude, with most of the land being no more than 500 ft. (150 m) above sea level. It does provide stark contrast, however, from the vast Saharan desert of the north and the savannah of the east and south (which provide the hunting ground for the more well-known big cats) to the rainforests of the center. The small cats of Africa seem to prefer the dry and open, sandy, or rocky areas over the more sheltered rainforests.

Caracal (Felis caracal)

The caracal, also called Persian lynx or African lynx, is a fiercely territorial, medium-sized cat. It is labeled as a small cat, but it is one of the heaviest as well as the fastest. The name caracal is derived from a Turkish word—"karakulak"—meaning "black ear." The cat was once tamed and trained for bird hunting in Iran and India. The caracal is capable of leaping into the air and knocking down ten to 12 birds at one time.

RIGHT

The caracal's name is derived from a Turkish word that refers to its distinctive black ears.

Characteristics

The caracal is often referred to as the desert lynx, but it does not have the same physical features, such as the typical ruff of hair around the face. Instead it has a short, dense coat, usually a uniform tawny brown to brick red, and black individuals have been recorded. As the name implies, the backs of the ears are black and topped with long black tufts. This tuft is the characteristic that caracals share with the members of the lynx family. It is the largest and most formidable member of Africa's small cats. Males typically weigh around 28–40 lbs (13–18 kg), while females are slightly smaller. The caracal is 2 ft. (65 cm) in length, plus the 1 ft. (30 cm) tail. The life span is 19 years.

Habitat

Although this cat is found all over Africa, except in the sand deserts and equatorial rainforests, the caracal is especially common in South Africa. It is widely distributed from the Arabian and Sinai Peninsulas, Israel, Jordan, Lebanon, Syria, Kuwait, Iraq, Iran, and Turkey through Turkmenistan, Afghanistan, and south to the Punjab and central India. Animals of essentially dry areas, caracals are found in woodlands, savannah, hilly steppes, and acacia scrubland. They prefer the drier savannah and woodlands areas and are not found in the tropical rainforests or in deep deserts. They are also found in arid mountains at heights up to 1.5 mi. (2,500 m).

Diet

Caracals prey on a variety of mammals, with the most common being rodents, hares, hyraxes, and small antelopes. Unlike the other small African cats, caracals will not hesitate to kill prey larger then themselves, such as adult springbok or young kudu. These cats have also been reported on occasion, although this is an exception, to store their kills in trees, as leopards do.

LEFT
Caracals are fiercely territorial and are prolific hunters, frequently taking on prey larger than themselves.

These cats are mostly nocturnal, but they have been seen in daylight in protected areas. Caracals use the Big Cat technique of a throat bite to kill mountain reedbuck. These antelopes are about twice the size of a caracal and form an important part of their diet. In one study, mountain reedbuck was found in 20 percent of caracal scats. Small cats usually hunt prey smaller than themselves; therefore, they do not need to use the throat bite to subdue a larger animal.

Conservation Status

Because it is so easily tamed, the caracal is sometimes kept as a pet and is said to adapt easily to living with humans. Farmers in Africa look upon it as vermin because it frequently climbs over fences to eat chickens and other poultry.

This cat is almost impossible to see in the wild, not because there are so few of them but because it hides extremely well. Game drives in countries such as Kenya and Botswana widely encounter other animals, but a sighting of a caracal is extremely rare.

The caracal has been hybridized with the domestic cat at the Moscow Zoo. The number in the wild is not known, but they are thought to be common throughout central and southern Africa, where humans have exterminated their main competitors—the black-backed jackals. In India the caracals have benefited from tiger reserves.

Serval (Felis serval)

Although the serval is much smaller than the cheetah, it has similar proportions and is easily mistaken for its bigger cousin when seen from a distance. Like the cheetah, the serval has long limbs, but these are not used for speed. They help the cat leap nimbly and provide a vantage point to see above the vegetation.

Characteristics

This long-legged cat has a small head and comparatively large ears, broad at the base with rounded tips. It is marked with dark spots and blotches on a tawny background, and these become elongated on the back to form stripes. Often referred to as "the cat of spare parts," this atypical but beautiful animal is among the feline family's most successful. The hind legs are longer than the front; the body is long and slender. The ears are black on the back, with a distinctive white spot, and the tail has six or seven black rings and a black tip. The coat color is pale yellow with black markings, either of large spots that tend to merge into longitudinal stripes on the neck and back, or of numerous small spots, which give a speckled appearance. These speckled servals from West Africa, called servalines, were once considered to be a separate species *Felis brachyura*, until it was shown that the speckled pattern was simply a variation. The life span is 20 years.

Habitat

The serval inhabits the plains and forests of the north African countries of Algeria and Morocco, and in central and southern Africa, excluding the southernmost tip and the rainforest belt in central Africa.

Servals are found in well-watered savannah, long-grass environs, and are associated with reed beds and other riverbank vegetation. They live in a variety of habitats all connected with water sources. They range into alpine grasslands and can penetrate dense forests along waterways and through grassy patches, but they are absent from rainforests. Servals will make use of arid areas in extreme cases and have occasionally done so in parts of southwestern Africa.

BELOW

The serval's long limbs enable it to leap vertically and occasionally catch birds from the air.

LEFT

Servals have remarkably good hearing and are able to locate and stalk their prey without seeing it.

Diet

The servals' big ears are unparalleled in the cat world. Its hearing allows it to locate (echolocation) small mammals moving through the grass or underground and to hunt its prey without seeing it, until the final pounce. It also has the ability to leap vertically and catch prey such as birds right out of the air. They do this by "clapping" their front paws together and striking with a downward blow. Primary prey for the serval includes rodents, birds, reptiles, fish, frogs, and insects. Servals have a hunting success rate of 50 percent.

Conservation Status

The serval is reasonably widespread and relatively common throughout Africa. It also breeds well in captivity. The north African serval *F (L) s constantinus* is listed as endangered, but all other servals are "least concern." In the Cape region of southern Africa, servals were historically restricted to the coastal belt and inland to east of 24 degrees east longitude. This is where most of the human pressure is concentrated. They are now extinct in the Cape Province of South Africa. Natural repopulation seems unlikely, so reintroduction is the only option. Caracals seem to have been able to adapt to the habitat degradation better than the servals.

A serious threat to servals and other small wildcats is the fur trade, which continues to demand large numbers of the beautifully marked skins. To make a coat from these small wildcats requires a very large number of skins because of the intricate process of matching spots, stripes, and bars. Servals have shown up in the pet trade.

Fascinating Facts

Australia and Antarctica are the only continents that have no native cat species. It is believed cats were living in parts of Australia before European settlement, possibly escapees from shipwrecks or traders' boats, where they had been employed to catch rats.

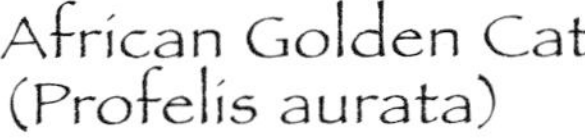

African Golden Cat (Profelis aurata)

While the name implies a golden-colored coat, the golden cat is polymorphic—its base coat coloration varies extensively depending on its location. It goes from a golden/reddish brown to slate/silver gray.

Characteristics

The African golden cat is a medium-sized cat and can grow to 35 in. (90 cm) in length and weigh up to 39 lbs (18 kg). The African golden cat has long been regarded as closely related to the Asian or Temminck's golden cat, but a recent review of cat taxonomy separates the two into different genera.

Two subspecies are described: *F. (P.) a. aurata* (Congo to Uganda), *F. (P.) a. celidogaster* (West Africa). Each of the subspecies has two different characteristic coat patterns. *P. a. celidogaster*: Type 1 is spotted all over; Type 2 has indistinct spots on the back and neck, with a few large, clear, flank spots. *P. a. aurata:* Type 1 has no pattern on the neck and back, but it has numerous small spots on the lower flanks; Type 2 has virtually no pattern, except on the stomach. The life span is 15 years.

Habitat and Diet

The main habitat of the golden cat seems to be the tropical rainforest belt, which traverses the African equator; however, there is also evidence of the cat moving into the adjoining tropical dry forests and savannah scrub.

The cat catches its prey by stalking and rushing, mainly at ground level. Their diet includes small to mid-sized mammals such as rodents, monkeys, duiker, hyrax, and a variety of birds. They may also scavenge other predators' kills.

Conservation Status

The African golden cat status is "insufficiently known," and due to its relatively restricted natural habitat, it must be considered at risk until more data is available as to its true population and distribution. Their primary threat is deforestation.

LEFT

The primary habitat of the African golden cat is the tropical rainforests of equatorial Africa.

African Wildcat (Felis silvestris lybica)

The African wildcat, also known as the desert cat, is a subspecies of the wildcat *F. silvestris*. Some individuals were first domesticated around 10,000 years ago in the Middle East, and they are the ancestors of the domestic cat we know today.

Fascinating Facts

For the first time ever, two unrelated clones of a wild species have bred naturally to produce healthy babies. Two litters of kittens produced by natural breeding of cloned African wildcats have been born at the Audubon Center for Research of Endangered Species. The first five kittens were born on July 26, 2005, to the African wildcat Madge, who is a clone of the wildcat Nancy. The second litter, consisting of three kittens, was born on August 2 to the African wildcat Caty, also a clone of the wildcat Nancy. The father of both litters is Ditteaux, a clone of the African wildcat Jazz.

Characteristics

The African wildcat is sandy brown to yellow gray in color, with black stripes on the tail. The fur is shorter than that of the European subspecies. It is also considerably smaller: the head/body length is 18–29 in. (45–75 cm), the tail 8–15 in. (20–38 cm), and the weight ranges from 7–14 lbs (3–6.5 kg). The cat is the wild prototype of a tabby cat. It is distinguished from domesticated tabbies by longer legs, a more upright seated posture, and reddish, unmarked, translucent ears. The life span is 15 years.

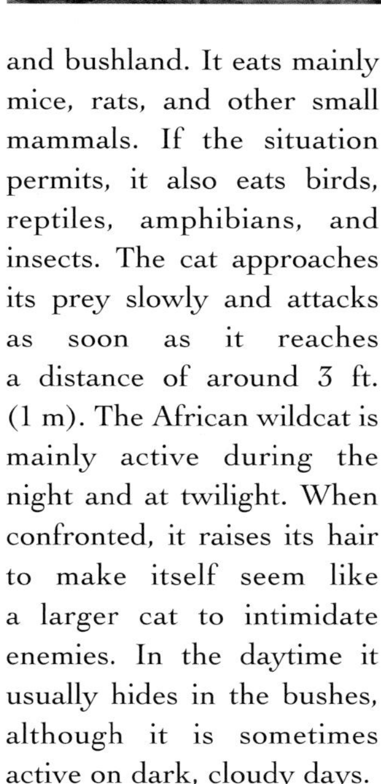

Habitat and Diet

The African wildcat is found in Africa and in the Middle East in a wide range of habitats: steppes, savannah, and bushland. It eats mainly mice, rats, and other small mammals. If the situation permits, it also eats birds, reptiles, amphibians, and insects. The cat approaches its prey slowly and attacks as soon as it reaches a distance of around 3 ft. (1 m). The African wildcat is mainly active during the night and at twilight. When confronted, it raises its hair to make itself seem like a larger cat to intimidate enemies. In the daytime it usually hides in the bushes, although it is sometimes active on dark, cloudy days.

Conservation Status

The African wildcat is listed as "threatened." There is concern that interbreeding between the African wildcat and domestic cats may have been sufficiently extensive to threaten the status of the wildcat as a genetically distinct population.

ABOVE

African wildcats predate mainly on rodents, stalking them to a distance of around three feet before pouncing.

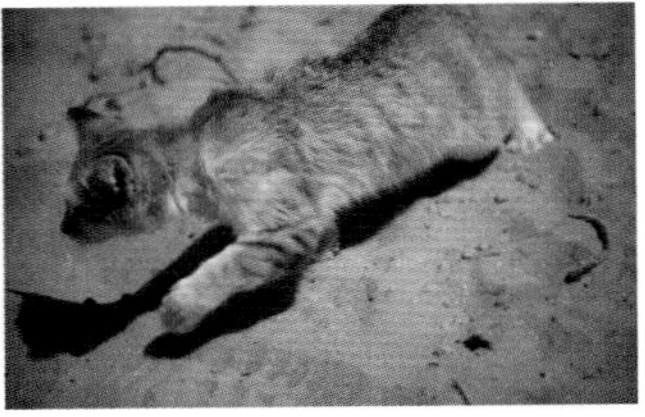

ABOVE

The extensive hair on the sand cat's feet protects it from the hot sand and makes its footprints invisible.

Sand cat (Felis margarita)

This cat is difficult to study in the wild. Their foot coverings leave their footprints almost invisible. They have learned to crouch down and shut their eyes when a light is shone on them, which prevents reflection. That, combined with their protective coat color, makes them blend into their habitat.

Characteristics

The sand cat is very small, with short legs. It has a large, wide head and huge ears that sit low on either side of the head. The dense, soft fur can be any color, from sandy to a light gray in ground color, with bands of dark brown to black around its legs, dark bands coming from the corner of each eye on the sides of its face, and a white muzzle. The cat also has black tabby markings on its face and body. It has extensive amounts of hair covering the pads of the feet to protect them from the searing hot sands. Its life span is 13 years.

Habitat and Diet

Sand cats inhabit arid regions that are characterized by rolling sand dunes, flat stony plains, and rocky deserts. They seem to display a preference for regions of shifting sand and areas of sand dunes covered with sparse vegetation. There is no freestanding water throughout the majority of the range of the sand cat. They rely on getting enough moisture from their prey.

The diet consists of small rodents, lizards, insects, and snakes, which they stun with rapid blows to the head before killing. They usually hunt at night.

Conservation Status

Zoo populations are dwindling, and the cats are extremely inbred. It's likely that they have descended from only one wild-caught pair. Sand cats can be seen at the London Zoo and Twycross Zoo in the U.K. All international commerce in sand cat products is strictly regulated.

Fascinating Facts

Cats are terrible at catching butterflies because they leap at them and their feet leave the ground. When this happens, they can't control their movements, and butterflies move in a darting motion. Cats rarely catch them.

Black-footed Cat (Felis negripes)

The smallest of all the felid species, the black-footed cat is one of the most fascinating. It is also known as the anthill tiger, or little spotted cat, and it has a reputation of being fierce.

RIGHT

Despite being the smallest felid, the black-footed cat is a fierce hunter and is capable of killing sheep.

Characteristics

This cat has a large, broad head in proportion to its small body. Its coat varies from light sandy brown to reddish brown, and it is covered with dark-spotted patches that sometimes blend into broken stripes. The legs are barred with dark horizontal stripes, and the tail is broken with dark rings and ends in a black tip. The pads of its feet are black and surrounded by long black hairs, which give the small feline its name as well as protecting its feet from the heat of its semi-desert home. The life span is unknown.

Habitat

The black-footed cat is typically associated with open, sandy, grassy habitats with sparse shrub and tree cover, such as the Kalahari and Karoo regions. Long grass with high rodent and bird populations is the best habitat.

Diet

The diet consists of shrews, gerbils, hares, lizards, and beetles. Highly opportunistic, black-footed cats will take any prey that they can overpower. Uneaten food is stored for later. They have been observed to scavenge springbok carcasses and take birds in the air. Black-footed cats are regularly reported to hang onto the throats of sheep until they pierce their jugular veins. They will drink if water is available, but they usually get all the moisture they require from their prey.

Conservation Status

Many experts describe the black-footed cat as a rare species, but other reports indicate that they are common in parts of their range. Poison and traps that are indiscriminately laid out for the African wildcat and jackal are affecting black-footed cats in certain areas. This cat is listed as "least concern."

Useful Addresses

Cat Registries and Organisations

The Governing Council of the Cat Fancy (GCCF)
5 King's Castle Business Park
The Drove
Bridgwater
Somerset, TA6 4AG
UK
Tel: +44 (0)1278 427 575
www.gccfcats.org

Fédération Internationale Féline (FIFe)
www.fifeweb.org

Co-ordinating Cat Council of Australia (CCC of A)
Secretary
P.O. Box 347
Macedon, Victoria 3440
Australia
Tel: +61 (0)3 5426 1758
http://cccofa.asn.au/

New Zealand Cat Fancy (NZCF)
Membership Coordinator
264 Cannon Hill Crescent
Christchurch 8008
New Zealand
www.nzcatfancy.gen.nz

Cat Fanciers' Association (CFA)
PO Box 1005
Manasquan, New Jersey 08736
USA
Tel: +1 980 528 9797
www.cfainc.org

American Cat Fanciers Association (ACFA)
PO Box 1949
Nixa, Missouri 65714
USA
Tel: +1 417 725 1530
www.acfacat.com

The International Cat Association (TICA)
P.O. Box 2684
Harlingen, Texas 78551
USA
Tel: +1 956 428 8046
www.ticaeo.org

Cat Fanciers' Federation (CFF)
PO Box 661
Gratis, Ohio 45330
USA
Tel: +1 937 787 9009
www.cffinc.org

Canadian Cat Association (CCA)
289 Rutherford Road, S #18
Brampton, ON
L6W 3R9 Canada
Tel: +1 905 459 1481
www.cca-afc.com

International Society for Endangered Cats
124 Lynnbrook Road SE
Calgary, Alberta T2C 1S6 Canada
Tel: +1 403 279 589
www.wildcatconservation.org

American Association of Cat Enthusiasts
PO Box 213
Pine Brook, New Jersey 07058
USA
Tel: +1 973 335 6717
www.aaceinc.org

Feline Conservation Federation
7816 N. County Road 75 W
Shelburn, Indiana 47879
USA
www.felineconservation.org

International Progressive Cat Breeders' Alliance
PO Box 311
Upton, Kentucky 42784
USA
Tel: +1 270 531 7966
www.ipcba.8k.com

Welfare and Rescue Organisations

Royal Society for the Prevention of Cruelty to Animals
Wilberforce Way
Southwater
Horsham
West Sussex, RH13 9RS
UK
Tel: +44 (0)300 1234 999
www.rspca.org.uk

Cats Protection
National Cat Centre
Chelwood Gate
Haywards Heath
Sussex, RH17 7TT
UK
Tel: +44 (0)8702 099 099
www.cats.org.uk

The Original Cat Action Trust
The Old Smithy
Rattery, South Brent
Devon, TQ10 9LE
UK
www.catactiontrust.org.uk

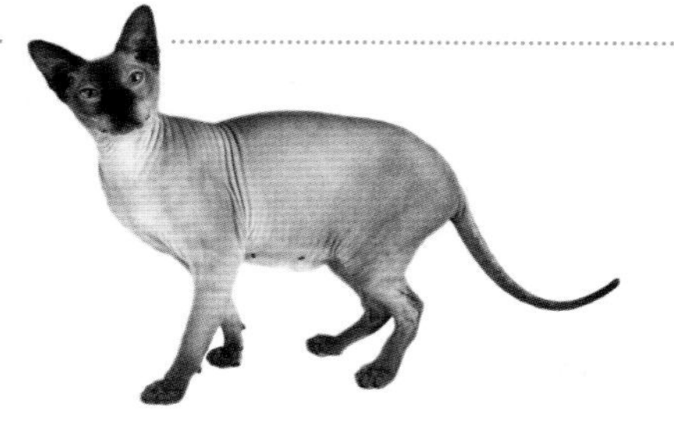

American Humane Association
63 Inverness Drive East
Englewood, Colorado 80112
USA
Tel: +1 303 792 9900
www.americanhumane.org

The Humane Society of the United States
2100 L Street NW
Washington, D.C. 20037
USA
Tel: +1 202 452 1100
www.hsus.org

Big Cat Rescue
12802 Easy Street
Tampa, Florida 33625
USA
Tel: +1 813 920 4130
www.bigcatrescue.org

Advice and Information

Feline Advisory Bureau
Taeselbury, High Street
Tisbury, Wiltshire, SP3 6LD
UK
Tel: +44 (0)870 742 2278
www.fabcats.org

Cat World Magazine
Ancient Lights, 19 River Road
Arundel
West Sussex, BN18 9EY
UK
Tel: +44 (0)1903 884 988
www.catworld.co.uk

Pet Website
18 Shepherds Close
Grove
Oxfordshire, OX12 0NX
UK
www.petwebsite.com/cats

Cat Channel
477 Butterfield, Suite 200
Lombard, Illinois 60148
USA
Tel: +1 630 515 9493
www.catchannel.com

Cats International
193 Granville Road
Cedarburg
Wisconsin 53012
USA
Tel: +1 262 375 8852
www.catsinternational.org

Pet Place
20283 State Road 7, Suite 400
Boca Raton
FL 33498
USA
Tel: +1 561 237 2940
www.petplace.com

Show Cats Online
PO Box 4971
Blaine
Washington 98231-4971
USA
Tel: +1 604-535-7469
www.showcatsonline.com

Terrific Cats
PO Box 15124
New Bern
North Carolina 28561
USA
www.terrific-cats.com

Further Reading

Altman, Roberta, *The Quintessential Cat*, Hungry Minds Inc. (New York, New York), 1996

Bard, E. M., *Test Your Cat: The Cat IQ Test*, HarperCollins (New York, New York), 2005

Becker, Marty; and Spadafori, Gina, *Why Do Cats Always Land on Their Feet?: 101 of the Most Perplexing Questions Answered about Feline Unfathomables, Medical Mysteries, and Befuddling Behaviors*, HCI (Deerfield Beach, Florida), 2006

Bessant, Claire, *The Cat Whisperer*, Blake Publishing (London, UK), 2004

Burn, David, *An Instant Guide to Cats*, Gramercy Books (New York, New York), 2000

Christensen, Wendy, *The Humane Society of the United States Complete Guide to Cat Care*, St. Martin's Griffin (New York, New York), 2004

Choron, Sandra and Harry, *Planet Cat: A CAT-olog*, Houghton Mifflin, 2007

Church, Christine, *House Cat: How to Keep Your Indoor Cat Sane and Sound*, John Wiley & Sons (Somerset, New Jersey), 2005

Cutts, Paddy, *The Complete Cat Book: An Encyclopedia of Cats, Cat Breeds & Cat Care*, Lorenz Books (London, UK), 2000

Edgar, Jim, *Bad Cat*, Hodder & Stoughton (London, U.K.), 2007

Edwards, Alan, *The Ultimate Encyclopedia of Cats*, Lorenz Books (London, U.K.), 2003

Elliot, Charles, *The Cat Fanatic: Quirky Quotes on Frisky Felines*, JR Books Ltd (London, U.K.), 2007

Elridge, Debra; Carlson, Delbert; Carlson, Lisa; and Griffin, James, *Cat Owner's Home Veterinary Handbook*, John Wiley & Sons (Somerset, New Jersey), 2007

Fogle, Bruce, *The New Encyclopedia of the Cat*, Dorling Kindersley (London, U.K.), 2007

Halls, Vicky, *Cat Confidential*, Bantam Books Ltd (New York, New York), 2005

Hotchner, Tracie, *The Cat Bible: Everything Your Cat Expects You to Know*, Gotham (New York, New York), 2007

Johnson-Bennett, Pam, *Cat vs. Cat: Keeping the Peace When You Have More Than One Cat*, Penguin (New York, New York), 2004

Johnson-Bennett, Pam, *Psycho Kitty?: Understanding You Cat's Behavior*, Crossing Press (Trumansburg, New York), 1998

Loxton, Howard, *Cats: 99 Lives: Cats in History, Legend and Literature*, Duncan Baird Publishers (London, UK), 2001

Malek, Jaromir, *The Cat in Ancient Egypt*, British Museum Press (London, U.K.), 2006

Neville, Peter; and Bessant, Claire, *The Perfect Kitten*, Hamlyn (London, U.K.), 2005

O'Neill, Amanda, *Cat Biz*, Barron's Educational Series (Hauppauge, New York), 2006

Pilbeam, Mavis, *The British Museum Little Book of Cats*, British Museum Press (London, U.K.), 2004

RSPCA, *Care For Your Cat*, HarperCollins (London, U.K.), 2006

Somerville, Louisa, *The Ultimate Guide to Cat Breeds*, Chartwell Books, 2007

Sunquist, Mel and Fiona, *Wild Cats of the World*, University of Chicago Press (Chicago, Illinois), 2002

Tabor, Roger, *Understanding Cat Behavior*, David & Charles Plc (Devon, UK), 2003

Verhoef-Verhallen, Esther, *The Complete Encyclopedia of Cats*, Chartwell Books, 2005

Zuffi, Stefano, *The Cat in Art*, Harry N. Abrams Inc. (New York, New York), 2007

Glossary

accepted
A characteristic accepted in a breed standard.

ACFA
American Cat Fanciers Association.

acute disease
A rapidly progressing illness.

adult cat
Any cat over the age of eight months old, in most cat registries, for show purposes.

afterbirth
Expelled after the delivery of each newborn kitten, this matter consists of fluids and membranes that surround kittens in the uterus.

agouti
Cat color that results from each individual hair follicle having contrasting bands of color.

agouti gene
The gene that produces striping or a tabby pattern.

ailurophile
A cat-loving person.

ailurophobe
A person that hates cats.

albino
A cat that is white because it lacks melanin pigmentation.

allergy
A reaction resulting from exposure to a certain allergen.

allowable outcross
A cat that is allowed by a cat registry to be mated to another breed of cat in order to produce a kitten with certain favorable characteristics. The Abyssinian, for example, is an allowable outcross for the Somali.

alopecia
Loss of hair, bald patches—usually due to illness.

alter
To spay or neuter a cat.

amino acids
The molecular building blocks of proteins that are essential for good nutrition.

anoestrus
The condition of not being in season for a female cat.

antibiotic
A substance that is derived from a living organism and is used to inhibit the growth of bacteria.

AOC (any other color)
Non-recognized accepted color or pattern in a certain breed of cat.

AOV (any other variety)
Cat association term to classify cats that are offspring of registered parents but are not eligible to enter championship cat show classes because they do not have the official requirements for coat color, coat length, or other physical characteristics.

asthma
A condition of the respiratory system that causes difficult breathing.

asymptomatic
Exhibiting no symptoms of a disease.

autoimmune disease
The body's own defense mechanisms attack normal tissues.

awn hairs
The part of the cat's undercoat that is longer than the downy undercoat but shorter than the primary guard coat.

awry
Crooked jaw formation.

back crossing
Inbreeding, where a cat is mated with a parent.

barring
Stripes associated with tabby markings.

base coat
The primary coat.

benched
When a cat is kept and displayed in a separate area from where it is judged.

benching cage
Show cage, where a cat is kept and displayed when it is not being judged.

best in show
Most points and winner of a championship.

best of breed
A cat, which in the judge's opinion comes closest to meeting the breed standard among all other competing cats of that breed.

BEW
Blue-eyed white.

bib
The part of the coat including the lower chin and the chest.

bite
The angle at which the upper and lower teeth meet and intermesh.

blaze
Stripe or splash of white on the cat's forehead or nose. (In blue-cream and tortoiseshell cats, a blaze is a vertical division of two colors (usually half red and half black) running down the middle of the face. "Checkerboard" is the term used when this pattern is reversed on the cat's chin.

bloodline
A cat's ancestry.

blotched tabby
Another term for the classic or marbled tabby.

booster vaccination
A follow-up injection that is periodically carried out after the primary injection to continue immunity to a disease.

boots
White markings on the hind paws or lower leg of a colored cat. Also called "gauntlets."

bracelets
Dark stripes on the legs of tabby-patterned cats.

break
Well-pronounced angle between nose and forehead. Indentation on the bridge of the nose occurring between or near the point between the eyes. Also called "stop."

breech birth
When a kitten is born tail end first.

breeches
The longer hair on the back of the thighs of longhaired or semi-longhaired cats.

breed
A subdivision of the species consisting of individuals with common hereditary characteristics. Cats sharing common ancestors and similar physical characteristics.

breed council
Cat association members who are actively involved in exhibiting and breeding cats of a specific breed.

breed ribbon
An award for "Best of Breed."

breed true
A breed is said to breed true when it produces kittens that have the same characteristics as their parents.

brandling
A mingling of different colored hairs in a coat.

bronze
Egyptian Mau color characterized by a rich, warm, red base color with darker spotting and flecking.

brush
The thick hair of the tail on a longhaired cat, especially Persian.

bull's eye
A mark found on the sides of the body of classic (blotched) tabby pattern cats that is characterized by a solid, circular spot of dark coloring surrounded by a ring of darker coloring.

butterfly
Mark found on the shoulders of classic (blotched) tabby cat that resembles a butterfly.

calling
The sound female cats make when they are interested in breeding.

cameo
A type of cat color that has a white base, with red on the outer part of the hair shaft.

cardiomyopathy
Genetically linked heart defect that causes heart failure.

carrier
A cat carrying a genetic defect or disease.

castration
Removal of testicles in a male cat. (Neutering.)

cataract
Clouding growth on the cat's lens on the eyeball.

cat association
An organization for the promotion of cats, cat breeds, cat shows, and cat health.

Cat Fancy
People who are involved in breeding, showing of cats, and cat clubs.

catnip
A plant of the mint family (*nepeta cataria*) that acts as a hallucinogen to cats.

cattery
A place where cats are bred and raised. Alternately a facility for boarding cats.

cattery name
The name of a cattery. Also used as the prefix or suffix of a registered cat's name to indicate the breeder and/or owner.

CCA
Canadian Cat Association/ Association Feline Canadienne.

CFA
Cat Fanciers' Association.

CFF
Cat Fanciers' Federation.

CEW
Copper-eyed white.

champagne
Rich, soft, beige color found in the Burmese breed. American term for chocolate/lilac Burmese.

champion
A title that is earned by a cat after accumulating a certain number of winner's points in cat shows. Considered as the first step toward becoming a Grand Champion. Some cat associations require six "winners" ribbons for championship, while others require a cat to "final."

championship finals
Top ten pedigreed adult cats are awarded rosettes in the judging ring.

championship status
Cats of a certain breed become eligible to compete for championship titles.

checkerboard
Vertical division of two colors (usually half red and half black) running down the middle of the cat's chin.

cherry eye
Prolapsed gland of the third eyelid.

chestnut
Solid, warm brown color of cat.

chinchilla
Cat that is white at the base, with a small amount of darker color on the tips. Lightest degree of tipping.

chocolate
Light chestnut brown.

chocolate lynx point
Medium chocolate brown coat, with underlying tabby pattern.

chocolate tortie point
Points primarily medium chocolate brown, with additional tortoiseshell colors.

chromosomes
Cell elements that control inherited characteristics.

chronic disease
A constantly recurring disease.

cinnamon
Rich, dark brownish red color.

classic tabby
A pattern with swirls and blotches of darker color over a lighter base color. Also called "blotched" or "marbled" tabby.

closed cattery
A cattery that does not allow cats to come in or out, including for shows or stud service. Can also refer to simply not offering stud service to outside cats.

coarse
A negative term for a cat that is not refined or harmonious in conformation.

cobby
Body type typically huge, short, muscular, broad chest and hips, heavy boned, and low on the legs.

colitis
Inflammation of the large intestine.

color class
Divisions created by cat associations to classify certain types of coat colors or patterns, such as shaded colors or parti-color.

colostrum
Mother's milk secreted by the mother during the first few days following birth, which provides the kittens with immunity to some diseases.

concaveation
Spayed female cat produces milk in response to the suckling of a kitten.

condition
Wellbeing of a cat, including muscle toning, grooming, and good health.

conformation
Structure of a cat's body, legs, and tail.

congenital
Any trait or condition that exists from birth. It may or may not be hereditary.

cottony
Refers to a coat that is long, fine, and flyaway, especially as on a Persian.

convex
Domed forehead.

CPC
Colorpoint Carrier, meaning that the cat carries the colorpoint gene.

cream
Diluted version of red that appears as a pale beige color.

cream lynx point
Points that are cream to pale red with underlying tabby pattern.

cross
Mating or breeding one cat with another.

cryptorchid
A male with either one or both testicles not descended.

cyst
A swelling that contains fluid other than pus.

cystitis
Inflammation of the bladder.

dam
Female parent.

dandruff
Scales of dead skin that can cause an allergic reaction in humans.

declawing
Surgically removing claws. A declawed cat is not allowed to enter in competitions.

dehydration
Loss of water from the tissues.

demodex
A mite that can cause mange.

dermatitis
Inflammation of the skin.

dewclaw
The first digit found on the inside of the leg above the front paws.

dilute
A paler version of a primary color. The dilute of black is blue, and the dilute of red is cream.

disqualification
Elimination from competition due to a serious fault.

division
A cat show term that signifies a subdivision consisting of two or more color classes.

DNA
Chemical substance that makes up chromosomes.

domestic
A non-pedigreed cat.

dominant
The prevailing gene member of a gene pair.

doming
The rounded part of the head between the ears. Also refers to the rounded part of the forehead.

down hairs
The shortest hair on the cat, soft and downy.

dyslapsia
Abnormal development of a part of the cat's body.

ear furnishings
Tufts of hair that grow in and around the ears.

ear mites
Tiny insects that feed on the lining of the ear canal.

ear tufts
Long hair originating from within the cup of the ear.

ebony
Black.

eclampsia
A disease caused by calcium deficiency that appears during pregnancy or shortly after the birth of kittens.

electrolytes
Bodily substances that contain vital minerals.

embryo
Undeveloped fetus.

enteritis
Intestine inflammation caused by bacterial infection.

enzymes
Chemical substances that are formed within living cells that allow for biochemical reactions.

epidermis
Outer layer of the skin.

estrus
Being in heat. A period of varying length where a female cat produces a watery secretion from the genital tract and is sexually receptive to male cats. If mated, she will ovulate.

euthanasia
Humanely ending a cat's life.

external parasites
Organisms, such as ticks and mites, that affect the outside areas of the body.

fault
An imperfection or deviance from the breed standard.

fawn
Pale buff, sandy, slightly pinkish tinge. Dilute of cinnamon.

Feline Immunodeficiency Virus (FIV)
Virus that attacks the cat's immune system.

Feline Infectious Peritonitis (FIP)
A coronavirus infection of the membrane lining the abdominal cavity. This disease leads to death.

Feline Leukemia Virus (FeLV)
A virus that causes one of the most lethal infectious diseases found in cats. It is directly and indirectly the cause of many feline illnesses, including cancer of the lymphocytes.

Feline Lower Urinary Tract Disease (FLUTD)
Urinary tract disease causing urethral blockage and kidney stone formation.

Feline Urologic Syndrome (FUS)
A disease of the urinary tract often responsible for blockage of the urethra in male cats. Life threatening.

feral
Cats living in the wild.

fetus
Unborn kitten that has developed to the point where it is no longer considered an embryo.

fever
Temperature in cats that is over 102° F (39° C).

fillers
Material that is added to pet food in order to increase volume.

flecking/flecked
Alternating bands of light and dark color on each individual hair, such as found on the Abyssinian.

follicle
The part of the skin from which hair grows.

foreign
Term describing a fine-boned, long-limbed, elegant cat, such as a Siamese or Abyssinian.

frill
A mass of long hair circling the neck, especially on a Persian. Also called "ruff."

fungicidal
A product that prevents the growth of fungi.

fungus
A primitive form of plant life that can be parasitic, for example, ringworm.

gastric
To do with the stomach.

gauntlets
White markings located on the hind paws or lower leg of a colored cat. Also called "boots."

gene
The individual hereditary units that control growth, development, and the physical characteristics of a cat. They are found in specific locations on a chromosome.

gene pool
Total of all of the genes, both dominant and recessive, that exist in a certain breed of cat.

genetics
The science of heredity.

genotype
Total of all the genes that a kitten inherits from its parents, recessive and dominant.

gestation
Period of pregnancy. Cat pregnancy lasts between 63 and 69 days.

ghost markings
Faint tabby striping or spots on a kitten's coat that disappear with maturity.

gloves
Solid colored markings, usually white, on the forepaws of a cat.

gingivitis
Inflammation of the gums.

goggles
The lighter colored hair encircling the eyes. Also called "spectacles."

grooming powder
A chalklike powder used in grooming to give volume, separate the cat's hair, and/or enhance the color.

ground color
Hair color that is closest to the body.

guard hair
One of three types of hair in a cat's coat. Usually outer, longer, and coarser than other hair.

harlequin bicolor pattern
Predominantly white cat with several patches of color scattered on the body.

heat
The period where a female cat is receptive to mating.

hemorrhage
Internal bleeding.

heterochromatic
Eyes of two different colors.

HHP
Household Pet.

hip dysplasia
Hip socket malformation causing crippling in cats.

histamines
Chemicals released by the body when antibodies encounter an allergen. These chemicals cause the familiar allergic reactions, such as sneezing and watery eyes.

hock
Cat's back leg joint, similar to the human ankle.

hormone
Substance that is produced in a particular region of the body, carried by the blood and which exerts influence on another area of the body.

household pet
Domestic or purebred cat that is not registered and is a pet. Household pets can compete in special categories in cat shows.

hot tortie/hot blue-cream
When color is dominantly red or cream. Also called "reverse tortie/reverse blue-cream."

hybrid
Result of mating cats of different breeds.

hybrid vigor
Increased vitality resulting from breeding cats of two different breeds together.

hyperthermia
Increased body temperature that can result from heat stroke.

IM
Intramuscular (injections).

immune response
Reaction to infection in the body.

immunization
Helping with artificial resistance to infection.

inbreeding
Mating of closely related individuals, usually brother to sister, mother to son, or father to daughter.

incontinence
Inability to control urine or defecation.

incubation period
Time between exposure to a disease and the time the disease shows symptoms in the infected cat.

inflammation
Changes that occur in tissue after an injury; indicated by pain, swelling, and redness.

inherited
Characteristic that is the result of genetic influences.

internal parasites
Larvae and worms that are living off of the host cat's meals or its blood.

IV
Intravenous (injections).

Jacobson's Organ
A sensing organ in the top of the cat's mouth involved in smell and taste.

jowls
Larger cheeks characteristic of unaltered, mature males.

judging cage
Cage in the judging area.

kitten
A cat up to the age of eight months old.

laces
White area on back of hind legs from foot to hock, especially on Birman and Snowshoes. *See also* "gauntlets," "gloves."

lavender
Cat fur color, gray with a pinkish cast.

lilac-cream point
Points that are a mixture of lilac and cream.

lilac-cream lynx point
Points that are a mixture of lilac and cream, with an underlying tabby pattern.

lilac lynx point
Points that are gray, with a pinkish cast and that have an underlying tabby pattern.

lilac point
Points that are gray, with a pinkish cast.

line breeding
Mating cats that are related by at least one common ancestor within the first three generations of their parents.

litter
Kittens born in the same birth from the same mother.

litter
Absorbent material used in a cat's waste box.

litter registration
Registering a litter of kittens with a cat registry organization, like the CFA or TICA.

luxating patella
Genetically transmitted problem that causes the kneecap to slip when the joint is moved. Can cause lameness.

lynx tip
Tuft of longer hair on the tip of the ear, especially on a Maine Coon or Norwegian Forest Cat.

lynx tufts
Hair furnishings on the tips of the ears.

lynx point
Light body coat, with darker extremities that have tabby markings. Also called "tabby point."

mackerel
A tabby characterized by vertical stripes, like a fish-bone pattern.

mascara
Dark skin pigment found around the eye, typical of silvers and tabbies.

mask
Darker colored area of face of a colorpoint.

meezer
Slang term for a Siamese cat.

melanin
Dark pigment produced by the body, which gives color to the skin, hair, and eyes.

metabolism
Physical and chemical processes that take place in a living being.

mi-ke
Calico or tortoiseshell-and-white variety of Japanese Bobtail.

mink
The result of the influence of point and sepia genes on the self gene (solid color).

mitted
White feet.

modified wedge
A type of head that is triangular shaped and not as extreme as a wedge.

moggie
Non-pedigreed cat.

monorchid
Male cat with one testicle.

mutation
A genetic change that alters a cat's characteristics.

natural breeding
Breeding without the interference of selective breeding.

necklace
Continuous or broken stripes on the upper part of the chest in tabby varieties.

neuter
To remove a male cat's testicles by castration so that it cannot reproduce.

nictating membrane
Third eyelid that a cat can pull across its eye for additional protection.

non-agouti
Not a genetic tabby.

nose leather
The hairless tip of the nose and nostrils.

nose liner
Colored line of skin found across the top of the nose leather in silvers and tabbies.

not for breeding
A cat that has been sold or registered without breeding rights.

OE
Odd-eyed. Each eye is a different color.

outcross
Breeding two cats that have no common ancestors for at least three generations.

overshot jaw
When the upper jaw protrudes abnormally beyond the lower jaw.

parasite
Organism that lives off of another one, drinking blood or living in the digestive tract.

patched tabby
Cats that are any of the tabby patterns (classic, mackerel, flecked, or spotted), with patches of red coloring.

pathogen
Organism that is capable of causing a disease.

parti-color
A color division for cats at cat shows that usually includes bicolors, tortoiseshells and tortie, and whites. In any case the cat must have a solid block of color with additional colors, although the specific definition varies between cat associations.

pedigree
A document containing names, titles, colors, and registration numbers of cat's ancestors.

pedigreed
To describe a cat that has a pedigree document. Often used interchangeably but incorrectly with "purebred."

pericarditis
An inflammation of the membrane covering the heart.

phenotype
Visible characteristics of a cat's genetic makeup.

piebald
Basic white pattern, with areas of color.

pigment
Coloration.

pinking up
Describes how a cat's nipples turn bright pink when they have been bred, which happens about three weeks after mating.

placenta
The organ that allows oxygen, food, and waste material to pass between the mother cat and the unborn kittens.

platinum
A silvery-beige color.

points/pointed
Coat pattern in cats with a paler body color, with contrasting darker colors on the face, ears, tail, and legs.

progeny
Offspring of an individual cat.

provisional
Class at cat shows for cat breeds that have not yet been accepted for championship status by an individual cat association.

purebred
A cat whose parents are the same or allowable outcrosses.

quarantine
Time in which a cat is isolated from other cats in order to prevent the possible spread of a disease.

queen
Female cat used for breeding purposes.

quick
Vein that runs through a cat's claw.

rangy
Long body.

recessive
Gene not expressed unless both members of a specific gene pair are recessive.

red
Solid cat color.

red lynx point
Points that are reddish orange, with underlying tabby patterns.

registry
Cat associations register cats, issue registration numbers, determine breed standards, license cat shows, and license cat-show judges.

renal
Relating to the kidneys.

renal amyloidosis
Genetically linked kidney condition, which causes kidney failure.

reverse tortie/reverse blue-cream
When color is dominantly red or cream. Also called "hot tortie/hot blue-cream."

rex
Type of coat with no guard hairs but a soft and curly undercoat.

ringworm
Contagious skin disease caused by a fungus.

roll out doming
Nicely rounded forehead.

roman nose
Nose type with an arch and low-set nostrils.

ruddy
Dark orange-red color.

ruff
A mass of long hair circling the neck, especially on a Persian. Also called "frill."

sable
Dark brown cat color.

SC
Subcutaneous—under the skin. Also "SQ."

sclera
White portion of the eyeball.

seal lynx point
Dark, almost black points, with underlying tabby pattern.

seal point
Dark points, almost black.

seal tortie lynx point
Dark points, almost black, with tortoiseshell coloring and an underlying tabby pattern.

seal tortie point
Primarily dark points, almost black, with an underlying tortoiseshell color pattern.

selective breeding
Intentional mating of two cats in order to achieve a trait or to eliminate a trait.

self
Cat that is of one solid color from the base to the tip of the hair shaft.

semi-cobby
Having a slightly longer and leaner body type than cobby.

semi-foreign
Cat body type that is long and tubular but not as extreme as a cat with a foreign or oriental body type.

set type
Breeding term to describe the process of breeding successive generations of cats with certain characteristics in the hope of producing cats that will possess the trait and also be able to pass it on to their offspring.

sex-linked
A characteristic that is usually associated with only one of the sexes.

shaded
Cat that is white at the base, with the darker color starting halfway down the hair shaft and extending to the tip.

silver
Cat color usually the result of a white coat with black flecking.

single coat
One coat, usually the topcoat or guard hairs, without the downy undercoat.

sire
Male parent of a kitten.

slinky
Slang term for a cat breed that is long and slender, like a Siamese or Oriental.

smoke
Cat color that is white at the base and with darker coloring covering most of the hair shaft.

solid
One-color cat.

spay
Female cat that has been sterilized through a surgical procedure. To alter a female cat so she can no longer breed.

spectacles
The lighter colored hair area encircling the eyes. Also called "goggles."

spontaneous mutation
Genetic accident that permanently alters certain genetic characteristics.

spotted
Coat pattern featuring clear, non-overlapping, oval or round spots.

spotting
White areas in the coat.

SQ
Subcutaneous—under the skin. Also "SC."

standard
The written description of the ideal characteristics of a recognized cat breed.

stop
Well-pronounced angle between nose and forehead. Indentation on the bridge of the nose, usually between the eyes. Also called "break."

stud
Breeding male cat.

stumpy
Manx with a tail ⅜–4 in. (1–10 cm) long, consisting of one to three caudal vertebrae.

taurine
An amino acid that a cat needs in its diet for good eyesight.

TICA
The International Cat Association.

tipped/tipping
Color on the ends of hair.

toe tufts
Long hairs growing out from between the toes, both on the top and underside of the paw.

tomcat
Unaltered, male cat.

tuck up
Underbelly of a cat, curving up into the haunches.

tufts
Hair on the tips of the ears and/or between the cat's toes.

umbilical hernia
Hernia of fat and sometimes the intestines in the region of the naval.

undercoat
Soft and downy hairs next to the skin.

undershot jaw
When the lower jaw protrudes abnormally beyond the upper jaw.

van
A color pattern on a bicolor or calico, with color confined to head and tail, with only one or two small body spots.

variety
A subgroup of a breed. A cat that has registered parents but is not eligible for championship status because it does not conform to the breed standard.

vascular
Pertaining to the blood vessels.

weaning
When kittens learn to eat solid food and no longer rely on their mother to feed them.

wedge
Head type that has triangular-shaped dimensions.

weegie
Slang term for Norwegian Forest Cat.

whip tail
Long, thin, flexible tail tapering from the base to the tip, typical of a Siamese.

whisker pad
Area of the upper lip from which the whiskers grow. The fleshy part of the muscle on either side of the muzzle below the nose.

whisker pinch
The distinct demarcation between the cheeks and the muzzle.

white
Cat color that lacks pigmentation.

whole
A cat that is capable of reproduction and has not been spayed or neutered.

wry bite
Crooked jaw.

woolly
Thick undercoat.

zoonosis
An animal disease that can be spread to humans.

Picture Credits

Illustrations by **Ann Biggs**: 30 (b), 31 (c), 32 (t), 33 (t), 34 (bl), 41 (b), 45 (c), 97 (t)

All pictures courtesy of **Marc Henrie** except for the following:

Ardea: John Daniels: 105 (bl), 115 (l); Kenneth W Fink: 325 (r); Joanna Van Gruisen: 331 (tr); Jean Michel Labat: 111 (tl), 168 (tl), 171 (t, b); Richard Waller: 325 (l); M Watson: 146, 170 (bl)

Roger Baker: 250 (tl, c)

Bridgeman Art Library: Fenton House, Hampstead, London, UK/National Trust Photographic Library/Derrick E. Witty: 134 (cr); Musee Fragonard, Grasse, France/Giraudon: 25 (t); Kunsthistorisches Museum, Vienna, Austria: 24 (b); Musee d'Orsay, Paris, France/Giraudon: 25 (br); Rafael Valls Gallery, London: 25 (bl)

Christie's Images: 137 (tr, cl)

Corbis: 26 (tl, b), 28 (t), 29 (tl); O Alamany & E Vicens: 313 (tl); Annebicque Bernard: 92 (t); Yann Arthus-Bertrand; 3, 199 (bl), 261 (t, br); Bettmann: 29 (tr, b), 152 (c); Blue Lantern Studio: 27 (tr); Ed Bock: 133 (br); Tom Brakefield: 320 (l); Bureau L.A. Collections/Rhythm & Hues: 27 (c); C/B Productions: 151 (br); Christie's Images: 18 (cl), 24 (c), 151 (bl); DK Limited: 56 (l), 85 (tl); Pat Doyle: 32 (c); Fine Art Photographic Library: 18 (cr), 23 (c); Gianni Dagli Orti: 19 (cr); Philip Gould: 93 (b); Martin Harvey: 42 (t); Robert Holmes: 17 (bl); Hulton-Deutsch Collection: 28 (br), 107 (b), 135 (c); Krista Kennell/ZUMA: 32 (b); Don Mason: 80 (tr); Joe McDonald: 171 (c); Mediscan: 101 (c); Robert Pickett: 313 (tr); PoodlesRock: 23 (bl); Carl & Ann Purcell: 17 (t); Walter Rawlings/Robert Harding World Imagery: 24 (t); Reuters: 313 (b); Walter Rohdich; Frank Lane Picture Agency: 63 (br); Kevin Schafer: 320 (r); SGO/Image Point FR: 107 (t); Paul A Souders: 55 (b); Stapleton Collection: 18 (b); Eric Thayer/Reuters: 136 (br), 144 (tl); Seth Wenig/Reuters: 93 (tr); Roger Wood: 15 (b)

DK Images: 5 (tl, tr, crt, bl), 7 (t), 12 (tl), 19 (tl, tr), 36 (bl, br), 38 (flt, flct, flc, flcb, flb, ctl, ctr, frt), 39 (lt, lb, ct, cc, cb), 40 (lc, lb, tr), 47 (br), 52 (b), 55 (t), 58 (t), 63 (bl), 70 (bl), 72 (t), 77 (t, c), 78 (l), 82 (bl), 85 (tr, br), 90 (tl, br), 91 (tr), 93 (tl), 94 (br), 95 (br), 98 (tl, tr), 101 (t), 104 (bl), 106 (tl, tr), 109 (t), 118 (bl), 120 (tl, br), 121 (tr), 122 (tl, b), 123 (br), 124 (br), 126, 127, 128, 129 (t), 131 (br), 140 (t), 141 (cl), 147 (c), 148 (tl), 150, 152 (tl, b), 153 (t, br), 154, 155, 156 (t, c), 158, 159 (t, bl), 160 (b), 161 (t), 162 (bl, br), 163 (tl, tr, c), 164 (tl, c, bl), 165 (t, cr), 166 (t), 172 (bl, br), 173 (c, b), 174 (c), 175 (t, r), 176 (cl, cr), 177 (b), 178 (br), 179 (c, b), 181 (tr, cl), 182 (cl, bl), 183, 184 (cl, b), 185 (br), 186 (c), 192 (c), 195 (tl), 197 (tr, b), 198 (cl, bl, br), 202 (c, br), 203 (b), 204 (tl), 205 (t), 206 (br), 207 (tr, bl), 208 (b), 209 (t, br), 211 (bl), 212 (cl), 215 (c), 217 (b), 218 (tl), 221 (br), 222 (cl, cr, b), 223 (tr, bl), 224 (tl, bl), 225 (t, br), 226 (br), 227 (br), 229 (tl, tr), 230 (cl, cr, b), 231 (b), 232 (bl), 233 (br), 235 (t), 236 (c, bl), 237 (tr, bl), 238 (c), 239, 240 (tl, cr, b), 241 (bl, br), 242, 244 (c, br), 247, 253 (tr), 255 (br), 258 (tl, c), 260 (tl, cl, cr), 261 (bl), 262 (b), 263 (t, bl), 264, 266, 267, 268 (t), 272 (bl, br), 273, 275, 283 (t, bl), 285 (bl), 286, 289, 290 (bl), 291 (t, c), 292 (b), 293, 294 (tl, c), 298, 302 (tl), 304 (b), 309 (b), 314 (tl), 316 (tl, r), 321, 323 (tl), 328 (b), 332 (tl, b), 334 (t), 341 (tl, br), 348

Helmi Flick: 138 (b), 250 (cl, b)

FLPA: Jim Brandenburg: 332 (cr); Hans Dieter Brandl: 312 (b); Thorsten Eckert: 112 (bl); Yossi Eshbol: 338 (tl); Armin Floreth: 54 (bl); Foto Natura Catalogue: 46 (c); 100 (br); 137 (b); 184 (tl); 185 (t); David T Grewcock: 60 (br); Tony Hamblim: 315 (t, l); Angela Hampton: 63 (c), 73 (b), 86 (b), 87 (t), 168 (cr), 169 (bl, br); Hannu Hautala: 312 (tl); David Hosking: 132 (t), 217 (t), 324 (b), 338 (tc); Wayne Hutchinson: 11 (l), 39 (rt), 43 (b); Mitsuaki Iwago: 11 (r), 21 (b), 57 (b), 132 (bl), 170 (t), 187 (bl), 334 (cr); Heidi & Hans-Jurgen Koch: 40 (bl); Giesbert Kühne: 74 (bl); Gerard Lacz: 30 (c), 167 (b), 201 (t), 210 (c), 213 (tr), 214 (cl), 256 (tl), 260 (b), 297 (b), 301 (t), 327 (tr); Frank W Lane: 322 (b); Mike Lane: 83 (bl); Frans Lanting 339 (tr, br); Linda Lewis: 163 (b); Yva Momatiuk/John Eastcott: 301 (br), 333 (cl); Elliott Neep: 153 (bl), 335 (bl); Mark Newman: 309 (cr); Panda Photo: 38 (flb), 74 (br), 222 (tl), 223 (br), 270 (c); Fritz Polking: 334 (bl); Malcolm Schuyl: 14 (b); Jurgen & Christine Sohns: 132 (br), 256 (tr, b), 257 (t, cl), 312 (c), 317 (b); Sunset: 5 (crb), 229 (bl), 257 (br); Roger Tidman: 31 (b); Terry Whittaker: 14 (t), 301 (bl), 326 (bl, br), 327 (tl, b), 328 (tl), 329 (t, b), 332 (tl), 336 (tl, tr), 336 (b), 338 (bl), 339 (bl); Martin B Withers: 108 (t), 170 (br); Konrad Wothe: 11 (c), 43 (t), 44 (b), 63 (tr), 75 (br), 133 (bl)

Fotosearch: 323 (br)

iStock: 125 (br)

Richard Katris: 186 (cr, bl), 187 (t, br), 188, 189, 190, 191 (b), 210 (tl, bl), 211 (t, br), 212 (tl, cr, b), 213 (bl, br), 243 (tr, cl), 249 (cr, bl), 251, 276, 277, 288, 294 (b), 295, 296

Mary Evans Picture Library: 17 (br), 18 (t, b), 23 (t, br), 134 (bl, br), 135 (t), 148 (b)

Ulrika Olsson: 136 (t, bl)

Alan Robinson: 1, 9 (t), 198 (tl), 200, 201 (b), 227 (bl), 230 (tl), 231 (tl, tr), 236 (tl, br), 237 (br), 246, 252 (r), 253 (tl), 265, 268 (bl, br), 269, 287, 291 (b), 292 (tl, cr), 299, 341 (tc, tr)

RSPCA Photolibrary: 102 (t); Des Cartwright: 117 (tl); John Downer: 131 (cr); Geoff du Feu: 100 (bl); Andrew Forsyth: 108 (b), 111 (b); Angela Hampton: 102 (b), 105 (t, br), 109 (b), 110 (t, b), 111 (tr), 113 (tr), 116 (br), 117 (tr, bl), 168 (bl); Becky Murray: 112 (br); Jonathan Plant: 169 (tr); Alan Robinson: 125 (tl); Nick Withey: 116 (cl)

Jim Sanderson: 322 (tr), 323 (bl), 330 (t, b), 331 (tl, b)

Karen Sausman, Kingsmark Bengals and Serengetis: 249 (tr, cl)

Shutterstock: aceshot1: 82 (tl); Utekhina Anna: 37 (t), 244 (tl, br); Frank Anusewicz: 169 (tl); Anyka: 22 (t); Dan Bannister: 319 (tl); Iva Barmina: 69 (tr); Galina Barskaya: 72 (b); Simone van den Berg: 30 (tl), 35 (b), 161 (br); Stuart Berman: 309 (t); Nick Biemans: 305 (cr); Mary Bingham: 46 (b), 79 (br); Vera Bogaerts: 122 (c); Joy Brown: 65 (r), 103 (t); Tony Campbell: 45 (t), 75 (tl); Ferenc Cegledi: 324 (c); Ekaterina Cherkashina: 38 (cb), 39 (lc), 138 (t), 157 (tr), 167 (t), 172 (tl), 173 (tr), 196 (b), 204 (cl), 243 (b, cr), 245, 297 (tr, c); Lars Christensen: 133 (t); Richard Costin: 308 (bl); Alexey Demidov: 5 (clb), 79 (t), 104 (t); Oshchepkov Dmitry: 131 (cl); Rusty Dodson: 303 (tl), 335 (t); Anna Dzondzua: 35 (t); EcoPrint: 303 (tr); Steffen Foerster Photography: 149 (b), 310 (tl, cr); fotorro: 87 (b); Alexander Garanin: 40 (rc); Andreas Gradin: 311 (bl); Jerko Grubisic: 8, 157 (cl); Natalia V Guseva: 40 (bc); Joanne Harris and Daniel Bubnich: 157 (br); Margo Harrison: 130 (b); Joshua Haviv: 316 (b), 317 (tl, tr); Jonathan Heger: 149 (tl), 302 (cl), 311 (t); J Helgason: 51 (t); Patrick Hermans: 335 (br); Ben Heys; 80 (br); Shawn Hine: 48 (tl), 54 (br); Nancy Hixson: 125 (rcb); Miroslav Hlavko: 56 (t); R Hughes: 300 (c), 305 (tl); Iconex: 304 (c); Vasily A Ilyinsky: 306 (t); Eric Isselée: 36 (t), 41 (t), 164 (cr), 181 (bl), 185 (bl); Pavel K: 41 (c); Ilyas Kalimullin: 47 (t); Vita Khorzhevska: 22 (bl); J Kitan: 10, 59 (t); Graham S Klotz: 37 (b); Lois M Kosch: 73 (c); Cheryl Kunde: 209 (bl); Erik Lam: 39 (lb), 165 (b), 180 (l), 258 (b), 259 (cl, b); Leach: 45 (b); Leo: 306 (b); Polina Lobanova: 94 (bl); Dwight Lyman: 85 (bl); Brian McEntire: 4, 186 (tl), 191 (t); Stephen Meese: 309 (cl); Vladimir Melnik: 69 (b); Sharon Meredith: 71 (t); Stanislav Mikhalev: 48 (bl); Michelle D Milliman: 66 (b), 112 (t); Tatiana Morozova: 46 (t); Nando: 306 (t); Ariusz Nawrocki: 80 (cc); Rafal Olkis: 75 (tr); Michelle Pacitto: 34 (br); Perrush: 80 (cr); Photobar: 311 (br); PK Photo: 125 (rct); Vova Pomortzeff: 314 (c, b), 315 (cr); Pavel Pustina: 308 (br); Robert Redelowski: 119 (t); Robynrg: 206 (c), 300 (r), 319 (tr, b); s-dmit: 42 (bl); Kristian Sekulic: 302 (b), 304 (t), 308 (t, cl), 333 (br), 341 (bl); Gleb Semenjuk: 91 (tl), 228 (b); Misha Shiyanov: 12 (cr); Igor Sivolob: 82 (tc); S.M.: 89 (rcb); Caroline K Smith: 318; Forest L Smith III: 31 (t); Denis Sokolov: 89 (tr); Solos: 252 (l), 259 (tr); SouWest Photography: 300 (l), 337; Wally Stemberger: 333 (t); Igor Stepovik: 62 (t); Stiggy Photo: 125 (tr); Johan Swanepoel: 302 (cr); Magdalena Szachowska: 147 (l), 159 (br), 195 (tr); Denis Tabler: 114 (bl), 225 (bl); Graham Tomlin: 149 (tr); Nikolay Tonev: 305 (tr); Suzanne Tucker: 281 (tl); H Tuller: 43 (c); Nat Ulrich: 44 (tr), 89 (tl), 204 (cr); Jiri Vaclavek: 90 (bl); Claire VD: 89 (rct); Zhorov Igor Vladimirovich: 96 (tl), 98 (b); VR Photos: 124 (tr); K West: 306 (b); Wrangler: 310 (b); Feng Yu: 125 (rc); Dusan Zidar: 64, 71 (b)

TopFoto: 27 (tl, b), 160 (t); Alinari: 5 (clt), 16 (b); ARPL/HIP: 16 (tl), 151 (tl); The British Museum/HIP: 16 (tr), 19 (cl), 151 (tr); ImageWorks: 117 (br), 141 (r, bl), 145 (cl), 148 (c); Michael Le Poer Trench/Arena Images: 26 (tr); PA: 28 (bl)

Index

Page numbers in **bold** refer to main entries, page numbers in *italics* refer to picture captions.